MW01130952

THE COMPLETE BOOK OF THE

FRESHWATER
AQUARIUM

THE COMPLETE BOOK OF THE
FRESHWATER
AQUARIUM

≈

A comprehensive reference guide to more than 600 freshwater fish and plants

VINCENT B. HARGREAVES

THUNDER BAY
P·R·E·S·S

San Diego, California

Thunder Bay Press

An imprint of the Advantage Publishers Group

5880 Oberlin Drive, San Diego, CA 92121-4794

www.thunderbaybooks.com

Copyright © Salamander Books 2006
An imprint of Anova Books Company Ltd

Text copyright © Vincent B. Hargreaves

Copyright under International, Pan American, and Universal Copyright
Conventions. All rights reserved. No part of this book may be reproduced or
transmitted in any form or by any means, electronic or mechanical, including
photocopying, recording, or by any information storage-and-retrieval system,
without written permission from the copyright holder. Brief passages (not to
exceed 1,000 words) may be quoted for reviews.

All notations of errors or omissions should be addressed to Thunder Bay Press,
Editorial Department, at the above address. All other correspondence (author
inquiries, permissions) concerning the content of this book should be addressed
to Salamander Books, 151 Freston Road, Road, London W10 6TH, United
Kingdom.

ISBN-13: 978-1-59223-514-8
ISBN-10: 1-59223-514-X

Library of Congress Cataloging-in-Publication Data
available upon request.

Printed in China
1 2 3 4 5 11 10 09 08 07

Additional Captions
Page 1: A pair of Red flame dwarf gourami *(Colisa lalia)*.
Page 2: A Red-finned shark *(Epalzeorhynchos frenatum)*.
Page 3: A Blue-eyed plecostomus *(Panaque suttonorum)*.
Pages 4–5: A Decorated catfish *(Synodontis decorus)*.

Contents

Introduction

The guidelines given to me to make this book were generous in the extreme; my choice was to be as comprehensive as possible, yet at the same time rely completely on my own personal experiences of fifty years of fishkeeping. The modern hobbyist is richly provided with guides and works of reference, particularly about tropical freshwater aquariums. The idea was not to compete in this field, but simply to endeavor to answer four questions. If I were to set up a new aquarium housing tropical freshwater fish, how would I go about it? What decor and plants would I choose? Which fish would I choose for the system? What would I do to maintain the standard of the water, livestock, and plants? A guide, yes, but a very personal one.

I have fulfilled these terms of reference as best I could, but it would not have been possible to do it so well had I not been able to depend on the valuable help of friends admirably equipped to assist me in this project. These people are acknowledged at the end of this work.

One purpose dominated the writing of this book—to present a modern systematic treatment for setting up an aquarium. The same objective prevailed in researching and writing the sections on aquatic plants, freshwater invertebrates, and fish. The acceptance of my previous book, *The Complete Book of the Marine Aquarium*, as a guide and reference to fish, invertebrate, and algae classification by many teachers of courses in ichthyology (or fish biology) and by many ichthyologists, botanists,

and other zoologists has been increasingly gratifying. Many other important works have been published since then and we have a better understanding of the aquarium hobby than we did a decade ago. However, only further work will enable us to judge whether all of our new ideas are actually advances.

Another objective was to produce a work that would be valuable to the novice, but equally valuable to the experienced or advanced hobbyist. I feel that I have achieved this objective, yet made it concise enough that it remains a single volume. Keeping tropical fish and aquatic plants is relatively easy in the twenty-first century, even with the minimum of equipment. Like I said in my previous book, just don't rush it!

Finally, this hobby can be one of the most satisfying and calming free-time occupations that exist. The peaceful effect of a well-planted aquarium containing beautiful and attractive fish is second to none. It is a relaxing hobby and one with a great deal of reward—a living picture! The budding hobbyist must remember one important point, though. Practical fishkeeping is really not what it implies. We are primarily water-keepers, not fish-keepers. Keep the water healthy and the fish and plants will do fine. After all, they have been doing that for a couple of hundred million years!

I hope that the reader will enjoy this book as much as I have enjoyed writing it.

Vincent B. Hargreaves

A quartet of Bleeding heart tetra (Hyphessobrycon erythrostigma). *These fish are ideal in a peaceful community aquarium with other species of similar size. They are happiest if kept in a shoal in soft, slightly acidic water.*

part one

SETTING UP
THE AQUARIUM

What kind of aquarium?

Before attempting to establish an aquarium, a little thought should be given as to what kind of aquarium is going to be set up. There are three different systems in the hobby at the moment. The first of these is the oldest and most common kind of tropical fish tank. The second and third are usually more complicated and often rely heavily on a higher degree of expertise and technology.

In the first system—the aquarium—the accent is on a successful and pleasing arrangement of decor along with a few hardy plants. The main attraction of this kind of aquarium is, however, the fish stock. Tropical fish are those that are found in lakes, rivers, and streams throughout the tropical world. Often, they are brightly colored, sometimes bizarre in shape, and generally attractive. This kind of aquarium is usually the first system that a new hobbyist goes for.

The second system is a brackish aquarium. In this kind of aquarium, an attempt is made by the hobbyist to establish a system that will more realistically duplicate a natural environment where there is a high concentration of salt in the water, the conditions that are found in tidal estuaries. This is a most interesting and satisfying side of the hobby, but the tank is not as easy to set up and get functioning correctly at the start. Nevertheless, to be able to re-create a small portion of a brackish-water environment within the confines of a living room, albeit in a synthetic manner, is a challenge that few hobbyists can turn down once they have the knowledge required to be able to set one up.

The third system is often termed a "Rift Lake aquarium." This is because it replicates the environment that African Rift Lake fish enjoy. It contains water that has a high alkaline content.

The purpose of this book is to provide a guide to the three systems and the installation and maintenance of the equipment required, and also the successful upkeep of the various plants, fish, and invertebrates involved. Before this is dealt with in detail though, a thought should be given to the position of the aquarium. This is an extremely important factor. When a tank is filled with water it is usually far too heavy to be moved around. So this should be one of the first considerations along with the size of the intended tank.

Advanced aquarium technology has shown us the importance of correct and controlled lighting. If the tank is placed near a window, for instance, that control is lost to a certain degree. Nuisance algae may form due to excessive light and on hot days the sun will heat the aquarium water to sometimes dangerous temperatures. A similar problem may occur if the aquarium is next to a central heating radiator or warm air-duct. These are basic considerations, of course, but they are often overlooked.

One of the most common mistakes that the beginner makes is to place his aquarium well away from the nearest power source. Then, when the tank is set up and filled with water, the only alternative is to use unsightly cable extensions in order to provide electrical power to the aquarium.

A little thought beforehand can make life a lot easier, both for the aquarist and for the aquatic life he or she intends to keep.

Typical aquariums on sturdy cabinets that are available in different types of wood finish. The cabinets can be utilized for books.

The tank

Two examples of well-constructed bow-fronted all-glass aquariums.

Size is an important factor when choosing an aquarium. As a rule, a tank with less than 22 gallons (100 liters) limits the amount of livestock that can be kept in it. From the outset, it is advisable for the aquarist to choose the largest tank that he can afford, or that will fit into the living room decor. There are certain criteria that are not often considered here, though. The first of these is the depth of the aquarium in relationship to its width and height. A depth of over 24 inches (60 cm) is unrealistic for most hobbyists for a specific reason: deeper tanks are difficult to service. One has only to look at the problem in a practical way. The length of an average person's arm is usually from 26 to 28 inches (65 to 70 cm). Grasping something at the bottom of the tank will make this distance considerably shorter. So unless a large show aquarium is intended, with all its inherent problems, the hobbyist should take this into consideration. Unless, of course, he is prepared to climb into the aquarium to set up the decor or service the tank. This may seem an obvious point, but it is one that is often overlooked, even by the most experienced aquarist.

Very large aquariums are often costly to run and can be time-consuming. A good all-around tank will have a capacity of 50–70 gallons (250–350 liters). The ideal dimensions would be 40 x 20 x 20 inches (100 x 50 x 50 cm) or 56 x 24 x 20 inches (140 x 60 x 50 cm), where the width and length of the tank both exceed its depth. This gives a larger surface area and allows the water to absorb considerably more oxygen from the surrounding atmosphere. Where lighting is an important factor, and in most aquariums it is, a flat constructed aquarium allows better light penetration than a tall, deep fabricated one.

Choose silicone-sealed frameless tanks with 2–3 mm expansion seams at the joints. One liter of water weighs one kilogram; therefore 50 gallons (250 liters) will weigh a quarter of a metric ton! The weight of this water will be dissipated throughout these expansion joints, so they need to be well constructed. The thickness of the glass should have been calculated during manufacture to prevent bowing once the tank is filled with water and, where they are of a lightweight construction, strengthening bars and crosspieces should be in place around the upper edge of the sides. Go for black silicone-sealed joints where possible. Not only are these more attractive, they are also more effective.

Recently, there has been another technological advance in aquarium manufacture: the all-glass bow-fronted tank. A template is prepared to the size required and then a thick sheet of glass is heated up and allowed to sag slowly to form the bow. It is then tempered to produce a strong, scratchproof front glass that allows good viewing of the aquarium, even from an acute angle.

The base

Having given some thought to the placement and size of the aquarium, the base construction should be considered. Bearing in mind what has been said before about the weight of an aquarium filled with water, it is necessary that the base construction is solid enough to support this weight. More important, however, especially where a large show aquarium is to be installed, is the floor on which it is placed. Many older buildings have problems with bearing loads of, say one ton of water, on the four load-bearing feet of an aquarium stand. The aquarist should check the strength of the floor before proceeding to fill the tank with water. In addition, it is a good idea to place the tank on the base with foam rubber or polystyrene in between. This will act as a shock absorber when the tank is filled and stop unnecessary vibrations if the room has a wooden floor or if the room is subjected to vibration from heavy traffic from a nearby road. It will also ensure that the aquarist's precious charges remain stress-free when they are later introduced.

The base itself can be a stand, a brick construction, or a cabinet with a steel, aluminum, or wooden frame. A cabinet is the most advantageous solution for the beginner. It offers a great deal of versatility and storage space. Advanced aquarists will construct made-to-measure units and some—with DIY flair—will integrate the aquarium and base into the living room decor through the use of wood paneling and brickwork. It is up to the individual aquarist to decide his or her needs but it should always be kept in mind that the base must be strong enough to support the weight of the aquarium once it is filled with water. It goes without saying that the stand or base should be level before attempting to place an aquarium on it. Check this with a spirit level from side to side, front to back, and also diagonally. If the floor is uneven, Perspex or metal shims should be used under the base to correct this. These should never be placed between the base and the tank itself.

An added advantage of a cabinet, whether self-built or store-bought, is that it serves as a space in which a filter sump can be installed. Sump filtration systems, along with other forms of filters, will be dealt with later. Alternatively, there are cabinets designed for other uses.

Three examples of sturdy bases for aquariums. Below left is designed to fit in a corner of a room. The one above left is for a standard rectangular aquarium, and it may be recessed to allow the tank to be sunk into it when using a deep sand filter bed. The one below shows that stands are available in fancy shapes, in this case hexagonal.

Heating and cooling

It is important to maintain a stable water temperature in an aquarium. These days, all commercially produced submersible heaters have built-in thermostats so that a given water temperature can be reached with the twist of a control screw. Most heaters are preset by the manufacturers to the approximate temperature required for a tropical fish tank. Nevertheless, it is a good idea to keep an eye on the water temperature, especially in a newly set-up aquarium, and to make the necessary adjustments as required. When choosing the size of the heater for a given aquarium capacity, the aquarist should allow roughly one watt for every two liters of aquarium water (or 100 w for a 50 gallon or 225 liter tank). Tropical fish and plants may be kept quite happily in water temperatures ranging between 73°F and 84°F (23°C and 29°C) but an attempt should be made to keep the water temperature relatively stable at around 79°F (26°C) for the best results. To this end, a submersible or external thermometer is required with which to monitor the actual water temperature. There are many inexpensive ones available.

Small biological filter systems often come with a built-in thermostatically controlled heater. In such a case there is no need to protect the heater from the danger of wandering invertebrates attaching themselves to it when it is switched off. However, if the heater is placed in the aquarium without some form of protection, there is a real danger, particularly in the case of large ornamental snails, that one will attach itself to the heater module. Then, when the heater switches on again, they will be burned and in severe cases will die. Where the system uses a filter sump, however, this ceases to be a problem, since all such items of equipment can be placed in the filter sump well away from the important and valuable livestock.

It should be pointed out here that in certain areas the air temperature might be high enough to cause an increase in the temperature of the water. This is particularly the case with aquariums set up in warmer climates or on particularly hot days during the summer. In such cases it may be necessary to cool the aquarium water rather than heat it. If the warm period is only temporary, then ice cubes sealed in a polythene bag and floated in the tank— or better still, in the filter sump—will suffice to reduce the temperature. If the problem is a permanent one, however, a cooling unit will be required to bring the water temperature down to manageable levels.

These units are also used in cold water setups to maintain the necessary low temperatures that are required by cold water fish and plants. Most aquarium stores will be able to order these units if they are required, although they are not cheap.

Lighting

This is perhaps the most important aspect of a successful aquarium. Surprisingly enough, aquarists have been slow to appreciate the importance of correct lighting over an aquarium. This is because of a lack of understanding of the fundamental theory of light itself. In this section, an attempt will be made to explain this in simplified terms.

Light is composed of magnetic waves, which are measured in nanometers (nm). It consists of all the spectral colors, and each of these colors represents a given wavelength. Visible light starts at violet (roughly 380 nm) and ends at red (780 nm). Together with the intermediate colors such as indigo, blue, green, yellow, and orange, these produce the color spectrum. The efficiency of light is measured in units of light flux (lumens) and its intensity is measured in lux. Lux is calculated as follows: 1 lux = 1 lumen over an area of 1 square meter. In terms of rivers, streams, and lakes, the light at the water surface at midday may be 100,000 lux in tropical climates. At a depth of one meter, the light intensity will fall by about 50 percent to 50,000 lux and at a depth of 10 meters only about 1 percent of the light intensity remains. In the past, aquarists used a luxmeter to measure the amount of available light in an aquarium, but this item isn't very effective because it only measures the light intensity, not its color composition and this, as will be explained, is extremely important.

In recent years, the importance of the color composition of light for an aquarium has become fully appreciated and hobbyists have a better understanding of what is required. Strictly speaking, the color composition—or color temperature, to be precise—of aquarium lighting is just as important as the correct filtration system. To illustrate the difference between light intensity and color temperature, consider a fluorescent tube or a metal halide burner. When these reach the end of their serviceable life, there will be a noticeable difference in the light that is emitted. This is even visible with the naked eye, as anyone who has changed a metal halide or fluorescent tube in a series of

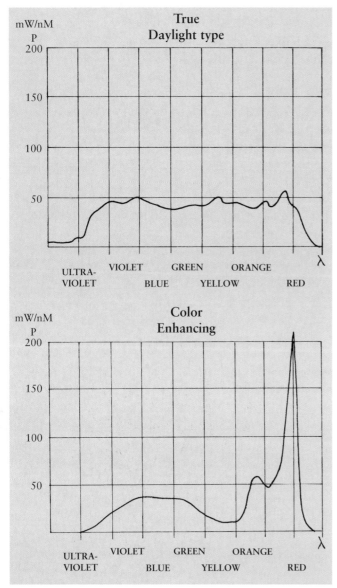

The differences between daylight and color-enhanced fluorescent tubes is shown here with the two graphs. "Warm" light promotes good plant growth, and this is toward the higher end of the color spectrum. However, it can also produce unwanted growth of nuisance algae.

this is that the warmer light wavelengths, such as red and orange, are being filtered out at depth. These light wavelengths have a lower color temperature and because they are being filtered out, the color temperature of available light has a tendency to rise. It can be said then that the color temperature of light is inversely proportional to the depth of water.

This is easy to understand when one considers that the deeper one dives underwater, the bluer the available light becomes. Diving from the water surface into a deep lake, the first colors that disappear are the reds and oranges, followed by the yellow and green light until, at a depth where some light is still available, it is limited to blue or indigo. Of course, in a murky river with overhanging undergrowth, mangroves, and other trees, the model result may differ.

Remember: Warm light (red, orange, etc.)
= Lower color temperature
Cold light (blue and actinic)
= Higher color temperature

Plants require the correct light for growth. Plants that grow in shallow water require warm light because the

such will confirm. The light is different. Even so, there will be no measurable difference in the light intensity; it is the color temperature that has altered.

The color temperature of light is measured in degrees kelvin, where the higher the color temperature, the colder the light—for example, blue, which is usually thought of as being a "cold" color, has a higher temperatures than red, which is regarded as a "hot" color. To clarify this, the color temperature of light at the water surface of the Amazon river at midday may be 6,000 kelvin. At a depth of 16 feet (approximately 5 meters), however, the color temperature will have risen to about 8,000 kelvin, and at a depth of 50 feet (15 meters) it may be 10,000 kelvin. The reason for

Integrated lighting units, incorporating actinic tubes and metal halides.

Metal halides are important for some aquariums. The ones shown here have a color temperature of 10,000 kelvin.

light intensity is high, but the color temperature is relatively low. It goes without saying that fluorescent tubes with an accent toward the red end of the color spectrum, such as "Gro Lux" and "Warm White," are ideal for freshwater aquariums if the hobbyist wishes to promote plant growth.

If an attempt is being made to duplicate the color temperature of the light from deeper lakes and rivers, a higher color temperature is desirable. This means that the light in an aquarium should have a color temperature of between 6,000 and 10,000 kelvin, depending on the depth at which the aquarium inhabitants were collected.

Fortunately, there are lighting systems that cater to these requirements and your local dealer should be able to advise you as to the optimal lighting system for your aquarium. As a rule of thumb, fluorescent tubes do not produce as high a color temperature as do specially produced metal halides. A combination of blue (actinic) fluorescent tubes along with "daylight" tubes will produce a color temperature of up to 7,500 kelvin, but above this there is a requirement to use specially produced metal halides along with, of course, blue fluorescent lighting. In such systems it is easy to produce a color temperature of up to 10,000 kelvin.

Whether the aquarist uses fluorescent or metal halide lighting, it is important to remember that as they become old, the color temperature can alter drastically. Replace them at regular intervals or whenever a noticeable change

in the light occurs. This is important for delicate plants and cave-dwelling fish, which rely heavily on the consistency of light for their continued well-being.

In summary, there are two basic lighting options for a tropical freshwater aquarium. The first alternative, to achieve a higher color temperature that is required by some deepwater plants and fish, is a combination of metal halide lighting and blue fluorescent tubes. The second option, and by far the most common lighting system for normal aquariums, is a combination of "daylight" and "color-enhanced" fluorescent tubes in a ratio of 2 to 1, respectively. Systems using this kind of lighting are optimally suited for promoting good plant growth and also for enhancing the colors of the fish and plants in the tank.

High-quality fluorescent tubes are available to the hobbyist. The color composition of these is an important factor in an aquarium.

Filtration

The treatment of aquarium water in order to keep the tank inhabitants healthy and in an environment approaching that of the natural habitat offers many possibilities. Mechanical filtration of the water is the least effective form of filtration in an aquarium, since it will not remove the various chemical contaminants that build up over a period of time. This leaves us little alternative but to use one of the various forms of biological filtration.

Biological filtration

Before a description of the various types of biological filters is given, it is prudent at this stage to mention the biological processes that occur within the aquarium and the effect that a biological filter has on these. To this end, a diagram is given here to simplify things.

For the beginner making his first attempts with a

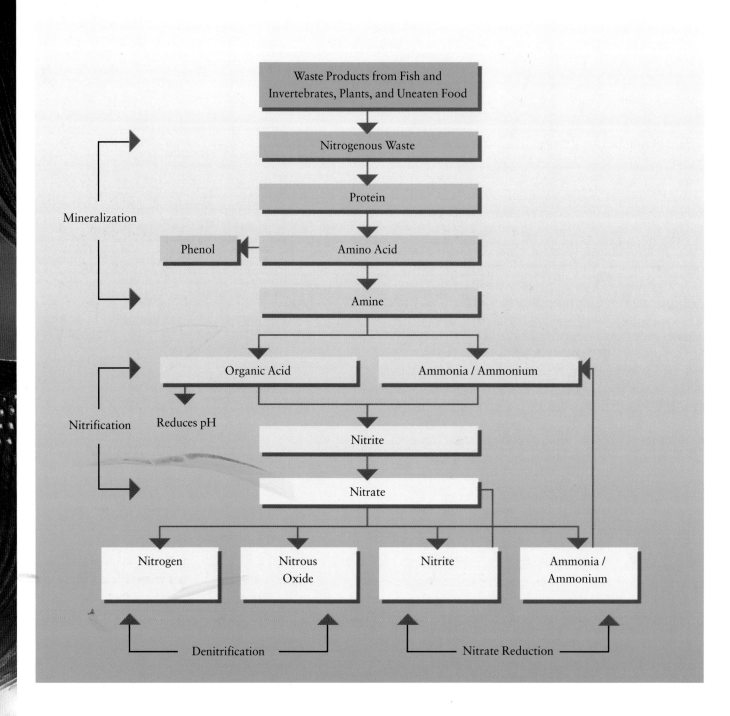

"Aquaballs" Trickle Filter medium from Aqua Medic, Loveland, USA.

tropical freshwater aquarium, it is essential that the fundamentals of biological filtration be fully understood. This will ultimately save a lot of time and money. Before any tank can be stocked with fish and plants, it needs to be "fully cycled," or matured. This is a process where bacteria are allowed to form in sufficient quantities to perform the function of biological filtration. How the bacteria do this is explained below using the diagram on page 18 as an aid.

To clarify the diagram, it can be seen that the uneaten food and waste products from fish and small invertebrates—such as snails and freshwater crustaceans, along with dead or dying plants—are absorbed into the water as nitrogenous waste. Healthy bacteria colonies present in a mature aquarium will start the process of mineralization almost immediately. The bacteria responsible for mineralization convert this proteinous waste into amino acid and amine during the mineralizing stage. As a by-product of this, phenol is produced and will gradually build up over a period of time. In any great quantity, phenol discolors the water and is unhealthy for the tank inhabitants. To check for excess phenol in an aquarium, look for it using a white dinner plate or sheet of white plastic. If the water shows a yellow tinge against the background of the white plate when it is immersed in the tank, there is too much phenol present. This can be reduced by changing part of the aquarium water or by

introducing an activated charcoal filter, which will be dealt with later in this section.

Amino acid provides the foodstuff for bacteria and as they utilize this they break it down to produce ammonia, ammonium, and organic acid. Organic acid has a tendency to reduce the pH of the water. The pH of freshwater is normally 7.0. However, there are some fish, such as discus and African Rift Lake cichlids, where the pH plays a much more significant role in their husbandry. Depending on the pH, ammonia, which is harmful to fish and invertebrates, will convert to ammonium. This is not as dangerous as ammonia and is in fact utilized by plants as a food source. It must be pointed out at this stage that ammonia and ammonium occur in some quantity in a newly set-up aquarium. This is a natural phenomenon and simply means that the aquarium is starting to mature correctly. There are test kits available to test the levels of ammonia in an aquarium and it is advisable that the beginner purchases one at the start.

After mineralization has taken place, a group of aerobic bacteria, *Nitrosomonas* spp., oxidize the ammonia into nitrite. This is the first part of the nitrification phase. The second bacteria in the nitrification phase, *Nitrobacter* spp., are responsible for oxidizing the nitrite into nitrate, a relatively harmless end product.

In a newly set-up aquarium it is necessary to monitor the level of nitrite in the water. This will rise to almost

A modular wet/dry filter designed to be fitted into a filter sump.

through the normal water circulation and gas exchanges on its contact with air. Using aerobic heterotrophs for denitrification is the ultimate way to control the environment within an aquarium and it will be dealt with in detail later.

The other way, nitrate reduction, is undesirable and in some ways dangerous. The end products of nitrate reduction are nitrite and ammonia/ammonium—in other words, a reversal in the nitrification process. It does not often occur in an aquarium, but it is not unknown. If a large fish has died unnoticed and rots in some hidden part of the aquarium, or if there are areas of the tank that are entirely free of oxygen and have become anaerobic, nitrate reduction can take place. This is brought about by the bacteria utilizing the essential gases from the nitrate to produce a reversal of the oxidizing process. This should not be allowed to happen. It could result in a rapid buildup of nitrite and ammonia in the water. In such cases the first indication that the aquarist has that all is not in order is when his precious charges start to die.

Initially there are no bacteria present in a newly set-up aquarium. These colonies have to be introduced or allowed to grow under the right conditions. This is often a natural process and more will be said about this later. It is important to remember that without any bacterial filtration in an aquarium, there will be no success.

Wet/dry filters (trickle filters)

The so-called wet/dry filters are often referred to as trickle filters. These units, in various forms, are in widespread use. They offer an excellent filter area for aerobic bacteria to colonize and grow and, by their inherent construction, they have an unbeatable potential to break down organic waste into inert solids, and this is what is required from a modern filter system. In effect, with this kind of filter, almost everything in the way of proteinous waste is mineralized and subsequently oxidized into nitrate.

The construction of this kind of filter takes on different forms depending on the manufacturer. Originally the filter consisted of several sand- or gravel-filled trays placed on top of each other so that the water drawn from the aquarium could trickle through the various porous trays, which offered a large surface area for bacterial colonization. The fact that the trays were not immersed in water but, rather, outside the aquarium to offer good aeration possibilities, gave rise to the term "wet/dry filters." After the treated water had reached the bottom tray, it was then returned to the aquarium via a circulation pump. In its original form this was not a bad idea since, depending on the water flow and the compactness of the sand in the filter, anoxic areas could be created according to the depth of the trays and the sand.

lethal levels before the tank is fully cycled. If fish are introduced at this stage they will become weak and prone to disease. Once the level of nitrite falls, it means that the tank is fully cycled and, although not fully matured, it is well on the way to becoming so. Again, the beginner should test the nitrite level in the aquarium water every day. Over the cycling period it may rise quite high but it will eventually fall to zero if the tank has been set up properly.

Having stated that nitrate in the aquarium water is relatively harmless, this must be qualified. Over a period of time the nitrate level will gradually rise unless steps are taken to hinder this. While most fish can stand relatively high levels of nitrate (up to 500 mg/liter for short periods of time), some species are not so tolerant. Although nitrate has already been referred to as an end product, it is not really so. Nitrate can be reduced or it can be denitrified and in such cases aerobic heterotrophs and facultative anaerobic bacteria are utilized. In an aquarium where there are anoxic areas, this type of bacteria will form quite naturally. Deep within rocks and bogwood there is little in the way of oxygen and in these areas the bacteria can survive to perform an important function. They are able to utilize the oxygen contained in the nitrate compound and the result is a residue of nitrogen, which can be gassed off

The modern version, which uses plastic "bioballs," is a much better idea. Everything is mineralized and oxidized and there is no facility, through their construction, for them to be anything other than aerobic bacterial filters. The end product of this is nitrate, which, in considerable amounts, can prove harmful to some tropical fish. However, the amount of nitrate can be controlled through healthy plant growth, which will use this as a source of nutrients. In addition, phosphate is produced, which will also be utilized by plants. Despite its efficiency, the hobbyist should be aware of the fact that any excess nitrate and phosphate will result in an "algae bloom" that will quickly cover the sides of the aquarium with a green, slimy algal growth. The trick here is to do a partial water change to remove the excess nitrate and phosphate from the water. This will also keep the aquarium plants healthy.

In summary, the trickle filter offers one of the best oxygenation possibilities in the world of filters. In addition, it has exceptional nitrification potential and a fully matured trickle filter has an excellent biological "skin" over the filter medium. This skin is comprised of protozoa, fungus, and aerobic bacteria and, when the innovative biological polypropylene balls are used, provides a greatly increased filter surface area. Furthermore, the construction of the balls enables any excess bacterial growth to be simply washed away if it gets too thick and starts to harbor anaerobic zones. As the water trickles slowly over this skin, it absorbs oxygen from the air to saturation point and through the biological filtration, nitrogenous wastes present in the water are converted into inert solids. This process, carried out through several steps (some of which are poisonous to aquatic life), produces the relatively harmless nitrate, phosphate, and sulfate, thereby providing a fertilizer for algal growth. In spite of these advantages, it is questionable whether or not the trickle filter offers the best possibilities in terms of water treatment for a tropical fish aquarium. Through the high rate of mineralization and nitrification, the carbonate hardness (KH) is affected and sinks dramatically in some cases. This can be a major problem with some setups, such as those housing African Rift Lake cichlids, which need hard water. In addition, protein-coupled trace elements are oxidized and the end products of this are minute quantities of nitric and sulphuric acids. These acids would destroy the buffering system within the aquarium water in this kind of tank. Because of its high nitrification potential, the trickle filter mineralizes everything, and one of the end products is nitrate, which, in greater quantities, is a poisonous substance for both marine life and humans (the permitted level of nitrate in drinking water in the United States and Europe is 50 mg/liter). The other products mentioned, phosphate and sulfate, are equally damaging to aquatic

life. Little denitrification can take place because of the oxygen-rich environment within the filter. As has been stated previously, this is not a good basis for the culture of anaerobic (denitrifying) bacteria, certainly not in enough quantity to be able to denitrify the daily dose of organic waste from an aquarium. And for the filter to become fully effective, it requires several days' maturation time and generally has a high heat loss and evaporation rate. This means that the aquarium water must be constantly topped up to compensate for the loss of water through evaporation. If the trickle filter is fitted inside the tank, it is important to install an automatic top-up system, otherwise when the water level evaporates flush to the level of the weir, the filter will cease to function correctly. Nevertheless, it would be wrong, because of these drawbacks, to say, "The trickle filter doesn't work," or, "Throw out your trickle filter." On the contrary, I have seen many beautifully set-up aquariums using these filters and it would be unjust to question the theories of many experienced aquarists. When the trickle filter is used in a system with a good denitrification potential, it is in a class of its own.

Diatom Filter

There are popular misconceptions about this type of filter and because of this they have never been popular. They are relatively expensive but, nevertheless, no serious aquarist should be without one. The importance of this type of filter is based on two facts:

- It is not intended as a permanent filter.
- The filter and filter bag do not filter. It is the diatomaceous earth, which one must add, that does the actual filtering.

They are, however, very effective. In a test aquarium, I was able to verify this over a period of four months. Diatomaceous earth, which is made up of the minute skeletons of one-celled diatoms, is able to filter the water so effectively that no particle larger than 1 micron (0.001 mm) will pass through it. The advantages of this are obvious when one considers that the swarming or free-swimming stage of *Oodinium pilularis* (freshwater velvet disease) is 20–100 microns and the larvae of *Ichthyophthiriasis* (white spot or "ich") is between 200–1000 microns.

In the test aquarium, I was able to filter out the *Oodinium* (on one occasion) and *Ichthyophthiriasis* (on two occasions). This was done by deliberately taking infected fish from a local dealer and introducing them to the aquarium. Later, I was able to verify another desirable effect of using this filter: it eliminates algal blooms that can take over an aquarium in a very short time, causing green water and green slimelike growths. It is difficult to eliminate but the diatom filter does it effectively or, at worst, reduces it to manageable proportions.

The rules of use are as follows:

- For *Oodinium* and *Ichthyophthiriasis*, etc., use the filter for a minimum of 10 days. Change the earth every three to four days because this can become blocked depending on how dirty the aquarium is. In order to prevent a reoccurrence of the disease, I would advocate the use of this filter for 30 days in order to ensure the removal of all free-swimming spores.
- For excess algae, use the filter for 21 to 30 days, changing the earth every two days.

Mechanical filters

Mechanical filters still have a place in this hobby and can be relied upon to produce the desired effect; namely that of clearing murky water caused by large particle impurities. They are particularly useful in a newly set-up aquarium for clearing the water in the beginning and then

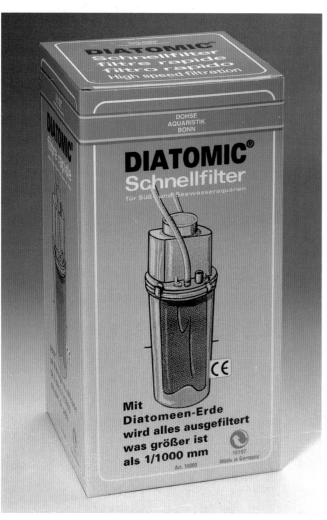

Diatom Filter from Dohse Aquaristik, Bonn, Germany.

later as an effective filter for excess algal growth. There are three main types of mechanical filter. The first is the mechanical sump filter, a row of three or more plates, or "baffles," placed in the filter sump vertical to the flow of water. This type of filter has its drawbacks, however. Despite regular cleaning—and for this job I would recommend removing the plates to the bathroom or backyard and spraying them strongly with a hose—they have a tendency to clog up. This is particularly the case when a calcium reactor is in use for African Rift Lake fish because minute particles of calcium find their way into the fine pores of the filter and within a few months they have to be replaced—a more expensive proposition than normal filter wool. I have tried cleaning them even to the point of drying them out and beating the calcium out with a hammer! Within a few weeks they were again blocked. (Recently I was surprised to find this type of filter being recommended as a biological filter, a job for which they were not designed.)

The second type of mechanical filter available is the outside filter. These may be of a similar design to the canister filter or may be open-topped. They are very effective but, as a rule, more time-consuming to dismantle and clean than the third type of mechanical filter. This is the inside filter, a compact and effective filtering unit normally in a small canister fixed to a power-head or turbo-filter. The advantages of this type of mechanical filter are both its small size—it can be hidden away quite easily in the sump or in the aquarium itself—and the ease in which it can be cleaned and serviced. The most important point to remember is that the filter wadding should be cleaned at least once a week, even more often if the aquarium is particularly dirty. For this I would again recommend the same spray cleaning process mentioned previously. Furthermore, it should be noted that failure to clean a mechanical filter regularly can result in it functioning as a poor biological filter and, through inevitable blockage, it will cease to filter at all.

The final mechanical filter is also the cheapest and simplest form. This is the sponge filter that clips onto the inside of the tank with an air line attached to it. Air from a pump is then supplied to the lower part of the outlet tube. As the air bubbles in the tube rise, an air lift takes place, carrying water upward and drawing water through the sponge, trapping large particles within the sponge. The sponge can easily be removed and rinsed under running water on a weekly basis. Although this kind of filter is not effective for larger aquariums, it is ideal for small ones and has proven to be successful in fry-raising tanks where tiny fry suffer a real danger of being sucked up into a more powerful filter system.

Power filter

These are sometimes referred to as canister filters and are normally closed-unit filters, mostly sealed with an O-ring and mounted on the outside of the aquarium. As the name implies, they are powered and have a high water turnover rate. Nevertheless, I would not recommend them for a freshwater aquarium for which they were not specifically designed. The reason for this is that because of their construction, and by that I mean a sealed unit, oxygen is not able to enter the filter, except what there is in the water itself. This means that the effect of the biological process is greatly reduced because aerobic bacteria cannot colonize the filter in the same quantity as, for instance, in a trickle filter. There is simply not enough oxygen in the water to go around!

Added to this, the biological filtration that does take place uses up a great deal of the oxygen present in the water and the result is that the water that is returned to the aquarium is extremely poor in oxygen. This is something that by definition we cannot afford to have in an aquarium. They are worthy of a mention, though, because they can be used to the aquarist's advantage as an effective charcoal filter.

Charcoal filter

Charcoal filtration is often used in an aquarium for the specific purpose of removing harmful chemical elements or compounds from the water. For this, "activated charcoal" is used. Carbon-based filters have been used for many years where the base element is activated charcoal. The respirator or gas mask used by the emergency services and the army has activated charcoal as its filter base. In addition, the nuclear, biological, and chemical warfare protection suits in use by both scientists and armies worldwide are made with activated charcoal–based material. The special properties of this form of carbon have for some time been utilized in the aquarium hobby. Through the process of nitrification by aerobic bacteria in an aquarium, products are created, which in large amounts can prove detrimental to both fish and plants. These chemicals—principally phenol-based compounds that are responsible for the yellow coloring in the aquarium water— can be easily removed through the installation of a charcoal filter. Care must be taken, though, when choosing charcoal for this type of filter. Much of the charcoal available in aquarium stores can do more harm than good in an aquarium. This is because even with some of the better quality material on offer, an unacceptable amount of phosphor leaches into the water during its use and causes excess algae growth in the tank, which will soon become unsightly. The aquarist is advised to take great care and if

Aqua Carbon from Interpet, in Dorking, England, and Baltimore, Maryland, is an activated filter charcoal.

necessary consult the dealer or manufacturer to ensure that it is phosphate-free, if it is not marked on the pack as such.

There are differing opinions about the use of activated charcoal in aquariums. Some experts say that it removes important microelements from the water, thereby restricting plant growth. This has not been proven and in any case it is the only tool we have to remove harmful phenol or other poisonous substances from the water. In addition to this, I have not been able to establish any difference in plant growth in any of my aquariums or in those of my colleagues. In terms of how much charcoal one should use in an aquarium, I recommend 200–250 grams per 100 liters of aquarium water. The charcoal should be placed in a nylon bag and then in the filter compartment of the aquarium or in a canister filter. If the system has an aquarium sump, it is easier to simply place the bags in the sump. After a period of three to six months, depending on the quality of the charcoal, it ceases to be effective and will have to be replaced. The idea that activated charcoal can be "recharged" by placing it in a hot oven for an hour is incorrect. Also, the theory aired frequently on the Internet that if the old charcoal is left in the filter system it will become an effective anaerobic or denitrifying filter is simply not true.

Biological filter

The term "biological filter" is misleading since most filters utilize bacteria to function effectively. But what is meant here is a general term to cover a wide range of filters that have superseded the canister or power filter. (To confuse matters even more, the biological filter is also called a "power filter" on occasions.) The composition of the filter medium varies greatly, as does the filter form and size. There are inside filters and external ones and some even

The Interpet Prime filter, one of the modern series of biological filters available to the marine aquarist.

have a built-in trickle filter, such as the Hagen Biolife. Others, like the Interpet Prime filter (above), are extremely effective. They all have one thing in common, however, and that is the way the water is treated. The water passes through several stages of mechanical and biological filtration before being returned to the aquarium. The list of filter media available is endless but includes filter wool, activated charcoal, ceramic, foam, polypropylene, and ion exchange resins. The effectiveness of these filters for a freshwater aquarium can also vary from filter to filter and even this is dependent on which filter media are used. Therefore, it is not possible to comment in general terms with so many variables. Those filters that I have tested have ranged from poor to excellent in their results but the two filters mentioned above appear to be rather more cleverly thought out than most.

Undergravel filter

The undergravel filter (or subsand filter, as it is sometimes referred to) has been around for a long time. Originally it consisted of a porous base plate covered with a thick layer of gravel. It had one or more air tubes and was powered by a strong air pump (see diagram at right). Later this was modified, and instead of using air, the filter was driven by a turbo-pump, making it more effective.

With the advent of reverse-flow UG filtration, the whole circulation was reversed with the filtered water rising up through the gravel instead of down through it. Although popular in the UK and United States, it never really caught on in continental Europe. Nevertheless, it is still one of the most widely used filters, despite its critics and its problems. No other filter offers the same filtration area as that of the UG filter. The fact that it has an

excellent nitrification potential is not the only advantage; denitrification also takes place within the filter medium.

The major drawback is that after a year or so the filter medium becomes blocked and channeling of the water flow occurs, reducing its nitrifying capability. Over the same period of time, the denitrification potential increases inversely proportional to the reduction in its nitrifying potential and this can be considered as an advantage for a tropical freshwater aquarium. But it is important not to allow the filter medium to become foul through loss of circulation. This balance between blockage and the increase in nitrification potential, which is so desirable for an aquarium, is best overcome when the gravel is replaced in a particular way, and this after exactly 12 months. I stress *replaced* and not just washed, as the latter will not be effective. Over a period of time the pores and holes in the gravel also become clogged, reducing the effective biological surface area, so it has to be replaced as well. The best method of doing this is to mentally divide it into four or five strips and replace one strip per month with the help of a net. In this way the bacterial culture is not destroyed by a total tank strip-down, which is the greatest criticism. It is surprisingly easy to do and takes little time.

An additional drawback to this type of filter is that instead of oxygenating the water, it actually removes oxygen during its nitrification process, and this in no small amount. Therefore, additional aeration should be used to compensate for this. Many modern power-head pumps have a small air tube included in the box. Once attached to the pump (a very simple process), additional and effective aeration can be provided to compensate for the oxygen removed by the undergravel filter.

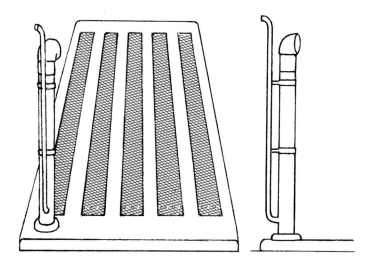

The basic concept of the undergravel filter.

Other biological filters

There are many other filters that utilize bacteria to break down organic waste into more or less inert solids. Quite a lot of them are unsuitable for aquariums. This is because during the mineralization and oxidization processes of the organic waste, oxygen is removed from the aquarium water. Cartridge filters are becoming increasingly more popular for tropical aquariums. The two basic types are the mechanical filtration units, where the filter medium has to be regularly replaced or cleaned, and the biological filtration units. Although biological cartridge filters once suffered from the same problem as sub-sand filters— where the water that was returned to the aquarium was extremely poor in oxygen—the new generation, such as the Maximal Bio-System series, appear to have overcome this through the inclusion of an integrated air diffusion system. Cartridge filters are mounted inside the aquarium or in the filter sump and the water is drawn through a series of bacteria-rich filter media before being returned to the tank again. They are capable of a high turnover rate of filtered aquarium water and are easy to maintain.

Another filter that has become popular with marine aquarists over the past few years is the fluidized bed filter. This is a compact unit that, liter for liter, may be up to 20 times more effective than the trickle filter. Water is drawn into the unit and kept moving over the thin film of bacteria that cover the fine silica or similar particles contained within the unit. Because the water is constantly kept moving, there is little in the way of clogging and no buildup of detritus. Unlike the recently developed cartridge filters, because of their construction they are unable to provide denitrification in any form and everything is oxidized into nitrate. I would recommend this type of filter for a large-capacity aquarium; they produce excellent results.

Freshwater plenum systems (the BGC reactor)

No aquarium book would be complete without it covering the most up-to-date ideas and technological systems. The reader who has carefully read through this section will realize that suggestions have been made, but no dogmatic recommendations. Instead, the advantages and disadvantages of the different systems and equipment have been listed so that readers are left to draw their own conclusions as to what is most suitable for their own aquarium. What follows is also described from a neutral position. It is hoped that this system will be of some help to the aquarist considering keeping brackish-water fish or African Rift Lake cichlids.

The BGC reactor is a modified version of the plenum filter used in tropical marine aquariums. It has several

Modern biological cartridge filters, such as these, have an integrated air diffusion system to allow the water to have increased oxygen saturation before it reenters the aquarium.

differences to the conventional plenum, the major one being its flow system. For aquariums up to 55 gallons (250 liters), two power-heads are required for water circulation. On larger aquariums, three or more power-heads should be used. It must be stressed that this is less of a filter and more of a purification plant. It is a reactor employing the accurate and finely calculated use of bio-geochemical (BGC) avenues. One of the power-heads should be fitted with a cartridge filled with filter wool. This serves as a mechanical filter to remove suspended particles from the water. The filter wool needs to be washed in fresh water on a weekly basis to prevent it from becoming blocked; for it to function as a biological filter it is not cleaned and aerobic bacteria are allowed to grow on it. A second power-head can be fitted with a canister to hold activated charcoal or a good-quality phosphate remover such as Rowephos. As an option, an additional canister filter can be used for this purpose. Even an old trickle filter box could be used after removing the contents; they do have a use after all! This is the only filtration that is required.

The BGC reactor removes waste products from the water and converts them into nitrogen, which is gassed off as the water circulates to the surface. All the work has been done for the aquarist if the reactor is built to the exact specifications, given later. We know that a zero nitrate reading is undesirable for plant growth, but too much nitrate is harmful to some fish. The reactor, which can be built to fit any aquarium, is simple to construct. It will keep nitrate levels to around 0.5 to 3.5 mg/liter. The system should also include an activated charcoal filter and a facility to remove phosphate from the water. The system is self-buffering so that there is often no need to add "Kalkwasser" or other pH buffers. Even a calcium reactor is often unnecessary.

Construction of the reactor plate is simple. A plastic "egg crate," the kind used as light diffusers in office buildings and stores, should be cut to fit the inside of the aquarium leaving about ½ inch (1.2 cm) all the way around. Bioballs from a trickle filter should then be affixed to the underside of the plate using plastic cable ties so that the upper surface is exactly 1¼ inches (3.2 cm) in height. These may need to be cut down to achieve the correct height. They should be spaced about 5–6 inches (12–15 cm) apart throughout the area of the plate for stability. The finished plate is then wrapped in a single layer of 1 mm mosquito screen and the sides and end sewn together with nylon monofilament line (fishing line) to form a tightly closed bag. This cassette is then placed in the aquarium. The sand used over this has been tried and tested at several different grades and various depths, but there is only one grade that works properly, and only one thickness that allows the correct formation of bio-geochemical avenues and gradually depleting oxygen levels.

There are two materials that can be recommended for the sand bed. The first of these is crushed coral sand. This should be graded using a 1 mm sieve, and then again using a 4 mm sieve. Any sand that falls through the 1 mm sieve, or remains in the 4 mm one, should be discarded. This 1.1–3.9 mm mixture is ideal for the reactor. The second material that can be used is aragonite. This is sand obtained from fossilized reefs. It should be graded in the same way as coral sand. Apart from the fact that it is often less expensive than coral sand, it begins to dissolve at pH levels under 8.2. Coral sand requires a much lower pH before it releases calcium carbonate into the water and this is often viewed as a disadvantage as far as pH buffering is concerned because the result sometimes means the loss of pH control.

The pH within the sand bed is lower than that of the bulk aquarium water and, if aragonite is used, the result is that calcium carbonate is dissolved in the water more readily, producing an increase in carbonate hardness along with a decrease in carbon dioxide. Because of this, I recommend that aragonite be used. Crushed coral and coral sand begins to dissolve at much lower levels, often below pH 7.8. Less pH control is possible and the water is not as evenly and gradually buffered.

Whichever sand is used, it should be washed and placed on the reactor plate to a depth of exactly 2 inches (5 cm) throughout the whole aquarium. A piece of the same 1 mm window screen that was used to wrap the reactor plate should be cut to fit the inside of the

aquarium, leaving edges slightly short of the front glass. This hides the screen once the second layer of sand is added. After this, the remaining 2 inches of sand can be added, making a total of 4 inches (10 cm) in all. The reactor unit is complete. The surface of the sand should now be 5¼ inches from the bottom of the aquarium if the work has been carried out correctly.

Once the tank is filled with water, the sand will settle somewhat. This allows the hobbyist to add living sand to bring it back to the required level. By doing this, the sand will become seeded with bacteria and the reactor will cycle and mature over a period of about 90 days. Live sand can be purchased, or it can be obtained from another aquarium. Some dealers are often prepared to supply it from their own tanks for a small fee.

The reactor works by allowing water to diffuse through the sand and into the void under it created by the reactor plate. Because of the grading of the sand particles, the oxygen saturation becomes depleted gradually in the lower levels until only 1 or 2 percent remains.

The upper level of sand is referred to as the aerobic zone and the lower level as anoxic. But in fact there are no such zones, just differing oxygen levels throughout the depth of the sand. The bacteria in the lower levels breathe oxygen from the nutrients in the water rather than from the oxygen present in the upper areas. The separating screen is there to prevent burrowing animals and fish from disturbing these lower layers.

Filter sump

One of the tidiest ways of setting up an aquarium is with the use of a filter sump. This is basically a small aquarium or similar container that is usually situated under the main aquarium, often in the base or cabinet. The top of the main aquarium is fitted with an overflow weir and the water overflow is transported by gravity, through a series of pipes, down into the filter sump. From here, a submersible circulation pump transports the water back up into the aquarium through a second series of pipes. In this case, though, there is usually a nonreturn valve fitted to prevent any flooding of the sump, should there be a power or pump failure.

The advantages of this circulating system are enormous. Unsightly filters can be installed here, freeing space in the main aquarium. Heaters, activated charcoal filters, mechanical filters, and electrodes for control equipment can be fitted here and neatly stored away. Even a second sub-sand filter can be installed to supplement the one in the main aquarium. For enthusiasts who like to propagate additional plants, the sump can be used as a nursery if additional lighting is used above the sump area under the main aquarium.

This aquarium is fitted with an overflow weir, which leads down into a filter sump.

The sump can also double as a confinement tank where boisterous fish—or increasingly aggressive ones—may be housed until they are placed elsewhere. This reduces the stress on other tank inhabitants.

Water top-ups or partial water changes can also be done directly into the sump so that the overflow water from the main tank automatically reduces any slight chemical or pH differences before it is pumped back into the main aquarium.

In hot weather, bags of ice cubes can be floated in the sump to reduce the temperature of the water carried to the aquarium. By installing the heater/thermostat in the sump, the main show tank remains free of any unsightly equipment and remains a truly natural and aesthetically pleasing environment for the hobbyist.

Water

Water is not just water from a faucet, it is much more. Often there are contaminants or additives that may harm plants and fish. Chlorine/chloramine or other chemicals are often added to make the water safer for human consumption. Simply filling the aquarium with water from a tap and then adding plants and fish is not enough. What is needed is water conditioning. This is done in two ways. First, the water needs to be strongly aerated for 24 hours to oxidize most of the contaminants. Second, additives can be used to make the water even safer. There are a lot of "tap water conditioners" on the market and the aquarist is advised to use one of these before adding any livestock whatsoever. The trick is to ensure that the water in the aquarium will not harm any fish or plants that are added to the aquarium after the initial setting-up stage. Allow the water in the aquarium to settle down and let the filtration run for a minimum of two days before taking the next step by adding plants. After this period, let the tank settle again before introducing the fish that have been chosen. This will allow time for the bacterial filtration system to become established. Even so, it will not be fully effective, so introduce the livestock slowly over a few weeks so as not to overload the biological system too quickly or heavily.

Water management

Good oxygenated water with plenty of movement and current flow is a prerequisite for a successful aquarium.

Along with this, water management and control should be exercised at regular intervals. Test kits are widely available that measure or test most of the water parameters. In addition, electronic control equipment can be used and although these units are initially more expensive, they provide very accurate results and can work out to be cheaper in the long run.

During the maturation period of an aquarium, the water should be checked on a daily basis and the results recorded for later reference. With a fully matured aquarium, however, a weekly check should suffice. The main tests that should be carried out to ensure good water quality and provide a healthy freshwater environment are as follows:

- **Temperature**
- **pH**
- **Carbonate hardness (KH, sometimes referred to as dKH)**
- **General hardness (dH)**
- **Carbon dioxide (CO_2)**
- **Calcium (Ca^{2+})**
- **Phosphate (PO_4^{3-})**
- **Specific gravity (SG—brackish water aquariums only)**
- **Ammonia (NH_3^-)/Ammonium (NH_4)**
- **Nitrite (NO_2)/Nitrate (NO_3)**
- **Iron (Fe)**

The importance of these tests and the ways to measure them will be covered in the following sections. If you are a newcomer to this hobby, it is a good idea to practice using these test kits during the initial cycling period of the aquarium.

In this way you will quickly become adept in interpolating the results and be aware of the quality of the water before attempting to introduce fish and plants. Any attempt to add livestock too quickly to a newly set-up aquarium may result in fish deaths due to "new tank syndrome," which is not a disease in itself but it can bring about losses of fish for no apparent reason.

It must be stressed at this stage that without carrying out these tests at regular intervals, the aquarist runs a very great risk of a breakdown in water quality. This will inevitably result in the loss of some, if not all, of his precious charges. This leads to disenchantment, which leads in turn to the would-be aquarist leaving the hobby, sometimes for good. With the correct items of equipment and test kits, this can be avoided, and most successful aquarists find the routine water quality checks and tests to be an interesting and enjoyable pastime.

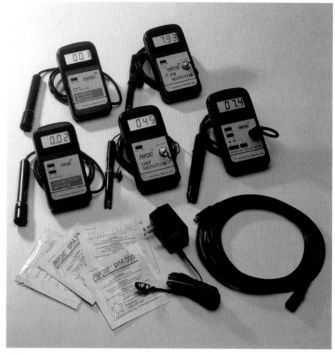

Electronic control units such as these are ideal for the enthusiast and advanced aquarist.

Temperature

In the earlier section on heating and cooling, this topic was covered in some depth. However, it is important that the aquarist maintains a periodic check on the temperature of his aquarium, particularly in hot weather and in situations where the aquarist has compromised in his choice of location, perhaps choosing a place affected by sudden temperature changes. Ideally, the temperature should be 77–80°F. Overheating an aquarium can be a very real problem. Water control means total control; in such situations, the aquarist loses this control without periodic checks.

Another method is with the use of a temperature controller such as those shown at right. These units are more than just a thermostat. First of all, the temperature of the aquarium is accurately displayed in a liquid crystal or light-emitting diode window, so that it can be easily read at any time. More important, most of these units have the facility to be coupled directly to heaters and/or cooling units so that the temperature can be brought under control at any time of the year. This is through the use of magnetic switching units, to which the temperature controller gives information, telling it to switch either the heater or cooling unit on or off. Of course, these controllers are not cheap, but then again, when they are used they can reduce stress on the fish and plants that is caused by continuous changes in temperature. The more

that stress is reduced, the more chance we have of success with our aquarium inhabitants. Any rapid or constant changes in the basic water parameters will only serve to increase this stress.

The Temperature Controller 7027 from Tunze Aquarium Technical Systems, Germany, incorporates a microprocessor for regulation.

pH

The dictionary gives the definition of pH as "the negative decimal logarithm of hydrogen-ion concentration in moles per liter, giving the measure of acidity or alkalinity of a solution." This may sound complicated to some and the formula, $pH = -log_{10}[H^+]$, perhaps even more so. But it is quite simple, really. When water disassociates itself, we have positively charged hydrogen ions (H^+) and negatively charged hydroxide ions (OH^-).

$$H_2O <> (H^+) + (OH^-)$$

The hydrogen ions (H^+) function as acidic and the hydroxide ions (OH^-) as base, or alkaline. In pure water, both ion groups are in equal quantities and the water is neutral, i.e., pH = 7.

$$[H^+] \times [OH^-]$$
$$= (1 \times 10^{-7}) \times (1 \times 10^{-7}) = (1 \times 10^{-14})$$

As soon as acidic or alkaline material is added to the water, the H^+ and OH^- ions become unbalanced. When, for instance, water has a pH value of 8 (i.e., alkaline) the amount of OH^- ions is higher than H^+ ions.

$$[H^+] \times [OH^-]$$
$$= (1 \times 10^{-8}) \times (1 \times 10^{-6}) = (1 \times 10^{-14})$$

In any case, the aquarist need not get involved with the exact chemical reactions when the acidity/alkalinity of a solution is altered. What is more important is the relationship of pH to CO_2 and also to the carbonate hardness (KH). These three are bound together. Any aquarist who tries to break this bond chemically (such as by adding buffering agents to the water to raise the pH without affecting the KH) will find it harder than trying to split an atom! The stability of the pH is dependent on carbonate (CO_3^{2-}) and hydrogen carbonate (HCO_3^-) ions.

With regard to the formula above, when the pH rises from a value of 7 to a value of 8, for instance, it means that its alkalinity has increased tenfold! From this it is logical to assume that abrupt or drastic alterations in the pH value in an aquarium will have a considerably adverse effect on the animals contained therein. The normal pH of a fish tank should be 6.8 to 7.2. Constant control of the pH value in a tropical freshwater aquarium is required in order for the fish and plants to remain healthy. There are many test kits available that are inexpensive and serve this purpose remarkably well. These test kits usually consist of a reagent and test vial along with some sort of color

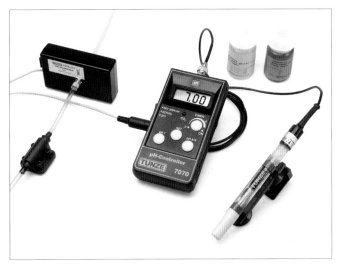

The pH Controller 7070 is available from Tunze, Germany, with magnetic switching unit and calibration fluids.

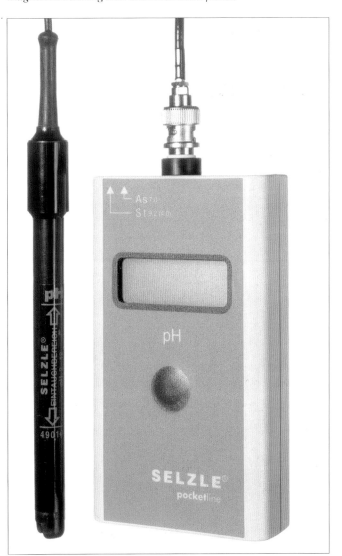

The pocket pH Meter from Selzle, Germany.

comparison chart, allowing the aquarist to compare the reaction color in the test vial. The value is then simply read off the test chart against the corresponding color.

Meters are now widely available and make the measurement of pH values far easier. They have to be calibrated periodically to retain accuracy and this involves placing the electrode in calibration fluid preset to a given pH value (normally pH 3, pH 7, and pH 9) so that the necessary adjustments can be made to the instrument.

Many tropical lakes, rivers, and streams, particularly in South America, have very soft water that is slightly acidic. Keeping fish and plants that are used to this environment means that the pH will have to be lowered

to make them feel healthy and happy in their captive environment.

If you are intending to incorporate a calcium reactor in the aquarium system for buffering purposes—to keep a high pH—it is advisable to obtain a pH control unit like the one shown on the previous page. These units may be preset to a particular pH value and, through a magnetic switch, the dosage of calcium carbonate from the reactor can be electronically controlled. This form of pH control is very effective and the advantage is obvious: fish are not subjected to the same stress as when buffering agents are added directly to the aquarium water.

Carbonate hardness (dH or dKH)

The carbonate hardness of water in a tropical freshwater aquarium can be looked upon as being the pH stabilizer. Total water hardness consists of carbonate and noncarbonate hardness. The measurement of carbonate hardness is given in degrees of German hardness (dKH) or often dH. An increase in the buffering capacity of the aquarium water means an increase in the dKH and a more stable pH. The biochemical processes that are constantly taking place within an established or maturing system affect the level of the carbonate hardness. These processes produce acids and this can create problems in a Rift Lake tank. Natural seawater has a carbonate hardness of between 7 and 9 dKH, whereas in an African Rift Lake aquarium it may be as high as 18 dKH. In such an aquarium, try to maintain a buffering capacity with a reserve at some point between 9 dKH and 12 dKH. The amount of carbon dioxide present in the water, as CO_2 gas and carbonic acid (H_2CO_3), determines the amount of calcium (Ca_2^+) that is dissolved from calcium carbonate ($CaCO_3$). This calcium then forms a bond with the carbon dioxide to produce hydrogen

Carbonate hardness test kit from JBL GmbH, Germany.

carbonate (HCO_3^-). When the amount of HCO_3^- increases, the carbonate hardness also increases. It can be seen from this that carbon dioxide plays an important role in pH stability.

Carbonate hardness test kits usually consist of a test vial and a dropper bottle of reagent fluid. With a measured amount of aquarium water in the test vial, drops of the reagent fluid are counted in until a color change takes place, say from blue to yellow. The number of drops required for this to happen is the carbonate hardness, i.e., 9 drops = 9 dKH.

General hardness (GH)

General hardness, or GH, is the measure of calcium (Ca^{2+}) and magnesium (Mg^{2+}) ions in the water. GH is commonly expressed in parts per million (ppm) of calcium carbonate ($CaCO_3$) or degrees hardness (dH). However, it may also be expressed in milligrams per liter (mg/l), which is the same numeric value as ppm. Depending on the kind of aquarium that is being set up, the general hardness can vary a great deal according to the requirements of the fish and plants.

This table shows the relationship of the GH to hard and soft water.

dH	ppm	Water
0–4	0–70	very soft water
5–8	71–140	soft water
9–12	141–210	medium hard water
13–18	211–320	fairly hard water
19–30	321–530	hard water

Carbon dioxide (CO$_2$)

Carbon dioxide is the end product of photosynthesis. Plants take CO$_2$ from hydrogen carbonate (HCO$_3^-$). During the maturation period of an aquarium there is an overproduction of carbon dioxide because of the formation of bacteria and other microorganisms. At this stage, its introduction into the tank by artificial means is not only unnecessary but also dangerous: at this stage an oversupply of CO$_2$ will only serve to reduce the pH.

In normal tap water there is little free CO$_2$ (3–4 ppm). I have already mentioned that it is unbreakably bound together with the carbonate hardness and pH; therefore, removal of CO$_2$ will result in a rise in the pH. In the aquarium, direct sunshine accelerates photosynthetic processes, resulting in a fall in the pH, which is one of the reasons why an aquarium should not be located too near a window. To clarify this, when CO$_2$ is added, the pH falls. When it is removed, the pH rises.

CO$_2$ reacts with water to produce carbonic acid (H$_2$CO$_3^-$) and increases the carbonate and hydrogen carbonate ions. Therefore, the addition of CO$_2$ results in an increase in H$^+$ ions and makes the water more acidic. CO$_2$ utilized in photosynthetic processes produces the opposite effect, although plants use the CO$_2$ from the hydrogen carbonate (HCO$_3^-$) present in the water (with a pH of 8.2, 90 percent of the CO$_2$ is in the form of hydrogen carbonate).

Obviously, carbon dioxide is important to the general well-being and stability of the aquarium. We can also use it as a tool to stabilize the pH and provide a buffering reserve when used in conjunction with a calcium reactor. The idea that the addition of CO$_2$ can produce sporadic outbreaks of hair or thread algae is not true except in the case of its addition to an aquarium that is not fully matured. CO$_2$ is extremely important for plant growth and a level of 10–25 ppm is recommended. Levels above 25 ppm, however, are harmful to fish and the other tank inhabitants.

Calcium (Ca^{2+})

The level of calcium in natural seawater on a coral reef is about 420 mg/l. In a brackish water aquarium it is usually about half this value, at 200 mg/l. We need to duplicate this as closely as possible in such an aquarium. With newly mixed sea salt and water it is no problem because there is enough calcium reserve built into the mixture to provide this level at the very least. Unfortunately, in an established aquarium this calcium level is quickly depleted. Mollusks and crustaceans need calcium in the form of calcium carbonate (CaCO$_3$) in order to build their skeletons—in fact, a high percentage of their shells and carapaces is made up of this. But it is not only these animals that use it. Fish require calcium for bone growth, so we must be constantly aware of the calcium level in the aquarium. This means periodic testing and the subsequent control of this level. Calcium test kits are now available to facilitate this. All of the kits that I have used have produced very similar results, so that one can say that they are quite reliable. This was not the case a few years ago. A typical calcium test kit comprises a titration solution, a dry reagent, and a fluid reagent. A small amount of aquarium water is put into a test vial and one of the solutions is added along with the dry reagent. Then drops of the second solution are counted into the test vial until a color change occurs, usually from pink to red. Each drop is equivalent to 20 mg/l of calcium:

10 drops = 10 x 20 = 200 mg/liter. In the African Rift Lakes, levels of calcium range from 40–80 mg/l in Lake Malawi to 200–360 mg/l in Lake Tanganyika.

The depletion of calcium adversely affects the buffering system of the aquarium water and although we may have enough calcium in the tank, in the form of calcium carbonate in coral sand and rock, it is of little use in this case. In water with a pH of 8.2 or more, assimilation of calcium from calcium carbonate is very slow. The idea of providing enough buffering capacity in an aquarium by simply using coral sand and rock is wrong. It doesn't work that way. A pH of 7.5 or lower is required and a pH of 6.0 would be even more effective. But Lake Tanganyika cichlids wouldn't like it very much. In fact they wouldn't survive very long! So calcium needs to be replaced on a regular basis in this kind of aquarium.

The Calcium Test Kit from JBL GmbH, Germany.

Calcium reactor

The calcium reactor is really a rather cultivated solution to the problems of pH, carbonate hardness, and calcium levels that have plagued the aquarium hobby. And it works. I have not had any problems in any of my aquariums for the last six years due to the calcium reactor. Nor do I use buffering agents; they are no longer necessary.

For the uninitiated, a calcium reactor consists of a diffusion chamber filled with calcium carbonate ($CaCO_3$) and a low-wattage circulation pump. There is an inlet to carry water from the aquarium into the diffusion chamber, and a return outlet. The theory behind this system is that water is allowed to flow from the aquarium into the reactor, where it is circulated repeatedly over calcium carbonate granules (coarse crushed coral or shell works just as well since it is made of calcium carbonate). The idea is to retain the water as long as possible in the diffusion chamber so that the calcium carbonate becomes soluble. But it has already been explained that at a pH of 8.2 or more, calcium carbonate will not become soluble, so it has to be given some help. This is done by injecting CO_2 gas from a gas bottle into the diffusion chamber at a slow rate. In effect, this creates an artificial atmosphere within the reactor unit and produces a localized drop in the pH level to about 6.0. And this water, still circulating, can dissolve calcium carbonate and does so quite effectively to produce calcium bicarbonate ($Ca[HCO_3]_2$).

The injection of CO_2 gas is carried out with the use of an armature and reduction valve connected to a bubble counter. A bubble counter is a simple piece of equipment consisting of a container, normally filled with distilled water, through which the gas is allowed to flow, producing bubbles in the liquid. It is installed in the gas line between the bottle and the calcium reactor and by careful adjustment of the reduction valve, the bubbles can be visually counted into the diffusion chamber. With regard to the flow rate of water through the calcium reactor, it should be very slow and controlled exclusively from the inlet and not the outlet. This stops any chance of a buildup of excess gases within the reactor unit that could arrest the circulation of water through the pump housing. The actual flow rate can be adjusted to allow a return to the aquarium of between 50–100 drops per minute. When this is coordinated with the input of gas through the bubble counter to be roughly the same rate, a maximum effect will be achieved. The results of a well set-up calcium reactor can be astonishing and the water being returned to the aquarium will have values of 550 to 650 mg/liter calcium and a carbonate hardness of between 20 and 30 dKH. The diffusion chamber needs to be recharged periodically according to its size, as the reactor can consume up to half a pound (225 g) of crushed coral or shell per month.

These units can be controlled in several ways according to the individual aquarium parameters. By increasing the water flow in and out of the reactor, greater amounts of calcium will be brought into the aquarium, but only if the flow of CO_2 is increased proportionally. Failure to do this will reduce its efficiency. Remember: high flow—more carbon dioxide, low flow—less carbon dioxide.

A calcium reactor is not a piece of equipment that needs to be run continuously. At night, for instance, the aquarium requirement for CO_2 is not the same as during the day and the calcium requirement also drops during this "quiet period" for the fish and plants. Because of this, it is possible to connect the reactor into the light switch circuit so that the unit is switched off with the aquarium lights.

By far the best method of control is with a pH meter incorporating a microprocessor. In this way, continuous monitoring of the pH is carried out automatically and, through a magnetic switch, the supply of gas to the reactor can be interrupted when the pH sinks below a given level. The calcium reactor not only makes the adding of buffering agents obsolete, it also stabilizes the pH to a remarkable degree.

A calcium reactor and bubble counter on the left, with CO_2 bottle, armature, and magnetic switch on the right. A pH control microprocessor is shown in the foreground.

Phosphate (PO$_4^{3-}$)

Phosphate is a compound of phosphorus and oxygen (PO$_4^{3-}$) and all living things need it in minute quantities. In tap water the level of phosphate is 0.01 mg/liter or less. But even in such small amounts it is the major nutrient for plants. It should not be looked upon as being poisonous, but in quantity it can lead to over-fertilization of the water. Unfortunately, this is very common in some aquariums and the cause can be traced back to its organic origins. Too much phosphate in the water leads to almost uncontrollable outbreaks of hair and slime algae, which grow all too well under these conditions. There are many causes for an overproduction of phosphate in an aquarium and it may be that the root cause is a combination of many different things. The major cause is overfeeding by the enthusiastic aquarist, leading to detritus. However, when plants and other organisms die off, phosphate is produced. These examples are organically based. There are other ways that phosphate can be inadvertently introduced into an aquarium and these could be termed inorganic. Most of the commercially produced aquarium products are phosphate-free but there are still some available that are not, therefore care should be taken when buying them. Make sure that the words "phosphate-free" are stated clearly on the packaging. A lot of activated charcoal currently available has a high phosphate content. If you are not sure if it contains phosphate, place it in a bucket of water for an hour or so and then do a test. If it does contain phosphate, change products.

Phosphate test kits are quite inexpensive and easy to use. A test vial is filled with a sample of the water to be tested. Reagents are then added and agitated. After allowing the reaction color to develop, it is compared with the color chart that comes with the test kit.

Biological filtration has no effect on its removal except where oxygenated water is trickled over a bed of calcium carbonate. This method of phosphate removal is only effective when the calcium carbonate bed is periodically replaced. Iron (Fe) may also be added to the aquarium to reduce phosphate to iron phosphate (FePO$_4$), which is inert. By far the best way of reducing phosphate is to lower both the stocking and feeding rates of the tank.

A phosphate test kit is important to have on hand, especially if excessive amounts of algae are present in the aquarium. Photograph courtesy of JBL GmbH, Germany.

Specific gravity (SG)

The specific gravity of water is unimportant for normal tropical fish tanks. However, it is a major factor in the success of a brackish water aquarium. Brackish water, such as in tidal estuaries and rivers, has a higher salinity than freshwater. Generally, it is impractical to mix fresh seawater with freshwater to achieve this. The problems of transporting and purifying the large amount of water necessary for successful maintenance of life would be prohibitive. Besides, there are commercially produced salt mixes that will duplicate its composition with a great deal less trouble. The specific gravity (SG) of brackish water lies usually between 1.005 and 1.015. What this means is that it is 1.005 to 1.015 times heavier than freshwater, which has an SG of 1.000. Seawater, on the other hand, has an SG of 1.024 to 1.025. Brackish water also has a high alkalinity; this can be measured using a pH meter or

test kit, as has already been explained. A pH of 7.8 to 8.3 would be normal for brackish water, and the pH of seawater is around 8.2 to 8.4.

Most commercially prepared marine salt mixes are made up to produce a pH reading of 8.1 to 8.3. Considerably less salt is required to produce brackish water, so a lower pH can be expected once this is mixed to the correct SG. Take care in choosing the correct marine salt mix. Only those that state that they are nitrate- and phosphate-free are suitable for aquarium use. There are many proprietary brands available to the hobbyist, such as Kent Sea Salt, Instant Ocean Sea Salt, Red Sea Marine Salt, and, perhaps the most well-known and certainly the most widely used, Tropic Marin. Note that one liter of brackish water contains about 10–16 grams of dissolved salts.

Two factors are important during the preparation and mixing of brackish water for the aquarium. The first is that the specific gravity must be constantly checked. This can be done with a hydrometer. One type is shaped rather like a fisherman's float and is weighted internally so that it floats upright in the water to give the SG reading along the stem that is level with the water surface. They are not very accurate—two instruments from the same company can often give differing readings. A great improvement is the dial-type hydrometer, which is fixed to the inside glass of the aquarium. These are available from most pet stores.

The float type has a weight at one end and, not surprisingly, floats on the water. There are a series of marks to indicate the specific gravity, and the point where the surface of the water is along the neck of the hydrometer corresponds with the water's specific gravity. Most of these instruments are calibrated to be accurate at a water temperature of 77°F (25°C). It is a good idea to look at the instrument from a point above the water level rather than down onto it. This will produce a more accurate result.

If the aquarist has several aquariums, it may be a good idea to buy a specific gravity meter. These are pocket-sized instruments that are extremely accurate. At the time of writing, this item of equipment is only available from one manufacturer and it is revolutionary. It represents state-of-the-art technology in this hobby and is relatively cheap and easy to use.

The SG meter is a sophisticated, battery-powered instrument. One of the great advantages to this device is that it is temperature-compensated, which means that whatever the aquarium temperature, it will give an accurate SG reading. The unit can also be switched to read the temperature as well as the specific gravity of the water. The unit is extremely accurate, giving temperature readings to a tenth of one degree. The specific gravity readings are given to four decimal places.

Obviously, this instrument eliminates any vagueness in specific gravity readings through conductivity conversions or inaccurate hydrometers, and its portability makes it ideal for testing the water in your local dealer's holding aquariums. It is very light and fits into most pockets. The single drawback—if it can be called that—is that the electronic probe must be the same temperature as the water under test, to enable quick and accurate specific gravity test results. This is no great problem, since by holding the probe in the water for a minute or so the temperatures will equalize and an accurate reading can then be taken.

Tropic Marin Sea Salt is used in most public aquariums and zoos and is renowned for its pH stability.

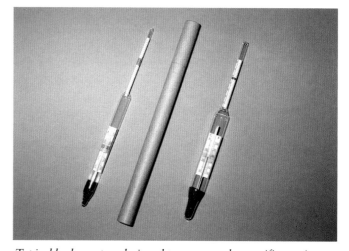

Typical hydrometers designed to measure the specific gravity of seawater.

Ammonia (NH$_3^-$) /Ammonium (NH$_4$)

When the aquarium is going through the maturation or cycling phase, ammonia is often present in quantity within the first three to five days. It is one of the intermediate stages of mineralization and nitrification. In an established tank, though, no ammonia should be detectable. Ammonia and ammonium always occur together and, depending on the temperature and pH of the water, ammonia can change into ammonium and vice versa. Ammonia (NH$_3^-$) is highly toxic to fish but as the pH is lowered, more and more of it changes to ammonium (NH^4). In this form it is relatively harmless and is utilized by many plants as a nutrient.

It is important to remember the ability of ammonia/ammonium to interchange, especially with regard to the introduction of fish to an aquarium (see section on choosing and introducing fish and plants).

Ammonia test kits measure the total ammonia present in an aquarium (ammonia + ammonium). As with most test kits, reagents are used to provide a color comparison to a color chart using a measured sample of the aquarium water.

This ammonia/ammonium test kit from JBL GmbH, Germany, is designed to measure the total ammonia.

Nitrite (NO₂)

Nitrite is normally only present in any quantity in a newly set-up aquarium. Levels of between 0.5 and 5 mg/liter are damaging on a long-term basis, with some species not being able to withstand levels above 0.25 mg/l. Quantities higher than this are lethal. When a fish is suffering from nitrite poisoning, it will swim around with folded fins and clearly display breathing difficulties, which can be identified by the increased rate of gill movement (or gill beat). The stricken fish may hang around at the water surface for periods of time and may occasionally give a short, wild dash around the aquarium. The fish is suffocating because the excess nitrite in the water causes its blood hemoglobin to change to methhemoglobin. Hemoglobin is the red, oxygen-carrying substance in the blood. Methhemoglobin is unable to carry oxygen and so the fish cannot respire.

Nitrite test kits are available from most pet stores and with a newly set-up aquarium the water should be tested daily. Once the tank has fully cycled, a weekly test will suffice for the first six months and after that, only occasional checks will be necessary.

Nitrite can be removed by the use of ozone; however, this will hinder the production of nitrate and should only be used as a quick fix. Once the aquarium filter system is functioning bacterially, the nitrite level will fall quite naturally. On the rare occasion where nitrite levels rise again in an established aquarium, it is usually an indication that all is not well with the bacteria cultures in the filter. Other reasons could be a blocked filter, or it may be that one of the larger fish has died and is decomposing, hidden behind the aquarium decoration. In such cases the problem must be found and immediately rectified.

Nitrate (NO₃)

Nitrate is the end product of nitrification and some fish can withstand levels of up to 800 mg/liter for short periods of time. Nevertheless, in an aquarium, nitrate should be kept to an absolute minimum. At levels of only 300–400 mg/l, African Rift Lake cichlids will begin to die. Nitrate stops cell development in fish and some of the more delicate fish are uncomfortable when the nitrate in the water rises above 80 mg/l.

Nitrate is also a plant nutrient, but most aquatic plants do not require such high levels to grow correctly and healthily. Excess nitrate produces hair and slime algae that will grow over much of the aquarium glass and even over the ornamental plants. The only solution to this problem is to change part of the water on a

weekly basis until the nitrate level falls to manageable proportions.

Weekly checks should be made using a nitrate test kit. These are inexpensive and most pet stores have them in stock, but unfortunately many of these kits are inaccurate: thirty-five different kits from various manufacturers throughout the world were tested together under controlled conditions using solutions with known and calibrated levels, and only four of these test kits gave the correct readings. Two repeatedly failed to give any reading at all! All the other kits read too high; none gave a low reading. The reason for the latter is, I suspect, that manufacturers have gone too far in their endeavors to come up with a product that is safe to use. Added to this are the tight government conservation controls that force manufacturers to replace or reduce the amount of poisonous substances used in test kits. This has led to the marginal use of these chemicals, resulting in test kits that can barely be relied on. The hobbyist should be aware of these shortcomings when purchasing one of these test kits and, if necessary, consult an established dealer or experienced aquarist as to which test kit to use. As an alternative, test strips can be employed. These are small plastic strips with reaction zones on them. They have the advantage of being quick and easy to use and they are fairly accurate. The end of the strip containing the reaction zone is immersed in the aquarium for about one second. After this, the color is allowed to develop for a further 60 seconds and it can then be compared to the color chart supplied with the packaging.

Iron (Fe)

In 2.2 lb (1 kg) of aquatic plants, the iron content of an aquarium can vary between 11 and 19 mg. Iron is important for plant growth and in small quantities is a significant factor in the process of photosynthesis. It is not utilized in the photosynthetic process itself, but it does allow it to occur more efficiently. Most plants absorb it into their cell structure to maintain a healthy growth. Groundwater can contain in excess of 20 mg/liter of iron, whereas water for domestic use often has less than 0.1 mg/l. Faucet water is purified, filtered, and then oxygenated. Through the oxygenation process, iron is oxidized and no longer available. In contrast, groundwater is rainwater that has filtered through the soil with very little oxygen but a great deal of carbon dioxide (CO_2) that dissolves iron in the ground; thus it becomes rich in iron. But groundwater is seldom used for aquariums, so most hobbyists rely on water from the faucet, which means that any available iron will be depleted very quickly. When all the iron has been used up in the aquarium water, the green or red colors of the plants will gradually fade to yellowish green or brown and eventually they will start to die off. To stop this and to maintain an iron concentration of about 0.1–0.5 mg/l, iron must be added to the aquarium water. Most aquarium stores sell iron additives and substrate fertilizers but the specific composition of the latter are usually vague. It is better to purchase a chelated solution containing only iron. Drops or doses are added according to the volume of the aquarium and the manufacturer's recommendations. Repeated doses may be required if the aquarium is heavily planted. To maintain a check on the iron content of an aquarium, an iron test kit is required.

Iron test kits are easy to use and usually contain just one reagent, which is added to a sample of aquarium water. The test vial is set aside for some minutes to allow the color to develop, after which it can be compared to a color scale. If the iron content is under the ideal level, iron should be added. If, however, the iron content is too high for some reason then a partial water change may be necessary in order to reduce this. Testing should be carried out periodically, and also before and after the use of iron additives, because too much iron in an aquarium can cause as many problems as too little.

Aquarium decoration

This is the stage where the hobbyist can really exercise creative skills. There are, however, certain limitations and basic guidelines that every aquarist should be aware of. These should be mentioned so that ingenuity and originality do not become hazardous to the plants, fish, and small invertebrates that are to be included in the tank.

Water is the ultimate solvent, so anything that dissolves in water has the potential to pollute the tank environment. Soluble materials such as textiles, fabrics, and paper-based items should not be used. Potentially toxic materials should also be avoided. Chemicals can dissolve in water in a few seconds and can kill livestock. Exposure to some metallic substances and objects can, even in minute quantities, prove detrimental to water quality and weaken a fish's immune system so that it becomes prone to disease. Metallic objects such as toys, figurines, and other items that contain exposed metal must be avoided. Items that have been dyed should not be placed in an aquarium. When they are wet, there is a real threat that the dye will leach into the aquarium water. Oily items, such as crayons, modeling clay, and wax figures should also be avoided. It also goes without saying that household detergents, cleaners, solvents, and pesticides have no place in a tropical freshwater aquarium.

It is easy to be misled by some items that are seen for sale at your local dealer. Driftwood, bogwood, rocks, shells, and pieces of coral should be treated with the utmost suspicion. Naturally occurring items, such as those that come from a nonaquatic environment, may be carrying microorganisms, mineral deposits, and parasites that can affect the water quality. Rocks, shells, and corals may seem like creative additions to the tank but they consist of calcium carbonate; this chemical can leach into the tank and raise the pH to unacceptable proportions for some fish and plants, particularly those that are used to soft, slightly acidic water.

Bogwood and driftwood may also seem like excellent choices to add a dramatic effect to a waterscape. However, there are many available that are entirely unsuitable. Some that are available to the hobbyists have been ostensibly "cleaned" but are still toxic to some fish, particularly some species of *Tetra*. Wood-based ornamental items contain tannins, which will leach into the water, causing an orange-brown stain that will persist for months—or years—even with frequent water changes.

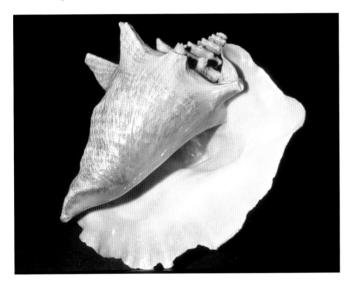

Beautiful shells such as these may look attractive in a freshwater aquarium but they are composed of calcium carbonate, which can make the aquarium water extremely hard over a period of time.

Rock work

There are many types of rocks that can be used to decorate an aquarium. Dolomite, tufa, and fossilized reef rocks all have a high calcium carbonate content, however, so unless the hobbyist is planning to build a brackish water tank or one containing African Rift Lake cichlids, this kind of rock should be avoided. For the usual tropical freshwater aquarium, there are many alternatives to these rocks. These include slate, volcanic lava, granite, sandstone, desert stone, onyx, basalt, petrified wood, and many others. Explain what is required to your local aquarium supplier and he will be able to advise you accordingly. If you are unsure whether or not the rock is calcium-rich, try splashing some white wine vinegar on the dry surface of it. If it sizzles or produces white or yellowish foam, it is almost certainly calcium-based.

All rocks should be boiled and left to cool before being placed in the tank. This will ensure that no microorganisms are inadvertently introduced into the aquarium water. Porous rock needs to be boiled for about half an hour before it is clean. Porous rock is lightweight and can contain many fissures that are ideally suited for the growth of bacteria that will help break down organic waste into relatively inert and harmless solids in the aquarium. Hard and compact rocks such as granite do not have this capability, although the rock may be extremely attractive.

In the last few years "glass rock" has been introduced into the aquarium trade and there are two distinct kinds. The first is manufactured imitation rock produced from glass and molded into aesthetic forms suitable for a decorative aquarium. The second type of artificial rock, and one that is much more ecologically desirable, is actually a by-product from various manufacturing industries. This highly porous, somewhat glasslike rock is reddish-brown in color and chemically inert. It is also very attractive and offers a good surface area, both on the surface of the rock as well as in the porous fissures, for bacteria to form and keep the water healthy and free of organic pollutants.

Arranging rock in a tank is a matter of common sense. Rock work is not necessary in some tanks, such as those that are going to be predominantly waterscaped using plants. In others, such as tanks containing cichlids, rock work is vitally important. First, many cichlids lay their eggs on or under rocks. Additionally, many species burrow, dig pits, and disturb plants—often to the point where they are uprooted or eaten. However, by cleverly arranging rocks to protect plants, this mayhem can be kept to a minimum.

When rocks are to be arranged on the substrate for decoration, it is a good idea to think about the project first. Many hobbyists add the substrate first and then embed the rocks into the gravel or sand. Others build the rock formation first and then add the substrate. There is no hard-and-fast rule here. The important thing is to create a waterscape that is both pleasing to the eye and useful in its construction. If the project is thought about and the rocks are carefully examined, lovely effects can be created. One such effect can be produced if the aquarist takes care to examine the grain, or more correctly, the strata of the rock being used. Slate, for example, is usually sold as flat rocks with strata horizontal to the flat plane. If slabs of slate are placed at random in the tank, the result is

You can create some dramatic effects by using substantial rocks to form a fitting background for solid-looking fish. Here a Blue-eyed plec seems at home against a heavy granite waterscape.

unnatural. The various strata planes conflict with one another, giving a disruptive appearance and one that is out of harmony with nature. If, however, these rocks are placed on plastic supports, each at a 30° angle to the base of the tank using pieces of egg crate, the overall effect is much more pleasing. The uniform rock strata gives an overall impression that is more in tune with the natural world.

When other pieces of slate are added to create caves and grottoes, they should all follow the same angle, even if they are placed on top of one another. After the substrate is added, the pieces of plastic are no longer visible and when the aquarium is cleverly planted, the result will be impressive.

Base medium (gravel and sand)

The substrate or base medium material can be looked on in two ways: it can be purely decorative or it can serve a specific purpose. Decorative sands and gravel come in a variety of colors, sizes, and grades. While they do indeed help decorate an aquarium, they are not always the most practical or the healthiest for fish and plants. Many small-grained, colored sands and gravel have very sharp edges and some are glass-based. Fish such as cichlids like to burrow and disturb sand and the sharp edges can inflict damage on the fish and this can subsequently cause disease.

Planted tanks should utilize coarse, natural, washed sand or gravel and should be calcium- or lime-free. Gravel that is pea-sized or larger can cause problems because uneaten food and detritus can fall through the spaces between the individual stones, where it will decay and affect the water quality. Natural gravel that has a mean diameter of a ¼ inch (6 mm) appears to be the most widely used. Some aquarists prefer a finer grade and this is ideal where a deep sand bed or a plenum filtration system is used. However, if an undergravel filter is part of the system, then the 6 mm grade is perfect.

For aquariums that need hard water, such as brackish water and African Rift Lake setups, the substrate should be calcium-based. Crushed coral and aragonite are the ideal solution and both are available in various grades. Coral sand can be used to maintain hardness and higher pH levels in a hard-water setup. Again though, it is often sharp when it is newly purchased. After a while, however, it has a tendency to become more rounded and smoother through constant disturbance and also the action of calcium depletion.

Soft-water aquariums containing South American fish that prefer slightly acidic water should be provided with a gravel that can cope with this. Laterite is composed of laterite clay and comes in a convenient granular form. It can be mixed with regular aquarium gravel and is ideal for a soft-water aquarium. Plants do extremely well in this base medium, too.

There are many other choices of substrate available to the hobbyist, such as fluorite, crushed onyx, and volcanic gravel to name but a few. There are even sands and gravels that have been precoated in a shiny resin that makes them chemically inert. However, because this resin actually blocks the individual pores in the material, far less

bacteria can settle both in and around this gravel. This will subsequently limit the amount of biological filtration that can take place within the substrate. Nevertheless, it is up to the individual to decide which is the most pleasing and decorative base medium to use, or which type will serve the most useful purpose for the setup chosen. If the hobbyist has any further doubt, it is a good idea to seek advice from a local aquarium store.

Whichever base medium has been chosen, it should be washed thoroughly before being placed in the tank. A good tip here is to pour about three or four inches of dry gravel at a time into a bucket and run clear water over it, stirring it up until the water runs clear. This process should be repeated until all the gravel is clean and inserted in the tank.

Unusual decoration

Aquarium decoration has a culture of its own. Within the hobby there are many trains of thought. There are those that endeavor to set up a tank using only the natural beauty of carefully selected plants as a backdrop to their living natural waterscape, whereas others wish to contrive something surreal and unnatural, using a combination of bright colors and plastic extras. If a tank is being set up for a child, then it is perfectly reasonable to use the odd plastic sunken galleon or plastic mermaid sitting atop an oyster that opens and closes every few seconds to release a few bubbles that hurry to the surface. Archways and caves of brightly colored plastic, along with scuba divers hovering in midwater, have their charm to some people. But remember that plastic items, while chemically inert, do take up space and, since many of these items are connected to air lines to produce intermittent bursts of bubbles, they can be disturbing to fish and some species of plants. Of course, after a few days, newly introduced fish will get used to this commotion and settle down. But eventually most of these objects cease to function correctly and adjustment is required. This disturbs the fish and plants again and the whole process is repeated.

From an aesthetic point of view, tropical fish and plants come from a variety of habitats. They are found in such places as the African rift lakes; the streams, rivers and lakes of Africa; North and South America; and Asia, Australia, and Indonesia. Not many mermaids and sunken galleons are found in such places. Of course, it is unnatural but some aquariums set up in this way do have a certain charm—even though many hobbyists would view the decorations as kitsch.

Plastic replicas of plants, on the other hand, do have a role to play in certain setups. In brackish-water

Used in an aquarium, bogwood creates a natural-looking background and provides an excellent focal point. You can also use vine roots, which are thinner and more textured.

aquariums, or African Rift Lake tanks, plants that can survive the hard water conditions are difficult to find and even more difficult to grow. Many species that are kept in these kinds of aquariums are herbivorous, or will uproot plants during their constant burrowing. Natural plants that have not evolved a resistance against this will quickly die. So if vegetation is required, plastic substitutes are sometimes the only option.

Bogwood and driftwood are very acceptable in tropical freshwater aquariums. The only drawback has been mentioned previously: some untreated types of wood leach tannin or other compounds into the water, which will give the aquarium an unsightly brownish-orange cast and can often prove detrimental to the health of the aquarium inhabitants. Even water changes will not eradicate this problem and often the only solution is to remove the offending piece of wood. Experienced aquarists will only choose wood that is being displayed for sale in an aquarium and can be seen to be of sufficient quality and suitably inert for use in a tank. One other alternative is to question the store owner or manager and establish its quality. Recently, bogwood that has been specially treated with an inert resin coating has been introduced to the aquarium world. Prior to this, bogwood was given a coating of silicone varnish to prevent it from leaching, but this gave it an unnatural shiny appearance. Of course, this is not to say that all bogwood and driftwood will cause problems in a newly set-up aquarium. Many of the items that are currently for sale at aquarium stores are ideal, but it is always better to know the potential drawbacks.

Choosing the system

For novice hobbyists, the choice is limited to a very simple setup containing hardy plants and fish with various decorative items and substrate, along with a filter to serve the needs of the system. Children, along with novices, will not usually dwell on the aesthetic aspects of a fish tank—they are only too happy to see and appreciate the bright colors and the constant movement of a tropical freshwater aquarium, whatever its design or however it is constructed. However, they often become curious and interested after a certain period of time. Some go on to become quite expert at keeping fish and plants. Others carry the hobby further and become experts in breeding and propagation. This hobby has to cater to them all.

Enthusiasts who have several months or years of experience often get interested in the extremities of the hobby. Many fish-keepers wish to push the envelope a little bit further. They may be drawn to semicommercial fish breeding, or they may wish to become specialists—or even experts—in a particular branch of this fascinating hobby. For these aquarists, the choice and diversity within the hobby is great. Specializing in one particular aspect of the hobby can be the most rewarding approach of all; what follows is a brief insight into the diversity of aquariums that can be set up if you are enthusiastic enough and wish to develop greater expertise.

The traditional tropical freshwater aquarium

A traditional tropical freshwater aquarium is usually the first choice for beginners. It is also the easiest to set up and maintain. It is estimated that there are millions of tropical freshwater aquariums worldwide. It is a very basic system that has no special requirements and can be set up using normal water that has been dechlorinated. The aquarium is set up using basic substrate, rock work, and perhaps a couple of pieces of driftwood that have been cured so that they do not leach any tannin into the water. Water is added slowly so that the substrate does not become disturbed. When the tank is about half full, the rock work and driftwood are added. Once this has been done, the aquarium is filled and allowed to "run in" for a period of about 24 hours. By that time the water is pretty much free of chlorine if the pumps and filtration units are running correctly.

The next step is to decide what plants are needed to make the aquarium attractive and lifelike, but there are questions to be answered. Is this tank being set up for a child? Is the intent to set up an aquarium to house a

A typical freshwater tropical community aquarium with natural growing plants among granite rocks. This type of aquarium is the easiest to set up and maintain.

selection of compatible community fish and plants? Or is the intention of the aquarist to set up a tank housing South American fish that inhabit soft water?

If the tank is for a child, there are many plastic decorations that are available at your local pet store. These items are often driven by an air line and are designed to please younger aquarists. The list is endless, from a fully suited diver bobbing up and down in the water and driven by an air pump, to a mermaid sitting gracefully on an oyster that opens and closes as a single air bubble is released.

The brackish-water aquarium

Brackish-water aquariums are increasing in popularity faster than most systems. The numbers of fish, invertebrates, and plants that can be kept in such an aquarium has been found to number in the thousands, rather then the few dozen that were considered suitable five years ago. A brackish-water aquarium can be spectacular when it is constructed correctly.

Brackish water is water that contains more sea salt than freshwater, but less than in the open sea. Moreover, a brackish-water environment is subject to major variations in water parameters, much more so than the sea, rivers, streams, and lakes. These are all relatively stable environments. The areas where brackish-water fish and plants are collected are diverse, but the most well-known are the estuaries. An estuary is the part of the river that meets the sea. It is usually subject to tides and is typically sluggish, silty, and full of organic nutrients. As a result, estuarine water is seldom clear and often a muddy brown color. The salinity is constantly fluctuating because of the tide and the amount of freshwater entering from rivers and streams or from rainfall. It is also subject to fluctuation through evaporation. Because of this, many brackish-water fish and plants are extremely tolerant of changes in water parameters. Most brackish-water fish species are very hardy and great numbers of them actually benefit from salinity changes and the amount of dissolved organic material in the water.

If the hobbyist wants to construct such an aquarium, a few things need to be pointed out. An all-glass tank is required, since salt will corrode any metal-framed one. Thankfully, this kind of aquarium seems to be a thing of the past. The hood on top of the tank has to be plastic and not metal for the same reason. Brackish water absorbs considerably less oxygen than freshwater because of its density (specific gravity). Therefore, good oxygenation is required. Air pumps and fast-flowing power-heads can

The Green puffer (Tetraodon nigroviridis) *from Southeast Asia is a typical brackish-water species.*

supply this requirement. The filter system is virtually the same as that of a marine aquarium and there are many alternatives, including the wet/dry filter. An undergravel filter is also a good alternative, but the water that is returned to the aquarium will be poor in oxygen because of bacterial activity, so it needs to be aerated.

The best substrate for this kind of system is aragonite. This comes in variety of different grades, but it should not be too fine. Some authors recommend using fine silica sand as an alternative. However, this has been found to produce mass outbreaks of diatomaceous algae (brown algae) that looks unsightly and can be difficult to eradicate from an aquarium.

Freshwater has a specific gravity (SG) of 1.000. Seawater has an SG of 1.024 to 1.025. Brackish water can be anywhere between these two extremes. Most fish and plants prefer that the SG be around 1.010 to 1.015.

To replicate this in a tank, the hobbyist needs some marine sea salt mix intended for aquarium use and a hydrometer to test the water once it has been mixed to the correct specific gravity. The rule of thumb here is: SG too low, add more salt. SG too high, add more water. Once the salt has been mixed, it should be aerated for 24 hours prior to addition to the aquarium. This is to ensure that all the different salts involved in the mixture have completely dissolved.

The African Rift Lake aquarium

The term "African Rift Lake aquarium" generally refers to an aquarium containing fish, predominantly colorful cichlids, that are found in the African Rift Lakes. There are a great many lakes in the African Rift Valley, but the three largest ones—Lake Victoria, Lake Tanganyika, and Lake Malawi—contain the greatest diversity of fish species.

The largest lake is Lake Victoria, which is bordered by Uganda, Kenya, and Tanzania. Although it is not, in the strictest sense, an African Rift Lake, it does lie between the eastern and western branches of the Great Rift Valley and has a very similar water chemistry to that of the true rift lakes. Lake Victoria is about 250 miles (402 km) long and roughly 110 miles (176 km) wide, roughly the size of

Ireland. It is also the youngest of the three rift lakes and the shallowest; its deepest point is only 250 feet (76 meters).

Lake Tanganyika is the second-largest lake in Africa and is roughly 410 miles (659 km) long. Its widest point is about 45 miles (72 km). This lake is over 4,700 feet (1,432 meters) deep. These features make it the longest lake in the world and also the second deepest. It currently supports over 200 described species of cichlids, but this number is sure to increase as more are discovered. The lake has only one outlet; therefore, the water has a higher mineral content than the other two lakes. The reason for this is that minerals are left behind as the water evaporates and these make the water harder and increase the alkalinity.

The third-largest lake is Lake Malawi, which is 365 miles (587 km) long and 53 miles (85 km) wide at its widest point. It probably supports the greatest freshwater fish diversity anywhere and is home to over 500 species of cichlids. It has a depth of 2,300 feet (701 meters). The water chemistry is similar to that of Lake Victoria, which is why many aquarists keep species from both these lakes together in the same aquarium.

By nature, African cichlids are very aggressive, so the aquarium should be as long as possible, with the width and depth playing a lesser role. The additional length will significantly reduce any territorial squabbles. Because the pH of the African Rift Lakes is very high, the base medium, or substrate, should comprise a material that will allow for pH buffering. This means that it should consist primarily of calcium carbonate. There are many choices here but crushed dolomite, coral sand, crushed shells, and aragonite are the most popular.

The decoration for this type of aquarium often presents a problem. Driftwood and bogwood will lower the pH

A group of Golden mbuna (Melanochromis auratus). *This fish is quite pugnacious, one male should be kept with several females in a "Malawi tank" with other similar species.*

and should be avoided. Most of the fish are herbivorous, so any plants will be quickly consumed. However, there is a great selection of artificial plants available and some are almost indistinguishable from the real thing. These are made of PVC and the fish will leave them alone.

The water chemistry of the African Rift Lakes is entirely different to freshwater anywhere else on the planet. It is more akin to a marine environment than freshwater. Because of this, salts should be added to increase the hardness, the alkalinity, and the pH. There are several theories about how best to do this. These include formulas for mixing epsom salt, baking soda, water, and sea salt in different ratios. The preferred way is to buy one of the proprietary brands of cichlid salts and mix it with water according to the direction on the package. This saves a great deal of hassle. Despite this advice, there will be many old diehards who prefer to concoct their own formulas—and good luck to them.

The table shown here gives the relative water parameters of the three African Rift Lakes. An important point to note here is that due to the high alkalinity in Lake Tanganyika, an excessive water temperature will severely reduce the amount of oxygen in the water. Lake Tanganyika cichlids cannot survive temperatures in excess of the upper limit shown here.

Water parameter	Lake Malawi	Lake Tanganyika	Lake Victoria
Temperature	75°–84°F (24°–29°C)	75°–82°F (24°–28°C)	70°–81°F (21°–27°C)
pH	7.8–8.6	8.6–9.5	7.2–8.6
Carbonate hardness	5–8 dKH	16–19 dKH	2–8 dKH

Osmosis

With the three main types of aquarium—traditional tropical, brackish water, and African Rift Lake—we can see that there are widely differing water parameters. Even among the three African aquariums there are great differences. From being in soft, slightly acidic water to that of almost being in seawater, fish would have to be able to alter their metabolism and other processes to compensate for the swings in water parameters. Many fish cannot do so and quickly succumb if they are subjected to extreme conditions. However, quite a few species can, and are extremely adaptable. How are they able to do this?

When a semipermeable membrane separates a low-concentration solution from a high-concentration solution, water molecules will move through the membrane from the low solution to the high solution in an attempt to equalize it. At the same time, the salt ions will move in the reverse direction from the high to the low solution. This process is called osmosis.

A fish is composed mainly of water and it lives in water. Its body walls and gills function as a semipermeable membrane. In the case of a freshwater fish, its body fluids contain more minerals than the surrounding water, so energy is used to stop the water from flooding in through its body tissue. In order to retain the correct balance of body fluids, as the fish absorbs water it must excrete abundant amounts of weak urine. A saltwater fish is the opposite. Its body fluids are a weaker solution than the surrounding water and it uses energy to stop its body fluids from flowing out into the water and dehydrating it. To do this it must drink copious amounts of water and produce only a little but very concentrated amount of urine. In the process of drinking water, specially developed cells in the kidney and gills of the fish extract the salt. The way that a fish controls the balance of its body fluids is called osmotic regulation. It is important to understand this and to bear it in mind when introducing fish into your aquarium. If the fish is to be introduced into a brackish-water tank, or one containing African Rift Lake cichlids, then the differences in the water in the transport bag and that of the water in the aquarium have to be equalized. If the tank water has a different density to that in the transport bag containing the fish, then osmotic shock will occur unless a gradual transfer is undertaken. This could result in the loss of the fish or at the very least create undue stress so that the fish becomes weak and prone to disease. Many fish have a highly effective system of osmotic regulation and can adapt to new water parameters, but they do need a certain amount of time in which to do it.

Choosing and introducing fish and plants

A dealer's reputation is based on the quality of the items he sells and on the service he gives. A newcomer starting out in this hobby should not be afraid to ask his advice. The dealer should also be forthcoming about the quality of his water and also its chemical parameters such as pH, dKH, SG, and other values. The fish should be chosen with care. Any specimens that have signs of disease should be left alone. A distressed fish often loses its natural body colors and if the cause is not just a bullying tank-mate, it could be an indication of something more serious. Fish with visible damage such as lesions on their head or body will often develop infections from which they may subsequently die. These should also be passed over. The fish you choose should be fat, healthy, and feeding. But don't ask to see it feeding, as this can cause problems during transportation if you buy; the freshly digested meal will usually be excreted into the transport bag on the way home. This will increase the ammonium content of the transport water and in doing so will lower the pH dramatically. Instead, ask the dealer if the fish is feeding and then take his word for it. After all, he wants you to come back! Fish that are not feeding and those that have a pinched or emaciated look should be avoided. Look carefully before buying; watch the fish and take time

doing so. Only then can you make the correct decision.

Before a fish can be introduced into an aquarium, it has to be acclimatized to the water. There will probably be a difference in the specific gravity of the water in the bag and that in the tank if you are buying African Rift Lake fish or those from brackish water. This has to be slowly equalized. If the fish has been in the bag for over an hour, and this is often the case, then the pH will have dropped dramatically because of the fish's excrement and urine in the water. This will be in the form of ammonium (NH^4) and does no permanent harm. However, a rapid rise of the pH will cause the ammonium, by this time also in the body fluids of the fish, to change to ammonia (NH_3^-). If this happens, the fish has little chance of survival. Even experienced aquarists sometimes do not take this into account, and if the fish is not dead by the next evening, it will die a week or so later from disease due to the lowering of its natural body resistance. When the dealer's tank has a pH of 7.8, the aquarist is wrong in thinking that when he arrives home two hours later the water in the bag will still be 7.8. In fact, it will be a great deal lower.

In the past the bag was always floated in the aquarium until the temperature had equalized. Then it was opened and the top rolled down to form a flotation collar. Over

A tank-bred Marbled angelfish (Pterophyllum scalare) *is ideal for the average community, being not overly aggressive.*

a period of 15 to 30 minutes, water from the aquarium was allowed to enter the bag periodically until the pH, hardness, and specific gravity had also equalized. After this the fish was released into its new surroundings. This method was fraught with problems not only because of ammonia. Often the bag would partially collapse, sometimes trapping the fish in a small space and inducing stress. Other tank inhabitants would come to investigate the bag and, seeing the distressed fish through the clear sides, would often proceed to bully it even before its release.

The modern way to acclimatize a fish is to use a bucket or small plastic aquarium and immediately tip the contents of the bag into it. Then, using a ¼ inch (6 mm) tube like those used with an air pump, water from the aquarium is allowed to siphon drop by drop into this container. A small clamp on the tube can be used to control the speed and the process should be carried out over a period of about 15 to 25 minutes until the fish is swimming in 90 percent aquarium water. At this stage and with the aquarium light switched off for the rest of the day, the fish can be coaxed gently out of the container into the aquarium. With any luck the fish will feed quite happily the next day. The transfer to the aquarium should not be done with a net, as this can cause damage. Nor do I recommend using your hands. Warm, dry hands on the skin of a fish will strip the slime coating and have the effect of a major burn on its body.

Plants should also be chosen with care. They should be healthy looking, with bright colors and strong leaves and stems. If bunched plants are being chosen, they are usually bundled together with lead. If there is some discoloration or rotting around the lead weight, they should not be purchased. This usually means that they are far from fresh and have been out of the substrate too long, or worse, they are dying.

Potted or rooted plants should be inspected for any signs of disease or decay. Rooted plants are a lot easier to plant if lead is wrapped around the base of the roots. Lead strips should never be wrapped around the bases of the leaves or the inflorescence. If a potted plant has a root system and pot that is buoyant because it has dried out during transportation, placing strips of lead around the inside of the pot can make it easier to plant. All potted plants do much better if they are planted with their pots in a deep substrate. Whatever species of plant is being introduced, it should be inspected for damaged, decaying, discolored, or dead leaves before planting. These should be stripped from the plant and discarded so that only healthy blades, stems, and root systems are introduced into the aquarium.

Care and maintenance

This is really just common sense. Having gone to the trouble of learning all about aquariums to the point of setting one up, a certain amount of routine aquarium maintenance is required if you are to keep the fish and plants in a healthy condition. This means the periodic addition of trace elements such as iron and other plant fertilizers. Regular topping up with water will also be necessary to replace water lost through evaporation. Since it is only the water that evaporates and not any dissolved salts or nitrate, this topping up should be done with fresh, nitrate- and phosphate-free water.

In the first year after an aquarium is set up, it is a good idea to do a daily count of the fish; any that do not appear at feeding time should be searched for. Monthly checks should also be carried out on any circulation pumps, power-heads, and air pumps in operation to make sure that they are running properly. The air pump filter wadding should be replaced if it is blocked or dirty. If limewood diffusers are used, such as those used in a sponge filter, they will have to be replaced every six to twelve weeks, depending on the quality. Most important of all, however, are the periodic partial water changes.

Magnetic glass cleaner from Tunze, Germany.

These will be dealt with in the following section.

The wise aquarist keeps his aquarium clean—this is simply good housekeeping. But it means more than just cleaning the viewing glass when the tank inhabitants can no longer be seen because the glass is covered with algae! Apart from glass cleaning, which can best be done using a

Even an aquarium containing hardy fish such as the Sumatra barb (Puntius tetrazona) *shown here requires regular maintenance.*

glass-cleaning magnet like the one shown on the previous page, filter wool must be changed regularly, or at least washed when any mechanical filters are in use. Detritus should also be removed whenever possible. To do this, it is good practice to "fan" the rocks and other aquarium decoration. Place your hand in the aquarium and, keeping your fingers closed, wave it from side to side over the rocks. In this way any detritus in the decoration will be dislodged and it can be siphoned off after it has had time to settle on the bottom.

Water changes

Like marine hobbyists, freshwater aquarists often dispute the necessity for carrying out partial water changes on a weekly or monthly basis. The argument is usually, "My water is so good that I don't need to change it." But we simply do not know enough about what happens to the water over a period of time in an aquarium. We do know that it changes its composition. The point is that we have no way at the moment of measuring all the parameters and components of water to determine whether or not it is actually "so good." We know well enough that water ages, and a gradual buildup of nitrate and phosphate occurs, but what of the other hidden elements and compounds that can build up in a mature tank? Through biological processes, phenol and other pollutants can gradually increase in a tank and delicate fish start to die. What of other elements that can build up in an aquarium, like molybdenum, titanium, cobalt, selenium, lead, and vanadium? How much of these elements is important for a healthy aquarium and how much is detrimental? What is their level after the aquarium has been running for six months or more? We have no practical way of finding out, and until we have a way to determine the total composition of the water in our aquariums, we must replace those elements that are removed by the plants and fish and remove the unwanted elements and compounds that build up in the aquarium over time. The indiscriminate addition of proprietary vitamin supplements for fish, and plant nutrients and fertilizers, is not the way.

A partial water change every month will ensure that a portion of the old water is regularly replaced. The amount should be restricted to 10 percent of the actual water volume—even better is when 2.5 percent of the water volume is changed every week.

New water should be strongly aerated for 24 hours before use. This will oxidize any additives such as fluoride and make the water safer to use. Prior to its addition, the same amount of water should be removed from the aquarium. The water that is removed need not be thrown away immediately; it still has several uses. For instance, with a little added salt, it can be used for brine shrimp cultures. It can also be used in the garden or for potted plants.

Whenever any water is mixed for an aquarium, it should not be used directly from the faucet without first establishing how much the water is contaminated by nitrate and phosphate. In some areas where lead and copper pipes are still used, there can be a lethal amount of other poisonous substances in the water. The amounts vary considerably from area to area. Measured levels of lead and copper have often been found that actually exceed the World Health Organization's limit for human consumption. Neither the United States nor Europe has set any legal limit on the amount of these contaminants in domestic tap water, and until they do it will continue to be a problem.

Reverse-osmosis units

Water from the faucet often contains contaminants that may be harmful to delicate fish and plants, especially if it is used during the initial setting up of an aquarium. It can contain quite high levels of nitrate, phosphate, chemical additives, and insecticides, and if these chemicals are found, the water needs to be treated and purified. Water can be treated effectively with a reverse-osmosis unit such as the one shown below. These units work by allowing water to be forced the wrong way (hence the name) through a semipermeable membrane. The water pressure needs to be at least 3 bars in order to overcome the osmotic pressure. In this way, small, pure water molecules are allowed to pass through the membrane while the larger molecules that contain contaminants pass over the membrane. There are two outlets to these units, the first of which is the rejection outlet. The second outlet releases the purified water to be collected. One of the drawbacks of using these units is that up to five times more water is rejected than that which is purified. Nevertheless, the rejection rates of pollution can be up to 98 percent depending on the type of membrane that is used. The rejected water need not be thrown away. It can be directed into the toilet flushing system or into the garden. Many aquarists use it for watering houseplants or for washing the car.

There are two types of reverse-osmosis units, with two different types of membrane. Units that use cellulose triacetate (CTA) membranes are usually cheaper but they are not so good, having a pollution rejection rate of only 90–95 percent. In addition, they need to be run constantly to prevent the membrane from drying out and becoming brittle and porous. If this happens, they only function as a

In an aquarium, the water quality must be optimal in order to keep plants and fish like these with any degree of success. Much of this depends on the quality of the freshwater that is used for topping up and partial water changes.

coarse sieve. In addition, these membranes will be broken down by bacteria over a period of time and have to be replaced.

The second type of membrane is much better. This is known as the "thin film composition" (TFC) membrane. These units are more expensive but have a higher pollution rejection rate, 95–98 percent. They are a great deal more resistant to attack from bacteria and only need to be replaced every three to six years. The difference in time depends on whether or not prefilters are in use. A good reverse-osmosis unit will come complete with a sediment prefilter to remove large particles from the water before they can reach, and possibly block, the membrane. It will also have a carbon prefilter. This is very important, because it will not only remove some of the heavy metals and larger organic molecules from the water, it will also remove the chlorine. Chlorine is capable of ruining a membrane by making it porous in a short period of time. By using a carbon prefilter, the life of the membrane will be extended. All reverse-osmosis units have a rating in gallons or liters per day.

The Standard 90 reverse-osmosis unit from Aqua Medic comes complete with sediment prefilter and carbon filter.

Deionizing units

There are two kinds of deionizing units available to the aquarist and both involve the use of ion exchange resins. Ion exchange resins are either "anion," which remove the negatively charged ions from the water, or "cation," which remove the positively charged ions. These two types of resins form the basis of the deionizing unit. In the first type, both resins are combined in one chamber and when they become saturated and ineffective they have to be replaced. With the second type of unit, two chambers are used to keep the resins separate. The advantage of this is that the resins can be recharged using strong acid and base solutions. With mixed resins this is not possible.

There are, however, several drawbacks to using deionizing units. The first is that the resins need to be continually replaced or recharged, and this takes time and resources. Not so obvious, though, is the fact that any contaminants, such as pesticides, that are neutrally charged will not be removed. Deionizing units should never be used to full capacity since they may begin to release some of the contaminants that they have removed back into the purified water again. In comparison to a reverse-osmosis unit, the main advantage is that deionizing units filter all the water passing through, not just a percentage. Even so, they have never really caught on in the aquarium hobby.

Ultraviolet sterilizer modules

Ultraviolet light (UV-C), with a wavelength range of 100 to 280 nanometers, has long been known to have damaging, sometimes lethal, effects on living cell tissue. By exploiting this, it is possible to achieve a sterilization effect. UV-C light splits the molecules and upsets the synthesis of the gene-carrying threadlike structures so that the inherited characteristics of the cell are destroyed. When the cell splits, the genetic information is no longer there and it dies. This knowledge has enabled us to produce effective ultraviolet sterilizing units for use against bacterial infection.

The ultraviolet sterilizing units for the aquarium hobby are designed to combat fish parasites, plankton, bacteria,

and microalgae by destroying their reproductive capabilities. The unit is designed to allow water to be pumped around an ultraviolet light source.

During the construction of the light source, quartz or crystal glass is employed to filter out the unwanted wavelengths and leave a specific and effective wavelength of 253.7 nanometers. With a 6-watt light source it is possible to sterilize a 100-gallon (450-liter) aquarium effectively, depending on the flow of water through.

In a properly set-up aquarium, with good water quality, an ultraviolet sterilizing unit is an excellent addition. Fish parasites, bacterial fish infections, and explosion-like growths of unwanted algae will not occur.

Foods and feeding

Once the fish have been settled in the aquarium, they need to be fed regularly. The rule of thumb here is that fish should be fed once or twice a day but sparingly so that all the food is taken within a matter of about a minute. Do not allow food to settle in the bottom of the aquarium and remain uneaten. If this happens, it should be removed immediately, and thereafter the fish should be fed even more frugally. In an aquarium where there are only a few herbivorous fish, another rule applies. There is usually enough natural microalgae present in the tank that feeding may only be required every second or third day. There are many types of food that can be given to fish and most of them fall into four main categories:

Flake and granulated food: These are commercially prepared foods made especially for tropical fish and there are many varieties available. They are an ideal supplement to live or frozen foods that form the staple diet of carnivorous aquarium fish. Both flake and granulated foods normally contain up to 1 percent phosphate, which in the case of overfeeding makes it a very good microalgae fertilizer! Nevertheless, they are rich in the protein, carbohydrates, fat, and vitamins that are essential for energy and cell growth. Some medicinal flake foods contain malachite green chloride so that treatment for gill and skin parasites can be given orally. This has the advantage that treatment of these manifestations can be carried out in the aquarium without removing the stricken

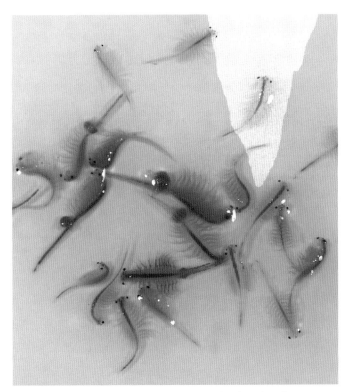

It is recommended that fish be given live food such as brine shrimp, but make sure that it is thoroughly washed and free from disease.

fish to a quarantine tank. However, its effect is limited to parasitic infections.

Frozen (frost) food: The main diet of carnivorous fish should consist of a variety of frozen foods and there are many to choose from. By having an assortment of these in the freezer, you can be sure that your fish will have a balanced diet. These foods are very convenient to use; they come in flat packs that can be easily broken up into daily portions. Recently, pop-out cube packs that are already separated into feeding portions have entered the market. A typical assortment to have in the freezer could consist of the water flea (*Daphnia*), adult brine shrimp (*Artemia*), bloodworms, and frozen greenstuff. Frozen portions should not be put directly into the aquarium; they should be first thawed out. I have found that the best method is to use a small plastic sieve. Place the frozen food in the sieve and then hold it under the tap where cool water will quickly thaw it out. This has the added advantage of washing away the phosphate-rich ice and frost coating that would normally find its way into the aquarium. It is interesting to note that as soon as the fish see the small, white plastic sieve that I use, they become agitated even before I cross the room.

Live food: An occasional feeding of live food is advantageous to most carnivorous fish and there are

some, such as garfish, that will only accept live food in the beginning. As a rule, though, these fish can soon be coaxed to take frozen food when live food is not available.

Typical live foods that are often available from a handler are freshwater shrimp, *Daphnia*, bloodworms, white worms, and brine shrimp (*Artemia*). Unlike frost foods, which are usually irradiated to prevent the transfer of disease to an aquarium, there is always a small chance that fish can become infected by eating live foods. When their origin is from freshwater, they should be washed thoroughly before use. With brine shrimp there is such a slender chance of this happening that it can be ignored for our purposes.

Green foodstuff: These are vegetable foods such as lettuce, spinach, and algae. Some fish are herbivores while many others are omnivorous, sustaining themselves on a mixed diet of plants and fresh protein. In order to fully satisfy the feeding requirements of these fish, lettuce and greenstuff can be introduced if the aquarium algae is too sparse. The lettuce or spinach leaf should be blanched in hot water first and it is a good idea to clamp it between the two halves of a glass-cleaning magnet before placing it in the bottom of the aquarium. In this way the fish can bite and tear at it much easier. The reason it needs to be blanched first is to eliminate the cellulose. Carbohydrate in the form of cellulose is found in the cell walls of plants and this is indigestible for fish. Spinach is a very good substitute for algae and is high in iron and calcium. The alternative is to set up a separate tank to grow cuttings of plants and place them in the main aquarium at regular intervals to satisfy the needs of large herbivorous fish. Most fish are content if their diet is supplemented with frozen greenstuff, so this is only advice to those aquarists who are having difficulty feeding their precious plant-eating charges.

Feeding newly arrived fish: When one considers that most land animals are only able to convert about 10 percent of their daily food intake into body flesh, then it may come as a surprise that fish can convert up to 50 percent to flesh. Because of this, they require a high-protein diet. Often, a newly bought fish will refuse to feed in the first few days. It is essential in this case to understand the reasons why a fish feeds in the first place. There are six main reasons and knowing these will help the fish to feed and also to understand why it is not feeding.

The first and obvious reason is hunger. Lack of hunger can be caused by the end phase of a disease or through shock and fright.

The second reason why a fish feeds is habit. At a particular time of day there may be a current change, bringing food-rich water to the fish or it may have its own particular rock on which it grazes. These are no longer there when it is introduced into a new aquarium and so the fish has to be encouraged to feed at a different time and in a different place. The wise aquarist can overcome this problem by making his feeding strategy as attractive as possible for the fish. In this way the fish must, in effect, alter its behavioral characteristics. This takes time and patience on the part of the aquarist, and hunger on the part of the fish.

The third reason is as a reflex action, or conditioned reflex. This is usually caused by something moving in close proximity to the fish that, while perhaps no longer hungry, snaps at the morsel in a reflex action. The lesson to be learned here is that movement of food at feeding time makes it much more attractive for the new arrival.

Curiosity is the fourth reason that a fish will take food. In this case a fish may not be hungry or may even be in a state of shock. But something very near is wriggling or swimming and if it is attractive enough, the fish will investigate. It will take it into its mouth briefly and spit it out again as if testing it and if it tastes good it will eat it, even if it is a live adult brine shrimp which it has probably never before encountered. The trick here is to use live food in various forms for the "difficult fish" in the hope that it is tempted to begin to feed. And when it does, it is a much less difficult proposition to wean it onto frost foods.

The fifth reason why a fish feeds, but only in human terms, is jealousy. The new arrival may be the only fish in the aquarium or there may be only one or two small tank-mates that are unobtrusive at feeding time. This new fish may be used to having to compete for its food in a feeding commotion with others of its kind or even other fish. In an aquarium this may be no longer the case. The answer here is obvious: add a few small but hungry tank-mates. They will create such a commotion at feeding times that the new arrival will be unable to resist competing.

The sixth and final reason could be loosely termed "anger." A fish is incapable of anger in the way that a human experiences it. Rather, it is a defense mechanism where feeding is triggered as a response to a threat. Some animal behaviorists would term this a reflex action, but I disagree. It sees something as a threat but it is provocatively small, so instead of driving it off, it simply eats it.

A typical case in point here is the salmon lure that is often used by anglers. A fresh-run river salmon is not hungry; it is there to spawn. And the salmon lure is usually a concoction of brightly colored tinsel and feathers; it is unlike anything the fish has ever seen. Yet it will strike at it and swallow it if it is presented in the right way. The moral of this is to make feeding times as provocative as possible for these new arrivals.

Diseases

Most aquarium books deal with fish diseases in great detail. The modern way of thinking dictates that we have a slightly different approach. Aquarium fish diseases will not be covered in any great detail in this work since we now know that 99 percent of all fish diseases that manifest themselves in an aquarium are totally unnecessary and can be avoided. They are, as a whole, caused by mistakes by the aquarist and bad water quality.

In a well-matured aquarium with good water quality, disease will not break out unless the aquarist makes a mistake such as allowing a fish to have a diet deficiency, or by introducing a new fish to the aquarium that is in a stressed state.

The major causes of disease in an aquarium are bad water quality, stress, incorrect diet, overstocking of the aquarium, and, most common of all, stocking the aquarium before it has fully settled down. The latter is obvious, since the majority of disease problems that the beginner encounters occur in the first six months. After that time, the tank will have settled down. The biggest mistake is rushing things, but overcrowding the aquarium

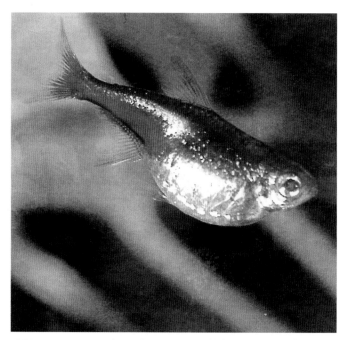

A Neon tetra (Paracheirodon innesi) *suffering from abdominal dropsy, where excess fluid has accumulated within the body.*

is asking for trouble as well. Keep the water quality to a high standard, don't make mistakes, and there will be no disease problems. This cannot be stressed enough.

In spite of this advice there are diseases that do occur. This is because nothing and no one in this hobby is completely infallible. Therefore, the following six disease descriptions have been included, along with their symptoms and the respective methods of eradication. These are the ones that the novice aquarist is most likely to meet.

Ichthyophthiriasis **sp.** (White spot disease or "Ich")

DESCRIPTION: A parasitic ciliate protozoan that goes through several stages in its life cycle, including a free-swimming (swarming) stage. Very contagious.

SYMPTOMS: Small, white, pinhead-sized spots on the fins, head, and body of the fish. Loss of appetite. In later stages, clustering lesions on the fins, increased gill beat rate, and finally, death.

CURE: Remove the affected fish to a quarantine tank and treat with a copper-based cure or malachite green.

Oodinium pilularis (Freshwater velvet disease)

DESCRIPTION: A parasitic dinoflagellate protozoan that is believed to be actually a kind of alga. It also goes through a free-swimming stage in its life cycle. Extremely contagious.

SYMPTOMS: Peppery dusting of minute gold-brown spots on the sides, head, and fins of the fish, giving it a velvety appearance. There is an increase in the gill beat rate and the fish usually swims around with fins folded, occasionally flicking itself off the rocks in an attempt to rid itself of the irritation. Often fatal.

CURE: Quarantine this fish and treat it with a copper-based cure.

Epistylis **sp.,** *Saprogenia* **sp.,** *Flexobacterial infection* (Cotton wool disease)

DESCRIPTION: Cotton wool disease can be any of three disorders. Epistylis is a microscopic parasite that grows in compact bundles and appears the same as cotton wool disease. Saprogenia are fungal organisms that attack fish with low immune systems. They can only grow on damaged areas of the skin and fins. Flexobacteria grow in bundles or stacks and can appear as cotton wool disease.

SYMPTOMS: White cotton wool balls, usually on the fins and tail. In later stages of the disease, the growths will spread and turn gray or reddish-brown. Mouth fungus is also known as cotton wool disease. Highly contagious and, if left untreated, it is fatal.

CURE: Topical application of potassium permanganate solution, gentian violet, or treatment with a proprietary fungicidal medication.

Exophthalmus (Pop eye)

DESCRIPTION: Not considered to be a disease but rather a symptom. However, it can also be caused by cyanobacteria entering the membrane of the eye, or by bad netting of the fish.

SYMPTOMS: Very obvious swelling of one or both eyes, which become opaque. Loss of appetite and in severe cases it can be fatal. Recovery from this disease sometimes results in blindness of the affected eye.

CURE: Remove the affected fish to a quarantine tank and reduce lighting to a minimum for 14 days. If this is not possible, shorten the light duration in the aquarium and make sure that there are plenty of places for the fish to hide. Light reduction will usually cure the problem.

Neobenedenia sp., *Benedenia mellini* (Gill and skin flukes)

DESCRIPTION: Small, wormlike parasites that attach themselves to the skin and gills of a fish. In extreme cases this can prove fatal.

SYMPTOMS: Gills colored pink instead of the usual bright red. Increase in respiratory rate; the fish will flick itself off rocks repeatedly to try to displace the parasites.

CURE: Treat with the addition of methylene blue or formaldehyde-based cures, or cures containing a combination of the two.

Gram-negative and gram-positive bacterial infections

DESCRIPTION: Bacterial infections that can affect the fins and body of a fish as well as the internal organs. Gram (+) bacteria and gram (-) bacteria differ in the kinds of infections they produce and in the types of antibiotics that are likely to kill them.

SYMPTOMS: Fin rot and tail rot, along with internal stomach swellings and redness of a particular area of the body are all indications of a bacterial infection of one kind or another. Gray slime, scratching, and open sores can also be indicative of bacterial growth on or within a fish's body.

CURE: Remove to a hospital tank and treat with a proprietary brand of broad-spectrum antibiotic, such as tetracycline, amoxicillin, nifurpirinol, or erythromycin.

General treatment

For diseases that have a free-swimming stage, such as gill and skin flukes, velvet or white spot disease, the use of a diatom filter can be helpful, especially in a tropical freshwater aquarium. This is because at the free-swimming or swarming stages, the disease can be literally filtered out of the water. For more information about the installation and maintenance of a diatomaceous filter, see page 21.

Copper-based cures

A word of warning: copper-based cures should be used with extreme caution and never in a tank containing freshwater invertebrates. Copper is lethal to most invertebrates, even in minute quantities. It can also be poisonous to fish if the dose is too high, so it should only be administered as a last resort in a separate aquarium. Always use a copper test kit to monitor the level.

Broad spectrum antibiotics

Recently, broad-spectrum antibiotics have become available to the hobbyist. Many of these are in capsule form and—particularly in the United States—are available without a prescription. Antibiotics combat microbes that cause diseases in aquarium fish. They are manufactured for aquarium use, usually in 250 mg capsules, placed directly into the aquarium at the rate of one capsule or tablet for every 10 gallons (38 liters) of aquarium water.

Many familiar antibiotics can be used to treat fish, including penicillin, ampicillin, tetracycline, amoxicillin, cephalexin, erythromycin, and ketoconazole. The packages usually contain 100 doses and, considering the high prices paid for other veterinary medicines, they are inexpensive. Most nonspecific fish diseases can be eradicated using this kind of medication. Also, fish that have been treated with antibiotics tend to be much more resistant to infection.

There are also "bio-bandages" available nowadays. This kind of treatment quickly and effectively treats open wounds and cysts. They are much more effective than open baths or dip treatments. Bio-bandages are gel-based topical wound preparations that contain a combination of the antibiotic neomycin and a proprietary vitamin-polymer formula for quicker healing. However, the utmost care is needed in their application.

Other life-saving remedies

Every hobbyist should have a first-aid kit that includes a small container for use as a weak salt bath for fish that have parasitic infections. Salt baths should only be used on species that are salt/pH resistant. This excludes most fish from South America. Other items in the first-aid kit should include a pair of tweezers, a soft net, a soft paintbrush (for applying topical medications), and pair of scissors.

Good standby medications should include:
- Methylene blue
- Malachite green
- Aniline green
- Acriflavine
- Formaldehyde
- Victoria green
- Chelated copper
- Gentian violet

Malachite green is always useful for sterilizing nets if the hobbyist has more than one tank. It is good practice to have a bucket or other suitable container filled with a mild solution of water and malachite green. After use, the nets can be dropped into this solution. This prevents any disease from being transferred from one tank to another.

Scientific classification

The eighteenth-century Swedish naturalist Carolus Linnaeus devised a system of classification for the animal kingdom, the basis of which is still in use today. In this system he grouped like creatures together. These groups, called phyla, could then be split into different classes of creatures which, in turn, could be further subdivided until it was possible for scientists to place every known living creature in its correct place in the animal kingdom. Of course, this was an enormous step forward in man's understanding of the surrounding world, and it was destined to become the universally accepted method of recognizing a particular animal in any discussion. Each creature was given a Latin name consisting of two parts. The first part referred to the genus (the generic name of that particular branch of the family) and the second part to the species (the specific epithet for the animal itself). For instance, in Germany a fish may be called a "Siamesischer kampffisch"; in the United States it may be referred to as the "Betta"; and in England it would usually be called the "Siamese fighting fish." Its systematic

The "Siamesischer kampffisch," as it is known in Germany, is also called a "Siamese fighting fish" in England and, in the United States it is known as the "Betta." Its systematic name— Betta splendens—is, however, recognized throughout the world.

or Latin name, however, is *Betta splendens*, and it is this name that is recognized worldwide. Although I have used common names for fish and plants in this book, they are always accompanied by the Latin name in italics to prevent confusion. Taking the fish *Betta splendens* as an example, it could be systematically displayed thus:

KINGDOM: ANIMALIA
 Phylum: Chordata
  Subphylum: Vertebrata
   Superclass: Gnathostomata
    Grade: Teleostomi
     Class: Actinopterygii
      Subclass: Neopterygii
       Division: Teleostei
        Subdivision: Euteleostei
         Superorder: Acanthopterygii
          Series: Percomorpha
           Order: Perciformes
            Family: Belontiidae
             Subfamily: Macropodinae
              Genus: *Betta*
               Species: *Betta splendens*

The modern system that has been used for the fish listed and described in this book follows that of Joseph Nelson's definitive work, *Fishes of the World* (1994), with more recent research and current information to update this. This is the most sensible system at the moment and that which is most often used and understood by aquarists.

For the plant research and identification, a synthesis of information has been used, which includes modern DNA analyses and many recent works of reference, as well as ongoing discussions with botanists and naturalists throughout the world.

Identification of the plants in the following chapter, and later in chapters on the fish and invertebrates, should always be done using these scientific names. The common names also included have little scientific meaning and are intended only to represent a cross-section of those names applied to fish and invertebrates in English-speaking lands throughout the world. They do not form the base of any form of reference as they vary a great deal from country to country and even region to region. But they may be of some help to the beginner.

The plants and fish included in this book have been chosen for their suitability for a tropical freshwater aquarium, irrespective of any form of conservation control or environmental pressure groups; however, most of those described are available to the aquarium trade without control. Fish suitable only for public aquariums, because they subsequently grow too large for the average aquarist, have not been included.

The sizes of fish and plants that are given are the maximum known size that they will grow to in their natural habitat. In plants, this is the height from the substrate to the tip of the highest leaf. In fish, it is the measurement from the tip of the snout to the base of the caudal fin. When the range of a plant or fish is given, it is intended to indicate where the particular species is found to be endemic. Isolated or unusual occurrences have not been taken into consideration, nor have those instances where species have been artificially introduced into certain areas. The number of bubbles at the side of each species' photograph refers to the degree of difficulty in which a particular species can be kept in a healthy state in an aquarium. The quick glance visual help code indicates the following:

◖—Easy, a good organism for beginners as well as experienced aquarists.
◖◖—Not difficult for aquarists with six months or more experience.
◖◖◖—Quite difficult to keep. Only for experienced aquarists.
◖◖◖◖—Very difficult. Require optimal aquarium conditions.
◖◖◖◖◖—Almost impossible for all but the most experienced aquarist.

Notes on taxonomy

Only painstaking research, examination of the plants and fish themselves, a great deal of correspondence, and reference to the most up-to-date scientific literature can form a solid foundation that is reliable in terms of species identification. The listings given in the following chapters will, I hope, reflect these efforts. The 600 or so species named here should at least help to clarify some of this confusion.

The diagram shown on page 55 is for reference purposes, since there are certain terms used in the

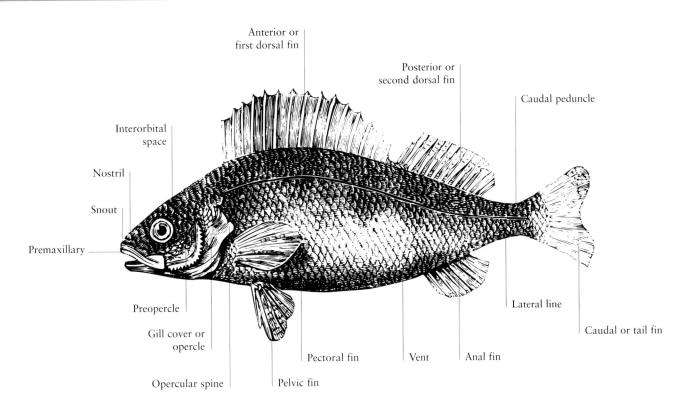

Anterior or
first dorsal fin

Posterior or
second dorsal fin

Caudal peduncle

Interorbital
space

Nostril

Snout

Premaxillary

Preopercle

Gill cover or
opercle

Opercular spine

Pectoral fin

Pelvic fin

Vent

Anal fin

Lateral line

Caudal or tail fin

accompanying fish descriptions with which the reader may not be familiar.

In order to fully understand the way this book is laid out in terms of the descriptions of the plants and fish, it is necessary to first explain the order in which the various families appear. To some this will be unusual, since most aquarium books in the past have simply listed the families in alphabetical order. This is not strictly correct because it does not follow the systematic methods used by botanists, biologists, and ichthyologists throughout the world. Because this book has been written to set parameters in terms of aquarium science, I have followed the accepted method.

It is not possible in a single volume to cover and describe all of the more than 6,000 species of aquatic plants or 9,300 or so species of fish that are found in tropical freshwater environments throughout the world. Nor is it necessary, because a good 70 percent of them are unsuitable for a home aquarium. One reason is because many grow too large for the average aquarium, although they may often be kept in zoos and large public aquariums. Other reasons may be that they are too rare, unsuitable, or impossible to keep alive in an aquarium. It could also be that they are simply too drab and uninteresting to the average dealer and aquarist. This leaves us with about 900 species that are really suitable for a tropical fish tank. But even this is too many to describe in a single volume.

What I have tried to do in this work is to cover a cross-section of the species that the hobbyist will find at his local dealer or that the dealer will find on export/import lists. This has not been an easy task because this book is aimed at both the U.S. market and the European market, so the "local dealer" could be in any of these lands. This will inevitably lead to some species being unavailable to the reader. However, this work caters for similar species of the same family, in terms of care and keeping in an aquarium. Also, some species of fish can become out of bounds to aquarists because they are considered invasive if released into the wild; such is the case with the Eel catfish, now banned in the United States.

Regarding the descriptions of the various species covered in this book, it has been difficult to establish some sort of uniformity across the groups. This is often the case when it involves not only fish but also invertebrates and plants. For example, in the section on plants in the aquarium, their cultivation plays a secondary role, since most plants will grow and can be readily cultured. Where this is not the case, it is mentioned in the body text. Fish, however, breed in many different ways, so a brief description has been given for each species described, if it is known.

Plants present another problem. Plant growers and wholesalers misname many of them. These errors get passed on to the hobbyist through the various retail outlets. Where this is relevant, it has been pointed out in the description.

Sometimes a plant will be a variety of a species and, in this case, the word "var." is written after the specific epithet and before the name of the variety. In other cases, a plant may lack a specific epithet altogether and just be given a variety name such as *Echinodorus* "Kleiner bär." This is because the plant is the result of cross-culture of tissue from two different species.

part two

AQUARIUM
PLANTS

The importance of aquarium plants

Plants are as important in an aquatic environment as they are on land. Think of a place without plants. The only places are very arid deserts, the deep oceans, and wastelands of the Arctic. Plants populate everywhere else, from the rain forests to the tundra. It is plants that produce and maintain our environment. The most obvious characteristic of plants is their green color, the result of a pigment called chlorophyll. Plants utilize this to capture light energy, which fuels the manufacture of food, such as sugar, starch, and other carbohydrates. Without these food sources, most life on earth would cease to exist. Oh, perhaps there would be fungi and some algae, but there would be no fruits, vegetables, grains—or animals—because these ultimately rely on plants for food, too. An aquarium without plants is not a fully functional biosystem. It is also a lot less attractive.

Kingdom: Plantae

Plantae encompasses all land and aquatic plants. It includes mosses, ferns, conifers, deciduous trees, and flowering plants. They have a truly amazing range of diverse forms. With more than 250,000 species, the kingdom is second only in size to the arthropods, the jointed-leg animals, which include all the insects of the world. Plants have been around for a very long time. The first terrestrial plants began to appear in the Ordovician period some 500 million years ago, but they did not begin to resemble modern plants until the late Silurian period 90 million years later.

By the close of the Devonian period about 360 million years ago, there was a wide variety of shapes and sizes of plants. These included small creeping plants and tall forest trees. In the table shown to the right, by no means all plants are represented. This list includes only those families that are important to the tropical freshwater aquarium hobby.

Division: Chlorophyta (green algae)

Ancient algae appeared almost two billion years ago. It is the brown algae, *Heterokontophyta*, that seem to be the most recent line of phylogenetic development, with the earliest fossilized records of diatomaceous algae occurring at the beginning of the Cretaceous period, 120 million years ago.

The division incorporates almost 8,000 species in about 500 genera. There are 10 current classes and a total of 17 orders. These algae all have chlorophyll as the predominant pigmentation. There are about 1,100 species to be found in seawater and the pigmentation consists of beta-carotene and the chlorophylls "a" and "b." The cell walls are made up of pectin compounds and cellulose. Some species have calcium carbonate within the cell tissue. These are generally referred to as calcareous algae and are entirely marine living. In this division there is only one order that contains species which are of interest to the tropical freshwater aquarist.

Green algae of the division Chlorophyta are what one could term opportunistic plants. They are found in a variety of habitats in both fresh and seawater. They occur in brackish-water estuaries and on land. Everyone has seen old, algae-covered gravestones, but this is not the only example. The trunks of trees in damp woods and forests often have a greenish film of algae on their bark. This is usually green algae of the genera *Trentepohlia* or *Trebouxia*. In the springtime, ponds sometimes have a greenish cast in the water and in the summer, wool-like growths of greenish slime. These are all algae belonging to the division Chlorophyta. Some are able to survive in extreme conditions such as ice and snow. In the high mountains *Chlamydomonas nivalis* gives old snow a somewhat reddish color. A mixture of carotene-based pigments (hematochrome) causes this because it effectively masks the chlorophyll present in the algae. Arctic and Antarctic ice is often tinted pastel green and blue; this is sometimes caused by the presence of algae from this large group.

The green algae, through their special characteristics, form an almost natural division that differentiates them from all other algae. They do have a close affinity to the mosses and the demarcation here is a great deal more difficult to establish with some species. Algae can be colony-building or single-celled. They may be planktonic, multicelled, or microscopic; they can occur as epiphytes on other algae. The presence of some species

Plantae

Division: Chlorophyta
Class: Cladophorophyceae
Order: Cladophorales
Family: Cladophoraceae

Division: Bryophyta
Class: Bryopsida
Order: Hypnales
Family: Hypnaceae

Class: Hepaticopsida
Order: Marchantiales
Family: Ricciaceae

Division: Lycopodiophyta
Class: Isoetopsida
Order: Isoetales
Family: Isoetaceae

Division: Magnoliophyta
Class: Liliopsida
Order: Alismatales
Family: Alismataceae

Order: Aponogetonales
Family: Aponogetonaceae

Order: Hydrocharitales
Family: Hydrocharitaceae

Order: Arales
Families: Acoraceae, Araceae, Lemnaceae

Order: Arecales
Family: Arecaceae

Order: Cyperales
Family: Cyperaceae

Order: Xyridales
Family: Mayacaceae

Order: Asparagalis
Family: Ophiopogonaceae

Order: Asteliales
Family: Dracaenaceae

Order: Amaryllidales
Family: Amaryllidaceae

Order: Pontederiales
Family: Pontederiaceae

Class: Magnoliopsida
Order: Caryophyllales
Family: Amaranthaceae

Order: Nymphaeales
Families: Cabombaceae, Nymphaeaceae

Order: Apiales
Family: Apiaceae

Order: Myrtales
Families: Lythraceae, Onagraceae

Class: Piperopsida
Order: Ceratophyllales
Family: Ceratophyllaceae

Class: Rosopsida
Order: Asterales
Family: Asteraceae

Order: Araliales
Family: Hydrocotylaceae

Order: Capparales
Family: Brassicaceae

Order: Menyanthales
Family: Menyanthaceae

Order: Primulales
Family: Primulaceae

Order: Urticales
Family: Urticineae

Order: Violales
Family: Violaceae

Order: Lamiales
Families: Acanthaceae, Lamiaceae, Scrophulariaceae

Order: Haloragales
Family: Haloragaceae

Order: Rhizophorales
Family: Rhizophoraceae

Division: Polypodiophyta
Class: Polypodiopsida
Order: Aspleniales
Family: Lomariopsidaceae

Order: Marsileales
Families: Marsileaceae, Salviniaceae

Order: Parkeriales
Family: Parkeriaceae

Order: Polypodiales
Family: Polypodiaceae

---

can indicate organic pollution, whereas the presence of others may indicate a constant influx of clean, clear water.

Their colors range from bright apple green to leaf green, but yellow, bottle-green, or greenish-black forms are also found. Many of the species live in freshwater. Mostly these are the algae of the classes Zygnematophyceae, Charophyceae, and most species of the class Chlorophyceae.

Order: Cladophorales

The order is made up of algae that are very varied in both shape and size. In the family Cladophoraceae, there is only one genus containing species that are of interest to the aquarist. In the genus *Chaetomorpha*, the growth form is often a confused tangle of small, relatively thin thalli that are made up of short cells that are cylindrical in shape. The algae occur in varying shades of green and are found in mat-formed or bushy colonies. These afford a haven for small fish and invertebrates, which can hide within their snarled growths. The second genus, *Cladophora*, contains mostly marine representatives, although there are also some freshwater species. The growth is usually less tangled, with thin, tubular branches that form tufts on harbor pilings and rocks. Their color may vary from light to dark green and uncontrolled growths can cover vast inshore areas.

The second family, Valoniaceae, encompasses algae that are spherical or oval-formed with balloonlike vesicles consisting of a single large cell. These cells, which can be anything up to 2 inches (5 cm) in diameter, are considered to be the largest single living cell in the world. The surfaces of these vesicles are often colonized by microalgae (epiphytes). They may be attached to the substrate by hairlike rhizomes or they may be pelagic (free floating). Some species are found in both the pelagic and benthic (attached to the substrate) forms. They are to be found in all warm seas of the world to depths of at least 265 feet (80 meters).

Cladophora aegagropila

Common names: Moss ball, Marimo ball, Marimo algae
Family: Cladophoraceae
Range: Tropical Indo-Pacific, particularly Southeast Asia. Also known from European waters and throughout the Mediterranean Sea
Height: 2–10 inches (5–25 cm)
Description: This species forms a clustered ball of algae. It is normally found in shallow lakes where the waves caused by the prevailing winds roll the plant into a tight spherical form.
Aquarium suitability: If the aquarist wishes to keep this plant in its original shape, it must be turned regularly. If this is not done, it will attach to rocks and stones and form a green carpet. Although it is a very slow-growing species, larger plants can be broken up to form new plants.

Division: Bryophyta (mosses)

Apart from ferns and flowering plants, mosses are the most diverse group of plants with more than 10,000 species in about 700 genera. As a comparison, they are twice as diverse as known land mammals. They have no vascular tissue or wood to give them structural support, nor do they have well-developed leaves or cones, or flowers. For this reason, they do not receive the same interest and attention as flowering plants, ferns, and trees. This does not mean that they are not important to our environment—they are extremely important.

Mosses require an abundance of water for their growth and reproduction. Nevertheless, they can tolerate extreme dry spells by drying out. One group, the *Sphagnum* mosses, can hold large amounts of water in the dead cells in their leaves. These look insignificant and unimportant but they have become very dominant in certain habitats. *Sphagnum* is currently estimated to cover 1 percent of the earth's surface, half the land area of the United States.

Mosses play important roles in our natural habitat. They help to insulate the Arctic permafrost, reduce erosion along the banks of streams, and assist in water and nutrient cycling in tropical rain forests. Most mosses are land dwelling, but there are a few that inhabit freshwater. A few species are present in tropical streams, lakes, and rivers and these belong to the family Hypnaceae. One of these species, Java moss, is a firm favorite among aquarists.

Bryophyta are present in most terrestrial habitats, even deserts. The leaves are usually only one cell thick but the midrib section can be several cells thick. This does not mean that the midrib section contains conducting tissue like the vein of a leaf. Mosses may also have rudimentary rhizoids and they can also be multicellular, but they do little more than serve as holdfasts for the plant.

Order: Hypnales

This is a very large order that encompasses some 39 families containing a total of 265 genera of mosses, many of which are terrestrial and of little interest to the tropical freshwater aquarium hobbyist. One family is of special interest, however. This is Hypnaceae, which has 20 genera. These mosses are very variable in form but they are all small, creeping mosses. Their leaves are irregular or pinnately branched and usually curved to one side of the stem, often tapering to a long, fine apex giving a plaited appearance to the shoot. For this reason, species from this family are referred to as "plait mosses." One genus in particular is interesting. This is *Vesicularia*, which contains species that live at the water's edge, often submerged, on bogwood and rocks near stream margins. These mosses are very attractive and ideal for a freshwater hobbyist. Some of the plants from Southeast Asia make good aquarium specimens.

Vesicularia dubyana

Common name: Java moss
Family: Hypnaceae
Range: Southeast Asia, in particular Indonesia
Height: 2 inches (5 cm)
Description: A bright green moss with fine, fernlike branching leaves that grow as tangled clumps on rocks and submerged wooden structures. It is also found on the moist margins of tropical streams under many different light conditions.
Aquarium suitability: Low to high lighting. Simply attach the plant to driftwood or bogwood with fishing line until it remains there. Once it is established, remove the line and it will spread, eventually covering whatever it is attached to. By removing a small part of the plant and reattaching it elsewhere, it is very easy to propagate. For the fish breeder, Java fern provides an excellent hiding place for young fry.

Order: Marchantiales

The order Marchantiales is grouped into two suborders. These are the complex Marchantiineae and the more simplified Ricciaceae. The latter is of interest to some aquarists. These plants are what are colloquially termed the "liverworts" and a few species from this group are floating plants. They can be fixed to rocks or entirely submerged, so that they will grow underwater wherever the hobbyist wants them to. More important, these are ideal floating plants for the fish breeder who wants to provide a safe haven for young fry as they grow. In particular, *Riccia* spp. allow a dense floating mat of interwoven clumps that is ideal for surface egg-layers such as anabantids. *Riccia* spp. can be tied to rocks and driftwood, where it will anchor and grow in attractive clumps that are up to 6 inches (15 cm) across.

Riccia fluitans

Common names: Crystalwort, Riccia
Family: Ricciaceae
Range: Circumtropical and subtropical in a variety of aquatic habitats
Height: Spreads in floating mats that can be 2 inches (5 cm) deep and up to 20 inches (51 cm) in diameter
Description: Riccia is an attractive shade of bright green. It comprises short individual plants that interlock together to form dense carpets at the water surface. Propagation is by division and this plant can multiply very quickly.
Aquarium suitability: Riccia is a firm favorite among aquarists, particularly fish breeders. It provides an excellent floating anchor for anabantids such as *Betta splendens* to build their bubble nests. It is also an ideal breeding ground for infusorians, on which the newly born fry can feed.

Division: Lycopodiophyta (clubmosses, quillworts)

The division Lycopodiophyta is a tracheophyte subdivision of the kingdom Plantae. It includes some of the most primitive of all living vascular plants. They reproduce by shedding spores and possess macroscopic alternations of phases of a single generation, meaning that they consist of two separate, free-living plant bodies that are able to facilitate reproduction. Nevertheless, some species are homosporus whereas others are heterosporus.

There are three classes within this division and these are Lycopodiopsida, Selaginellopsida, and Isoetopsida. These plants have a long evolutionary history and there is a worldwide fossil history, particularly in coal deposits. Most of the known genera are now extinct.

Lycopodiophytans extended onto land during the Silurian and Devonian periods. Once on land and without water, dessication became a real possibility, so more structural support was needed to protect the plant. Most adaptations of the primitive lycopodiophytans can be attributed to these changing conditions. All of the plants in this group have relatively simple leaves because of the development to adapt roots to obtain nutrients on land. Many species remained in water, however, including many from the class Isoetopsida, which are the quillworts.

Order: Isoetales

This order includes the quillworts with the extant genus *Isoetes*, which encompasses about 70 species. They have a worldwide distribution and are small, usually aquatic plants with short stems and elongate leaves. Very similar fossils have been discovered from the mid-Cretaceous period. These belong to the genus *Isoetes*. The plants have greatly reduced stems that are bulbous and lack vegetative leaves. Plants of this order are quite advanced in development and they have many features common to the great Carboniferous scale trees. These include secondary tissue development of wood and bark, bipolar growth, an upright plant habit and a modified shoot system that acts as a root system.

With only the difference in form and size, these plants resemble—and could actually be treated as—miniaturized versions of the mighty scale trees of a bygone age. Even though the giant scale trees died out during the Carboniferous period, these aquatic relatives have survived to the present day as living fossils. One species stands out among this group as being ideally suited to aquarium life and will be described next.

Isoetes lacustris

Common names: Octopus plant, Lake quillwort
Family: Isoetaceae
Range: North America to Europe in subtropical or temperate lakes
Height: 8 inches (20 cm)
Description: The plant produces up to 30 leaves that are grasslike and dark green in color. The stem is a two-lobed corm that stores starch. Because the stem is so much reduced, there is very little actual plant between the leaves and the root. This small area does, however, grow thicker with age and may even develop bark. The roots are produced from furrows in the corm and are considerably different from the roots of higher plants. They may be considered to be modified leaves rather than actual roots.
Aquarium suitability: This is a great plant that needs good water movement to thrive and a nutrient-rich substrate that is not too coarse and not too fine. Reproduction is from spores and since these plants produce spores of both sexes, they can be propagated in an aquarium environment.

Division: Magnoliophyta

The plants in the division Magnoliophyta are also referred to as "angiosperms" and include flowering plants that are found on land or in water. They have leaves, stems, and roots with seeds that are usually enclosed in a shell-like coating. Wind, water, animals, and birds may spread the seeds so that they can germinate in new places to grow into new plants. This is a vast division that includes grasses, crops, grains, garden and roadside weeds, and broad-leaved trees and shrubs.

The division, Magnoliophyta is split into two main classes. The first of these classes is Liliopsida, which includes grasses, lilies, orchids, cattails, greenbriers, sedges, and bulb plants. Many of these are also found in aquatic environments. Plants in this class are also referred to as "monocots," which is short for "monocotyledons." This means that young seedlings have only one seed leaf. The second class, Magnoliopsida, is the largest class of flowering plants. In this group the plants are sometimes called "dicots," which is short for "dicotyledons." Young seedlings in this class have two seed leaves. They include aquatic plants as well as oaks, violets, and blackberries.

Two other classes also encompass tropical aquatic plants. Although they are not as large as the two main classes of Magnoliophyta, they are important to the aquarium hobbyist. These two smaller classes are Piperopsida and Rosopsida and contain some of the most ornate and beautiful of all aquarium plants. They include the *Cardamines* and the *Hydrocotyles*.

Order: Alismatales

The order Alismatales contains a group of monocots called alismatids. These were originally classified into three families, although this has recently proved to be incorrect. Many of the species grouped into these families had too many differences and because it was proved that one or more families were polyphyletic, the order had to undergo radical taxonomic changes. The alismatids are now classified into no less than 14 families with about 165 genera that have a cosmopolitan distribution. Most of these plants are comprised of herbaceous nonsucculent species that are commonly found in aquatic or semiaquatic environments. Most of the plants that the aquarist will instantly recognize from this group are very ornamental and include those of the genera *Echinodorus* and *Sagittaria*.

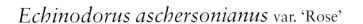

Echinodorus aschersonianus var. 'Rose'

Common names: Rose sword, Indian red sword
Family: Alismataceae
Range: South America (cultivated)
Height: 10–16 inches (25–40 cm)
Description: This plant is actually a cultivated hybrid of two plants that was first produced in 1986 by Hans Barth in Dessau. The original plants were *Echinodorus ascersonianus* and *E. uraguayensis*. New underwater leaves are pink and as they develop they become suffused with reddish-brown spots. Older leaves are bright green with lighter colored ribs.
Aquarium suitability: *Echinodorus* 'Rose' is relatively undemanding in its aquarium requirements, and therefore is a good choice for the novice aquarist. The lighting can be medium- to high-intensity and the pH of the water can vary from 5.5 to 8.0. A high-nutrient substrate will promote good plant growth.

Echinodorus barthii

Common name: Red melon sword
Family: Alismataceae
Range: South America (cultivated)
Height: 10–20 inches (25–50 cm)
Description: The red melon sword is a highly decorative plant that has been cultivated for its color. Young leaves are dark red and these lighten with age. Older leaves gradually become green and eventually dark green.
Aquarium suitability: Excellent as a solitary show plant, this one needs enough light to develop a good color. The substrate needs to be high in nutrients. Large specimens will take away a great deal of light from smaller plants that are underneath them, so they may require regular pruning. This plant is quite tolerant of wide swings in pH and water hardness. It is also unaffected by temperature fluctuations.

Echinodorus berteroi var. 'lanceolatus'

Common name: Burhead sword
Family: Alismataceae
Range: United States, Caribbean, and Central to South America, in lakes, rivers, and slow-running streams
Height: 28 inches (70 cm)
Description: The leaves are variable in form but submerged leaves are bright green. They are often fragile and can be translucent (hence the German name *zellophane-pflanze*, meaning "cellophane plant").
Aquarium suitability: In mature aquariums, this plant will do particularly well. Normally, it is sold in a plastic pot that needs to be embedded in the substrate. Leaves that reach the surface offer shade for other plants that require low-light conditions.

Echinodorus bleheri

Common name: Broad-leaved Amazon sword
Family: Alismataceae
Range: Tropical South America
Height: 8–10 inches (20–25 cm)
Description: A broad-leaved plant that is midgreen to deep green with adventitious shoots. Common throughout its natural range in nutrient-rich, claylike substrate.
Aquarium suitability: Amazon swords should be used as background specimen plants in larger aquariums. They are very attractive and hardy. There are several variegations, including the *Echinodorus bleheri* 'Compacta,' which may be used as a foreground plant because of its smaller size. This species is quite easy to grow and not very demanding in a mature aquarium. As with all sword plants, nutrient-rich substrate is a must. Try to obtain one in its own plastic pot for the best result.

Echinodorus bleheri var. 'compacta'

Common name: Dwarf broad-leaved sword
Family: Alismataceae
Range: South America
Height: 6–8 inches (15–20 cm)
Description: Very similar to the previous species in form. The leaves are smaller and are often lighter in color. The width of the plant can be similar to its height and the overall impression of its growth is much more compact. This species can produce up to 50 leaves.
Aquarium suitability: This is an ideal plant for the middle range of an aquarium. It requires moderate to high light intensity and neutral or slightly acidic water for it to thrive. It is easily reproduced when small plants extend out from rhizomes. These can be severed, leaving a piece of the rhizome present on each new plant, and placed elsewhere in the aquarium.

Echinodorus cordifolius var. 'Radican'

Common names: Radican sword, Spade-leaf sword
Family: Alismataceae
Range: North America, Mexico
Height: 24 inches (60 cm)
Description: This plant is quite easy to identify, since it is the only *Echinodorus* species with arching to decumbent inflorescences. Quite apart from this, it is the only one with papillate veins on the sepals. In its natural habitat, this plant flowers in late summer to early fall.
Aquarium suitability: Immersed plants readily produce seeds that will often form new plants in nutrient-rich aquariums. If the plant has been "dry-shipped," the leaves will often die off. Although this may be alarming at first, if patience is used, new submerged leaves will grow. The roots should be pruned regularly to slow and limit growth.

Echinodorus cordifolius var. 'Marble queen radican'

Common name: Marble queen radican
Family: Alismataceae
Range: Central America
Height: 20 inches (51 cm)
Description: This variety of the Radican sword has multiple large leaves that have a marbled green and white coloration. It is an amphibious plant that will lose its submerged leaves once the taller ones reach the water surface.
Aquarium suitability: Ideal for a large aquarium, the Marble queen radican needs space. It will extend its leaves to the surface, where they will begin to float. At this stage they need to be removed to prevent the submerged leaves from dropping off. It can survive with only a moderate amount of light, but requires an iron-rich fertilizer for it to do especially well.

Echinodorus var. 'Kleiner bär'

Common name: Kleiner bär
Family: Alismataceae
Range: Central and South America (cultivated)
Height: 10–16 inches (25–40 cm)
Description: *Kleiner bär* is German for "smaller bear," but this plant is far from small. The lanceolate leaves are supported by long petioles that are yellowish-green. The leaves themselves can be broad or narrow and young leaves are red in color. Older leaves are usually dark green to reddish-green with yellow veins.
Aquarium suitability: A very attractive plant that needs a good substrate fertilizer for it to grow well. Try to obtain one in a pot if possible, as these seem to do much better than those specimens that are supplied with bare roots. Aquarium lighting is not a problem with this species and it will grow quite well in only moderate light.

Echinodorus martii

Common name: Ruffle sword
Family: Alismataceae
Range: Central and South America, particulary Brazil
Height: 6–12 inches (15–30 cm)
Description: The Ruffle sword is characterized by its elongated bright green leaves with fluted margins. The leaves are generally somewhat transparent with bright yellow ribs.
Aquarium suitability: This plant requires nutrient-rich substrate for it to do well. With the addition of CO_2 into the aquarium to lower the pH and produce slightly acidic water, it will flourish. The lighting should also be quite intense to promote plant growth. It is sensitive to iron deficiency, which can be seen by yellow appearing between the leaf veins. Therefore regular additions of iron-rich liquid fertilizer will ensure its continued well-being. This is not a plant for the novice aquarist.

Echinodorus var. 'Oriental'

Common name: Oriental sword
Family: Alismataceae
Range: South America (cultivated)
Height: 8–12 inches (20–30 cm)
Description: This plant appears to be a color mutation of *Echinodorus aschersonianus* var. 'Rose' that was first found in 1992 at the Oriental Aquarium in Singapore. The leaves are varying shades of red, with young leaves being almost transparent pink.
Aquarium suitability: Most aquatic plants are copper-sensitive and this species is particularly so. Care should be taken when treating fish diseases in a tank that contains plants such as the Oriental sword. Although it requires only moderate lighting, like other swords it needs a good, rich substrate. Faster growth can be promoted under more powerful lighting.

Echinodorus osiris

Common name: Melon sword
Family: Alismataceae
Range: South America, particularly Brazil
Height: 10–20 inches (25–50 cm)
Description: This is one of the few colored plants that occur naturally rather than as cultivated varieties. The youngest leaves are often bright red, whereas older leaves are deep green in healthy plants. The emergent leaves are egg-shaped but as they age they become increasingly more elongate with ruffled margins. *Echinodorus osiris* is triploid, meaning that no fertile seeds are produced. Propagation is effected through adventitious plants on the inflorescence or those developed on the rhizomes.
Aquarium suitability: The Melon sword will grow well in a substratum that has a high nutrient content. It is also a good indicator of the iron content in the water.

Echinodorus var. 'Ozelot'

Common name: Ozelot sword
Family: Alismataceae
Range: South America (cultivated)
Height: 8–16 inches (20–40 cm)
Description: A variable and decorative hybrid of *Echinodorus schluteri* 'Leopard' and *E. barthii* that has elliptical spots on red-brown or bright green leaves. Unlike other variants of the *Echinodorus* genus, this plant retains its spots even at low light intensity. The spots are the darkest on younger leaves and these have given it its common name, 'Ozelot.'
Aquarium suitability: A good plant for beginners, this plant can grow in a variety of aquarium conditions and is very hardy. Even at low light intensity with a wide range of pH conditions (pH 6.0–9.0), this species will flourish. It can withstand a wide range of water hardness and temperatures.

Echinodorus quadricostatus

Common name: Broad-leaf chain sword
Family: Alismataceae
Range: South America
Height: 10–12 inches (25–30 cm)
Description: A broad-leaved dwarf Amazon sword that is a rosette-formed plant with long lanceolate leaves on relatively long petioles. This species produces one to two rhizomes per month, on which new plantlets develop. The blades are bright green when they are new but become dark green in color once they are mature. In low-light areas, the leaves become somewhat ruffled on their margins.
Aquarium suitability: A great plant for the aquarium and one that will survive most beginners' mistakes. It produces about one new leaf per week, so after a few months it will need regular pruning.

Echinodorus parviflorus var. 'Tropica'

Common name: Rosette sword
Family: Alismataceae
Range: South America (cultivated)
Height: 2–6 inches (5–15 cm)
Description: The leaves of this plant each have a "hammered" appearance when the plant is healthy and the tips of the leaves are pointed and small. The plant spreads and reproduces by sending out rhizomes that will later develop into smaller, sister plants. The size of the plant is dependent on the available light.
Aquarium suitability: This is quite an easy plant to keep, but it is not recommended for the complete novice. Being relatively small, it looks best if it is planted in groups of three or more. It is not particularly fussy about water quality and will survive drastic temperature fluctuations as well as swings in pH and water hardness.

Echinodorus rigidifolius

Common names: Rangeri sword, Radican sword
Family: Alismataceae
Range: South America
Height: 12–24 inches (30–60 cm)
Description: The long petioles support broad lanceolate leaves that have somewhat ruffled margins. The leaves themselves are bright green in moderate light and deep green when the light intensity is high.
Aquarium suitability: The Rangeri sword is ideal for the beginner. It is relatively undemanding in its water and lighting requirements and is a very attractive plant. If the tank is relatively new, purchase one that is in a plastic pot, because there will be sufficient nutrients in it to serve its needs until the tank has fully matured. This sword is robust and grows quickly, so it needs plenty of space.

Echinodorus var. 'Rubin'

Common name: Ruby red sword
Family: Alismataceae
Range: South America (cultivated)
Height: 8–16 inches (20–40 cm)
Description: This beautiful and ornamental sword is a hybrid between *Echinodorus uraguayensis* 'Red' and *E. barthii*. The leaves are somewhat transparent and ruby red, with lighter leaf ribs that give off an exceptionally deep and intense sheen.
Aquarium suitability: Although this is an aquarium hybrid, it does have some special requirements in order for it to grow well. Growth is stimulated through the addition of CO_2 and this variant does best in an aquarium with a substratum that is nutrient-rich. Light requirements are medium to high but the pH level is not so critical to its well-being. *Echinodorus* 'Rubin' is extremely pH-tolerant (pH 5.5 to 8).

Echinodorus tenellus

Common name: Narrow leaf chain sword
Family: Alismataceae
Range: North America
Height: 2–4 inches (5–10 cm)
Description: The Narrow leaf chain sword is a small plant with grasslike leaves 1–2 mm wide. In bright sunlight the blades are reddish in color. In shady areas, however, they will be green. This is a very prolific plant under ideal conditions and can send out two rhizomes per week, on which new plants will develop.
Aquarium suitability: The small size of this species makes it an ideal candidate for use as ground cover in a planted aquarium. Given time and care, it will form an attractive carpet over much of the substrate. Also, it is hardy and robust and will survive most beginners' mistakes.

Echinodorus uruguayensis

Common name: Uruguayan sword
Family: Alismataceae
Range: South America
Height: 8–24 inches (20–60 cm)
Description: The leaves of this plant are usually broad and lanceolate, although they can vary in length and width considerably. In strong light the older leaves are dark green with ruffled margins; new ones are lighter in color and relatively straight. Recently, several other plants that had previously been considered separate species, such as *Echinodorus horemanii*, are now considered synonymous with this species.
Aquarium suitability: With sufficient nutrients this plant will grow bushy with many leaves. It prefers water that is slightly acidic, although it will also grow in hard water. It is not a plant for the complete novice and will do well in a mature aquarium.

Sagittaria platyphylla

Common name: Chileansis sagittaria
Family: Alismataceae
Range: North and Central America
Height: 6–16 inches (15–40 cm)
Description: The plant forms broad, green, grasslike leaves from a central root. In ideal water conditions rhizomes are sent out into the surrounding environment, on which new plants are formed. These then attach themselves to the substrate and will eventually form into a dispersed carpet. In areas low in nutrients, the blades or leaves will be lighter in color.
Aquarium suitability: If this plant is allowed to grow out of the water, it will produce broad oval leaves on petioles that bear white flowers. Kept submerged, it is an ideal foreground plant for larger aquariums and one that is robust and hardy. It is also a good starter plant for aquarists with hard water.

Sagittaria subulata var. 'Narrow leaf'

Common name: Narrow leaf sag
Family: Alismataceae
Range: South America (cultivated)
Height: 2–12 inches (5–30 cm)
Description: This is a cultivated variety of the previous species and, as the photograph shows, the bright green leaves are narrower than those of the original plant.
Aquarium suitability: A great plant that provides dense areas of growth for spawning fish and is an ideal choice as a foreground plant if it is regularly pruned. The Narrow leaf sag needs plenty of light to grow well and taller specimens should be trimmed back to allow smaller ones to get enough light. In an aquarium it will sometimes send long flower stems to the surface, where small white flowers unfold just above the water.

Sagittaria subulata

Common name: Dwarf sagittaria
Family: Alismataceae
Range: South America
Height: 2–12 inches (5–30 cm)
Description: The Dwarf sagittaria is a small plant with short rhizomes that are developed horizontally to the substrate and on which new plants are formed. These are normally spaced about 1 inch (2 cm) apart. Older plants remain quite small until they flower. At this stage of maturity, shoots are sent out to the surface and small white blooms are exposed to the air. Each flower has a light yellow center.
Aquarium suitability: Individual plants should be placed about 1 inch (2 cm) apart in the foreground of large aquariums. In smaller tanks they can be planted in the middle foreground. The species is easy to keep and is undemanding.

Order: Aponogetonales

Plants belonging to the order Aponogetonales are often referred to as the "Cape pondweeds." This does not seem to be a very appropriate common name for a group that encompasses some of the most attractive and striking of all the aquatic plants. Some botanists group these plants in the order Najadales, the "Water nymphs," which is a much more attractive name. However, in this book the correct classification must be adhered to and Aponogetonales is currently viewed as a monotypic taxon encompassing the family Aponogetonaceae. Whatever the common name, family name, or order actually is, the plants are beautiful indeed. Some species, such as the Madagascar lace plant, do not have the usual mesophyll (the normal internal dividing cells of a leaf, usually containing chlorophyll). Instead, they develop a lattice full of holes that makes them delicately attractive and breathtakingly beautiful aquarium plants. These are not small plants; some of them grow into show plants that are over 24 inches (60 cm) in height, with a width of 18 inches (45 cm).

Aponogeton boivinianus

Common name: Boivinianus
Family: Aponogetonaceae
Range: Appears to be principally from Madagascar, although there are conflicting reports of it growing in the slow-moving streams of eastern Africa
Height: 10–12 inches (25–30 cm)
Description: This species has broad, green, heavily fluted leaves with ruffled margins that often resemble growths of kale. The bulb produces up to 20 blades that are initially light green in color, but darken depending on the amount of available light.
Aquarium suitability: It is a difficult species to keep alive and have flourish in an aquarium, although some specimens prove to be an exception to the rule. Nevertheless, this is not a plant for the novice and a mature aquarium with a rich substrate is required for any degree of success.

Aponogeton longiplumulosus

Common name: Long-plumed aponogeton
Family: Aponogetonaceae
Range: Africa, mainly Madagascar
Height: 12–24 inches (30–60 cm)
Description: The petioles can be quite long in this species and these give the plant the height and spread that it needs to absorb sunlight for its growth and to develop a good root system to extract nutrients from the bottom. It has broad, mid- to dark-green leaves with moderately ruffled margins.
Aquarium suitability: A great plant for a centerpiece in a tank. Although it does best in soft, somewhat acidic water, it does not make too many demands on water quality. However, it does seem to do best when the lighting is of medium to high intensity.

Aponogeton madagascariensis

Common name: Madagascar lace plant
Family: Aponogetonaceae
Range: Africa
Height: 6–16 inches (15–40 cm)
Description: A broad leaf plant that, instead of the usual mesophyll, develops a lattice full of holes, making it a delicately attractive aquarium plant. In the wild, it is found under shady banks and brooks with little or no direct sunshine.
Aquarium suitability: This is one of the most difficult plants to keep in an aquarium. It requires a nutrient-rich and calcareous substrate with frequent water changes because it tends to shed the older leaves in water that has a high nitrate concentration. It should be kept as a solitary plant in a specialized aquarium. There are many different varieties, each requiring its own environmental conditions.

Aponogeton natans

Common name: Natans
Family: Aponogetonaceae
Range: Asia, especially Sri Lanka and India
Height: 14–24 inches (35–60 cm)
Description: The petioles are long, enabling the leaves to reach and float below or at the water surface. In ideal growth conditions, only the slender petioles are visible below the water line with the leaves floating. This effectively blocks the light to other competitive plants that may intrude into its growth area. The convoluted leaves are bright green when they are new, but as they grow older they become deep green to reddish-green.
Aquarium suitability: A very hardy plant for a mature aquarium with many hybrids. In ideal conditions this plant needs to be cropped quite regularly so that other plants in the aquarium get their fair share of light.

Aponogeton rigidifolius

Common name: Rigidifolius
Family: Aponogetonaceae
Range: Southeast Asia, principally Sri Lanka
Height: 12–24 inches (30–60 cm)
Description: Leaves are produced directly from the rhizome. These are long and dark green or red in color with fluted margins. As the name implies, these are stiffer and more rigid than those of others of this family.
Aquarium suitability: A hardy plant that will survive in both hard and soft water. Unlike other *Aponogeton* species, it does not need a dormant period. A large aquarium is necessary for this plant to have the space it needs to grow well and develop properly. New plants are produced from the rhizome but these should be left on the plant until strong roots are formed. They can then be separated from the parent plant.

Aponogeton ulvaceus

Common names: Ulvaceus, Madagascar water lettuce
Family: Aponogetonaceae
Range: Madagascar
Height: 12–16 inches (30–40 cm)
Description: At first sight this appears to be a robust plant with broad, bright green, convoluted leaves that extend from narrow bases directly from the tuber. It is far from robust though, and will die off in winter unless its climate and habitat are not optimal. The leaves are slightly translucent and quite delicate. During the growth season, up to 50 leaves may be produced.
Aquarium suitability: Not a plant for the novice; it is very difficult to keep alive in an aquarium unless its period of rest is understood. During the winter, the tuber must be removed from the tank and the leaves and roots cut off, then left in a dark place for two months before replanting.

Order: Hydrocharitalis

This order contains flowering plants that comprise the family Hydrocharitaceae, with 19 genera and about 110 species of submerged and emergent freshwater, brackish water, and saltwater aquatic herbs. Most are found in tropical environments but there are exceptions. Plants belonging to this order generally have separate male and female flowers, although in rare cases they can be hermaphrodite. Pollination generally occurs above the water surface, although there are about 10 species confined to salt water, where pollination is carried out below the water level. Some of the more ecologically significant plants belong to this order, including those of the genera *Egeria* and *Hydrilla*. *Egeria* spp. are generally found in tropical aquariums. In ponds and lakes in the wild they are important plants that provide cover for fish as well as a food source for birds. *Hydrilla* spp., on the other hand, can cause major ecological problems. As a result of their rapid growth, they can clog waterways and disrupt the stability of native vegetation in a given area.

Egeria densa

Common names: Anacharis, Common waterweed, Brazilian elodea
Family: Hydrocharitaceae
Range: South America, including Brazil, Argentina, Paraguay, and Uruguay
Height: 9–11 inches (23–28 cm), with frequent pruning
Description: Previously known as *Elodea densa*, this plant secretes an antibiotic that prevents the growth of blue-green algae (*Cyanobacteria*.) The growth rate of this plant depends largely on the amount of light and nutrients that are available.
Aquarium suitability: It grows very quickly; individual tendrils can reach a height of 6 feet (200 cm) or more. It is very easy to keep and an ideal plant for the complete beginner. This is a bunch plant that is usually available in a group of five or six tendrils that are weighted and buried in the substrate.

Vallisneria americana

Common names: Corkscrew vallisneria, Jungle vallis
Family: Hydrocharitaceae
Range: North America, from Alabama to Florida and also the Caribbean
Height: 10 inches (25 cm)
Description: This propagates rapidly, producing runners (rhizomes) to daughter plants. One variety reaches a height of 39 inches (100 cm). The leaves are straplike, bright green, and spiraled. In areas where there is a lower light level, there are fewer twists to the individual leaves.
Aquarium suitability: A very prolific and hardy plant, but one that is not entirely suitable for beginners. It requires bright lighting and the substrate should be plain gravel. Additionally, the aquarium should be mature with good biological filtration for this species to do well.

Vallisneria asiatica

Common names: Twisted vallis, Contortion vallis
Family: Hydrocharitaceae
Range: Asia, particularly Japan
Height: 16 inches (40 cm)
Description: The leaves of this plant are very tightly spiraled, green, and straplike. In lower light conditions, the leaves will have a lighter color with fewer twists. Daughter plants grow on rhizomes that extend along the substrate from the inflorescence.
Aquarium suitability: Like all *Vallisneria* species, this attractive plant is ideal for providing a background to the general waterscape of the aquarium. Individual specimens should be planted in loose groups or rows toward the rear of the tank. The aquarium water can have a neutral pH or be slightly acidic, but this species does not seem to do so well in hard water.

Vallisneria gigantea

Common names: Giant vallis, Jungle vallisneria
Family: Hydrocharitaceae
Range: Asia, including New Guinea and the Philippines
Height: 39 inches (100 cm)
Description: The Jungle vallisneria is a tall plant that usually grows two new leaves per month. The blades are straplike and bright to deep green in color. Daughter plants are produced from runners, or rhizomes.
Aquarium suitability: Most species from this family prefer fine gravel rather than a coarse grade. In finer gravel, more nutrients become trapped and available for plant growth. This species needs to be frequently pruned and requires iron supplements and relatively bright lighting for it to do well in a tropical freshwater aquarium. Because of its size and slender leaves, this is an ideal background plant.

Vallisneria spiralis

Common names: Italian vallis, Straight vallis
Family: Hydrocharitaceae
Range: Originally southern Europe and northern Africa, now worldwide in tropical and subtropical regions.
Height: 18 inches (46 cm)
Description: A fast-growing plant with relatively straight leaves for those of this genus. The blades are straplike, narrow, and bright to deep green, depending on the light conditions. Daughter plants are produced from short, robust rhizomes.
Aquarium suitability: The lighting requirements of this species are the same as for others of this genus. The water temperature is not as critical, though, and this plant will do well at temperatures from 59°–86°F (15°–30°C). Plant in small groups, or rows of five or six, as a background to the aquarium. Prune the longer outer leaves quite regularly for the best results.

Order: Arales

The order Arales has recently been included in the order Alismatales, which encompasses the families Araceae and Lemnaceae. However, the more traditional approach to this classification is retained here because of many phylogenetic differences that have yet to be conclusively proved. The Arales is the sister group of the order Alismatales and is an order of monocot flowering plants, many of which are aquatic living, such as arrowheads, arums, burheads, and duckweed. Nevertheless, the order also encompasses terrestrial plants including herbs, climbing shrubs, and marsh plants. Like their aquatic relatives, most of these live in tropical environments. Arales may even have common evolutionary ancestors with the palms (order Arecales) and the Panama hat palms (order Cyclanthales). Although some authors would disagree, this order is classified here to include over 2,000 described species in three families. These are Acoraceae (Calamus family), Araceae (Arum family), and Lemnaceae (Duckweed family).

Acorus gramineus var. 'Ogon'

Common name: Golden sweetflag
Family: Acoraceae
Range: Eastern Asia, principally Japan (cultivated)
Height: 24–36 inches (60–90 cm)
Description: The narrow leaves are rushlike and the coloration is green with a golden sheen. The blades are produced directly from the rhizome and they are stiff to the touch. *Acorus* species form luxuriant clumps of bristlelike leaves that are emergent.
Aquarium suitability: An excellent plant for an open-top aquarium, where it can be allowed to grow out of the water under suspended lighting. If it is completely submerged rather than emerged, it will die over a period of time. New plantlets can be separated at the rhizome and planted elsewhere.

Acorus gramineus var. 'Pusillus'

Common name: Dwarf Japanese rush
Family: Acoraceae
Range: Eastern Asia, principally Japan, in marshes and on the banks of streams
Height: 18 inches (46 cm)
Description: The genus *Acorus* is believed to be the most primitive extant form of the monocots. This dwarf form lacks the distinct midrib. The rhizome is slender and the leaves seldom exceed ½ inch (1 cm) in width. The bloom of this plant has a cream-colored spike.
Aquarium suitability: A hardy plant if it is kept emerged rather than completely submerged. It should be potted and then elevated so that portions of the leaves are above the water surface. The Dwarf Japanese rush is great for waterscaping where planting at different levels is needed to add extra dimension.

Acorus gramineus var. 'Variegatus'

Common names: Variegated Japanese rush, Green and white fan, Variegated sweet flag
Family: Acoraceae
Range: Eastern Asia, principally Japan (cultivated)
Height: 24–36 inches (60–90 cm)
Description: The leaves are narrow and rushlike, with white and green coloration. They are produced directly from the rhizome and are stiff. Primarily, this plant is bog dwelling, forming lush clumps of bristlelike leaves out of the water.
Aquarium suitability: Although this is not a true aquarium plant, it has been included here because it is an excellent plant for an open-top aquarium, where it can be allowed to grow out of the water under suspended lighting to create a dramatic effect. If it is completely submerged it will eventually die. New plantlets can be separated at the rhizome.

Anubias afzelii

Common name: Afzelii
Family: Araceae
Range: Tropical western Africa
Height: 4–16 inches (10–40 cm)
Description: Often confused with the many varieties of *A. barteri*, and there is really very little difference. However, this is recognized as a completely separate species and is much smaller and more compact than most other *Anubias* species. It is a beautiful plant that has a strong inflorescence (flowering stalks) and long, narrow leaves.
Aquarium suitability: This is a very forgiving plant under most aquarium conditions. As with other *Anubias* species, it requires very little light for it to grow. In optimal tank conditions, this plant will flower. Like others of this genus, the flower is white and leaf-shaped, resembling the calla lily.

Anubias barteri

Common name: Giant anubias
Family: Araceae
Range: Tropical western Africa from Senegal to Angola, but particularly Cameroon
Height: 14 inches (36 cm)
Description: Very similar to other *Anubias* species and often misidentified as *Anubias gigantea*. This is a bright green, broad-leaved plant with beautiful white flowers. It grows at the edges of streams, often with the roots attached to rocks and submerged tree trunks.
Aquarium suitability: This species is known for its hardiness and is often termed "the plastic plant that grows." It is an ideal plant to have in an aquarium and one that will survive most of the common mistakes that a novice hobbyist can make. Under fair to good tank conditions, this plant will flower quite freely.

Anubias barteri var. 'Barteri'

Common name: Cameroon anubias
Family: Araceae
Range: Cameroon and surrounding areas
Height: 18 inches (46 cm)
Description: This is one of the largest of all the *Anubias* species and the varieties within this genus. This is not a cultivated plant and actually grows in the wild as a separate variety of *A. barteri*. The petioles are much longer than in *A. barteri* and the ovate leaves are lighter in color and considerably shorter in relationship to its extended and slender petioles.
Aquarium suitability: Cultivated varieties tend to be much smaller than the natural plants. This makes them ideal for aquarium cultivation. This is an easy plant to keep and looks great in a reasonably large tank. Several specimens planted a few inches apart from one another make a beautiful backdrop.

Anubias barteri var. 'Caladiifolia'

Common name: Stilted anubias
Family: Araceae
Range: Tropical western Africa
Height: 24 inches (61 cm)
Description: Probably the largest of all the *Anubias* varieties and species and one of the most spectacular. The bright green leaves may be up to 9 inches (22 cm) in length on petioles that are up to 20 inches (50 cm) long. Adult specimens grow submerged as well as marginal plants in streams and rivulets. The white flowers are extremely attractive and bloom for a month or more in the wild.
Aquarium suitability: A large tank is a prerequisite for this beautiful plant, which can be a focal point in a well-planted artificial environment. Roots tend to extend downward, raising the rhizome so that mature plants appear to be raised on stilted roots above the substrate.

Anubias barteri var. 'Nana'

Common name: Nana
Family: Araceae
Range: Africa (cultivated)
Height: 4–6 inches (10–15 cm)
Description: Nana was first cultivated in the 1970s and is a very sturdy swamp plant that grows submerged or partially so. It develops its rhizomes above or on the surface of the substrate and these form new plants. The leaves are broad, rigid, and bright to deep green in color.
Aquarium suitability: Because of its relatively small size, this is an ideal plant for the center of the tank if it is a small aquarium. In a large aquarium it can be used as a foreground plant. In order to prevent growths of algae on its leaves, it should be given low light conditions or placed under a larger plant's shadow.

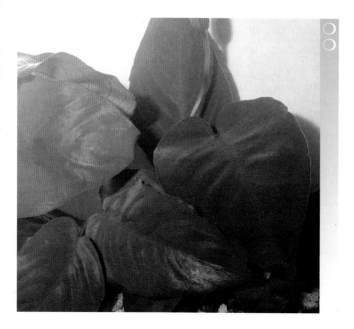

Anubias barteri var. 'Coffeefolia'

Common name: Coffee leaf anubias
Family: Araceae
Range: Tropical western Africa, from Senegal to Cameroon and extending into northern Angola
Height: 6–10 inches (15–25 cm)
Description: A naturally occurring variety of *A. barteri* that is striking in appearance. The broad, deep green fluted leaves arch in a curve over the root system. In contrast to many other *Anubias* species, this plant is quite short and stocky with shortish leaves that have ruffled margins. The petioles are brownish-red to wine-red, and new leaves are wine red in color.
Aquarium suitability: Flowers frequently underwater, and is a slow-growing variety like others of this genus. The attractive fir tree–colored leaves and wine-red petioles make it an ideal feature point for a well-planted tank. It is extremely hardy.

Anubias barteri var. 'Round leaf'

Common name: Round leaf anubias
Family: Araceae
Range: Africa (cultivated)
Height: 8–16 inches (20–40 cm)
Description: This variety has large, broad, rounded leaves with little or no angle to the tips of the leaves. The leaves are supported on long petioles that can often be longer than the leaf itself. The light to deep green plant grows well in below-average light and prefers water that is soft to neutral for its sustained growth.
Aquarium suitability: Aquarium specimens usually come in pots that contain a nutrient-rich substrate. They should be planted in their pots for the best result, with the upper lip of the pot about ¾ inch (1.5 cm) below the substrate surface. Propagation is from new plantlets formed on the rhizomes.

Anubias frazeri

Common name: Frazer's anubias
Family: Araceae
Range: Africa (cultivated)
Height: 8–16 inches (20–40 cm)
Description: The status of *Anubias frazeri* was questionable until recently. It is now recognized as a true species. This is a large plant with long petioles and broad, green leaves that are leathery and robust.
Aquarium suitability: A large aquarium is advisable for this species, as it grows quite tall. It should be planted with the rhizome above the surface of the substrate. Alternatively, it can be attached to a piece of driftwood with nylon fishing line and it will attach itself over a period of time, sending its roots into the substrate. The rhizomes of mature plants can be cut through and cultivated as separate plants.

Anubias gilletii

Common name: Arrowhead anubias
Family: Araceae
Range: Tropical western Africa, in Nigeria, Cameroon, Gabon, Congo, and the Democratic Republic of the Congo
Height: 12–24 inches (30–60 cm)
Description: Sometimes confused with *A. gracilis*, *A. gilletii* grows much larger and has green petioles, even on young leaves. The leaves themselves are much firmer to the touch, almost leathery in texture. Conversely, *A. gracilis* has much softer leaves and the petioles are characteristically red to red-brown. The lower lobes of the arrow-shaped leaves of *A. gilletii* are almost always turned upward.
Aquarium suitability: When planting, do not bury the rhizome. Trim all leaves that are emerged and the plant will stay quite small. This is a slow-growing plant.

Anubias gracilis

Common name: Dwarf arrowhead anubias
Family: Araceae
Range: Tropical western Africa, from Senegal to Angola and the Democratic Republic of the Congo
Height: 6–12 inches (15–30 cm)
Description: This plant is frequently sold under the name *A. hastifolia*, which will be described next, and *Anubias gilletii*, which was described previously. This species is an entirely different plant. The light green leaves are softer in texture than others of this genus and have a marked triangular shape.
Aquarium suitability: This is not a hardy plant and may not be kept in a tank containing herbivorous fish. It will not tolerate consistent handling or replanting. However, once the root system has developed, it is not a difficult plant to keep.

Anubias hastifolia

Common name: Hastifolia anubias
Family: Araceae
Range: Tropical western Africa
Height: 8–16 inches (20–40 cm)
Description: A large plant with leaves that are often 12 inches (30 cm) long, which sit atop petioles that are up to 24 inches (61 cm) high. Adult plants have leaves that are almost trilobed, with the middle lobe being lanceolate. Young plants have lanceolate leaves with heart-shaped bases.
Aquarium suitability: This is a huge plant that has only recently been introduced to the hobby. It is totally unsuitable for all but the largest show aquariums. However, it makes a spectacular display in a large tank and is a good choice for one containing large cichlids. Cichlids will not usually disturb this species or others of this genus.

Anubias heterophylla

Common name: Heterophylla anubias, Congo anubias
Family: Araceae
Range: Tropical western Africa
Height: 8–16 inches (20–40 cm)
Description: This plant is often incorrectly described as *Anubias congensis*, which is a separate variety of this species. This is a medium to large plant that has long, ovate leaves on slender but often short petioles. The leaves are bright green to deep green and are strong and leathery, often with lighter-colored veins through their centers.
Aquarium suitability: A plant that needs very little light. As with most *Anubias* species, it should be planted so that the rhizome is at the surface of the substrate, rather than under it. The exposed rhizome is then able to extend across the substrate and remain healthy to produce new leaves.

Anubias heterophylla var. 'Congensis'

Common name: Congo anubias
Family: Araceae
Range: Tropical western Africa
Height: 24 inches (61 cm)
Description: Probably the largest of all the *Anubias* varieties and species and one of the most spectacular. The bright green leaves may be up to 9 inches (22 cm) in length on petioles that are up to 20 inches (50 cm) long. It is very slow growing and may only add a few leaves each year.
Aquarium suitability: A large tank is needed for this beautiful plant, which can be a focal point in a well-planted aquarium. Roots tend to extend downward, raising the rhizome so that mature plants appear to be on stilted roots above the substrate. Some specimens are shorter with smooth leaves; others can be be tall with fluted grooves along the vein lines.

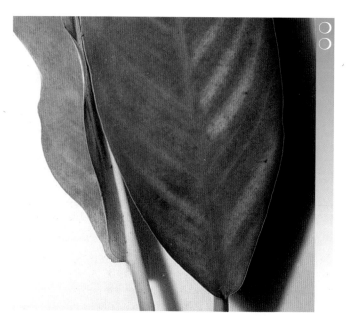

Anubias lanceolata

Common name: Lance anubias
Family: Araceae
Range: Tropical western Africa
Height: 9–11 inches (23–28 cm)
Description: The leaves are lanceolate and the petioles are about the same length as the leaf. Where the petiole is connected to the leaf, there is a slight angle that is somewhat swollen and lighter in color than the rest of the petiole. The veins within the leaf are quite prominent on the underside.
Aquarium suitability: A hardy and forgiving plant that requires very little light for it to grow well. It is ideal for a beginner's tank. As with other *Anubias* species, the rhizome should be left uncovered when planting. Most plants of this genus will survive in a variety of water conditions, from very hard water to soft, slightly acidic water.

Anubias lanceolata var. 'Tinkeso'

Common name: Tinkeso anubias
Family: Araceae
Range: Tropical western Africa
Height: 8–10 inches (20–25 cm)
Description: This variety of the previous species is very similar in description. However, the leaves are much more rigid and plasticlike to the touch. The veins within the leaf are not quite as prominent on the underside and the petioles are somewhat shorter.
Aquarium suitability: A very robust plant that can be grown in shady conditions. All *Anubias* species should be planted with the rhizome left exposed. They are a good choice for the novice because they can survive in quite poor water conditions.

Cryptocoryne ciliata

Common name: Crypto
Family: Araceae
Range: Southeast Asia
Height: 16–20 inches (40–50 cm)
Description: *Cryptocoryne ciliata* has a profusion of light green leaves with fairly acute tips. It is slow growing and only produces about six new leaves in a year. Propagation is effected when the plant sends out rhizomes that produce daughter plants.
Aquarium suitability: Unlike most of the Cryptocoryne species, this plant needs strong light. It is hardy and can tolerate hard or even brackish water, which makes it a good choice for an aquarium containing African Rift Lake cichlids. It is quite a large plant, so it should be used in the background or as a specialty plant in larger tanks.

Cryptocoryne crispatula
var. 'Balansae'

Common name: Balansae crypto
Family: Araceae
Range: Southeast Asia, principally southern Thailand
Height: 8–24 inches (20–60 cm)
Description: A relatively tall plant that usually has deep- to light-green leaves that are ruffled in appearance. Young leaves may be reddish-brown to light green depending on the nutrient content in the substrate. The leaves are long and slender, often much longer than the supporting petioles.
Aquarium suitability: Although this species originates from a hard water area, once acclimated it does equally well in hard or soft water. It is the oldest variety of *C. crispatula*. Groups of the Balansae crypto produce a striking background. Growth can be stimulated with the addition of CO_2.

Cryptocoryne moehlmannii

Common name: Sumatra crypto
Family: Araceae
Range: Sumatra
Height: 8 inches (20 cm)
Description: An attractive plant with bright green leaves and dark green petioles. The leaf form is variable, but usually broad and somewhat ovate. Older leaves have a heart-shaped base and a lanceolate upper lobe. There is often a narrow yellow stripe down the center of the leaf.
Aquarium suitability: Quite easy to keep if it is purchased in a pot. Plants sold with bare roots do not do well unless they are planted in a nutrient-rich substrate. Propagation is through runners, but this plant does not like to be moved too often. Allow the plants to root on the runners and then separate them, leaving a little of the rhizome on the new plant.

Cryptocoryne retrospiralis

Common name: Spiraled crypto
Family: Araceae
Range: Central Asia, mainly Sri Lanka and India
Height: 12–24 inches (30–60 cm)
Description: A narrow-leaved plant with stiff leaves that occasionally have undulating margins. Very similar in appearance to *C. spiralis*. The difference between these two is that *C. retrospiralis* has broader leaves than *C. spiralis*.
Aquarium suitability: The Spiraled crypto is one of the easiest plants to keep, but it grows quite large and should be used in groups of three or more as a background for other, smaller plants. Individual specimens should be planted a few inches apart to allow for growth. These will eventually form a thick clump, which gradually becomes a single attractive entity.

Cryptocoryne spiralis

Common name: Corkscrew crypto
Family: Araceae
Range: Southeast Asia, principally southwestern India
Height: 12–24 inches (30–60 cm)
Description: Although similar in appearance to the previous plant, the leaves are much narrower. Both species are found growing alongside one another, even in the rice paddy fields of India. The leaves are light- to medium-green, often with undulating margins.
Aquarium suitability: A good background plant and one that is very easy to propagate. Rhizomes are sent out at regular intervals. New plants form on these and once they have grown roots, they can be separated from the parent plant. Cut, leaving about 1 inch (2.5 cm) of the rhizome on either side of the new plant. It can then be planted elsewhere in the aquarium.

Cryptocoryne undulatus

Common name: Undulate crypto
Family: Araceae
Range: Southeast Asia, specifically Sri Lanka
Height: 4–6 inches (10–15 cm)
Description: The leaves of this plant are often deep brownish-red to maroon on the underside and green on top. The margins are undulated and grow on top of moderately long petioles. Although the leaves are generally narrow and lanceolate, there is a triploid variety available that has broader leaves that are flecked with black.
Aquarium suitability: This is a robust plant, ideal for the complete novice because it will survive most beginners' mistakes. It should be planted in groups of three or more as a foreground plant in large aquariums, or in front of the background plants in smaller tanks.

Cryptocoryne walkeri

Common name: Lutea crypto
Family: Araceae
Range: Southeast Asia
Height: 8 inches (20 cm)
Description: There are quite a few synonyms for this plant, such as *Cyptocoryne crispatula* var. 'Walkeri,' which is wrong, and *Cryptocoryne lutea,* which is now a junior synonym (the rule of nomenclature is that the first name to be published is the senior synonym; any others are junior synonyms of the species). It can be confused with *C. wendtii,* which does not grow so upright. The deep green leaves are lance-shaped with ruffled margins.
Aquarium suitability: This species is far less hardy than others of this genus. It does not like to be moved around after planting, so once it has rooted and taken hold, leave it alone.

Cryptocoryne wendtii

Common name: Tiny crypto
Family: Araceae
Range: Southeast Asia, Sri Lanka
Height: 5–16 inches (13–40 cm)
Description: The plant grows in areas where there is moderate to bright light. The broad leaves are firm and rigid. Depending on the variety and light conditions, they may be bronze, red, or green. This plant is very versatile and, contrary to popular belief, can adapt to water that is quite calcareous.
Aquarium suitability: As with all other species in this genus, this plant is very sensitive to sudden changes in water quality. Plants that have been cultured in an aquarium environment are much more robust than wild specimens and are easier to acclimate. The substrate should be of plain gravel, although most crypts are best grown in small plastic mesh baskets. There are many propagated varieties of this species, resulting in different mature plant sizes. Ask your local dealer for more information and choose plants according to required mature size. Old leaves should be removed before planting, as these no longer contribute to the plant's energy supply.

Cryptocoryne wendtii 'Red'

Cryptocoryne wendtii 'Bronze'

Cryptocoryne wendtii 'Green'

Cryptocoryne wendtii 'Red giant'

Spathiphyllum tasson

Common names: Brazilian sword, Peace lily
Family: Araceae
Range: South America, principally Brazil
Height: 9–16 inches (23–41 cm)
Description: An aquatic plant that grows in swamp areas rather than fully submerged underwater. It is slow-growing with broad, deep green leaves. The leaf margins are slightly ruffled and the veins of the leaves are lighter in color than the rest of the plant.
Aquarium suitability: Not a true aquarium plant, but if the new varieties are allowed to grow completely submerged, they will go through a transition, producing smaller aquatic leaves. These will then allow the plant to grow healthily underwater. However, semiaquatic specimens can be placed on a rock ledge at the rear of an open-topped aquarium. Ensure that the tips of the leaves are at the water surface.

Syngonium podophyllum

Common name: Arrowhead plant
Family: Araceae
Range: Central and South America, from Mexico to Brazil and Bolivia (cultivated)
Height: Generally 8–16 inches (20–41 cm) in an aquarium. Out of water, the plant is much larger
Description: Although it is often found in water margins of lakes, streams, and rivers, this is not a true aquatic plant. The cultured variety shown here adapts quite well to aquatic life. The leaves are sagittate (like an arrowhead), with the anterior lobe somewhat constricted at the base.
Aquarium suitability: This is a plant that really needs to be kept in a pot near the surface of an open-topped tank so that it can grow out of the water and provide a decorative, semiaquatic attraction in a show aquarium.

Lemna minor

Common name: Duckweed
Family: Lemnaceae
Range: Worldwide in ponds, rivers, and lakes
Height: Individual plants are ¼-inch (6 mm) ovals
Description: The oval green leaves of this invasive plant are flat, with the leaf margins often curled under. The root system hangs under the plant at the water surface. It is a very prolific plant that can do damage to waterways and irrigation systems by clogging the drainage ditches. It is an easy plant to identify and one that is often unwanted.
Aquarium suitability: Anabantids love this plant at egg-laying time. They use it to build their bubble nests and it helps, along with *Salvinia* spp., to keep the nests together until the fry hatch. Other than that, this plant should not be kept in an aquarium. It will soon take over the whole tank's water surface.

Pistia stratiotes

Common name: Water lettuce
Family: Lemnaceae
Range: South America, but introduced and now widespread in North America and Europe
Height: 2 inches (5 cm) from the water surface with a diameter of 6 inches (15 cm)
Description: Most floating plants are invasive and this species is no exception. It is a large plant with thick leaves that form a lettucelike shape. The leaves are pale green to bright green and they are covered in hair. The center leaves of the plant are folded around the flower, which are often difficult to detect. The Water lettuce has a clump of very fine roots that hang under the plant and these can be up to 12 inches (30 cm) long.
Aquarium suitability: A single plant in an open-topped breeding tank can work wonders in protecting newly hatched fry.

Order: Arecales

The order comprises a single family, Arecaceae. This is the palm family, with 217 genera and about 2,800 species. Typically, these are trees or shrubs with a single stem and pinnate leaves, whose stout petioles clasp the stem and younger leaf bases.

Most palms grow in tropical and subtropical areas of America, Asia, and, to a lesser extent, Africa. There are a few species that grow in temperate areas. They are economically important and are widely used to provide building materials, food, oils, and fuel. There is an almost complete fossil record of them stretching back 80 million years, although they were most abundant 60 million years ago. There are several species that are amphibious but very few are totally aquatic, and even less that are suitable for the home aquarium.

Chamaedorea elegans

Common names: Water palm, Parlor palm
Family: Arecaceae
Range: South and Central America
Height: Up to 20 inches (50 cm) in a semiaquatic environment
Description: The leaves are pinnate and the petioles wrap around the stem of the plant at the bases of new leaves. This is a bright to deep green true palm that can live in wetland areas in its natural habitat.
Aquarium suitability: *C. elegans* is normally grown as a houseplant and is not really suitable for an aquarium. However, they are regularly sold in the aquarium trade as aquatic plants. This is normally a hardy species, but if it is completely submerged in an aquarium, the roots and leaves will rot and the plant will die within a few weeks. Potted specimens do well if they are placed on a rocky ledge near the water surface.

Order: Cyperales

The order Cyperales encompasses plants that are commonly known as sedges. But this is an amazingly complex order that contains many species familiar to everyone. Cyperales includes sedges, bulrushes, reeds, grasses, bamboo, oats, rye grass, corn, and wheat. There are only two families: Poaceae, with about 8,000 species, and Cyperaceae, with almost 4,000 species. Only a few of these live in aquatic or semiaquatic environments. Many of the species are terrestrial and self-pollinating, whereas others are wind-pollinated. The flowers are arranged in spikes that represent reduced inflorescences. The leaves are reduced to a narrow blade, often with a surrounding sheath. Only two or three species are suitable for a tropical freshwater aquarium and these are the hair grasses, which are attractive thin-bladed plants.

Cyperus alternifolius

Common names: Umbrella palm, Umbrella flat sedge
Family: Cyperaceae
Range: Madagascar
Height: 4–6 feet (1.2–1.8 meters)
Description: This is essentially a semiaquatic bog plant. Young plants are very attractive, with pinnate leaves surrounding a central stem at regular intervals. The formation of the leaves on the central stem resembles a five-pointed star. The small yellow flowers bloom once the plant is above the water surface. This is a close relative of the papyrus.
Aquarium suitability: Many aquarists prefer this kind of plant in a cichlid tank because the leaves are often out of the water. The attractive plant stems can withstand any herbivorous fish's destructive appetite. Keep in an open-top aquarium with suspended lighting and plant in a nutrient-rich substrate.

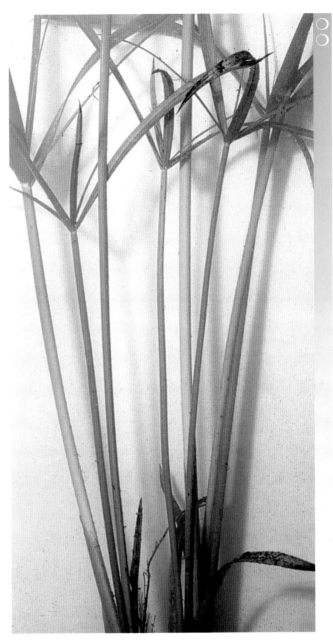

Eleocharis acicularis

Common names: Dwarf hair grass, Needle spikerush
Family: Cyperaceae
Range: Widespread in temperate and subtropical climates
Height: 4–6 inches (10–15 cm)
Description: A small plant with fine, needlelike leaves that are bright green to deep green in color, and mostly reddish at the base. If the plant is submersed it will not flower. It forms low tufted mats in brackish water, freshwater stream banks, and marsh areas.
Aquarium suitability: There are varying degrees of success reported with this plant. It does well in a nutrient-rich substrate, but will rarely live for more than a month in a new aquarium. Specimens should always be purchased in pots that have the correct substrate for this species. Loosely rooted plants or those that have been removed from their pots will not do well.

Order: Xyridales

The definition of this taxon is still unclear at the moment. Botanists and naturalists have recently disputed the families. This is an aquarium book and not a forum for botanical controversies about the specific taxonomic placing of plants, so the author's hypothesis is that it comprises four families. These are Eriocaulaceae, Mayacaceae, Rapateaceae, and Xyridaceae. It is an order of monocotyledonous herbs with few aquatic plants that would interest the aquatic hobbyist. Only one genus with about four species is worth consideration—the genus *Mayaca*.

Mayaca fluviatilis

Common name: Mayaca
Family: Mayacaceae
Range: South America
Height: 10–12 inches (25–30 cm)
Description: This is an attractive plant with a filigree appearance. The light green leaves have a silvery surface and the long, slender stalks can be reddish at the base and light green at the tips. The leaves themselves are pinnate, radiating out from the central column at short intervals.
Aquarium suitability: The Mayaca has proven itself to be an ideal plant for the novice. Unfortunately, it is quite rare and seldom seen on dealers' lists. It is sold in bunches that are without roots. Newly acquired bunches can be planted immediately in a substrate that is relatively new and poor in nutrients. This plant will survive many beginners' mistakes but will be eaten by most herbivorous fish.

Eleocharis montevidensis

Common names: Giant hair grass, Sand spikesedge
Family: Cyperaceae
Range: Widespread in marshes, estuaries, and on the banks of lakes, rivers, and streams in North America and Europe
Height: 8–20 inches (20–50 cm)
Description: It is similar to the preceding species and has the same coloration, dark green to bright green. This species, however, grows much larger and is more robust. There are many *Eleocharis* species and they are quite difficult to distinguish from one another. Similar nonaquatic species are often passed off as aquarium plants and usually die within a few weeks.
Aquarium suitability: This species needs medium to high lighting with a nutrient-rich substrate. It is suggested that iron be regularly dosed to balance any likely deficiencies, along with laterite, which is a good substrate fertilizer.

Order: Asparagales

This order encompasses four families that include nearly 5,000 species of aloes, day lilies, onions, and related plants. Structurally, they are one of the most diverse groups of all plants. The order provides us with asparagus, garlic, onions, daffodils, and many other diverse garden plants, including the agave, which can reach a height of more than 30 feet (914 cm). Most of the Asparagales grow a cluster of leaves at the plant base or at the top of a short trunk. On top of this, a long stalk develops and bears the flowers. To better visualize this, think of ornamental examples of the Amaryllis group of plants.

Ophiopogon japonicus

Common names: Dwarf mondo grass, Dwarf lilyturf
Family: Ophiopogonaceae
Range: Southeast Asia, principally Korea and Japan
Height: 12–15 inches (30–38 cm)
Description: Dwarf mondo grass has leaves that are up to 15 inches (38 cm) long and they are very slender, seldom exceeding ⅛ inch (3 mm) wide. The relatively rigid leaves are dark green and curved. It produces a rooting system that is tuberous with long substrate rhizomes. The flowers are white to light violet in color and the pea-sized fruits are blue.
Aquarium suitability: This is primarily a marginal plant, usually intended for pond use. However, it can also be utilized as an aquarium plant if it is placed on a rock ledge in the tank with the plant growing out of the water in an open-top aquarium and with suspended lighting.

Order: Asteliales

Until recently, plants of this order were grouped together in the order Asparagales. However, further analysis has proved that Asparagales is comprised of two separate clades. This has resulted in the removal of one group from the order and the creation of an entirely new order.

The name Asteliales has been chosen for this new order because it is the oldest recorded name for the group. The order is comprised of seven families of diverse plants but only plants from one family are of interest to the tropical freshwater aquarist: plants from the family Dracaenaceae. The family contains plants that are found in swamps and semiaquatic environments. They are often used as marginal plants for ponds, but they can also be fully immersed in tropical aquariums.

Dracaena deremensis var. 'Compacta'

Common name: Pineapple plant
Family: Dracaenaceae
Range: Sri Lanka (cultivated)
Height: 18 inches (46 cm)
Description: The Pineapple plant is an interesting one. It is similar in appearance to the previous species but with one difference: the central and marginal colors are reversed. This means that the leaves are deep green to dark green with deep cream to yellow margins. It gives the plant the same coloration as the pineapple plant, hence the common name.
Aquarium suitability: This is a strain that can be grown entirely submerged. Both this and the previous species have gained wide popularity amongst hobbyists, particularly in the United States. Earlier strains of the plant did not do well in an aquarium environment and usually rotted after a few weeks. This has now changed thanks to the tenacity of aquatic horticulturists in producing a hardy underwater strain.

Dracaena borenquensis

Common name: Green sandy dracaena
Family: Dracaenaceae
Range: Sri Lanka and India (cultivated)
Height: Rarely more than 24 inches (61 cm) in an aquatic or semiaquatic environment
Description: A terrestrial plant that is quite similar in appearance to both the bamboo and yucca plants. The broad, spear-shaped leaves are glossy and robust, with light-cream to yellow stripes down the center, and dark green margins.
Aquarium suitability: Although this is primarily a terrestrial plant that is often bought as a houseplant, it adapts quite well to an aquatic or semiaquatic environment. For some time now, plant nurseries and wholesalers have been culturing strains that will live in an increasingly aquatic environment.

Order: Amaryllidales

The order Amaryllidales encompasses a diverse group of plants that are similar to those of the Asparagalis and the Asteliales, but there is a fundamental difference. Plants of this group have an umbrella-like inflorescence that is subtended by a bract and has six stamens and three carpels. The bulbs have a scaly coating; the fruit is usually encapsulated. Plants of this group include cape cowslips, false garlic, hyacinths, lilies, liverseed grasses, and winter daffodils. They also include an attractive and interesting group of aquatic plants. These belong to the genera *Crinium* and *Zephyranthes* and are known as "onion plants" for their appearance, which is similar to that of the domestic onion.

The aquarist's variety of the onion bulb is planted with only the roots buried in the aquarium substrate. The rest of it is exposed in the water. After planting, the bulb will begin to sprout bright green, elongated leaves that can be smooth or convoluted, depending on the species.

Crinium calamistratum

Common name: Calamistratum onion plant
Family: Amaryllidaceae
Range: Western Africa
Height: 16–48 inches (40–120 cm)
Description: The roots are sturdy and the inflorescence is stout and onionlike but smaller than others of this genus. Its long leaves are emerald green and very narrow in proportion to their length. The margins of the leaves are ruffled, not unlike those of *C. natans*, although in that species the leaves are much broader.
Aquarium suitability: An ideal plant for a cichlid tank because they will not be eaten (apparently they have a bad taste). The aquarium lighting should be moderate to high. This species is a good choice for a brackish-water aquarium provided the salt concentration is relatively low.

Crinium natans

Common name: Onion plant
Family: Amaryllidaceae
Range: Southeast Asia and Thailand
Height: 12–18 inches (30–45 cm)
Description: This plant is very attractive and is quite closely related to the lily family. Propagation is effected through "bulb budding" from the parent plant. The convoluted and somewhat puckered leaves are bright green and 1–1½ inches (2–3 cm) wide. New leaves are produced at the rate of about one per month.
Aquarium suitability: Cichlids do not appear to like this plant, so it is a good choice for one of these specialist tanks. It is not often seen for sale but occasional imports make it a popular choice for a well-planted aquarium. The bulbs should be planted in the substrate so that the top protrudes into the open water. Several of these placed in a tight group make a very attractive show.

Crinium thaianum

Common name: Thaianum onion plant
Family: Amaryllidaceae
Range: Southeast Asia, principally Thailand
Height: 24–80 inches (60–200 cm)
Description: A very tall plant but one that is slow growing. The leaves are bright green to deep green and they are produced from large individual bulbs that can be white or reddish-brown in color. Mature plants produce small bulbs around the periphery of the main bulb that eventually break away to form new plants. This species produces leaves that have straight margins, unlike others of the genus.
Aquarium suitability: The Thaianum onion plant is an easy species to keep but it does grow quite large for the average aquarium. Nevertheless, groups of three or more, judiciously planted, look great in a large cichlid show tank.

Zephyranthes candida

Common names: Dwarf onion plant, Autumn zephyr lily, Fairy lily
Family: Amaryllidaceae
Range: South America, mainly Argentina
Height: 6–8 inches (15–20 cm)
Description: In a semiaquatic environment this plant will produce large white flowers that have six petals with a yellow center. It is a small perennial plant that will grow equally well underwater. The leaves are bright to deep green in color and the plant appears similar to *Crinium thaianum*. However, *Z. candida* seldom exceeds a height of 8 inches (20 cm).
Aquarium suitability: Because this is a perennial, it will die back for part of the year. The bulbs should be removed and stored in a dark, cool place with a light covering of compost to allow a resting period. After a few months, they can be replanted.

Order: Pontederiales

Plants of this order are commonly known as the "water hyacinths," but they also include mudplantain and pickerelweeds. These are monocot flowering plants that can be termed "aquatic herbs." It is a small order with only one family containing about 30 species in nine genera. The leaves can be well-developed or greatly reduced (in *Hydrothrix*). The leaves can be submerged, emergent, or floating.

The plants are found pantropical to subtropical and a few species in warm temperate zones. *Eichornia crassipes* (water hyacinth) is considered to be a water garden ornamental in colder climates, but it is a devastating weed in warm waterways around the world, often growing so dense that water navigation becomes difficult. It is thought by many to be one of the world's most pernicious weeds, invading lakes, ponds, canals, and rivers. It grows rapidly, forming extensive mats of interwoven plants that block drainage systems, clog irrigation pumps, and interfere with weirs.

Heteranthera zosterifolia

Common name: Stargrass
Family: Pontederiaceae
Range: South America, including Argentina, Bolivia, Brazil, and Paraguay
Height: 40 inches (100 cm)
Description: A beautiful aquatic plant that is bright green. It is aptly named because each petiole ends in an array of leaves that form star-shaped, densely tufted crowns. The leaves themselves are narrow and lanceolate in form. Once the leaves reach the water surface and the available light is sufficient, the plant blooms with a suffusion of small blue flowers.
Aquarium suitability: An excellent plant for a tropical freshwater aquarium and one that is revered by most hobbyists. It is not easy to keep because it needs bright light and a pH level between 6.0 to 7.5 for it to grow well.

Order: Caryophyllales

Surprisingly enough, this order encompasses a host of well-known plant groups, including the ice plant group, which is prolific in California, although it is not a native plant. It includes the cacti, cottonflowers, rhubarb, dock weed, and many other species. The order also includes the fig marigold family, the amaranths, and the carnation family. Strictly speaking, this is a very diverse group of plants that can survive in desert wastelands and in the swamps of the rain forests. By definition they are opportunistic plants that can adapt to a variety of environments and may eventually be proved to be the most successful of all the plants.

Alternanthera cardinalis

Common name: Cardinal temple
Family: Amaranthaceae
Range: South America (cultivated)
Height: 6–16 inches (15–40 cm)
Description: Young leaves may be tinged with red at the base of the upper surface, or bright green. The underside of each leaf is often deep red and the stems of the plant are red. Typical of *Alternanthera* species, water roots are developed at the junction of each of the paired leaves.
Aquarium suitability: The Cardinal temple is a beautiful mid-ground plant that needs high-intensity light for it to show its true colors. Once it grows too tall for a particular tank, it can be propagated by cutting or pinching off the upper part of the plant, ensuring that there is sufficient leaf-base rooting below the cut. The paired leaves around the root should be removed before planting this top section elsewhere.

Alternanthera ficoidea
var. 'Bonita hedge'

Common name: Green hedge
Family: Ameranthaceae
Range: South America (cultivated)
Height: 10–15 inches (25–38 cm)
Description: This is a cultivated variety of a terrestrial plant that has been adapted to aquatic conditions. Young leaves are lanceolate and older leaves have an elongated, heart-shaped form. The leaves are paired on opposite sides of the stem, with the following pair being 90 degrees opposed to the preceding pair.
Aquarium suitability: A difficult plant to keep because it is a strain of a nonaquatic plant. However, if care is taken to choose specimens that are already showing "water roots" from the bases of the leaves, then the plant should grow quite well in a nutrient-rich substrate.

Alternanthera reineckii

Common name: Amazon temple plant
Family: Ameranthaceae
Range: South American Amazon region
Height: 10–20 inches (25–50 cm)
Description: There are many cultured varieties of the original plant. The leaves are lanceolate and younger leaves have a reddish tinge to the underside and the tips. Older leaves are green, sometimes with a red underside to the uppermost leaves. The tall stems are light green to yellow-green.
Aquarium suitability: The Amazon temple is a natural plant and is a true aquatic one that grows well in an aquarium with a nutrient-rich substrate. The light intensity can be moderate to high, but the plant grows fast with high-intensity lighting. Cuttings can be taken from this plant and placed elsewhere in the aquarium and will grow with no special care.

Alternanthera ficoidea
var. 'Emerald hedge'

Common name: Emerald hedge
Family: Ameranthaceae
Range: North and South America, from Mexico to Argentina (cultivated)
Height: 8–12 inches (20–30 cm)
Description: Like the previous species, this plant is a cultivated strain of a nonaquatic plant, but does not grow as large. There are frequent water roots at the bases of the leaf pairs and the leaves themselves are deep green to very dark green.
Aquarium suitability: As with the Bonito hedge, water roots should be present before purchasing. This will indicate that it is a true aquatic species. For some time now, unscrupulous wholesalers have been supplying lower-grade, nonaquatic plants to the aquarium trade and this has given this plant a bad name.

Alternanthera reineckii
var. 'Roseafolia'

Common name: None
Family: Ameranthaceae
Range: South America (cultivated)
Height: 8–10 inches (20–25 cm)
Description: A beautiful plant whose leaves are pinkish-red on the upper surface and often purple underneath. It is a cultured variety of the previous species, and is grown for ornamental use. The leaves are lanceolate, and its well-defined central rib is lighter in color than the rest of the leaf.
Aquarium suitability: An excellent choice of plant to bring color into an aquarium. This particular variety, with its bright red and purple leaves, shows up in sharp contrast to a backdrop of green plants. Provide a mature substrate with plenty of nutrients and this plant will do well.

Alternanthera sessilis var. 'Rubra'

Common names: Scarlet hygro, Sessile joyweed, Red ivy
Family: Amaranthaceae
Range: Circumtropical, but widespread throughout the Pacific Islands as an invasive plant (cultivated)
Height: 8–20 inches (20–50 cm)
Description: This is a terrestrial plant that has been cultivated to grow in a submerged or a partially emerged environment. The leaves range from narrow and elliptical to lanceolate. The plant has strong stems and the leaves are light pink to deep red, depending on the environment.
Aquarium suitability: Reports of this plant being impossible to keep are an exaggeration. It is not a plant for the beginner because it is a strain originating from a terrestrial plant rather than an aquatic one. It can be grown in a nutrient-rich substrate, but ensure that strong water roots are visible before purchase.

Order: Nymphaeales

Egyptian priests and rulers were often buried with necklaces of the blooms of plants from this order. The order encompasses many aquarium plants, and those suitable for outdoor ornamental aquatic culture. Lotus and water lilies are the best known groups of this complex order. *Nelumbo* (lotus) is at the center of Hindu and Buddhist traditions. It is known as the "womb of gods" and is the symbol of a spiritual ideal.

The artist Claude Monet developed a passion for the lotus. Water gardens became popular in the early part of the nineteenth century and still are. Lotus and water lilies play a central part in their charm. All species in this order are aquatic, with leaves either floating on the surface or sometimes completely submerged, occasionally emerging above the water surface.

Cabomba caroliniana

Common name: Green cabomba
Family: Cabombaceae
Range: From southern North America to northern South America
Height: 78 inches (200 cm)
Description: The long tendrils are bright green with fernlike leaves around the central axis. The leaves are fine and needlelike, with slightly flattened blades. This is a popular aquarium plant because of its beautiful foliage.
Aquarium suitability: Green cabomba is fast growing, and needs to be pruned regularly. Brownish leaves at the base of the stem indicate that it is not getting enough light. Although it is the least demanding of all the *Cabomba* species, if there is insufficient light in the tank it will soon shed its leaves and die off. It is best planted in bunches near the back of the aquarium.

Cabomba palaeformis

Common name: Purple cabomba
Family: Cabombaceae
Range: Central America
Height: 9–11 inches (23–28 cm)
Description: Specimens have fine, filigree-like leaves attached to strong central stems that may be brownish-red to purple in color, depending on the amount of light that they have been subjected to. The bright green, branched leaves often have a bluish tinge to their margins, making the plant very attractive.
Aquarium suitability: The Purple cabomba comes into its own when it is planted in front of a brighter green backdrop of other plants. The subtle color combination is very attractive and pleasing to the eye. It is an easy plant to grow and is fast growing. If it gets too high, pieces can be pinched off from the tops of the stems and planted elsewhere in the aquarium.

Nymphaea zenkeri

Common name: Green tiger lotus
Family: Nymphaeaceae
Range: Western Africa
Height: 9–36 inches (23–91 cm)
Description: The leaves are bright green with dark purple spots. Initial growth is underwater with many leaves forming before it sends out runners to the water surface, where it will eventually bloom. The flower of this and the following species are usually white with a yellow center.
Aquarium suitability: In a large, open-topped aquarium with suspended lighting, this plant will really come into its own and will produce beautiful scented flowers, filling the living room with a magnificent aroma. In closed aquariums with tight-fitting hoods, the surface runners and also the roots should be pruned regularly to enhance underwater growth.

Nymphaea zenkeri var. 'Red'

Common name: Red tiger lotus
Family: Nymphaeaceae
Range: Guinea, western Africa
Height: 9–36 inches (23–91 cm)
Description: The leaves are rounded, with the two lower lobes being somewhat arrow-shaped. The color of the leaves makes this variety very attractive. They can be brownish-red to pink, with a suffusion of dark spots.
Aquarium suitability: The leaves start out quite low, but as the plant grows it will send runners toward the surface and some leaves will float, blocking the light. To avoid this, prune the runners before they reach the surface; this encourages bottom growth. The Red tiger lotus is a fairly hardy plant if it is kept at cooler temperatures in a freshwater aquarium.

Order: Apiales

Although there is little in the way of fossil records of the leaves and stems of this group, Apiales dates back to the middle of the Cretaceous period, about 100 million years ago. The order encompasses almost 4,000 species in three families. The Araliaceae is a group of 55 genera with about 700 species. It includes ivy and ginseng as well as temperate herbs, tropical trees, and shrubs. The second family, Apiaceae, is of great commercial significance. With almost 300 genera and 3,000 species, it is principally known for celery, fennel, carrots, parsley, hemlock, parsnips, and many herbs: dill, cumin, anise, and coriander also belong to this family. The third family is Pittosporaceae, with nine genera and 227 species. They include mainly Australian evergreen trees and shrubs.

Lilaeopsis brasiliensis

Common names: Micro sword, Grass plant
Family: Apiaceae
Range: South America
Height: 2–4 inches (5–10 cm)
Description: A small plant that has ribbonlike leaves on short stems, giving it a grassy appearance. The growth rate of this species is generally between one and two leaves per week. *L. brasiliensis* is often sold under the name *Lilaeopsis novae-zelandiae*, which is an entirely different plant with short, tubular leaves and is native to New Zealand.
Aquarium suitability: This plant is usually available in pots, loose plant bunches, or sometimes turf mats. It is excellent for foreground planting but it needs plenty of light and laterite/iron fertilization. Runners should be pinched off—this will help the plants to grow in bunches and reduce linear growth.

Order: Myrtales

The order comprises 10 families and approximately 9,300 species of flowering plants in the core eudicots. The two largest families are Melastomataceae, with roughly 4,500 species, and Myrtaceae, with about 3,000 species. Myrtaceae includes the Australian myrtle, guavas, and eucalyptus trees. Lythraceae, a smaller family, contains the pomegranate (*Punica granatum*) and many significant aquatic plants. These include the hedges, such as waterhedge, mini hedge, Borneo hedge, and the *Rotalas,* including the bizarrely named Indian toothcup, the difficult-to-keep Magenta rotala and the slightly-easier-to-keep Round leaf rotala.

There are many other plants represented in this order, including evening primroses and fuchsias, which belong to the family Onagraceae. The *Fuchsia* genus contains about 100 species but there are over 8,000 hybrids throughout the world that have been developed for their distinctive flowers. The most important plants in this family, as far as the aquarist is concerned, are those of the genus *Ludwigia*—including the easily grown *Ludwigia repens*—which have been firm favorites in freshwater aquariums for many generations.

Ammannia senegalensis

Common name: Red ammannia
Family: Lythraceae
Range: Tropical and subtropical East Africa
Height: 18 inches (46 cm)
Description: This is a herbaceous plant that can grow quite tall or become prostrate depending on the water level in which it is growing. The leaves may be elliptical to lanceolate. In nutrient-poor areas, the leaves will distort and become curled and twisted.
Aquarium suitability: This is not a true aquarium plant but it will grow quite well when it is planted in gravel and provided with strong lighting. It requires plenty of iron and a nutrient-rich substrate for it to grow well. It is one of the few aquarium plants that seems to prefer strong water movement. If it is pruned regularly it will grow bushy and look especially attractive.

Didiplis diandra

Common names: Waterhedge, Blood stargrass
Family: Lythraceae
Range: North America
Height: 4–10 inches (10–25 cm)
Description: A fine leaf plant with very thin stems. The leaves are almost pinnate and are bright green. In areas where the light is strong and the substrate is rich in nutrients, new shoots will develop that are tipped with pink to deep red, and the leaves will be longer.
Aquarium suitability: Waterhedge is quite difficult to keep, therefore this plant should be left to the more experienced aquarist. It needs a lot of light and prefers very soft water. Having said this, it is an ideal plant for a discus tank where soft water is a prerequisite. The addition of CO_2 on a regular basis will encourage plant growth.

Rotala indica

Common name: Indian toothcup
Family: Lythraceae
Range: Southeast Asia
Height: 4–12 inches (10–30 cm)
Description: *Rotala indica* should not be confused with *R. rotundifolia*. The main difference is that *R. rotundifolia* initially develops green leaves that are ovate or almost round. Later, it develops lanceolate to pinnate leaves that are pinkish-red. This species has pinkish-red, thin leaves throughout its life.
Aquarium suitability: This is not a plant for the beginner. Young plants are better kept than older, established ones. They seem to adapt better. As with other species from this genus, this plant needs a lot of light if it is to grow well. Plants bought in bunches should be separated before planting.

Rotala macrandra

Common name: Red rotala
Family: Lythraceae
Range: Southeast Asia, principally India
Height: 10–20 inches (25–51 cm)
Description: This is a beautiful plant with green basal leaves and brownish-red to bright red upper leaves. The taller the plant, the more red color in the leaves. Some of the transitional leaves may be red in the center and have green margins or vice versa. The leaf form is variable and may be elliptical or lanceolate.
Aquarium suitability: A difficult plant to keep for any length of time in an aquarium. Specimens need very high intensity lighting and individual plants need space between them to allow light to the lower leaves. This species needs soft water with a nutrient-rich substrate that is low in phosphate.

Rotala macrandra var. 'Magenta'

Common name: Magenta rotala
Family: Lythraceae
Range: Southeast Asia
Height: 10–18 inches (25–46 cm)
Description: Very similar to the preceding species but the leaves are narrower and lanceolate. The coloration of the leaves is a more intense red with a tinge of violet, giving an overall magenta color to the plant. The plant stems are green at the base and deep magenta toward the tips.
Aquarium suitability: This is quite a difficult plant to keep and it does not travel well. Ask the dealer to pack it in water, otherwise the delicate leaves will become bruised and die. Gravel that is high in nutrients but low in phosphate is a prerequisite for this plant and it needs high-intensity lighting if it is to do well. If these are provided, this is an excellent plant that shows well.

Rotala rotundifolia

Common name: Round leaf rotala
Family: Lythraceae
Range: Southeast Asia
Height: 15–22 inches (38–56 cm)
Description: Young plants are bright green with round leaves, hence the name. Older plants develop leaves that are more elliptical, even to a lanceolate form. As the plant grows, the upper, lance-shaped leaves also change color, taking on shades of orange-brown and sometimes a red coloration. This is a very attractive aquatic plant.
Aquarium suitability: The plant can become quite bushy and compact, therefore it should be pruned and separated at regular intervals to allow the growth of new leaves on the lower parts of the stems. A growth that is too bushy will not allow light through to facilitate new growth at the lower levels of the plant.

Rotala rotundifolia var. 'Borneo hedge'

Common name: Borneo hedge
Family: Lythraceae
Range: Southeast Asia (cultivated)
Height: 8–16 inches (20–41 cm)
Description: A relatively new variety of *R. rotundifolia*, new leaves are round and bright green when they appear, but as they grow they turn a much darker green. Sometimes they become ovate or elliptical when they are older.
Aquarium suitability: This plant is best arranged in small groups placed at regular intervals in the substrate. Bunched plants should be separated and planted individually without the use of lead anchors. Avoid constricting the roots, as this may cause them to rot. Like others of this genus, it requires good lighting and a substrate that is rich in nutrients but low in phosphate.

Rotala rotundifolia var. 'Mini hedge'

Common name: Mini hedge
Family: Lythraceae
Range: Southeast Asia (cultivated)
Height: 4–8 inches (10–20 cm)
Description: A very similar plant to the preceding species, but much smaller and compact. It has predominantly round leaves that are deep green to bright green. Older leaves can become ovate in optimal light.
Aquarium suitability: The Mini hedge is a very attractive foreground plant but not one that is easy to keep. It needs a lot of light and should not be overshadowed by other plants. Regular additions of iron and a nutrient-rich substrate should keep this plant happy with its surroundings. Keep the phosphate levels low with all *Rotala* species.

Rotala wallichii

Common name: None
Family: Lythraceae
Range: Southeast Asia
Height: 4–12 inches (10–30 cm)
Description: This is a very attractive species that has pinnate leaves that are soft to the touch. The central stems are green toward the roots and yellowish orange toward the tips. In high-intensity light, the tips of the stems are pinkish-red.
Aquarium suitability: Many aquarists have had difficulty with this genus. On the Internet, there are many reports and suggestions to keep the plants in a nutrient-poor environment. In fact, the opposite is the case. This and other *Rotala* species need a nitrogenous-rich substrate, but phosphate levels in excess of 0.7 ppm will kill them within a matter of days. If the tank has a high phosphate level, a phosphate remover should be used.

Ludwigia palustris

Common names: Water primrose, Water purslane
Family: Onagraceae
Range: North America
Height: 8–10 inches (20–25 cm)
Description: The plant has leaves that are opposing and elliptical to about 2 inches (5 cm) long. The leaf stalks are about as long as the leaf blades. Unlike the true water primrose (*Ludwigia hexapetala*), the plant stems are not hairy. Fibrous roots hang down from the lower stem joints of the plant stem. This species has a very inconspicuous flower that is usually located in the leaf base of an emerged stem.
Aquarium suitability: This species does well in a nutrient-rich substrate, but it does require high-intensity light for its continued well-being—"T5" lighting appears to be ideal. Propagation is effected by pinching off and rooting lateral shoots.

Ludwigia palustris var. 'Narrow leaf'

Common name: Narrow leaf ludwigia
Family: Onagraceae
Range: North America
Height: 8–10 inches (20–25 cm)
Description: This is a very attractive cultivated plant, deep green on the upper surfaces of the leaves and dark maroon-red to magenta on the under surfaces. The leaves themselves are broadly lanceolate in pairs on the stems. Older leaves are overall brownish-red. The stems of the plant are stout and green in color, but this is often of a lighter shade than that of the upper surfaces of the leaves.
Aquarium suitability: This variety is a great species to keep in an aquarium containing lots of green plants. It is relatively easy to keep and will provide a contrasting color if it is placed against the other plants.

Ludwigia palustris var. 'Needle leaf'

Common names: Needle leaf ludwigia
Family: Onagraceae
Range: North America
Height: 8–20 inches (20–50 cm)
Description: The surprising thing about this plant is that it is the entire color reversal of the previous variety. The leaves are also more pinnate. Each leaf is an overall green on the upper and lower surfaces, but it is the plant stems that are light red to deep red in color.
Aquarium suitability: A great plant for a tropical freshwater aquarium, but one that needs a great deal of light to keep its colors and grow correctly. Bunched plants should be separated and planted individually in a nutrient-rich substrate to allow the roots to take hold and develop. Planting these a few inches apart allows light to get to the lower leaves so that they can grow correctly.

Ludwigia repens

Common name: Broad leaf ludwigia, Water primrose
Family: Onagraceae
Range: Southern North America, native to Florida in shallow marshes and ditches
Height: 9–11 inches (23–28 cm)
Description: The leaves are small and fairly ovate or lance-shaped. They are often covered with soft hairs on the upper surface and underside. The slender stems may be branched or unbranched. As the tips of the plant reach toward the surface, they turn a delicate shade of red or reddish-purple.
Aquarium suitability: This is an undemanding plant that will survive most beginners' mistakes. It is decorative and very hardy and can adapt to most water conditions. Regular, but never drastic, pruning will keep this plant healthy and strong. It needs quite strong lighting and is easy to clip and replant.

Order Ceratophyllales

This order is distinct from the monocots, having weak roots that appear as vascular bundles in a closed stem (there is no intervascular cambium developing). It is a very small order with only one genus that encompasses about 10 species. Thought previously to be closely related to the genus *Cabomba*, which belongs to the Nymphaeaceae family, recent research has revealed that this single genus has no close relative to any other extant group of flowering plants. Fossilized fruits more than 120 million years old have been designated to this small order. This makes it the oldest extant angiosperm genus. So, as an old and highly specialized group of plants that are modified specifically to freshwater aquatic life, this group is very successful in tropical freshwater aquariums, as well as in backyard ponds.

Ceratophyllum demersum

Common names: Common hornwort, Hornwort
Family: Ceratophyllaceae
Range: North America and Europe
Height: 8–12 inches (20–30 cm)
Description: A brittle, rootless, submerged perennial herb with bright green leaves that have a coarse texture. The leaves are stiff and attached to the stem in whorls that curve upward and are more crowded toward the tip of the branch. Roots are entirely absent, although the plant may become attached to the substrate by pale modified leaves that have a rootlike appearance.
Aquarium suitability: This is a hardy floating plant that can be used in fry tanks to give them adequate shelter until they are large enough to fend for themselves. It is quite at home in varying temperatures and can survive equally well in soft or hard water.

Ceratophyllum submersum

Common name: Soft hornwort
Family: Ceratophyllaceae
Range: North America and Europe
Height: 8–12 inches (20–30 cm)
Description: This plant differs from the previous species in that the leaves are softer and the stems are more fragile. The leaves are usually lighter in color than *C. demersum* and they are positioned slightly farther apart. This is a floating plant that may attach itself to the substrate using modified rootlike leaves.
Aquarium suitability: The Soft hornwort is a hardy plant that requires very little light. Like the previous species, it is equally at home in a backyard pond as it is in an aquarium. If the light intensity is increased, this species will grow faster and remove excess nutrients from the water.

Order: Asterales

The best known of all the plants in this order is the daisy. Asterales is a group of core eudicots, often with a multitude of radiating petals. The order is very large with about 23,000 species and most of them are terrestrial; there are very few aquatic species. They occur in almost all parts of the world, usually abundant in areas that are not densely forested. Plants belonging to this order include asters, sunflowers, dandelions, and lettuces. *Campanulaceae*, with its bellflowers and lobelias, was once thought to belong to this group. The history of the asteralids dates back to the Cretaceous period. This was at a time when Australia, Asia, and Africa formed the supercontinent Gondwanaland. This is probably why species from this order are so numerous and widespread.

Shinnersia rivularis

Common name: Mexican oak leaf
Family: Asteraceae
Range: North and Central America, principally Mexico
Height: 16–24 inches (41–61 cm)
Description: A fast-growing plant that gets its common name from the oak-shaped leaves that surround the central stems. The plant stems are dark green at the base, becoming light yellow at the water surface. It can also be found as a marsh plant almost entirely out of the water. In strong light the leaves are closer together on the stem; in low light the reverse is the case. Leaf length is also affected by light strength.
Aquarium suitability: The Mexican oak leaf can be kept with ease in most aquariums. It is very fast growing and needs to be pruned regularly. Pinch off about the upper third of each branch and replant elsewhere.

Order: Araliales

This is a diverse order of plants that contains many species of commercial significance, including some common culinary herbs such as parsley and dill. The group also includes licorice root, Indian potato, parsnip, fennel, artichoke, and poison hemlock. Very few of these plants are able to live in a completely aquatic environment, but there are a few that are well-known to experienced aquarists. The most common belong to the genus *Hydrocotyle* and distinguish themselves by being equally able to float freely in the aquarium—as they do in rivers and lakes in the wild—or, as illustrated below, rooted firmly in the substrate of the aquarium.

At the moment there is considerable difference of opinion regarding the status of this order and several authors do not recognize it as a valid group. However, many modern authorities have recognized the order if the family Hydrocotylaceae is included. The majority of plants in this group are herbaceous, with many of them having hollow stems. The stems are seldom woody and even when they appear to be shrublike they are usually soft.

Hydrocotyle leucocephala

Common name: Brazilian pennywort
Family: Hydrocotylaceae
Range: South America
Height: 4–8 inches (10–20 cm)
Description: Wild plants are generally found floating in rivers and lakes. The leaves are bright green to yellowish-green, supported on short petioles from a central stem. Water roots can often be seen growing on the stems at regular intervals where the petiole base arises from the stem. The leaves are round- to heart-shaped depending on light intensity.
Aquarium suitability: This is a fast-growing plant that can be anchored in the substrate, where it will grow well, or it can be left as a free-floating plant to provide hiding places for fish fry. It is very adaptable to varying water conditions and temperatures and will also survive low light intensities.

Hydrocotyle vulgaris

Common names: Common pennywort, Marsh pennywort
Family: Hydrocotylaceae
Range: North America, Europe
Height: 6–16 inches (15–41 cm)
Description: The strange thing about this plant is that the leaves are attached to the petioles near the center of the underside. The leaves are virtually orbicular and bright green to deep green. This is a delicate and slender plant that grows in damp, shady places in the wild. The leaves are supported on relatively short petioles arising from a central stem.
Aquarium suitability: The Common pennywort is an easy plant to keep and will do well in an aquarium without any special care. It can also be used as a pond plant and will survive lower temperatures. Provide enough light and this plant will surprise you with its thick foliage.

Order: Capparales

The order Capparales encompasses some 15 families with over 4,000 species of flowering plants. This group contains many plants that are used in the kitchen. These include horseradish, turnip, cabbages, kale, oilseed rape, canola, Chinese cabbage, broccoli, mustards, Brussels sprouts, watercress, and many more vegetables and herbs. It is a diverse group that has considerable commercial significance. It is a relatively large order of plants, with some 390 genera and about 3,000 species worldwide.

The plants are widespread in distribution, but more common in temperate climates. These plants are herbs, but in many cases they may not appear so. Cabbages and broccoli are considered to be vegetables, for example, but they belong to this order of herbaceous plants.

Plants from this group are rarely "shrubby" and are sometimes aquatic, such as the watercress and the cardamine. Watercress is a great denitrifier in koi pond filters and grows quite well in such an environment. Cardamine is an exceptionally popular plant for the tropical freshwater aquarium.

Cardamine lyrata

Common name: Cardamine
Family: Brassicaceae
Range: Southeast Asia, principally Japan
Height: 8–20 inches (20–50 cm)
Description: Although this is essentially a marsh-dwelling plant, it thrives equally well submerged as it does on the surface. The leaves are bright green to deep green and are variable in form. Often, water roots form on the bases of the petioles that join the leaves to the central stems. These roots can be so strong and efficient that the plant can grow without being anchored to the substrate.
Aquarium suitability: Cardamine is a firm favorite among aquarists. It is a hardy plant that is popular for beginners and experienced aquarists alike. For the best results, plant small bunches of them in the tank substrate, but leave spaces between them to allow them to grow and spread. This is a fast-growing species that needs very little care so long as the aquarium does not get too warm. Temperatures above 82°F (28°C) will kill this plant.

Order: Primulales

The order contains three families with about 1,900 species of flowering plants. Generally, they have simple leaves and flowers with five petals. Species belonging to this order are found throughout the tropical and temperate world. The primrose family, Primulaceae, encompasses some 800 species that are typically found in temperate regions of the Northern Hemisphere. They have simple leaves, sometimes with serrated margins, and the flowers have pistils and stamens. The plants include creeping jenny, primroses, and cyclamen. The second family is Theophrastaceae, with about 100 species that are found principally in Hawaii and Central America. Myrsinaceae, the third family, has about 1,000 species that are the most common circumtropical and in the Southern Hemisphere. Plants from this family include the coralberry and the cape myrtle.

Lysimachia nummularia var. 'Aurea'

Common names: Golden creeping jenny, Golden pond penny
Family: Primulaceae
Range: Southern Europe (cultivated)
Height: 6–12 inches (15–30 cm)
Description: A golden variety of the previous species that has been cultivated primarily as a pond plant, but one that will grow equally well in an aquarium. The new leaves are golden-yellow, which darken to deep green with age. Like *L. nummularia*, the leaves are conspicuously veined and the bases are chordate. Young leaves are much smaller and may be more ovate.
Aquarium suitability: Like the previous species, this variation does grow quite slowly in the warm water of a tropical freshwater aquarium. In a pond, set as a marginal plant, it will grow much quicker because of the cooler temperature. Nevertheless, this is an ideal plant for the complete beginner.

Samolus valerandi

Common name: Brookweed, Seaside brookweed, Water pimpernel
Family: Primulaceae
Range: Brackish shores, coastal muddy banks, and freshwater coastal streams throughout North America
Height: 4–18 inches (10–46 cm)
Description: A marsh plant that is often found in brackish water. The leaves are relatively large and elliptical to lanceolate. The veins on the leaves are lighter green than the leaf itself and are supported on short petioles. Because it can live in a variety of habitats, this species is very hardy and undemanding.
Aquarium suitability: A great brackish-water plant that is ideal for that type of aquarium. In a traditional tropical freshwater tank, this species needs time to settle down, but is a relatively easy plant to keep.

Order: Urticales

The order encompasses six families with about 2,200 species. This is commonly known as the "nettle order" because among its members are the stinging nettles. Despite this, the order includes a wide diversity of plant life including from small herbaceous species to large trees. These include the mulberry, fig, and elm trees, as well as hop vines and the hemp, or marijuana plant. The six families are Moraceae (the mulberry family), Ulmaceae (the elm family), Cecropiaceae (the woody vine family), Barbeyaceae (a single terrestrial species that is found in northeastern Africa), Urticaceae (the nettle family), and Cannabacaceae (the cannabis family with three species).

Pilea cadierei

Common name: Aluminum plant
Family: Urticaceae
Range: Southeast Asia, principally Vietnam
Height: 8 inches (20 cm)
Description: This is a spreading-to-erect perennial herb that is closely related to the stinging nettle. The leaves contain an alkaloid which, when ingested by some animals, can result in poisoning. The leaves are green with mottled silver lines and streaks with the stems being green or pinkish-green. The flowers are small and insignificant.
Aquarium suitability: Essentially a terrestrial plant that does quite well completely submerged. It is the ideal plant for a cichlid tank once it has settled in. *P. cadierei* will shed most of its leaves when it is first planted in an aquarium. The hobbyist must persevere and remove large leaves that are dying. Once the plant takes hold and begins to grow, smaller submerged leaves will appear and the plant will do well.

Order: Violales

This is a diverse order encompassing 13 families and 593 accepted species. This is a diverse order with 18 families encompassing 272 genera and 4,283 valid species. The group includes some well-known plants, trees, and shrubs, many of which have enormous commercial significance. Papayas, melons, and cucumbers all belong to this order. Many of our favorite flowers belong to this group including begonias, pansies and violets. The seeds of the Hydnocarpus plants from Southeast Asia produce "chaulmoogra oil" that contains hydnocarpic acid. At one time this, along with the seed oil of Casearia sylvestris from Brazil, was important for the treatment of leprosy.

The seeds of Oncoba echinata, cultivated throughout the tropics, and of Caloncoba echinata, of west central Africa, are the sources of gorli oil, which was also used in the treatment of leprosy.

There are very few plants within this order that can be termed truly aquatic, or even semi-aquatic, but there are one or two species. The most important of these is the water violet, which is a true aquatic species

Viola cucullata

Common names: Water violet, Northern bog violet, Marsh blue violet
Family: Violaceae
Range: North America
Height: 5–10 inches (13–26 cm)
Description: A marsh plant that is often entirely submerged during the wet season. The leaves may be rounded or arrow-shaped, with the two lower lobes having acute angles. The true aquatic plant has leaves that bear a resemblance to the arrowheads (*Syngonium* spp.) but in miniature. The flowers are very attractive and are bluish-violet in the center.
Aquarium suitability: Often overlooked by hobbyists, it is very slow growing and most of the leaves will shrivel and die at first, so the hobbyist must persevere until new leaves emerge.

Order: Lamiales

A large order that comprises 12 families and in excess of 11,000 species. Most of the species are herbaceous but some are shrubs, vines, or trees. They have a wide distribution in a variety of habitats, including aquatic environments.

The olive tree, *Olea europaea,* belongs to this order and can grow to be hundreds of years old. Many other trees and shrubs belong to this group, including jacaranda, buddlia, forsythia, ash, jasmine, sesame, and lilac. Many well-known plants such as snapdragons, slipperworts, kittentails, and foxgloves also belong to this order. Aquatic plants include *Hygrophila, Bacopa, Glossostigma,* and *Limnophila*. Some of these are very popular and hardy aquarium plants. Some authors refer to this order as Scrophulariales.

Hemigraphis repanda

Common name: Dragon flame, Purple crinkle, Purple waffle
Family: Acanthaceae
Range: Southeast Asia, mainly Malaysia
Height: 8–12 inches (20–30 cm)
Description: This is essentially a terrestrial plant that will live submerged for short periods of time and emerged for up to two years in its natural habitat. The leaves are strongly lanceolate with ruffled margins. The upper surfaces of the leaves are grayish-green, the undersides are deep reddish-purple. The leaves are curved and attached to vertical robust petioles.
Aquarium suitability: If this plant is allowed to grow out of the water, it will survive and grow well. If it is totally submerged in an aquarium for long periods, it will die. This is a plant for an open-topped aquarium that has rock ledges to accommodate it. Cichlids will leave this plant alone.

Hygrophila corymbosa

Common name: Green temple
Family: Acanthaceae
Range: Southeast Asia
Height: 12–20 inches (30–50 cm)
Description: A fast, easy-to-grow plant that has broad, dark green leaves and strong stems. When the shoots reach the water surface, attractive blue flowers appear. *H. corymbosa* is the original plant for many varieties that have been cultured.
Aquarium suitability: A very attractive aquarium plant and one that is recommended for the complete beginner. If it is planted in small groups, it will do well in almost any kind of water quality. The hobbyist should ensure that the plants are not placed too close together or their subsequent growth will produce shaded areas. If this happens, the lower leaves of some specimens will not get enough light and will eventually die off.

Hygrophila corymbosa var. 'Siamensis'

Common name: Giant temple
Family: Acanthaceae
Range: Southeast Asia, principally Thailand
Height: 2½–15 inches (6–40 cm)
Description: An amazing plant that has broad underwater leaves that are light green to deep green with a velvety surface. The growth is usually quite dense in areas where the substrate is high in nutrients. Above the water surface, the leaves will be bluish-green and emerged shoots will produce small blue flowers.
Aquarium suitability: An excellent plant for the beginner. This species is normally sold in bunches with a piece of strip-lead attached. Plant the bunch as it is in the tank by simply pressing it into the gravel or sand. It will grow quite well. Once the roots have formed, the lead strip can then be removed.

Hygrophila corymbosa var. 'Temple narrow leaf'

Common name: Temple narrow leaf
Family: Acanthaceae
Range: Southeast Asia (cultivated)
Height: 8–12 inches (20–30 cm)
Description: This plant is sometimes called *Hygrophila corymbosa* 'Aroma' because of its emerged aromatic leaves. It is a narrow-leafed variety of the previous species and one that is very attractive. Submerged leaves are very long and narrow and they are grouped relatively close together. Emerged leaves are shorter, have a somewhat hairy surface, and are spaced wider apart from one another.
Aquarium suitability: The Temple narrow leaf is a stately and elegant plant but it is not as easy to keep as others of this genus. Its growth is slow and it needs a lot of light for it to do well.

Hygrophila difformis

Common name: Water wisteria
Family: Acanthaceae
Range: Widespread throughout Southeast Asia
Height: 8–20 inches (20–50 cm)
Description: The leaves are bright green, deep green, or light green. Light green leaves will only appear as new leaves or if the plant is in a substrate that is poor in nutrients. It is an attractive plant that grows in a variety of habitats. Unlike other members of this genus, the leaves are multilobed.
Aquarium suitability: This is very much a plant for complete novices and it will survive most beginners' mistakes. However, for its continued well-being in an aquarium it needs a nutrient-rich substrate. If the tank has a subsand filter, this will be no problem, as nutrients will occur naturally in the sand or gravel.

Hygrophila polysperma

Common name: Dwarf hygrophilia
Family: Acanthaceae
Range: Southeast Asia and India
Height: 8–10 inches (20–26 cm)
Description: *Hygrophilia polysperma* is ubiquitous throughout Southeast Asia, where it grows under a variety of conditions. In strong light the leaves are red, in lower light conditions they are pale to deep green. It is a tenacious alien species in the United States.
Aquarium suitability: This species should be planted in plain gravel in small bunches. It is self-propagating but can be planted elsewhere through cuttings from the parent plant. It is best kept as a background plant and requires frequent pruning. Because of its hardiness, this plant is ideal for the novice. It requires little care and will grow quickly provided it is given enough light.

Hygrophila polysperma
var. 'Tropic Sunset'

Common name: Tropic sunset
Family: Acanthaceae
Range: Southeast Asia (cultivated)
Height: 8–12 inches (20–30 cm)
Description: This plant is also known as *Hygrophila polysperma* 'Rosanervig.' It is simply a cultured version of the original species that has been patented. The coloration of the upper leaves is light pinkish red to brownish-red and they have light veins running through them. It is believed that the absence of color in the veins is caused by a virus that prevents chlorophyll from being produced in the cells that surround the leaf ribs.
Aquarium suitability: This is not an easy plant to keep and have flourish in an aquarium. It needs light to keep the leaves red and to keep it from dying off.

Nomaphila stricta

Common names: Giant hygro, Temple plant
Family: Acanthaceae
Range: Southeast Asia, from Thailand to Indonesia
Height: 10–16 inches (25–41 cm)
Description: A slow-growing plant with red stems and bright green to deep green leaves that have prominent veins on the undersides. This is a species that can grow submerged but will usually prefer a habitat where it can grow emerged to produce its small white flowers. The leaves are broad and lanceolate with new leaves lighter in color than the older ones.
Aquarium suitability: A hardy plant for a tropical freshwater aquarium, but one that needs to be able to grow out of the water at some point in its life. Provide a nutrient-rich substrate and it will do well. Any dead or dying leaves should be removed before planting to ensure that these do not rot in the tank.

Micromeria brownei

Common names: Creeping charlie, Aquatic mint, West Indian thyme
Family: Lamiaceae
Range: Caribbean, mainly Cuba
Height: 8–12 inches (20–30 cm)
Description: The plant stems are deep green at their bases, becoming light green toward the tips. The leaves are bright green to light green in color with marked lighter veins. Generally the leaves are round, often with chordate bases. This is a true aquatic plant and it is relatively fast growing.
Aquarium suitability: For the best result, this species should be planted in bunches of five or more stems in a nutrient-rich substrate as a middle-ground to background plant. Individual bunches should be placed about 4 inches (10 cm) apart from one another to allow light to the lower leaves of each plant group.

Bacopa caroliniana

Common name: Bacopa
Family: Scrophulariaceae
Range: North and Central America
Height: 8–12 inches (20–30 cm)
Description: *Bacopa caroliniana* is a broad-leafed plant that has deep green to light green leaves that grow in pairs along a central stem. It is an attractive submerged plant that can grow out of the water surface and bloom with blue to light violet flowers.
Aquarium suitability: For many years, hobbyists have used this slow-growing plant for aquarium decoration. Its broad leaves and slow rate of growth make it the ideal addition for any community set up that does not contain herbivorous fish. Like most bunched plants, it is best arranged in small groups. It does not need much attention and propagation is easy if a side shoot is taken and replanted elsewhere in the aquarium.

Bacopa monnieri

Common name: Moneywort
Family: Scrophulariaceae
Range: Circumtropical
Height: 10–20 inches (25–50 cm)
Description: This is an attractive, slow-growing plant with somewhat rounded, bright green leaves. It is found growing in lakes, streams, and river margins, and may be completely submerged or emerged. This species is also known to grow quite well in brackish water in estuaries and tidal rivers.
Aquarium suitability: The Moneywort is equally at home in an aquarium as it is in a garden pond. It is easy to propagate. All that needs to be done is to pinch off the outgrown long stems below the water surface and stick them back in the substrate. Each one of these will form a new plant. This species is best planted in small groups.

Glossostigma elatinoides

Common names: Glossostigma, Glosso
Family: Scrophulariaceae
Range: Australia, New Zealand, and Tasmania
Height: ¾–1¼ inches (2–3 cm)
Description: A stubby plant that is bright green with tiny, rounded leaves growing on short, lightly colored petioles that sway in a gentle water current. It is a small species that is very attractive.
Aquarium suitability: This species is one of the smallest aquarium plants, therefore it is an excellent foreground plant. It requires a nutrient-rich substrate to grow well. Once this is taken care of, it will send out soft rhizomes to form new plantlets. It needs quite a bit of light for it to stay low. If this is not provided, the plant will send out long runners to the surface and will look untidy. Not an easy plant to keep in an aquarium.

Limnophila aquatica

Common name: None
Family: Scrophulariaceae
Range: Southeast Asia
Height: 10–20 inches (25–50 cm)
Description: This is a very attractive plant with beautiful, light green leaves that are fine and filigree-like. The leaves circle a central stem that is robust and deep green. Surface shoots eventually flower, producing small blue flowers above the water surface.
Aquarium suitability: A fast-growing plant that can survive under a variety of water conditions. It does, however, require a nutrient-rich substrate for it to do well, and therefore is not recommended for the complete novice. Soft and slightly acidic water makes this species grow particularly well. Medium to high lighting will make this species produce lateral rhizomes.

Limnophila indica

Common name: Ambulia
Family: Scrophulariaceae
Range: Widespread throughout tropical Africa, Asia, and Australia
Height: 8–10 inches (20–25 cm)
Description: Ambulia is a common plant that is bright green with fine leaves that circle the stolons. This species is sometimes confused with *L. sessiliflora*. However, this species remains green at the tips of the plant nearest the surface, whereas *L. sessiliflora* develops a red tinge to the upper leaves.
Aquarium suitability: Should be used as a backdrop plant rather than a plant for the foreground because of its height. It is a plant that should be kept under quite intense light if it is to do well in an aquarium. Propagation can be carried out through cuttings from longer stems, but lateral shoots are also sent out.

Limnophila sessiliflora

Common names: Asian ambulia, Asian marshweed, Dwarf ambulia
Family: Scrophulariaceae
Range: Asia, Indonesia, Sri Lanka, Pakistan, India, and Japan, in a variety of habitats
Height: 7–9 inches (18–23 cm)
Description: This is an aquatic plant that thrives in bright light. The former name, *Ambulia sessiliflora*, should be considered as a junior synonym of this species. The bright green fronds are slender with narrow, branching leaves circling the central stem.
Aquarium suitability: Thrives best when an iron-based fertilizer is used. The tank should be kept clean and well filtered. It can be planted in bunches in plain gravel but requires a well-lit tank so that the plant tendrils do not become "leggy" and sparse. This plant is a good alternative to *Cabomba* spp.

Micranthemum micranthemoides

Common name: Baby tears
Family: Scrophulariaceae
Range: Southern United States and Cuba
Height: 2–4 inches (5–10 cm)
Description: A small plant with leaves that are arranged in clusters of four. The leaves are generally round, but new leaves can also be ovate. This plant is easily confused with *M. umbrosum* but it does not grow as large. The stems are robust and the leaves are bright green to deep green. This is a species that can grow emerged as well as submerged.
Aquarium suitability: A great foreground plant because of its small size. The only drawback here is that it requires very high-intensity lighting for it to grow well and develop into a thick foreground carpet. Provide the correct lighting and this species will grow into a spectacular green carpet in a show tank.

Order: Haloragales

The order comprises two families: Gunneraceae and Haloragaceae. Gunneraceae is a monogeneric family with about 50 species of terrestrial plants. Haloragaceae is a family of mainly aquatic plants with about 100 species, some of which are cosmopolitan in distribution (Myriophyllum). Both families have recently been placed in the order Saxifragales by some authors. However, it is believed that these two families, along with Podostemaceae, form an isolated group of highly specialized rosoids with a saxifragean origin. In this book, Gunneraceae has been kept in the Haloragales along with Haloragaceae, with Gunneraceae viewed as the basal unit in the group. Podostemaceae is assigned to the order Podostemales. It is felt that this is the most reasonable interpretation of this order at present.

Myriophyllum aquaticum

Common name: Parrot feather
Family: Haloragaceae
Range: South America
Height: 16 inches (41 cm)
Description: A fast-growing plant with very fine filigree leaves and deep green stems. The leaves are often light green or yellow and the uppermost leaves are bright green. Propagation is effected through lateral shoots from the parent plant.
Aquarium suitability: A bog plant that grows equally well in ponds as it does in aquariums. Plant in bunches at the rear of the tank to provide a fine foliage backdrop to other smaller plants. Ensure that there is enough space between the individual bunches, because it grows very fast. The aquarium lighting needs to be quite high in intensity for this species to grow well.

Myriophyllum heterophyllum

Common names: Red myrio, Red foxtail
Family: Haloragaceae
Range: Northeastern North America
Height: 8–10 inches (20–25 cm)
Description: This is a beautiful plant with very fine filigree leaves that are yellow at the bases and brownish-red at the tips. The stems are deep brick-red and the uppermost new leaves are bright green.
Aquarium suitability: The Red foxtail is a popular plant because of its attractive colors. It is moderately easy to keep but does have special needs. Plenty of water movement should be provided along with a nutrient-rich substrate. Propagation is through lateral shoots. High-intensity lighting is a prerequisite but it will not cope very well with blue-green algae infestation, so ensure that this is not present before introducing this species.

Myriophyllum pinnatum

Common names: Green myrio, Green foxtail, Cutleaf watermilfoil
Family: Haloragaceae
Range: Eastern United States
Height: 8–12 inches (20–30 cm)
Description: Easily confused with *M. tuberculatum* but that plant has red stems and green leaves. This plant, on the other hand, has green stems and delicate, bright green leaves. In the wild it grows in bright, sunny areas such as clear streams.
Aquarium suitability: Most species in this genus require a great deal of light for them to grow well in an aquarium; this species is no exception. Because of its ultimate height, it should be used as a background plant in a small aquarium and further forward in larger show tanks. The fine but dense foliage allows it to be used in front of unsightly heaters and filter tubes to hide them.

Myriophyllum simulans var. 'Brazilian'

Common names: Brazilian myrio, Brazilian watermilfoil
Family: Haloragaceae
Range: South America, principally Brazil and Uruguay
Height: 10–16 inches (20–41 cm)
Description: The leaves of this plant are bright green and finely pinnate. It is one of two varieties of *M. simulans*. The two differ in foliage and in size. This variety grows quite large and has very dense foliage that can often appear to be deep green. Lower leaves tend to be darker than the upper ones.
Aquarium suitability: A great plant for waterscaping because of its fine filigree foliage and bushy contrast to other, broader leaf plants. It is relatively undemanding and easy to keep, providing it has enough light. If this is the case, side shoots will appear to form new plants. Once these have formed roots they can be pinched off at the rhizome and planted elsewhere.

Myriophyllum simulans var. 'Filigree'

Common names: Filigree myrio, Common watermilfoil
Family: Haloragaceae
Range: Australia
Height: 8–10 inches (20–25 cm)
Description: The stems of this plant are light green at the tips and darker at the bases. The plant differs from the previous variety in that it does not grow as large. Apart from this distinction, the filigree effect of the pinnate leaf is much finer and more delicate.
Aquarium suitability: Another plant that needs a lot of light for it to grow strong and healthy. It should be planted in sand or gravel that has a high nutrient content. It is less hardy than the previous variety and is not a plant for the beginner. It looks especially attractive if it is planted next to other plants that have different leaf forms and colors.

Order: Rhizophorales

The order contains only a single family, Rhizophoraceae, with 14 genera and about 100 species of flowering plants, shrubs, and trees. Perhaps the best known of these are the 17 species of tropical shrubs and trees that are known as the mangroves. Only four of these, however, can be termed "true" mangroves (see *Rhizophora mangle* description, below). The others in this group are predominantly inland species such as the goatwood, with species from the pantropical genus *Cassipourea* the most numerous. The majority of the terrestrial species are considered to be parasitic.

The plants are woody with flowers that are adapted to pollination by insects because they each have a nectary disc, typically with five petals. Mangroves are quite amazing in their development. The red mangrove, for instance, produces a podlike fruit, which falls from the tree into the water. It can be carried thousands of miles through estuarine spates and ocean currents until it comes ashore and is embedded in the substrate of some distant land. Once there, it will sprout roots from its pod and begin to grow into a large and sturdy tree.

Rhizophora mangle

Common names: Red mangrove, American mangrove
Family: Rhizophoraceae
Range: Circumtropical and subtropical in coastal areas and tidal estuaries and bays
Height: 30–62 feet (10–20 m)
Description: This and three other similar species are the mangroves. These tropical trees or shrubs grow in coastal mud and sand with many tangled roots above the mud, or above the water surface in some cases. They are at home in brackish water, where they grow especially well. Their underwater root system plays an important role in the development of many fish fry and invertebrate larvae. The tangled root structures that extend underwater allow protection for many small animals. Nutrients that are harbored within the mangrove roots, both in the form of plankton and other organic debris, are vital to the ecology of some seashores and estuaries, providing food for myriad animals.
Aquarium suitability: For the ambitious amateur botanist or gardener, mangroves are one of the "impossible" plants in terms of propagation. For the aquarist, however, mangroves do not present a problem. They require brackish water, carrying enough nutrients to their root system so that the plant can flourish—easy for the aquarist with the right aquarium setup, very difficult for the gardener. In the last few years, more and more of these shrubs have appeared in stores. They are usually sold in small perforated plastic plant pots that the aquarist can place directly in an open-topped aquarium, among rocks and other plants, with the upper part above the water surface to allow the plant to grow. Metal halide lighting is a prerequisite and with it the mangrove will grow well. It is especially recommended for those aquarists who use a plenum-type filtration system.

Division: Polypodiophyta

This is the division of the plant kingdom comprising plants that are commonly known as ferns. These are vascular plants that have stems, roots, and leaves. Ferns can have stems that are up to 50 feet (16 m) high or they can be prostrate with the stem lying in or on the ground. Others may not look like ferns at all: *Salvinia* and *Azolla* are small plants that grow on the water surface. *Marsilea mutica* is commonly known as the water clover and is found in marshy areas, often submerged.

There are about 10,000 extant species of ferns, but they have been around for a long time. Ferns were abundant during the Carboniferous period. Usually the leaf or frond is divided into separate blades. New fern leaves generally unfurl gradually from the early bud stage, which is called a crozier, or fiddlehead. The spore cases, or sporangia, are developed under the leaves in groups.

The order Psilotales is tentatively included in this division, although they are so vastly different from living ferns that there is no universal agreement on this. It is believed that plants from the Psilotales, generally called whisk ferns, are a remnant of an otherwise extinct group of plants from the Devonian period.

Order: Aspleniales

Some authors believe that this order should only contain one family, Aspleniaceae. However, the conventional grouping has been retained here so that this order comprises nine families.

Ferns are found all over the world, from the temperate areas of Europe and North America to the equatorial regions of Africa and South America. The order includes wood ferns, spleenworts, holly ferns, and oak ferns, but there are many more species. Most plants in this order are terrestrial and there is only one plant that can be termed a true aquatic plant for the aquarium.

Bolbitus heudelotii

Common names: Bolbitus, Water fern
Family: Lomariopsidaceae
Range: Western Africa
Height: 6–12 inches (15–30 cm)
Description: A very attractive water fern with deep green leaves arising from a central horizontal rhizome. Young leaves are curled and gradually unfurl as they grow in typical fern fashion.
Aquarium suitability: This is quite a difficult plant to keep and should be left to the expert aquarist. When planting, avoid burying the rhizome in the substrate or the plant will die. The roots can be buried up to a few millimeters from the rhizome but not more. As a better alternative, the plant can be fixed to a rock or piece of wood using nylon fishing line. Once the roots have taken hold, the line can then be removed.

Order: Marsileales

The order was previously known as Hydroteridales, but modern rules of botanical nomenclature have caused the name to be changed. The ferns in this order are diverse in shape and form, often varying radically from species to species. Most of the plants do not look like ferns.

Marsileales is made up of three families of aquatic ferns. The Azollaceae (mosquito ferns) and the Salviniaceae (water-spangles) are floating plants (natant), whereas those of the family Marsileaceae (water clovers and pillworts) are submerged rooted ferns, often with emergent leaves. In some cases the natant species may grow in wet mud during periods of low water. Conversely, the Marsilaceae can be completely submerged for long periods of high water.

Marsilea mutica

Common name: Variegated water clover
Family: Marsileaceae
Range: Australia
Height: 6–8 inches (15–20 cm)
Description: This species has floating leaves with a distinctive pattern of red, yellow, and green leaves. In parts of Florida it is considered to be a nonnative, highly invasive fern. It is a herbaceous rhizomatous perennial that grows in marshy areas and shallow water.
Aquarium suitability: This is an attractive species that is relatively easy to keep. It is usually sold in a perforated pot—this can be placed in the substrate providing there is sufficient depth to cover the pot. Once it has rooted and taken hold, it will produce modified underwater leaves as well as the floating ones. These leaves may not have the typical four-leaf clover lobes.

Salvinia natans

Common names: Salvinia, Aquarium watermoss, Kariba weed
Family: Salviniaceae
Range: Asia and Southern Europe
Height: ¼–1½ inches (1–3 cm)
Description: This is a small floating fern that grows quickly if there are sufficient nutrients in the water and plenty of light. The small floating leaves are covered in minute hairs, which make them buoyant. Because they are fast-growing, they can cover large areas of water in a similar way to duckweed. In many areas, species of *Salvinia* are considered to be invasive and are a problem to the maintenance of waterways.
Aquarium suitability: As an aquarium plant, this species has its uses. It can produce shadowy areas where algae growth will be minimal. It is also good in breeding tanks and fry tanks as a place of refuge and safety.

Order: Parkeriales

This order is made up of seven families of ferns. Generally, the plants are small and rhizomatous with leaves that are often pinnate. Brake ferns and the attractive maidenhair ferns belong to this group along with lace ferns, creeping ferns, and Indian's dream.

Very few of the plants are aquatic but many marsh and wetland ferns can be emerged for most of their life and totally submerged for up to six months. Only one true aquatic genus is of interest to the tropical freshwater hobbyist and that is *Ceratopteris* (the water sprites). These are attractive plants that add a touch of the exotic to waterscaping, in terms of leaf form.

Ceratopteris thalictroides

Common name: Water sprite
Family: Pteridaceae
Range: Circumtropical
Height: 6–12 inches (15–30 cm)
Description: This particular fern is amazing in the way it grows underwater. It shows the typical unfurling of the new leaves, and older leaves will often float on the water surface and have a beautiful form. The leaves are finely branched, as with most ferns, and they are bright green to deep green depending on the light intensity.
Aquarium suitability: A great starter plant for the beginner if the specimen already has well-developed roots. If it is supplied as a bunched plant with a lead anchor, it may not do so well in a new tank. It grows fast under strong light and is ideal for a small tank. Because the leaves are not regular in shape, the water sprite can provide an excellent contrast when planted next to other broader-leafed plants.

Order: Polypodiales

Polypodiales is by far the largest order of modern ferns with roughly 250 genera and about 9,000 species. They are commonly referred to as the "true ferns." Some authors still use the name Filicales for this group, but this is a junior synonym. They are well represented in temperate and subtropical regions but they are particularly abundant in damp tropical areas. The form of these plants is very diverse and ranges from tiny gossamer structures to large, treelike growths. Some are epiphytes that live on the surface of other plants and there are others that are climbing species. Although they are called modern ferns, they date back to the coal deposits of the early Paleozoic period.

Microsorum pteropus

Common name: Java fern
Family: Polypodiaceae
Range: Asia, particularly Southeast Asia
Height: 6–12 inches (15–30 cm)
Description: This plant grows from an exposed blackish, horizontal central rhizome and the leaves are produced along its length. The leaves are broad, bold, and bright green. They are lanceolate in form with undulate margins and ripples throughout the centers of the blades.
Aquarium suitability: This is a hardy plant if it is planted correctly in an aquarium. The best way to do this is to tie the whole rhizome to a driftwood root or stone using nylon fishing line. Once it has taken root, the line can be removed. Do not bury the roots or the rhizome in the substrate because they will rot and the plant will die.

Microsorum pteropus var. 'Windeløv'

Common name: Lace fern
Family: Polypodiaceae
Range: Asia (cultivated)
Height: 4–8 inches (10–20 cm)
Description: This plant is a cultivated variation of the previous species and one that is very attractive and unusual. The leaves are broad at the base with the typical crinkled appearance on the surfaces and they may be bright green to dark green. Newer leaves tend to be lighter in color than the older ones. The finely branched, lacelike leaf tips make this plant an unusual variety.
Aquarium suitability: As with the Java fern, this species should be tied to a tree root or stone at first so that it can root correctly and grow. The rhizome should not be buried in the substrate and can be separated at strategic points to produce new plants, but it is recommended that at least three leaves remain on the separated portion.

Which plants do not belong in an aquarium?

There are many plants that are sold to the hobbyist as being "ideal" for his or her aquarium, but many of these plants cannot live for more than a few weeks if they are totally submerged in water. That is why all the plants that have been listed in the preceding section have been thoroughly checked for their sustainability and their hardiness under the conditions and parameters that have been provided in the advice on aquarium suitability sections. If there is a plant in your local dealer's store that you do not know anything about, then it is advisable to leave it alone until more information is available to you. It is better to keep disturbances within the aquarium to a minimum—whereas buying a plant that catches your eye in a garden center may be one of the joys of gardening, the aquarist has to take a more conservative view when buying plants for the aquarium.

The so-called water fern (there are actually two separate species in this photograph). Neither of them will live longer than a few weeks in an aquarium. They are terrestrial plants that prefer moist soil and plenty of sunlight to grow well. They will soon rot in a tropical freshwater aquarium in submerged conditions.

part three

FISH FOR
THE AQUARIUM

Fish for the tropical freshwater aquarium

The sizes of fish given are the maximum known size that a fish will grow to in its natural habitat, as measured from the tip of the snout to the base of the caudal fin. Where the range of a fish is given it is intended to indicate where the particular fish is found to be endemic. Isolated or unusual occurrences have not been taken into consideration, nor have those instances where species have been artificially introduced into certain areas. Once again, the "bubbles" positioned in the margin of each photograph refer to the degree of difficulty in which a particular fish can be kept in a healthy state in an aquarium. The quick-glance rating adheres to the following criteria:

○—Easy, a fish for beginners and experienced aquarists.
○○—Not difficult for aquarists with six months or more experience.
○○○—Quite difficult. Only for experienced aquarists.
○○○○—Very difficult. Requires optimal aquarium conditions.
○○○○○—Almost impossible for all but the most experienced aquarist.

Systematic classification of the Chordates

The superclass Gnathostomata is our first step into the systematics of fish. It is this class that holds the key to our own origin in cladistic terms, and that of all modern fish. I recognize three grades of Gnathostomata. The first of these is the grade Placodermiomorphi, which consists of a single class: Placodermi, a group of primitive fish with bony plates over much of their bodies that existed between the lower and upper Devonian period of the earth's formation, 395–350 million years ago. All fish of this grade are extinct and therefore do not appear on the chart on the opposite page. Fish of the second grade, Chondrichthiomorphi, swiftly replaced them at the end of the Devonian period, although this group has existed as a taxon since the Silurian period, 430–395 million years ago. Chondrichthiomorphi also consists of a single class—Chondrichthyes (cartilaginous fish) and there is an almost complete fossil record of its development since the end of the Devonian period, with some extant genera having their origins in the Cretaceous period 135–65 million years ago.

The third grade, Teleostomi, contains all true vertebrate animals. This not only means the tetrapods such as mammals, birds, lizards, and snakes, it also contains all modern bony fish. These will be covered in some detail after this section.

The class Chondrichthyes has two subclasses encompassing 10 orders, 45 families, 170 genera, and approximately 846 species. The first subclass, Holocephali, is made up of a single order and contains ancient and primitive deepwater fish that are known as ghost sharks and chimaeras. Most of these are unsuitable for life in an aquarium, although they are occasionally seen on offer in the trade as an "exotic saltwater fish." They do not usually live long in captivity.

Elasmobranchii, the second subclass, consists of nine orders and contains all the true sharks, rays, skates, and sawfish. The order Orectolobiformes (carpet sharks) contains the world's largest living fish, the whale shark. Most of the species are marine-living, although there are a few freshwater species and many others that enter into brackish water. However, most grow far too large for the average aquarium, so they have been excluded from this book.

Generally, the characteristics of this class are well known. The skeleton is cartilaginous, sometimes calcified, but never bone. There are five to seven gill slits and the scales are not made up of overlapping plates, as is the case with most fish. Instead, the scales consist of small tubercles (dermal denticles), which give rise to the sandpapery texture of the skin. The teeth are not embedded in sockets, they are fused in rows to tissue that is continually growing forward. In this way the teeth at the rear become erect, moving forward to replace broken or blunt teeth at the front, which are then shed. The teeth themselves are modified dermal denticles. There is no swim bladder present to offset the body weight, therefore the fish must swim in order to maintain its level in the water. In the case of sharks, the forward edges of the pectoral fins are inclined upward to produce a hydrofoil effect, helping give the fish lift.

Systematic classification of the chordates

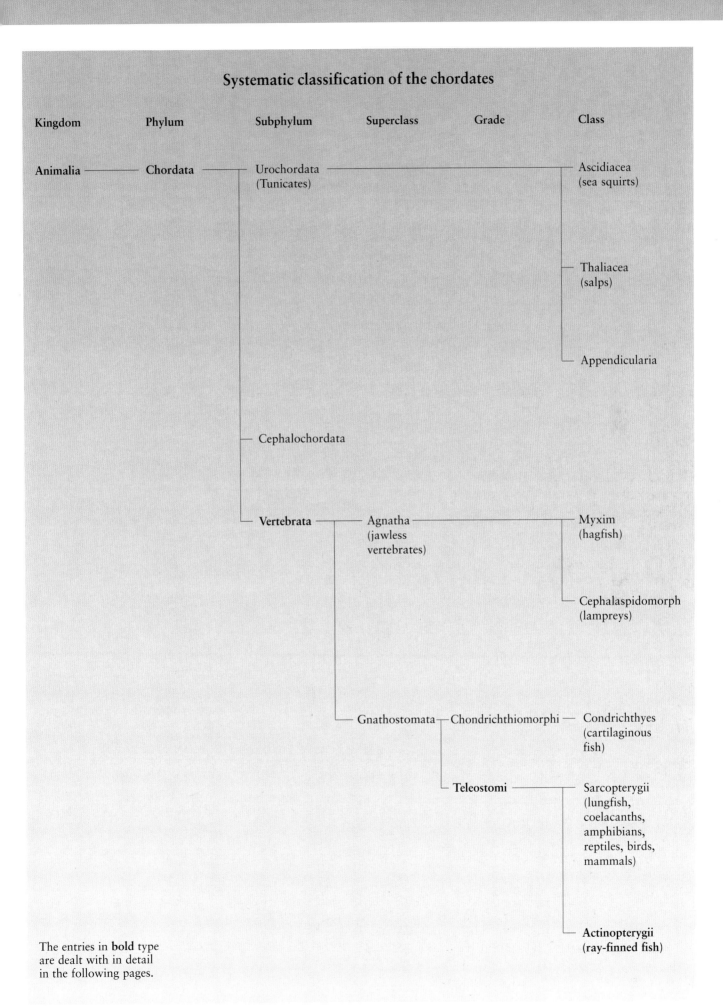

Kingdom	Phylum	Subphylum	Superclass	Grade	Class
Animalia	**Chordata**	Urochordata (Tunicates)			Ascidiacea (sea squirts)
					Thaliacea (salps)
					Appendicularia
		Cephalochordata			
		Vertebrata	Agnatha (jawless vertebrates)		Myxim (hagfish)
					Cephalaspidomorph (lampreys)
			Gnathostomata	Chondrichthiomorphi	Condrichthyes (cartilaginous fish)
				Teleostomi	Sarcopterygii (lungfish, coelacanths, amphibians, reptiles, birds, mammals)
					Actinopterygii (ray-finned fish)

The entries in **bold** type are dealt with in detail in the following pages.

Grade: Teleostomi

The second step in this systematic breakdown is the classification of the grade Teleostomi down to the various orders of fish. This is shown in the chart below. The chart has been simplified for ease of reference, but does give the aquarist a broad view of the taxonomic differences. It can be seen that all the relevant orders belong to the division Teleostei and it is an indisputable fact that practically all aquarium fish are true Teleostei, bony fish. This applies not only to freshwater aquarium fish but also to marine fish as well.

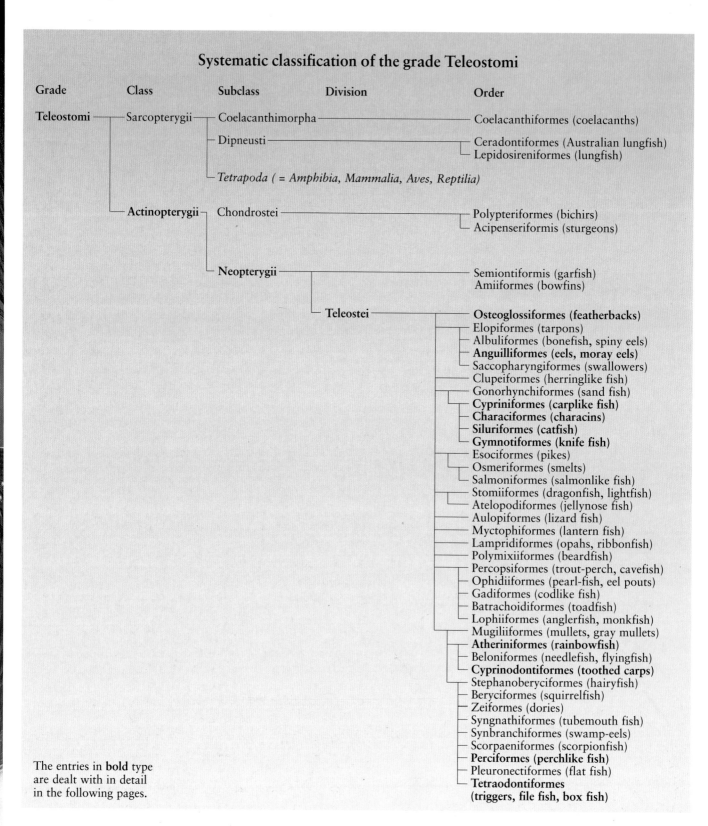

Systematic classification of the grade Teleostomi

Grade	Class	Subclass	Division	Order
Teleostomi	Sarcopterygii	Coelacanthimorpha		Coelacanthiformes (coelacanths)
		Dipneusti		Ceradontiformes (Australian lungfish)
				Lepidosireniformes (lungfish)
		Tetrapoda (= Amphibia, Mammalia, Aves, Reptilia)		
	Actinopterygii	Chondrostei		Polypteriformes (bichirs)
				Acipenseriformis (sturgeons)
		Neopterygii		Semiontiformis (garfish)
				Amiiformes (bowfins)
			Teleostei	**Osteoglossiformes (featherbacks)**
				Elopiformes (tarpons)
				Albuliformes (bonefish, spiny eels)
				Anguilliformes (eels, moray eels)
				Saccopharyngiformes (swallowers)
				Clupeiformes (herringlike fish)
				Gonorhynchiformes (sand fish)
				Cypriniformes (carplike fish)
				Characiformes (characins)
				Siluriformes (catfish)
				Gymnotiformes (knife fish)
				Esociformes (pikes)
				Osmeriformes (smelts)
				Salmoniformes (salmonlike fish)
				Stomiiformes (dragonfish, lightfish)
				Atelopodiformes (jellynose fish)
				Aulopiformes (lizard fish)
				Myctophiformes (lantern fish)
				Lampridiformes (opahs, ribbonfish)
				Polymixiiformes (beardfish)
				Percopsiformes (trout-perch, cavefish)
				Ophidiiformes (pearl-fish, eel pouts)
				Gadiformes (codlike fish)
				Batrachoidiformes (toadfish)
				Lophiiformes (anglerfish, monkfish)
				Mugiliiformes (mullets, gray mullets)
				Atheriniformes (rainbowfish)
				Beloniformes (needlefish, flyingfish)
				Cyprinodontiformes (toothed carps)
				Stephanoberyciformes (hairyfish)
				Beryciformes (squirrelfish)
				Zeiformes (dories)
				Syngnathiformes (tubemouth fish)
				Synbranchiformes (swamp-eels)
				Scorpaeniformes (scorpionfish)
				Perciformes (perchlike fish)
				Pleuronectiformes (flat fish)
				Tetraodontiformes (triggers, file fish, box fish)

The entries in **bold** type are dealt with in detail in the following pages.

Order: Osteoglossiformes

The order comprises six families with 29 genera and about 217 species, all of which are found in freshwater, although some notopterids are known to enter brackish water. This is a very old order that probably evolved around the middle of the Cretaceous period in our earth's history. The name of the order comes from the Latin for "bony tongues," because species of this group have toothed or bony tongues. They are distinct from other groups of fish in that the forward part of the gastrointestinal tract passes to the left of the esophagus and stomach, whereas in all other fish it passes to the right. One species, known colloquially as the Pirarucu or Arapaima (*Arapaima gigas*), is the largest known freshwater fish. Specimens have been recorded that were up to 14 feet 6 inches (4.5 m) in length!

Osteoglossidae (Bonytongues & Arowana)

The family encompasses two subfamilies. These are Heterotidinae with two genera and two species and Osteoglossinae also with two genera, but with five species. These are primitive throwbacks from the lower Tertiary period. Of the seven extant species, three are from South America, three are from Australia, and the final one is from Africa. These fish are almost entirely carnivorous, often being highly specialized surface feeders or "jumpers." Osteoglossum species have been seen to jump more than 6 feet (200 cm) from the water surface to seize monkeys from the overhanging branches in South America.

Osteoglossum bicirrhosum

Common name: Silver arowana
Range: South America, principally the Amazon Basin
Size: 40 inches (100 cm)
Description: The caudal fin is almost ovate and the scales are large and prominent. The back of this species is horizontal to the curved belly and the anal fin extends almost two-thirds of the body. The back is olive brown in older specimens, with silver flanks. The dorsal fin is shorter and smaller than the anal fin.
Aquarium suitability: This fish needs a big tank with a tight-fitting cover because it will jump out. It should be fed on meaty foods such as shrimp, mussels, prawns, and whitebait.
Breeding information: The males are mouthbreeders. Large eggs are cared for by the male until they hatch and the yolk sac of the fry has been absorbed, usually after eight weeks.

Scleropages jardini

Common names: Jardini arowana, Spotted barramundi, Australian arowana, Saratoga
Range: Australia, in freshwater creeks, rivers, and billabongs
Size: 36 inches (92 cm)
Description: The body is dark silver and the fins are deep grayish-black. Each scale has a small red spot on it and there are often white spots and blotches on the dorsal and anal fins. This fish has a large, upturned mouth and is a fierce predator.
Aquarium suitability: Much more placid than the previous species, except at feeding time, when it will become quite aggressive. Do not feed this fish by hand unless you want to be bitten. Feed floating pellets, crustaceans, and beef heart. It can be easily weaned onto most frozen foods.
Breeding information: This fish has not been bred in captivity. However, like all arowanas, it is a mouthbreeder.

Pantodontidae (Butterflyfish)

This is a monospecific family with only one species, *Pantodon buchholzi*. The pelvic fins are located under the pectoral fins and the swim bladder can act as an air-breathing organ. There is no suboperculum present and the pectoral fins are greatly enlarged. Recently there has been some discussion regarding the placement of this family. Many cladists believe it to form a monophyletic clade with the Osteoglossinae. Nevertheless, it has been decided to retain this family in its traditional position within the Osteoglossiformes because the evidence otherwise has not yet been fully presented. The single species in this family is a popular aquarium fish.

Pantodon buchholzi

Common name: African butterflyfish
Range: Western and central Africa, in calm water
Size: 5 inches (13 cm)
Description: The body coloration is marbled brown and beige. The pectoral fins are large and winglike, allowing this species to jump out of the water to catch flying insects. Its mouth is large and upturned because this is a surface-dwelling carnivorous fish.
Aquarium suitability: The aquarium should have good filtration and a tight-fitting hood, otherwise this fish will jump out. It is a shy fish that needs plenty of floating plants such as *Riccia* to make it feel more secure.
Breeding information: Females lay up to 200 floating eggs that hatch after two days. The fry need to be fed infusorians or enriched freshwater rotifers, such as *Brachionus* spp., for them to survive.

Notopteridae (Featherfin knifefish, Old World knifefish)

This family is made up of four genera containing eight species that are distributed throughout Southeast Asia and Africa in freshwater or sometimes brackish water. They are quite similar to other knife fish in body shape, but in this case the anal and caudal fins are joined together to form a single large fin and the fused caudal fin is greatly reduced. The four genera are *Chitala*, *Notopterus*, *Papyrocranus*, and *Xenomystus*. Generally, the body coloration is uniform with numerous spots, with curving stripes, or with large ocellated spots above the anal fin. The pelvic and dorsal fins are small and rudimentary or completely absent. Some species can reach a length of 5 feet (152 cm). Although they are popular with aquarists, they are really only suitable for large aquariums.

Chitala ornata

Common names: Clown knifefish, Featherback
Range: Southeast Asia, particularly Burma, India, and Thailand
Size: 40 inches (100 cm)
Description: The body coloration is silvery gray with as many as 10 large and distinct white-edged black ocelli on the flanks above the anal fin. The body itself is deeply compressed laterally and elongate, resembling a knife blade. The fins are dark gray to deep brown, depending on the age of the fish.
Aquarium suitability: Floating plants, dark areas, and plenty of hiding places are the key to success with this species. Provide all these in a large tank and this fish will do well.
Breeding information: Parent fish must be quite large before they will breed. The adhesive eggs are laid among floating plant roots or on hard surfaces. Fry should be transferred to a raising tank, where they will accept newly hatched brine shrimp.

Notopterus notopterus

Common names: Asian knifefish, Bronze featherback
Range: Widespread throughout Southeast Asia
Size: 14 inches (36 cm)
Description: This is one of the smaller knifefish, colored light brown to deep brown with a tinge of violet. The mouth is large and the fins are lighter in color when compared to the rest of the body. There is a light gray area around the lower part of the eye.
Aquarium suitability: Although this fish can be kept with other large fish, it does better in its own tank. It is aggressive toward its own species and is largely nocturnal. In a very large tank it will tolerate a female, but is very territorial. It will accept earthworms, tubifex worms, crustaceans, and floating pellets.
Breeding information: The Asian knifefish spawns at night with up to 200 eggs being dropped to the substrate and rocks. The male fish guards and fans the eggs, which hatch after two weeks.

Xenomystus nigri

Common name: African knifefish
Range: West Africa, including Zaire, Gabon, Niger, and Liberia
Size: 12 inches (30 cm)
Description: The body coloration is often bluish-brown to brown and is very similar in form to the preceding species. However, this species is easily recognized because it completely lacks a dorsal fin. Some specimens develop thin wavy lines or stripes across the upper part of the body.
Aquarium suitability: Free-floating plants should be provided to give this species a darker environment. It prefers soft water and plenty of swimming space. Do not keep small fish with this species because it will eat them.
Breeding information: 150–200 eggs are laid at night in crevices and holes. The male guards these until they hatch six to nine days later. Transfer eggs to a raising tank and feed with brine shrimp.

Mormyridae (Elephantfish)

The family consists of 18 genera and about 198 species. In mormyrids the mouth can vary from an elongated, proboscis-like mouth with a terminal snout to a rounded snout with a short lower jaw. Some of the bottom-dwelling species have a barbel on the chin. This is absent in mid-water species. Generally though, mormyrids are conspicuous by their snout, which is often extended into a proboscis and gives rise to their name. Amazingly enough, these fish have weak electrical organs situated on their caudal peduncles. Through this organ, mormyrids are able to communicate with one another, find prey, and detect the presence of predators in turbid water or after dark. Equally amazing is that these fish have very large brains, which are almost equal to the body mass-to-brain ratio of humans! Usually nocturnal, they soon adapt to daylight hours.

Gnathonemus petersii

Common name: Elephant nose
Range: Central to western Africa, Zaire, Nigeria, and Cameroon
Size: 9 inches (23 cm)
Description: The body coloration is bluish-black to brownish black with two vertical cream or white bars from the dorsal to the anal fins. There is also a thin white stripe that runs the length of the elongated caudal peduncle in some specimens. The small mouth is located above the end of the elongated proboscis and is used to forage for food.
Aquarium suitability: Initially a timid and reclusive fish that should be kept with others of a similar disposition, it needs plenty of plants and rocks for hiding places. Once it is happy with its surroundings, it can become incredibly tame.
Breeding information: Males and females identify each other by the electric signals they send out. In captivity these become reversed and so mating is almost impossible.

Order: Anguilliformes

The order Anguilliformes encompasses all the true eels, moray eels, and conger eels of the world. There are about 740 known species, combined into 141 genera that are further divided into 15 families. Only one of these families is of any interest to the marine aquarist and this is the family Muraenidae. This family contains all the moray eels.

All modern eels lack pelvic fins and have an elongated body. The dorsal fin has no distinct demarcation and is connected to the caudal fin along with the anal fin to form a continuous fin along the back and around the tail. Many eels, such as the morays, also lack pectoral fins.

Representatives of this order are found throughout the world and the best known and certainly the most ubiquitous in Europe is the common eel (*Anguilla anguilla*). This fish is migratory and is known for its marathon swimming ability, as it migrates to spawn many thousands of miles away from its natural habitat, even though this may be an inland river or lake. Although the flesh of some species are poisonous, many others are important food fish. A walk through the Sham Shui Po fish market in Hong Kong will reveal the extent of this. Here, at least three species of moray eel are seen for sale in quantity (usually *Gymnothorax favagineus*, *G. undulatus*, and *G. schismatorhynchus*). Some algal-eating fish extract toxic alkaloids from the algae and their flesh becomes poisonous. If these fish then fall prey to the moray, it becomes poisonous too.

Muraenidae (Moray eels)

Many moray eels grow too large for even the most generously sized aquarium and they are predominantly fierce saltwater predators. In the wild they are found in crevices or caves in rocks and coral. They are mostly nocturnal feeders and will lie in wait for their prey, darting quickly out of their holes to seize it in their large, powerful jaws. They will then drag it back to their place of refuge.

Generally the freshwater species are unpredictable creatures and cannot be trusted with small fish in the same aquarium for very long. Even small specimens have been known to bite. Often the moray will shake its head from side to side once it has seized its prey to tear and wrench a large piece of flesh from the rest of the body. They can also be disruptive to aquarium planting schemes.

The common features of the morays include a complete lack of pelvic and pectoral fins. The tubular anterior nostrils are at the front of the snout, the posterior nostrils in front of or above the eyes.

Gymnothorax tile

Common name: Freshwater moray eel
Range: West Pacific, in brackish-water estuaries and rivers
Size: 26 inches (66 cm)
Description: The body coloration is gray to grayish-brown with a suffusion of white to gold speckles on the head and sides. Juveniles are lighter in color and show less markings. Older fish have short dorsal fins and are often confused with *Gymnothorax polyuranodon* and *Echidna rhodochilus*. The head of this particular species is unusually small for fish belonging to this genus.
Aquarium suitability: Plenty of rock crevices and caves should be provided to make this fish feel at home. Although it is often seen on offer as a freshwater fish, this species is actually a brackish-water fish.
Breeding information: This species has never been bred in captivity and little is known about its breeding habits.

Order: Cypriniformes

Until recently the Cypriniformes included related families that are now considered to belong to separate orders. These include the catfish, which have now been placed in their own order, Siluriformes. However, the group is still paraphyletic, so new orders have been separated out and redefined. These include the orders Gonorhynchiformes, Characiniformes (characins and their allies), and Gymnotiformes (knife fish and electric eels). The most distinguishing features of this group is that there is a single dorsal fin and that the teeth are in the throat rather than the mouth. These teeth are called "pharyngeal teeth." Carps and minnows are included in this group. In all, there are five families and 279 genera encompassing about 2,675 species. These

belong to the family Cyprinidae, which is most notable because it is the largest family of fish with species found on all continents except Australia. Most species from this order occur in fresh water, although there are few brackish-water species around the world. The freshwater loaches (*Cobidae*) also belong to this complex group. Many of the fish in this order are popular aquarium fish.

Cyprinidae (Carps, Minnows, Rasboras, Danios)

This huge family encompasses many well-known fish, including the common carp, dace, chub, and other species that are much sought after by anglers. Loach, roach, and tench are also included in this family as well as goldfish, Koi carp, minnows, and freshwater bream. It is a very large family—probably the largest family of fish. There are 210 genera with about 2,025 species. Of these, about 1,275 species occur in Eurasia, with the greatest diversity in China and Southeast Asia. In Africa there are about 485 species in 24 genera; North America hosts 270 species in 50 genera. It encompasses bony fish with scaly bodies, naked heads, and toothless mouths. They are found in all parts of the world with the exception of South America.

Danio albolineatus

Common name: Pearl danio
Range: Southeast Asia, from India and Malaysia to Thailand
Size: 2½ inches (6 cm)
Description: The body is elongate and the tail is deeply forked. The belly is bluish and the back is somewhat darker with a tinge of violet under reflected light, giving the body color a pearl-like sheen. There is a fine, pinkish-orange stripe horizontally from the angle of the operculum to the caudal peduncle and a finer one below this to the anal fin base.
Aquarium suitability: An easy fish to keep and one that does better in small schools of five or six individuals. The tank should have a hood because this fish is a jumper.
Breeding information: The breeding tank substrate should consist of marbles so that as the eggs drop, the parents do not eat them. The pair should be removed after spawning.

Danio var. 'Frankei'

Common name: Leopard danio
Range: India, in clear, fast-flowing streams (as *Danio rerio*)
Size: 2½ inches (6 cm)
Description: The body is brownish-silver and the back is deep brown. The sides of this species are sprinkled with fine blue spots and the lower jaw protrudes, giving the mouth an upturned angle. This fish is actually a variety of *Danio rerio* that was first bred in Czechoslovakia in 1963.
Aquarium suitability: This is a fish for the complete beginner and most foods are accepted within an hour of introduction.
Breeding information: Danios scatter their eggs among fine-leafed plants. The parent fish should be well fed before spawning occurs and removed from the breeding tank once spawning and fertilization have taken place. The fry will hatch after 36–48 hours and become free-swimming after about six days.

Danio rerio

Common name: Zebra danio
Range: Eastern India and Bangladesh, in rice paddy fields and fast-moving streams
Size: 2½ inches (6 cm)
Description: The body is elongate and the tail is deeply forked. The back is a deep olive color and the belly is silvery white. There are alternating narrow blue and gold stripes along the sides of this species and this extends onto the caudal and anal fins.
Aquarium suitability: A very easy fish to keep and one that will survive most beginner's mistakes. Most foods are accepted, including flake food. A small school of five or six individuals looks very attractive in a well-planted tank.
Breeding information: A male and female will often pair for life. Females are somewhat deeper-bodied than males.

Devario aequipinnatus

Common name: Giant danio
Range: Sri Lanka and India, in slow-moving coastal rivers
Size: 4¾ inches (12 cm)
Description: The body is elongate and laterally compressed. The lower jaw protrudes and the back is grayish-green. The sides of the body are bluish-green with flecks and stripes of dull yellow. The margins of the median fins are transparent, sometimes with tinges of pink.
Aquarium suitability: This is quite an active fish that needs plenty of swimming space. Because it is very active, it should be kept with other active fish such as barbs.
Breeding information: Eggs are scattered among plants in the mid-morning. Add the female a day before the male and remove the parents after spawning, or feed them well with whiteworm to prevent them from eating the eggs.

Devario devario

Common names: Bengal danio, Sind danio
Range: Pakistan and India to Bangladesh, particularly the Indus and Assam rivers
Size: 6 inches (15 cm)
Description: The upper part of the body is brownish-gold and the lower half is blue, fading to bluish-white to golden-white ventrally. There is a horizontal dark blue stripe from the mid-body onto the caudal peduncle and the median fins are quite long but colorless.
Aquarium suitability: The tank should be quite roomy because this fish is an active swimmer that grows reasonably large for a danio. Food is not a problem, as this fish will eat anything that is offered. As with other danios, it is best kept in small groups.
Breeding information: Like the previous species, the Bengal danio is easily bred and the young fry hatch after 48 hours.

Devario regina

Common name: Queen danio
Range: Southeast Asia, from India, Thailand, and northwestern Malaysia
Size: 3 inches (7.6 cm)
Description: This species is found in the fast-flowing streams of the Mekong over sandy substrate. The mouth is upturned with the lower jaw protruding. The body coloration is deep violet dorsally with purple flanks. The median fins often have a light purple or violet tinge. There are four or five narrow gold bands on the sides of the fish.
Aquarium suitability: Ideal for a community aquarium. This fish is peaceful and easy to keep. However, it needs plenty of free-swimming space.
Breeding information: Very difficult to breed. There are no records of it being bred in captivity.

Tanichthys albonubes

Common names: White cloud, White cloud mountain minnow
Range: In clear streams in the White Cloud Mountain region of Canton, China
Size: 2 inches (5 cm)
Description: An attractive fish with bright red fins and a red snout. The body is dark olive dorsally and the belly is white. There is a large black spot on the caudal peduncle and a gold stripe extends from the eye to the caudal peduncle. The dorsal, anal, and pelvic fins have white or yellow margins.
Aquarium suitability: This is a very easy fish to keep and an ideal choice for the novice. It survives equally well in cool or warm water and is very hardy. It will accept most foods that are offered and that it can manage to swallow.
Breeding information: Breeding is easy. During spawning, the male curls his body around the female.

Boraras maculatus

Common names: Dwarf rasbora, Pygmy rasbora, Spotted rasbora
Range: Southeast Asia, from Malaysia to Borneo
Size: 1 inch (2.5 cm)
Description: A small rasbora, but very attractive and easily identified by the bright red blotch in the operculum region. There is a large black spot behind the operculum, and another at the base of the anal fin. In most cases there is a further one, but much smaller, on the caudal peduncle. The belly is white and the flanks and sides are pinkish-red. Dorsally, it is dark brownish-red.
Aquarium suitability: Heavy planting, including floating plants, is required to dim the lighting in the tank and make this fish feel at home. Ideal for a community tank containing other small and peaceful fish.

Rasbora borapetensis

Common names: Brilliant rasbora, Blackline rasbora
Range: Southeast Asia, principally the Mekong from the Chao Phraya and Mekong river basins; also northern Malaysia
Size: 2 inches (5 cm)
Description: The back is light olive and the belly is silver. There is a black stripe present from the operculum to the caudal peduncle and a narrow gold stripe above this. The caudal peduncle and caudal base is bright red in color.
Aquarium suitability: A very easy fish to keep and one that is very attractive if it is kept in small groups of six or more. It should be provided with plenty of places to hide and will thrive in a well-planted aquarium.
Breeding information: 60–80 eggs are laid among plants. These hatch after 72 hours and become free-swimming a short time later. The parent fish should be removed once the eggs are laid.

Rasbora dorsiocellata

Common names: Hi-spot rasbora, Emerald eye
Range: Southeast Asia: Malayan peninsula and Indonesia
Size: 1½ inches (4 cm)
Description: The body is olive-brown dorsally and silvery-white in the belly region. The eye is bright emerald green that flashes bright green when it swims through areas of natural sunlight. It is a small fish that has a high dorsal fin with a large black spot on it. The leading edge of this spot is preceded by a greenish-white crescent.
Aquarium suitability: This is quite a shy species that should be kept in a group of three or more. It should not be housed with aggressive tank-mates. Most aquarium foods are accepted provided the pieces are small enough for this fish to swallow. Crushed flake food seems to be a particular favorite for this species.

Rasbora pauciperforata

Common names: Red-line rasbora, Red-stripe rasbora
Range: Southeast Asia, principally Malaysia and Sumatra
Size: 2¾ inches (7 cm)
Description: A charming fish that has an olive green back and a silver belly. The sides of the body are light olive and there is a pinkish-red stripe present from the tip of the snout to the tail. The fins are relatively clear of color.
Aquarium suitability: This is a peaceful fish that prefers soft water and plenty of cover in which it can hide. It does well if it is kept with danios and hatchetfish. Flake food is readily accepted.
Breeding information: *Mayaca* and *Vallisneria* plants should be present for breeding. Keep several fish to determine the pair and remove the rest. Eggs are scattered among the plants and hatch after 24 hours. The fry are free-swimming after four days.

Trigonostigma heteromorpha

Common names: Rasbora, Harlequin fish, Red rasbora
Range: Shallow areas of slow-moving streams and swamps throughout Southeast Asia
Size: 1¾ inches (4.5 cm)
Description: The Harlequin fish is one of the all-time favorites in the fish-keeping world. The body coloration is silvery-olive with a bold, triangular wedge of black on the rear of the body that makes this fish unmistakable. The dorsal fin, caudal peduncle, and upper and lower lobes of the caudal fin are red. The rest of the fins are often tinged with red.
Aquarium suitability: This fish is quite susceptible to white spot if it is introduced to a newly set-up tank. In a mature system it is very easy to keep and feed.
Breeding information: Spawning takes place at sunrise and the eggs are deposited on the underside of broad leaves.

Rasbora trilineata

Common names: Scissortail rasbora, Scissortail, Three-lined rasbora
Range: Southeast Asia, including the Malaysian peninsula, Borneo, and Sumatra
Size: 4 inches (10 cm)
Description: The Scissortail rasbora is characterized by a black horizontal stripe that extends from behind the operculum to the caudal peduncle and the distinct, white-margined black spots on the upper and lower lobes of the deeply forked tail. The body color is light olive green, darkening dorsally, and the belly is silvery gray.
Aquarium suitability: This is a fast-swimming fish that needs plenty of room to swim. It is easy to keep and will accept most foods that are offered. Ideally, it should be kept in groups of three or more. Flake food and most other foods are eagerly accepted.

Barbonymus schwanenfeldii

Common name: Tinfoil barb
Range: Southeast Asia, principally the Malaysian peninsula, Borneo, and Sumatra
Size: 14 inches (35 cm)
Description: This is one of the largest barbs collected for the aquarium trade. The body is silver, sometimes with a greenish tinge around the region of the lateral line.
Aquarium suitability: Adult fish require quite a large tank but young fish do well in a smaller one. This species needs lots of free-swimming space and plenty of robust plants. It is an attractive fish, best kept in small schools of six or more.
Breeding information: Tinfoil barbs are quite easy to breed provided the tank is large enough. The pairs lay 2,000 to 4,000 eggs among plants but the parent fish will not eat the eggs. The fry hatch after 48 hours and can be fed on *Artemia*.

Leptobarbus hoevenii

Common names: Maroon shark, Gold shark, Mad barb
Range: Southeast Asia: Thailand, Sumatra, and Borneo
Size: 24 inches (61 cm)
Description: This is a strange fish with several common names. Juveniles are silver with a bold black stripe that extends from the operculum to the base of the caudal fin. Above this, there is a narrow gold line from behind the operculum to the caudal peduncle. The pelvis, anal, and caudal fins are pink or red, and the upper and lower lobes of the caudal fin are tipped with black. Adults lose the black line and the red fins fade to pink.
Aquarium suitability: In the wild this fish feeds from the seeds of the chaulmoogra tree (*Hydnocarpus* sp.). These seeds ferment in the body of the fish and it becomes intoxicated; however, this will not happen in an aquarium. This is a peaceful fish that will accept most foods that are offered.

Puntius arulius

Common names: Arulius barb, Longfin barb
Range: India, particularly the Cauvery and Tambaparani rivers
Size: 4¾ inches (12 cm)
Description: This species was formerly classified as an endangered species, but thankfully, no longer. The color pattern varies with age but is predominantly silver in young fish and darkens with age. There are several short bars and spots along the body and the anal fin has a red margin. The upper and lower lobes of the tail are also deep red. Older specimens have extended dorsal filaments.
Aquarium suitability: Relatively easy to keep and feed. This fish is not for the beginner, but it is ideal once the aquarium has settled down and is functioning.
Breeding information: Marbles should be used as a substrate so that the eggs can drop through the spaces to avoid being eaten.

Puntius conchonius

Common name: Rosy barb
Range: Southeast Asia, principally Bengal and Assam in northeast India
Size: 4 inches (10 cm)
Description: The nape and subdorsal region is greenish-gold and there is a black spot in front of the caudal peduncle. The rest of the body and fins, including the tail, is metallic orange-red. The anal and dorsal fins have broad, black margins.
Aquarium suitability: An active fish that will often eat fine-leafed plants such as *Riccia fluitans*. It is a schooling species that may disturb quieter fish. However, it is an easy fish to keep.
Breeding information: Use a substrate of marbles and lower the water level of the breeding tank to about 6 inches (15 cm). Then add the breeding pair in the evening. The pair will spawn in the morning, after which they must be removed immediately.

Puntius everetti

Common names: Clown barb, Everett's barb
Range: Southeast Asia: Borneo and Singapore in slow-moving or still water
Size: 4¼ inches (11 cm)
Description: The body is elongate and somewhat laterally compressed. Dorsally, the body is brownish olive and the belly is yellow or white. There are four or five bold, black bars present, with the first on the head and the fifth across the caudal peduncle. The fourth bar can often be present as a spot. In older fish, the fins are reddish in color.
Aquarium suitability: This fish is initially quite shy, so create some hiding places using rocks and plants. Once it is happy with its surroundings, it will be first at the feeding table.

Puntius laterstriga

Common names: T barb, Spanner barb
Range: Indo-Australian archipelago, from Thailand, Malaysia, Singapore, Sumatra, Java, and Borneo
Size: 7 inches (18 cm)
Description: The body is elongate and the mouth has two sets of barbels. The coloration is generally brownish-silver with two bold bars and a horizontal stripe that is deep black in color. The two bars are behind the operculum and do not extend past the first few rays of the dorsal fin. The mid-body stripe extends to the rear of these bars onto the caudal peduncle.
Aquarium suitability: An easy fish to keep but one that can become quite boisterous toward other, more peaceful tank-mates. It tends to become more solitary with age.
Breeding information: The courtship of the breeding pair is very active and as many as 3,000 eggs are scattered among plants.

Puntius nigrofasciatus

Common names: Black ruby barb, Purple-headed barb
Range: Southern Sri Lanka
Size: 2½ inches (6 cm)
Description: The Black ruby barb is quite high-backed and the body is laterally compressed. In adults the head is deep red and there are four bold, black body bars present. Juveniles tend to be much lighter in color. The dorsal, anal, and ventral fins are black with broad, clear margins. The tail is red in mature males and pink in females.
Aquarium suitability: This is an easy fish to keep, but one that can be quite aggressive toward other barbs. Kept in schools of its own kind, it is less likely to be aggressive.
Breeding information: It takes about two hours for the breeding pair to lay their 500 eggs, so be patient. As with most barbs, these are laid in the morning among fine-leafed plants.

Puntius pentazona

Common name: Five-banded barb
Range: Southeast Asia: Borneo and the Malay peninsula
Size: 2 inches (5 cm)
Description: The body is elongate with a high back. The flanks are orange-brown to silver at the throat; the belly and back are dark olive. There are five black vertical bars on the body. The first of these is the ocular bar and the last runs across the caudal peduncle.
Aquarium suitability: Can be somewhat shy at first and is better kept in small schools along with gouramis and loaches. It will accept most foods, including flake, tubifex, insect larvae, and small crustaceans such as brine shrimp.
Breeding information: These are egg scatterers. Males are slender and smaller with brighter colors. Plant the breeding tank with fine-leafed plants and a substrate of marbles.

Puntius tetrazona

Common names: Tiger barb, Sumatra barb
Range: Southeast Asia, from Borneo, Indonesia, and Sumatra
Size: 3 inches (7.5 cm)
Description: The body is somewhat disk-shaped and laterally compressed with four black vertical bars. The first of these is through the eye and the last is across the caudal peduncle. The dorsal fin is black with an orange-red to bright-red margin. The other fins are transparent orange.
Aquarium suitability: In a community tank this fish is a notorious "fin-nipper," so do not house it in an aquarium that has any fish with long flowing fins. It is a schooling fish that is less aggressive if housed in a larger tank.
Breeding information: The male exhibits more red color, but grows paler during the spawning period. Whiteworms should be fed to the parents during this time and the tank should have small, finer-leafed plants in it and marbles as a substrate so that the eggs can drop through the spaces to avoid being eaten.

Puntius tetrazona var. 'Green tiger barb'

Puntius sachsii

Common names: Gold barb, Goldfinned barb, Schubert's barb
Range: Southeast China
Size: 3¼ inches (8 cm)
Description: Many authors misname this species as *Barbus schuberti* or *Puntius schuberti*; neither name has any scientific validity. The body is golden yellow and the fins are darker, giving a more burnished gold appearance. There is a black blotch present on the caudal peduncle that is almost a bar. Numerous small spots adorn the sides of this species, and those in the region of the lateral line tend to be larger.
Aquarium suitability: An easy fish to keep if kept in small schools of six or more. Kept singly, they tend to be quite shy.
Breeding information: Pairs usually spawn during the morning, laying a few eggs at a time and then fertilizing them so that, over a period of two hours, up to 250 eggs are attached to plants.

Puntius titteya

Common name: Cherry barb
Range: Southeast Asia, mainly Sri Lanka
Size: 2 inches (5 cm)
Description: This is a beautiful barb that is brightly colored and can enhance any aquarium. Males are more colorful than females. There is a black stripe present that runs from the snout through the eye to the caudal peduncle. The rest of the body is cherry red, which darkens dorsally. The fins are pinkish-red to deep red.
Aquarium suitability: An excellent choice for a peaceful community set-up because this is not an aggressive species and will do little damage to any plant life.
Breeding information: Similar to the previous species, the parents should be fed on whiteworm, mosquito larvae, and bloodworm prior to spawning so that they do not eat the eggs.

Balantiocheilos melanopterus

Common names: Bala shark, Tricolor shark, Silver shark
Range: Southeast Asia, from Thailand, Malaysia, Borneo, and Sumatra
Size: 14 inches (36 cm)
Description: The body is elongate and laterally compressed with a tall, erect dorsal fin and a deeply forked tail. The body color is silvery gray and the pectoral fins are clear. The remaining fins are yellow with broad black margins on the trailing edges.
Aquarium suitability: The aquarium should have a cover fitted, because this species has a habit of jumping out of the water. The tank should be large and well planted with plenty of free-swimming space. It does not do any harm to plants and can be kept in a community setup. Most foods are accepted once the fish has settled down to tank life.
Breeding information: This fish has not been bred in captivity.

Epalzeorhynchos bicolor

Common name: Red-tailed black shark, Red-tailed labeo
Range: Southeast Asia, principally central Thailand
Size: 6 inches (15 cm)
Description: The body is elongate and high-backed with a deeply forked tail. The snout has two pairs of barbels and the upper jaw protrudes so that the mouth faces downward. This fish is easy to identify because it has a black body and a bright orange-red tail. The dorsal fin is high and somewhat sharklike in appearance.
Aquarium suitability: This fish is ideal for a community tank, but only one fish should be kept per tank because it is quite aggressive to its own kind or similar species. Older fish become increasingly aggressive to other fish.
Breeding information: A very difficult fish to breed in captivity because of its aggressive nature toward its own kind. A large tank is required with soft water, plenty of plants, and caves.

Epalzeorhynchos frenatus

Common names: Red-fin shark, Rainbow shark, Ruby shark
Range: Southeast Asia, principally the Mekong River in Thailand
Size: 5½ inches (14 cm)
Description: The body is elongate with a pointed snout. The coloration is grayish-brown to almost black with orange-red to red fins. Males have black on the margin of the anal fin. There is a short stripe present from the tip of the snout, through the eye to the operculum.
Aquarium suitability: Kept singly, this is a relatively peaceful, if somewhat territorial, community fish. If more than one specimen is to be kept, make sure they are in a large aquarium.
Breeding information: Soft, slightly acidic water is a prerequisite here. This is a difficult fish to breed. Spawning occurs with dim or no light in the tank in rock caves.

Epalzeorhychos kallopterus

Common name: Flying fox
Range: Southeast Asia; Borneo, Sumatra, and Java
Size: 5 inches (12.7 cm)
Description: The dorsal region is dark olive-brown and the rest of the body is golden yellow, lightening in color ventrally. A bold and broad black stripe runs from the tip of the snout to the tail. The upper part of the eye is often red in color and the dorsal, anal, and pelvic fins have white margins. This fish has a habit of swimming for short bursts and then resting on the substrate or plant leaf on its pectoral and pelvic fins.
Aquarium suitability: The Flying fox has been a firm favorite among hobbyists for many years and is a real character. It is a great algae-eater too, but not hair algae. It can be kept singly or in schools, but territorial aggression will often take place if the tank is too small for more than one specimen.

Gyrinocheilus aymonieri

Common names: Sucking loach, Indian algae eater, Chinese algae eater
Range: Southeast Asia, from eastern India to Thailand
Size: 9 inches (23 cm)
Description: The body color is somewhat drab and dull orange-brown that darkens to deep brown dorsally. There is a series of spots on the sides that runs from the snout to the caudal peduncle. The belly is white and the mouth has a cup-shaped suction mechanism, allowing this species to hold on to vertical objects with its mouth.
Aquarium suitability: This is one of the most frequently purchased aquarium fish because of its cleaning abilities. The Sucking loach helps control unwanted algae growth, particularly on the front viewing glass of an aquarium. It also removes algae from the leaves of slow-growing plants such as *Anubias* species.

Luciosoma spilopleura

Common names: Long finned Apollo shark, Apollo waterminnow
Range: Southeast Asia: Vietnam, Laos, Thailand, Malaysia, and Indonesia
Size: 10 inches (25 cm)
Description: The back of this species is olive green and the sides are silver. A row of black spots is present from behind the operculum to the caudal peduncle. These spots may be fused together to form an almost continuous stripe.
Aquarium suitability: The Apollo shark needs lots of free-swimming space—this means a large tank. Provide plenty of plants, including floating ones such as *Riccia fluitans*. It is intolerant of similar-looking fish and should only be kept with those that are similar in size because this fish is a predator.
Breeding information: Not known to have been bred in captivity.

Cobitidae (Loaches)

This is a small family that is closely allied to the carplike fish. However, they are characterized by having an elongated, often very narrow body, with an inferior mouth, which is surrounded with numerous barbels. There are two distinct forms: the eel-like body of *Pangio* spp., and the flat-bellied, relatively high-backed form of *Botia* spp. The jaws are without teeth and a single dorsal fin is present, usually in the mid-body region. Many loaches are nocturnal, particularly the European ones. Those species with their origin in Southeast Asia and North Africa may be active in the evening or also nocturnal. Some loaches are able to utilize oxygen from the atmosphere to breathe at lower water times, such as in marshes. To do this, they take in air at the water surface and pass it along their intestinal tract to extract the oxygen. Surplus air is voided at the anus.

Loaches possess spines under the eye that can be erected to deter predators. The barbels around the mouth are used as sensory "taste buds" to search the substrate for morsels of food. A few species develop a habit of resting on their sides for quite a long period of time.

Acantopsis choirorhynchus

Common name: Horse-faced loach
Range: Asia: India, Malaysia, Thailand, Borneo, and Vietnam
Size: 7 inches (18 cm)
Description: The body is elongate and slightly depressed, giving it a flat-bellied appearance. The eyes protrude and the nape angles down from these to a blunt snout with an inferior mouth. This gives the fish a vague "horse's head" profile. There is a row of 10 to 12 dark stripes running horizontally from behind the pectoral fins to the slightly reddish-colored tail.
Aquarium suitability: This is an interesting community fish that is quite peaceful but not very colorful. It requires plenty of hiding places—such as thick growths of plants, rocks, and driftwood—because it is mainly nocturnal. Floating plants are also a help because they subdue the light. A sandy substrate rather than a gravel one is preferable for this species.

Botia hymenophysa

Common names: Tiger loach, Banded loach, Barred loach
Range: Southeast Asia: Sumatra, Borneo, and Malaysia
Size: 8¼ inches (21 cm)
Description: The head is pointed and the tail is very large and deeply forked. The sides of this fish are marked with 10 to 12 black-edged dark bars, which extend downward from the back to below the lateral line, where they fade into a suffusion of dark spots and flecks.
Aquarium suitability: The Tiger loach is active during the evening and can be quite aggressive. Once established, this species can become diurnal (active during the day). It is a predator, so it should not be housed with small fish. It is also a bottom-feeding fish that will accept most foods that are offered and will clean up any morsels of food that other species have missed. At feeding time, it makes a loud clicking noise.

Botia lecontei

Common names: Red-finned loach, Le Conte's loach, Silver loach
Range: Southeast Asia: Laos and Cambodia
Size: 6 inches (15 cm)
Description: The body is elongate and laterally compressed with a flat belly and a tail that is deeply forked. The body coloration is predominantly powder blue to light blue with an iridescent green overtone. This species is often confused with *B. modesta*, which is more intense in color. Juveniles and females are a drab silver.
Aquarium suitability: This is quite a peaceful species that is best kept in groups of five or more of its own kind along with other robust species. Most foods are accepted within hours of introduction and it is quite hardy. However, it requires a lot of swimming space with plenty of hiding places.

Botia lohachata

Common names: Pakistani loach, Reticulate loach
Range: Pakistan and India, in rivers and slow-moving streams
Size: 4 inches (10 cm)
Description: The background body coloration is variable and may be pinkish-cream, olive green, or deep olive-brown. Like all *Botia* species, the caudal peduncle is very deep and the tail is deeply forked. The color pattern on the sides of this fish consists of a series of deep brown reticulated streaks and lines that run onto the dorsal, anal, and caudal fins as irregular wavy bars.
Aquarium suitability: A relatively small species that is often initially timid and withdrawn. However, once it has settled down in the tank it can become quite aggressive. It is nocturnal, but will often show its face in the evening and hide during the day. It can be housed in a community tank when its tank-mates are medium to large fish, such as larger barbs and Giant danios.

Botia macracanthus

Common names: Clown loach, Tiger loach, Clown botia
Range: Sumatra, Borneo, and Indonesia in slow-moving rivers and lakes
Size: 12 inches (30 cm)
Description: A very popular aquarium fish with a striking color pattern. Although this fish grows quite large in the wild, it seldom exceeds the size shown in an aquarium. The mouth has two pairs of barbels and the body color is light orange to pale yellow. There are three broad black bars through the body and head. The first of these runs from the nape through the eye to the throat.
Aquarium suitability: Kept in small groups of five or more, this fish does well. Single specimens are timid and difficult to keep. Although this fish is initially timid, it will soon learn to recognize its owner, especially at feeding time.

Botia modesta

Common name: Orange-finned loach, Redtail botia
Range: Southeast Asia; India, Malaysia, Thailand, and Indonesia
Size: 9 inches (23 cm)
Description: This is an attractive fish with a bluish-green body and bright red fins. The body is moderately elongate with a flat belly and a high back. The dorsal fin is high and the tail is large and deeply forked. The fish has a high-back appearance and the caudal peduncle is deep and more robust than many other species of fish. There is often a narrow curving bar between the bluish body and the red tail across the caudal peduncle.
Aquarium suitability: Quite a large fish to keep in a community tank and certainly not for the novice. It can be quite aggressive toward its tank-mates, especially barbs. Kept with other, larger species though, this fish will do well. Provide plenty of refuge and hiding spaces for the best result.

Botia sidthimunki

Common names: Chain loach, Dwarf loach
Range: Southeast Asia, principally India and Thailand
Size: 2 inches (5 cm)
Description: This botia is unmistakable because of its body pattern. The lower part of the body is dull yellow or cream and the upper part of the body is mid-brown to brownish-black with a row of six to eight large gold spots along the upper half of the body. These are often interconnected to give a pearl chain pattern. The head is cream and there is a deep brown stripe present from the snout through the eye that joins with the upper color pattern.
Aquarium suitability: The Chain loach is a small species that is relatively easy to keep and feed. It is best kept in groups of five or more. Single specimens do not settle down well.
Breeding information: Rarely spawns in captivity.

Botia morleti

Common names: Hora's loach, Skunk loach
Range: Southeast Asia, principally Thailand
Size: 4 inches (10 cm)
Description: The Skunk loach is not a very attractive fish when compared to others of this genus. The background body coloration is pale yellow to cream, sometimes with a greenish tinge. There are four black bars forward of the caudal peduncle in juveniles. These fade with age, leaving a bold black bar across the base of the tail. In adults there is a black stripe that extends from the tip of the upper jaw across the dorsal base to the tail.
Aquarium suitability: This fish raises interest among hobbyists because it does not grow too large and is a great fish for rooting out detritus and uneaten food from the substrate. Robust plants should be used with this species because in its search for food, it will uproot any plants that are not firmly anchored.

Botia striata

Common name: Zebra loach
Range: Southern India in slow-moving or still water
Size: 3½ inches (9 cm)
Description: A striking fish with a brown body and freckled fins. The caudal fin has several indistinct bars through it. There is a row of golden-yellow wavy bars of differing thickness from the snout to the deep caudal peduncle. This gives it a tigerlike appearance. The tail is deeply forked.
Aquarium suitability: Although this species is nocturnal, it soon learns to accept food during the daylight hours. Most foods are accepted, but live or frozen food should be used to supplement its diet. It is a peaceful species that can be kept in most community setups. It does well when it is housed with several of its own kind.
Breeding information: It has not been bred in captivity.

Pangio kuhlii

Common names: Coolie loach, Kuhli loach
Range: Southeast Asia: Thailand, Malaysia, Singapore, and Indonesia
Size: 4 inches (10 cm)
Description: This is a popular aquarium fish. The body is elongated and eel-like and the coloration is a variation of magenta, salmon pink, or orange, with the belly somewhat lighter. There is a series of 11 to 18 black, saddlelike bars present that extend almost to the belly region. There are four pairs of barbels around the mouth.
Aquarium suitability: Although this fish will hide for most of the day, it does come out at feeding time. It takes most foods that are offered but its diet should be supplemented with fresh protein or live food such as bloodworms.

Order: Characiformes

The order is quite large and very diverse. The origin of this group can be traced back to the Cretaceous period of earth's history, more than 100 million years ago. During this time the supercontinent known as Pangaea had already started to break up and the Mediterranean Sea was beginning to form.

Soon after this, though, the continents as we know them now began to divide up into their familiar shapes. South America broke away from Africa to drift westward, eventually joining with the North American continent and forming the Atlantic Ocean. During this time, about 80 million years ago, species began to diversify in order to adapt to differing conditions. This is why this group is represented in Africa as well as the Americas.

There is much controversy about the exact number of families in this order. Some authors recognize all the characiforms in one family and others as many as 20 families. The author's view here is based on mitochondrial DNA sequence data obtained through his studies done in 1998–99. The order comprises 10 families with about 238 genera and roughly 1,350 species. About 210 species are found in Africa and the remaining ones are from the southwestern United States, Mexico, and Central and South America.

Characiformes generally have an adipose fin and well-developed scales. Teeth are also present, since most of the species are either carnivores or omnivores. The anal fin can be short or long, but seldom exceeds 42 rays. Most of the smaller species are popular aquarium fish but there are larger species that are important food fish in various countries around the world. They are all freshwater fish and are unable to survive in saline environments. The tetras belong to this group, as do the headstanders, hatchetfish, pencilfish, and the voracious piranhas.

Citharinidae (Citharinids)

In many ways, fish belonging to this family can be considered to form a group that is a primitive sister group to all other characiformes. The family comprises two subfamilies, 20 genera, and about 100 species. Some species have nonprotractile upper jaws and are micropredators or herbivores, whereas others have movable upper jaws and are usually carnivores. The body form is varied, with some species being elongate and streamlined while others have deep bodies and relatively high dorsal fins. The three genera belonging to the subfamily Citharininae have reduced maxillae and lack teeth.

Very few species are seen in the aquarium trade and those that are encountered on dealers' lists or appear in aquarium stores usually belong to the genus *Distichodus*. These are often brightly colored and attractive fish that are relatively peaceful with other fish of a similar size.

Distichodus sexfasciatus

Common name: Sixbar distichodus
Range: Central Africa, from the middle and lower Congo in Zaire to Lake Tanganyika
Size: 30 inches (76 cm)
Description: The coloration of juveniles is much more intense than adult fish. The body is creamy white, darkening dorsally. There are six broad black bars present on the sides. The first of these is behind the operculum and the last is across the caudal peduncle. With the exception of the pectorals, all the fins are deep orange-red. In larger specimens, the adipose fin has a white margin.
Aquarium suitability: Small specimens are very attractive but they eventually grow quite large and are only suitable for big show tanks. Juveniles are not to be trusted with any tank-mates that are smaller than they are.

Anostomidae (headstanders)

This is a family that is widely distributed throughout South America. Typically, the body is elongate and torpedo-shaped with a small head and a terminal mouth that is often upturned. Most of the species in this group feed on plants and small invertebrates. They frequently adopt a "head down" position at an oblique angle. This gives them their common name, "headstanders." The angle of the fish in the water is often in excess of 45 degrees and can occasionally be up to 90 degrees. Most species display strong color markings that are usually black and white. Some species have horizontal stripes, whereas others have black and white vertical banding. The dorsal and anal fins are quite short.

Headstanders are very attractive, but they are not for the fainthearted aquarist. They are often very aggressive with a penchant for nipping fins and damaging the eyes and fins of their slower and more peaceful tank-mates. In a community tank, they should only be housed with robust and larger species, such as cichlids and larger characins, if damage to other tank-mates is to be avoided.

Abramites hypselonotus

Common names: Marbled headstander, High-backed headstander
Range: South America, in the Orinoco, Amazon, Paraguay, and Paraná river basins
Size: 6 inches (15 cm)
Description: The body is elongate and laterally compressed with a high back in adults. The background body coloration is beige to light brown with seven to nine irregular dark bands. The nape and adipose fin are often dull yellow. The dorsal and pelvic fins have black bars running through them, whereas the rest of the fins are colorless.
Aquarium suitability: Young fish may be housed in a community aquarium with no real problems. Older specimens tend to be more aggressive and will not tolerate their own kind or other similar species. This is a shy species that requires a well-planted tank with caves made from rocks.
Breeding information: Few records of breeding have been reported, although it is assumed that this species is not difficult to breed. The main problem is introducing a pair that is sexually mature and can tolerate one another.

Anostomus anostomus

Common names: Striped anostomus, Striped headstander
Range: South America: Brazil, Colombia, Guyana, Peru, and Venezuela, but principally the Orinoco and Amazon rivers
Size: 8 inches (20 cm)
Description: A very striking fish with a brownish-black body and three horizontal yellow stripes. The first of these runs dorsally from the nape to the tail and the other two stripes extend from the head, above and below the lateral line, to the caudal peduncle.
Aquarium suitability: Quite an easy fish to keep in a community setup. They can be kept in groups of six or more, but two or three of the same species will fight constantly. It should be provided with plenty of cover and places to hide.

Chilodus punctatus

Common name: Spotted headstander
Range: South America: Brazil, Guyana, Colombia, and Venezuela; most frequent in the Amazon and Orinoco rivers
Size: 4 inches (10 cm)
Description: The body is silver with numerous black spots over much of the body and fins. A black mid-lateral stripe is present from the snout to the caudal peduncle.
Aquarium suitability: This fish requires good water quality and it is quite sensitive to changes. Ideally, it should be kept at lower temperatures than usual and in soft, slightly acidic water in a well-planted aquarium.
Breeding information: The males have a somewhat elongated dorsal fin and the females are more rounded in appearance. Provide minor water changes prior to breeding and raise the temperature slightly to induce spawning.

Leporinus fasciatus

Common names: Black-banded leporinus, Banded leporinus
Range: South America, from the Orinoco to the Rio del Plata
Size: 12 inches (30 cm)
Description: This fish grows quite large and its body is elongate. The background coloration is light yellow to beige and there are eight to ten broad black bars present along the head and sides of the fish that slope slightly forward. Adult males often display an orange or red throat. The fins are colorless and the tail is deeply forked.
Aquarium suitability: Not a good fish for the beginner. This is a plant-eating fish that will soon strip the aquarium of plant life completely. The lighting should be of high intensity to promote good algal growth to supplement its diet. Nevertheless, this species is a good community fish.
Breeding information: No reports of successful captive breeding.

Leporinus octofasciatus

Common name: Eight-barred leporinus
Range: South America; northern Cubatão River in Santa
Catarina and upper Paraná River basin
Size: 9 inches (23 cm)
Description: Similar in coloration and markings to the previous
species. However, the black bands are thicker, almost vertical,
and there are eight bars rather than nine or more. Some bars
may have white saddles or break into two bars on the flanks.
The fins are generally clear of color but the tail may become
pink in older specimens.
Aquarium suitability: This is an excellent fish for a larger
show aquarium. It is slow moving and decorative, but newly
introduced fish tend to be quite shy for the first few days. Feed a
varied diet for the best results. Hardy, broad-leafed plants, such
as *Anubias* spp., will not be eaten but most other plants will.

Leporinus striatus

Common names: Striated headstander, Striated pencilfish
Range: South America, from the Orissanga, Paraná and
Paraguay river basins
Size: 10 inches (25 cm)
Description: Many aquarists confuse this fish with *Anostomus
anostomus*, which has very similar markings. In this case,
though, the fins are clear with no trace of red coloration. Also,
the first stripe occurs subdorsally and the belly is yellowish-
brown.
Aquarium suitability: The Striated headstander is best kept
singly. It is inclined to be a fin-nipper with its own kind. This fish
needs a well-planted aquarium with plenty of hiding places for it
to feel completely at home in captivity. Most foods are accepted,
including flake food, and it is a surprisingly good community
fish when it is housed with species of a similar size.

Lebiasinidae (pencilfish)

This family comprises six genera and about 51 species.
Unlike other characins, species from this group do not
possess an adipose fin. The family is found throughout
South America and includes mostly small- to medium-
sized fish that seldom exceed 5 inches (12.7 cm) in length.
Despite being a small family, many of the species are
popular aquarium fish. Some are brightly colored and
others have distinct markings that make them attractive to
the hobbyist. Fish from this family usually swim in the
middle to upper water levels so they require plenty of free-
swimming space.

Generally, these are peaceful fish that like to stay hidden
during much of the day. At dusk, however, they will leave
their hiding places in search of food. Day and nighttime
coloration can vary dramatically within the species.

Copella arnoldi

Common names: Splash tetra, Jumping characin, Spraying tetra
Range: South America, principally Guyana and the Rio Para
Size: 3½ inches (9 cm)
Description: The body is olive green to brown and the fins are long and flowing. There is a black stripe present from the snout to the operculum and a less defined dark stripe from the operculum to the caudal peduncle.
Aquarium suitability: A good community fish that is peaceful and can be kept in pairs or small groups.
Breeding information: The pair will jump out of the water and attach themselves to an overhanging leaf or the glass, pressing their bodies together and laying up to 10 eggs before returning to the water. This process is repeated until 150–200 eggs are laid. The male then gives them occasional splashes of water until they hatch after 36 hours. The fry then drop into the water.

Nannostomus beckfordi

Common names: Beckford's pencilfish, Golden pencilfish
Range: South America, from Guyana to Brazil
Size: 2½ inches (6.3 cm)
Description: The body coloration is olive-green to olive-brown with a bold black stripe that extends from the snout to the caudal peduncle. The belly is silver, often with tinges of red; the anal and caudal fin bases are also red.
Aquarium suitability: This species prefers soft water and a well-planted aquarium for it to feel perfectly at home. Small groups can be kept together and they are good community fish.
Breeding information: It is important that the eggs or the parents are removed after spawning has occurred, otherwise they will be eaten. Fine-leafed plants in the spawning tank can save some of the eggs, which hatch after about 30 hours. The fry become free-swimming after five to six days.

Nannostomus bifasciatus

Common name: Whiteside pencilfish
Range: South America, from French Guiana and Suriname
Size: 1¼ inches (3.4 cm)
Description: This fish has an olive-green to deep olive back, and white sides and belly. There are two stripes present. The first is narrow and extends from the nape to the upper area of the caudal peduncle. The lower stripe is bolder and runs from the snout to the tail. The caudal base is red.
Aquarium suitability: : A good community fish, but not one that is recommended for the complete novice.
Breeding information: Use fine-leaf plants in the breeding tank and lower the water level to 6 inches (15cm). Raise the temperature a few degrees to induce spawning and remove the parents once this has taken place. Alternatively, plants with the attached eggs can be transferred to a rearing tank.

Nannostomus eques

Common names: Three-striped pencilfish, Tube-mouthed pencilfish
Range: South America, from Guyana to Brazil and Colombia
Size: 2 inches (5 cm)
Description: An attractive fish with an elongated body and a tubular snout. The background color is pale brown and there are three horizontal rows of spots along the sides of the fish. These can fuse to form stripes; the mid-body row often forms a bold stripe from the snout to the caudal peduncle. The lower lobe of the tail is dark and makes it appear much larger than the upper lobe, which is transparent.
Aquarium suitability: This species needs plenty of hiding spaces or floating plants for cover. Most foods are accepted.
Breeding information: Spawning takes place on the underside of broad-leafed plants.

Nannostomus marginatus

Common name: Dwarf pencilfish
Range: South America, in the lower to middle Amazon River as well as Guyana, Colombia, Venezuela, and Peru
Size: 1½ inches (3.8 cm)
Description: The Dwarf pencilfish has a dull yellow body that darkens to olive green dorsally. Three black stripes adorn the sides of the fish. The upper stripe extends from the snout to the tail. The center stripe is bold and clearly defined and runs from the lower jaw onto the lower lobe of the tail. The third stripe is less distinct and extends from the throat to the anal fin. The dorsal, anal, and pelvic fins are tinged with red.
Aquarium suitability: A good fish for a community setup if it is kept in groups of five or more. Most commercially produced foods are eaten with relish.

Nannostomus unifasciatus

Common name: One-lined pencilfish
Range: South America, in the Amazon basin of Bolivia, Brazil, and Colombia and the upper Orinoco basin
Size: 1½ inches (3.8 cm)
Description: A tiny, attractive fish with a pale brown back and a gold stripe from the snout to the caudal peduncle. Immediately below this is a bold black stripe that extends from the jaw to the tail. The base of the lower lobe of the caudal fin is bright red.
Aquarium suitability: This pencilfish is peaceful by nature and it will be bullied if it is kept alongside more aggressive species. Freeze-dried foods along with flake, bloodworms, mosquito larvae, and glassworms are its favorite foods.
Breeding information: This is quite a difficult fish to breed but the general breeding care is the same as for others of this genus.

Gasteropelecidae (Freshwater hatchetfish)

This family is small and encompasses only nine species placed into three genera. Freshwater hatchetfish live in Panama and, with the exception of Chile, all the countries of South America. They are found in a variety of habitats in lakes, rivers, and streams. Generally, the pelvic fins are small and rudimentary and the body is strongly compressed laterally. In smaller species the adipose fin is absent, but it is present in the larger species. The tail is deeply forked and the anal fin is longer than the dorsal fin, which is set posteriorly. The pectoral fins are extremely large and are supported by an enlarged convex muscular pectoral girdle region. All species are capable of jumping out of the water and sailing for long distances to escape predators. They can also jump quite high, so their tank should have a tight-fitting hood.

Carnegiella marthae

Common name: Black-winged hatchetfish
Range: South America, in the Negro and upper Orinoco river basins
Size: 1¼ inches (2.8 cm)
Description: The black pectoral fins are large and elongated and there are numerous fine black spots on the sides of the fish. The back is generally olive-brown and there is a thin black stripe that runs from the throat under the belly to the caudal peduncle. Another black stripe runs from the pectoral base to the tail and there is a gold stripe present immediately above this.
Aquarium suitability: This is a peaceful, omnivorous fish that does well if it is housed with other peaceful fish. Pairs and small groups fare better than single individuals. Provide soft water and keep the tank covered because this fish can jump several feet out of the tank.

Carnegiella strigata

Common name: Marbled hatchetfish
Range: South America, in still or slow-moving waters of Peru and Guyana
Size: 2 inches (5 cm)
Description: The back is relatively straight and the belly is deeply convex. The pelvic fins are rudimentary whereas the pectoral fins can be up to half of the fish's body length. A yellow stripe is present dorsally and the sides are adorned with black patches and bars that give the fish a marbled appearance.
Aquarium suitability: Probably the hardiest of all the hatchetfish but still not recommended for the complete novice. Its tank should have soft, slightly acidic water and floating plants.
Breeding information: The eggs are laid on the leaves of floating plants and subsequently fall to the bottom, where they will hatch after 30 hours.

Gasteropelecus maculatus

Common name: Spotted hatchetfish
Range: Central and South America
Size: 3½ inches (9 cm)
Description: The back is slightly convex and there is a narrow black bar at the dorsal base. The background body color is olive-brown on the back, and silver on the sides and belly. In certain lighting, the sides of the fish may have an iridescent green or blue sheen. The upper flanks are covered in small black spots.
Aquarium suitability: Very often prone to white spot disease or "Ich," as it is sometimes known. Newly introduced specimens are particularly susceptible. Once settled in, however, it is hardy.
Breeding information: The parent fish should be conditioned on live food prior to spawning. They should be removed from the tank once this has taken place. The eggs hatch after 30 hours and the fry become free-swimming after five days.

Gasteropelecus sternicla

Common names: Common hatchetfish, River hatchetfish
Range: South America, principally Surinam, Peru, and Guyana
Size: 2½ inches (6 cm)
Description: This species is characterized by a black stripe that extends from the angle of the pectoral fin to the caudal peduncle. Above this the somewhat curved back is olive-brown. Below the stripe, the belly and flanks are silver with an iridescent sheen in certain light.
Aquarium suitability: One of the easiest hatchetfish to keep but still not a beginner's fish. It needs plenty of free-swimming space and a well-planted tank with soft water. This means a pH of 6.5–6.8.
Breeding information: Very difficult to breed in captivity and no reliable records are available at this time. Females can only be distinguished from the males during the spawning period.

Thoracocharax securis

Common names: Silver hatchetfish, Giant hatchetfish
Range: South America, particularly the lower Amazon basin
Size: 3½ inches (9 cm)
Description: This is the one of the largest members of this family. The back is relatively flat and olive-brown in color. The sides and belly are silvery-white and there is a horizontal yellow stripe present that extends from the pectoral base to the tail. Mature males often have yellow in the median fins.
Aquarium suitability: Ideal for a community setup if it is combined with other peaceful fish. Like all hatchetfish, this is a surface swimmer. Try to choose tank-mates that swim at lower levels and bottom-dwellers for the best result. It is best kept in small groups of three or more individuals.
Breeding information: Commercial breeding has been unsuccessful so far.

Characidae (Characins)

Nelson (1994) places the characins into 10 subfamilies with 170 genera and about 885 species. However, only three subfamilies will be handled here, as they group together some of the most popular aquarium fish. These subfamilies are Alestiinae, the African tetras; Tetragonopterinae, the South American tetras; and Serrasalminae, the pacus, silver dollars, and piranhas. Nelson also discusses a further subfamily, Characinae, but points out that this is particularly artificial. The author agrees with this and suggests that the subfamily is polyphyletic. Therefore the genus *Acestrorhynchus* is provisionally placed within the Tetragonopterinae subfamily group. The layout here follows this subfamily grouping, with the African tetras being discussed first, followed by the South American tetras, and finally the piranhas and similar species. Since Nelson's summation in 1994, new species have been discovered and described. This family now contains 1,032 species. It is a very diversified group and includes tiny fish that are popular in the aquarium hobby. Nevertheless, it also contains some potentially dangerous species.

Some characins possess an adipose fin while others lack it completely. Small tetras are often very colorful and these are firm favorites among hobbyists. An attempt has been made here to show a cross-section of which species are frequently available at your local dealer.

Phenacogrammus interruptus

Common name: Congo tetra
Range: Western Africa, in the upper Congo basin
Size: 3 inches (7.6 cm)
Description: Males are very colorful with iridescent blue backs and lateral bands of red and gold. The flanks and belly are silvery-blue. Females are less colorful and their fins are short. Males, on the other hand, have long, flowing dorsal fins and the center of the tail extends to form a central lobe.
Aquarium suitability: This is a beautiful fish, peaceful and spectacular if it is kept in groups of five or more individuals in a well-planted aquarium containing a carpet of healthy *Cryptocoryne wendtii* plants. It is also ideal for a community tank provided there are no fin-nippers present.
Breeding information: Spawning occurs in shallow water in the wild, so lower the water surface of the breeding tank.

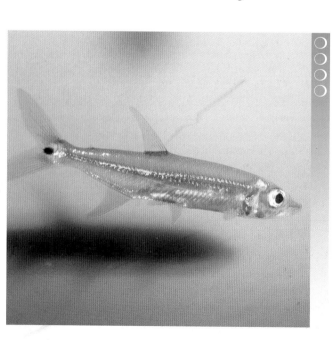

Acestrorhynchus falcatus

Common names: Freshwater barracuda, Spotted cachorro
Range: South America, found in the Paraguay River and Amazon basin
Size: 10 inches (25 cm)
Description: A large characin with an aggressive nature. The body is elongate and the dorsal fin is set far back on the body. An adipose fin is also present. There is a black stripe that extends from the eye to the tail and ends in a small ocellus at the base of the tail. This is often surrounded by an orange or red border in adults. Occasionally, the upper and lower lobes of the tail and portions of the dorsal fin are also red. The background body coloration of this species varies from pale yellow to silver.
Aquarium suitability: Suitable only for a tank containing hardy and robust species, such as cichlids, catfish, and other large characins, this is not a fish for the novice.

Acestrorhynchus nasutus

Common names: Slender freshwater barracuda, Big-eyed cachorro
Range: South America, in the northern Amazon basin
Size: 16 inches (40 cm)
Description: The body color varies from silver to yellow and the belly is white. This is a pikelike elongated fish with its dorsal fin set far back on the body, giving it a streamlined look and aiding in its speed of attack. This is an active predator that will attack and eat small fish. The tail is deeply forked and there is a black spot at the caudal base that is surrounded with bright yellow. This fish is more streamlined than the previous species.
Aquarium suitability: Unsuitable for all but the largest aquariums containing equally large show fish that are hardy and robust. Frequent feedings of live food and good filtration with plenty of water movement are essential for this species.

Aphyocharax anisiti

Common name: Bloodfin tetra
Range: South America, principally Argentina and the Rio Paraná
Size: 2¼ inches (5.7 cm)
Description: The body is somewhat elongate and moderately compressed laterally. The coloration varies between bluish-silver to yellowish-silver and the belly is white. The dorsal, anal, pelvic, and caudal fins are blood red with transparent margins. Adults often show a red blotch at the base of the operculum.
Aquarium suitability: The tank should have a tight-fitting cover, because this fish jumps if it is frightened. Provide adequate cover using rock work and plants so that it has places to hide. This species does well if it is kept in small groups.
Breeding information: Breeding is quite easy and spawning takes place near the water surface at dawn. It will lay 300–600 eggs.

Astyanax mexicanus

Common name: Blind cave fish
Range: Central America, known only from the three caves in San Luis Potosi, Mexico
Size: 3½ inches (9 cm)
Description: Amazingly enough, this is one of the world's most recent and evident examples of evolutionary diversification. *A. fasciatus* migrated into the caves of Mexico in search of food. In this dark environment they no longer needed the use of their eyes, so these organs became rudimentary and gradually disappeared. Now a separate species has been named. These fish hatch with functional eyes, but after 14 days they become distorted and enclosed in tissue. As the fish grows, the eyes shrink and become covered in tissue, leaving them blind.
Aquarium suitability: A good community fish that is occasionally aggressive toward fin-nippers.

Boehlkea fredcochui

Common names: Blue tetra, Cochu's blue tetra
Range: South America, particularly the Peruvian Amazon
Size: 2 inches (5 cm)
Description: The body is elongate and laterally compressed. The back is light olive-brown and the belly is bluish-silver. There is a broad blue stripe present that extends from the operculum and becomes more intense toward the caudal peduncle. At its terminus the tail shows minute traces of red above and below the line. In older fish, the upper part of the eye is orange.
Aquarium suitability: A very peaceful fish, ideal for a community tank if it is kept with other peaceful tank-mates. Difficulties can ensue after its introduction and some specimens will die if they do not feel perfectly at home with their surroundings. Once settled in, this is a hardy fish.

Chalceus macrolepidotus

Common names: Pink-tailed chalceus, Pink tail characin
Range: South America, from Guyana to Peru
Size: 10 inches (25 cm)
Description: The Pink-tailed chalceus is a fish with large scales along the sides and back. Ventrally, the scales are smaller in comparison. The body is elongate and moderately compressed, with a deeply forked tail. A dark spot is often present on the operculum. The dorsal and anal fins are pinkish-red and the tail is deep pink to red. In some specimens the pelvic fins are yellow.
Aquarium suitability: Not suitable for a community tank unless its tank-mates are large and robust species. This is naturally a predatory schooling fish best kept in small groups of seven or more individuals in a large show tank. If they are kept in smaller groups than this, fighting will often occur. This is a fish for the experienced aquarist.

Gymnocorymbus ternetzi

Common names: Black widow, Black tetra
Range: South America, in the Paraguay and Guaporé rivers
Size: 2 inches (5 cm)
Description: The Black widow is a small characin. The body is silver with two dark vertical bands. The anal fin is large and black. Mature fish may be a faded gray color.
Aquarium suitability: They should be kept in the same manner as most other tetra species, in schools of five or more. Tank size is not so important for such a small fish, but the aquarium should be decorated with plants and bogwood.
Breeding information: These are egg scatterers that have been successfully bred in the aquarium. Males have narrower and sharper dorsal fins than females. The female lays her eggs among plants. Fry hatch in 24 hours and should be fed newly hatched brine shrimp.

Hasemania nana

Common name: Silver tip tetra
Range: South America, mainly Brazil in the Rio Purus and Sao Francisco basins
Size: 2 inches (5 cm)
Description: The body color is dull yellow and there is a dark bluish-gold stripe present that runs from the operculum to the forked tail, where it ends in a black spot. The tips of the dorsal and anal fins have silvery-white margins, as do the tips of the upper and lower lobes of the caudal fin. The tail is deeply forked and mature males sometimes show tinges of red in the caudal fin.
Aquarium suitability: Quite a shy species; it can be difficult to acclimatize to aquarium life. In less than ideal conditions, this fish may succumb to disease. It needs a well-planted tank and good water quality.

Hemigrammus bleheri

Common names: Firehead tetra
Range: South America, principally the Rio Negro in Brazil and the Rio Vaupes in Colombia
Size: 2¼ inches (6 cm)
Description: The background body coloration is olive-brown, lightening to silver ventrally. A broad, brownish-gold stripe extends from the operculum toward the tail. In some specimens this can be very dark. With the exception of the lower jaw, the head is bright red. The tail is boldly marked with black and white stripes.
Aquarium suitability: The tank should have soft water and be fully mature for this fish to do well. It requires plenty of free-swimming space in a well-planted aquarium for it to feel happy. It is best kept in groups of five or six individuals.
Breeding information: Relatively easy to breed.

Hemigrammus erithrozonus

Common name: Glowlight tetra
Range: South America, from the Essequibo river in Guyana
Size: 1½ inches (4 cm)
Description: The Glowlight tetra is easily recognized with its silvery body and the bright, iridescent orange stripe that extends from the snout through the eye, to the caudal peduncle. The leading edge of the dorsal fin is often red and the rest of the fins are relatively clear of color.
Aquarium suitability: This species has been a firm favorite among aquarists for many years, and rightly so. It is a very attractive fish, especially if it is kept in small schools of up to 20.
Breeding information: Breeding this fish presents little problem if it is carried out in low-light conditions in a tank that has plenty of Java moss. Soft water is required and the parents should be well-fed and conditioned prior to their introduction.

Hemigrammus ocellifer

Common name: Head and tail light tetra
Range: South America, in the Orinoco and Amazon rivers as well as northwestern Argentina and French Guyana
Size: 2 inches (5 cm)
Description: A bluish-silver line runs from behind the eye to the tail. The background body color is silver and there are two black spots present. The first of these is behind the operculum and the second is on the caudal peduncle. The upper portion of the eye is bright red and there is a bright copper-colored spot on the upper portion of the caudal peduncle.
Aquarium suitability: The tank should be well planted, with plenty of free-swimming space. This is a peaceful schooling fish.
Breeding information: Raise the temperature of the breeding tank to induce spawning, which can produce 200–800 eggs.

Hemigrammus rhodostomus

Common name: True rummynose tetra
Range: South America, mainly the lower Amazon and Orinoco river basins
Size: 2 inches (5 cm)
Description: The body coloration is silver and the head is blood red in healthy individuals. There is a black horizontal bar from the caudal peduncle to the fork in the tail and the upper and lower lobes of the tail are also black. Between these markings the tail is white, giving it a checkerboard impression.
Aquarium suitability: A very attractive species that is peaceful and unassuming in a community setup. It requires excellent water quality and should not be bought for newly set-up aquariums. This fish is best kept in small groups.
Breeding information: The female lays very few eggs that hatch after about 30 hours. This is a very hard fish to breed.

Hyphessobrycon anisitsi

Common name: Buenos Aires tetra
Range: South America, principally Paraguay and the River Plate in Argentina
Size: 3 inches (7.6 cm)
Description: An attractive fish with a silver body that darkens to pale olive dorsally. There is a black stripe present that extends from the midbody region to the deeply forked tail, where it thickens on the caudal peduncle. In males, the flanks, dorsal, and anal fins are blood red, as are the upper and lower lobes of the caudal fin. In females, this color is translucent pink.
Aquarium suitability: An easy fish to keep and ideal for a community aquarium. However, this fish is an active plant-eater that can destroy most well-planted aquariums within weeks.
Breeding information: This is an easy species to breed but the parents must be removed after spawning is complete.

Hyphessobrycon bentosi

Common name: Ornate tetra
Range: Brazil, in the Amazon River basin
Size: 1¾ inches (4.5 cm)
Description: The body shape and size is typical of most other small tetras and is predominantly pink. The dorsal fin is black with a white margin and the pelvic and anal fins are red with white tips. The upper and lower lobes of the caudal fin are also red and the rest is clear or translucent.
Aquarium suitability: Often they will look faded if they are kept in poor, unhealthy conditions. Ornate tetras are best in small schools. They should be kept in neutral pH. A dark substrate is appreciated and subdued lighting is preferred—something that can be achieved by the use of floating plants. Feed a varied diet of mosquito larvae and bloodworms along with flake food.

Hyphessobrycon columbianus

Common name: Colombian blue flame tetra
Range: South America, known only from the tributaries and drainage systems of the Rio Acandi in Colombia
Size: 2¾ inches (7 cm)
Description: This relatively new species is found in Colombia and is very attractive. The body color is iridescent blue along the back and upper sides, and silver ventrally. The dorsal, anal, and caudal fins are red and the nape is light olive green. This species was originally described as *H. ecuadoriensis*, which is a separate species found in Ecuador.
Aquarium suitability: Does well in a community setup, even singly. It will remain peaceful and undisturbed, even when it is housed with aggressive tetras. It is one of the few tetras that is recommended for the complete novice.

Hyphessobrycon eques

Common names: Serpae tetra, Blood tetra
Range: South America: Amazon, Paraguay, and Guaporé river basins
Size: 1¼ inches (3 cm)
Description: Easily recognized by the dark bar behind the operculum and the white-tipped black dorsal fin. Mature fish have red tails and red pelvic fins. The anal fin is also red with black submarginally and white at the margin. The rest of the body may be blush-pink to gold. This is a sociable species that is found in relatively still waters.
Aquarium suitability: Excellent for a community aquarium. If too many are kept in the same tank with too little food, they will bite each other's fins in competition for any food that is offered. In the wild, this fish feeds on small worms, minute crustaceans, insects, and plants.

Hyphessobrycon flammeus

Common names: Flame tetra, Red tetra
Range: South America, particularly Brazil
Size: 2 inches (5 cm)
Description: Depending on the origin of the specimen, the body color can range from brown to red. The belly is silver and the posterior half of the body is blood red. The dorsal, anal, and pelvic fins and the tail are also red; the pectoral fins are clear.
Aquarium suitability: An easy fish to keep and feed if it is kept in small groups of five or more. It is a great fish for a community tank and one with an undemanding diet.
Breeding information: Very easy to breed in captivity. The anal fin of the female is lighter in color than the male's. Around 150–300 eggs are laid, after which the parents must be removed. The eggs hatch after about 60 hours and the fry hang from plants for three to four days before they become free-swimming.

Hyphessobrycon erythrostigma

Common name: Bleeding heart tetra
Range: Upper Amazon basin
Size: 2 inches (5 cm)
Description: The Bleeding heart tetra is a small, schooling characin. The body is elongated and pink. There is a small red spot present on the center of the fish's body, hence its common name of "Bleeding heart." It has a red dorsal fin with broad, black stripes edged in white.
Aquarium suitability: These tetras are active and hardy, making them a great addition to any community tank. Provide a good amount of swimming space and a varied diet of plant-based and protein-based flake food. Live foods are also greatly appreciated. A school of at least five is recommended per tank. The aquarium should be well lit and decorated with plants for shelter.

Hyphessobrycon herbertaxelrodi

Common name: Black neon tetra
Range: South America, mainly Brazil, in various rivers and tributaries
Size: 2 inches (5 cm)
Description: Above the lateral line, the body is olive-brown and the belly is silver. Between these colors there is a broad horizontal stripe of black that extends from the operculum to the tail. Above this is a narrow greenish-gold stripe that runs from the preoperculum to the caudal peduncle. The fins are relatively clear and there is a well-developed adipose fin present.
Aquarium suitability: This fish needs subdued lighting so that its colors can develop. The tank should be thickly planted and have plenty of free-swimming space. Small groups of five or more fish give the best results.

Hyphessobrycon megalopterus

Common name: Black phantom tetra
Range: South America, mainly Brazil
Size: 1¾ inches (4.5 cm)
Description: The body is pinkish-silver to gray and there is a large black bar behind the operculum. The dorsal, caudal, and anal fins have black margins and the pelvic, anal, and adipose fins are a bright red color in adults.
Aquarium suitability: It is essential that this fish be kept in small groups of six or more if it is to retain its intense color markings. Most foods are accepted but an occasional feeding of live brine shrimp and bloodworms will ensure the continued health of this species.
Breeding information: The eggs are laid on fine-leaved plants and hatch after about 36 hours. Soft water is essential in the breeding tank. The fry can be fed on most fry foods.

Hyphessobrycon pulchripinnis

Common name: Lemon tetra
Range: South America, in the Rio Tocantins and its tributaries
Size: 2 inches (5 cm)
Description: An attractive fish with a strongly compressed body and a deeply forked tail. The body is yellow and lightens to silver ventrally. The upper part of the eye is bright red and there is a light yellow to gold stripe present that extends from behind the operculum to the caudal peduncle. The leading edge of the dorsal fin is dull yellow and the leading edge of the anal fin is bright yellow with a black margin.
Aquarium suitability: A striking fish that is peaceful and recommended for a community setup. Since this is a schooling fish, it is best kept in small groups of eight or ten.
Breeding information: A shy fish that can be difficult to breed. In a well-planted tank, up to 200 eggs can be laid.

Impaichthys kerri

Common names: Purple emperor tetra, Blue emperor tetra, King tetra
Range: South America, mainly Brazil in the tributaries of the Rio Madeira
Size: 1½ inches (4 cm)
Description: A dark stripe extends from the snout to the tail. The area forward of the eye is black, but from the eye to the tail it is dark blue, broadening laterally. The upper half of the body is pale blue and the belly is silver in color. The pectoral, anal, and adipose fins are also blue.
Aquarium suitability: This species does not do well if it is housed with barbs or other notorious fin-nippers. It is better if kept with other peaceful fish in a small group of several individuals.
Breeding information: The males have longer fins and the females are more rounded.

Moenkausia sanctaefilomenae

Common name: Redeye tetra
Range: South America, principally Brazil in the Paranaíba River basin, and Paraguay
Size: 2¾ inches (7 cm)
Description: Characterized by a black bar through the tail and bright red eyes, this species is a very popular aquarium fish. The body is predominantly silver that darkens on the flanks in adult fish. Juveniles are uniformly silver in color but still exhibit the red eyes and the black bar on the tail.
Aquarium suitability: Kept in groups of five or more, this is an excellent aquarium fish that is gregarious and attractive. It can survive extreme pH, hardness, and temperature fluctuations once it has settled in and it is one of the fish that is recommended for the complete novice.

Moenkausia pittieri

Common name: Diamond tetra
Range: South America in Lake Valencia, the Rio Bue, and the Rio Tiquirito in Venezuela
Size: 2½ inches (6 cm)
Description: The body is strongly compressed and the dorsal fin extends over the adipose fin to the tail in males. The dorsal fin of the female is elongated but somewhat shorter. The upper part of the eye is red and the body can be iridescent silver, gold, or violet, depending on the amount of light and its color composition.
Aquarium suitability: The shimmering effect of the light reflected in the scales makes this a very attractive aquarium fish. Use a dark substrate and plenty of floating plants to filter the light and bring out the colors of this species.
Breeding information: Use peat-filtered water in the breeding tank and feed mosquito larvae to induce spawning.

Nematobrycon palmeri

Common name: Black emperor tetra
Range: South America, principally western Colombia
Size: 3 inches (7.7 cm)
Description: This is an attractive fish that is unmistakable in appearance. The first rays of the dorsal fin and the extreme upper and lower rays of the caudal fin are elongated and black in color. The central rays of the moderately forked tail are also extended in adults.
Aquarium suitability: The Black emperor tetra is a popular community fish that is easy to keep and feed. Males can be quite territorial toward other males, but this seldom results in injury.
Breeding information: A very easy fish to breed in captivity if the conditions are right. Pairs lay up to 150 clear eggs among the leaves of Java moss. These hatch after 24–30 hours and the newly hatched fry cling to the plants or glass for about three days.

Paracheirodon axelrodi

Common name: Cardinal tetra
Range: Venezuela and Brazil in the upper Orinoco and Negro river basins
Size: 1½ inches (3.8 cm)
Description: This species can be confused with the smaller Neon tetra, below. They display striking colors of blue and red usually only seen with coral fish. Their bodies are slender and moderately elongate with a blue upper half and red lower half. The fins are transparent.
Aquarium suitability: Cardinal tetras make a great addition to any community aquarium. It is recommended that these fish be kept in schools of six or more with other small tetras and *Corydoras* catfish. The tank should be dimly lit, with floating plants and driftwood if available. Because they are small, they should be fed on fine flake food and small aquatic invertebrates.

Paracheirodon innesi

Common name: Neon tetra
Range: South American jungle streams, especially tributaries of the Solimões River
Size: 1½ inches (3.8 cm)
Description: This is one of the most popular aquarium fish. It resembles the Cardinal tetra, except that the Neon tetra has a white belly and throat. A neon blue stripe extends from the snout to the upper surface of the caudal peduncle.
Aquarium suitability: Neon tetras are perfect for any community tank. A small school of six or more provides an attractive show of colors. These fish come from the Peruvian Amazon, where they live in shaded jungle waters, so they should be housed in a dimly lit aquarium. In their jungle habitat, water is replenished frequently by soft, fresh rain. To provide comparable conditions in the aquarium, frequent water changes should be made.

Paracheirodon simulans

Common names: False neon tetra, Green neon tetra
Range: South America, principally the upper Orinoco and Negro rivers
Size: 1 inch (2.5 cm)
Description: The dorsal region is light olive-brown and there is a broad blue stripe from the eye to the tail. In certain light this can show a greenish iridescence. The anal region is red, but not so pronounced as *P. innesi*. Some specimens lack this red color completely. The blue-green strip is also more pronounced than that of *P. innesi*.
Aquarium suitability: Not seen as often as the previous two species but the care and husbandry is the same. Provide plenty of plants and a dark substrate for the best results.
Breeding information: Breeding this species can prove difficult but not impossible. Soft water is a prerequisite.

Pristella maxillaris

Common names: Pristella tetra, X-ray tetra, Water goldfinch
Range: South America, in inland waters of Brazil, Venezuela, and Guyana
Size: 1 inch (2.5 cm)
Description: The body is translucent silver and pale olive-brown dorsally. It is easily identifiable by its flaglike dorsal and anal fins. These are yellow at the base, followed by a large black spot. The margins of the two fins are white. The pelvic fins also have black spots, but these are less distinct. The deeply forked tail is pinkish-red to bright red.
Aquarium suitability: This fish was previously known as *Pristella riddlei* and has long been a firm favorite among hobbyists. It is a robust character and peaceful by nature. Small schools are particularly attractive.

Rachoviscus crassiceps

Common name: Gold tetra
Range: South America, principally Brazil in the Amazon and its tributaries
Size: 1½ inches (3.8 cm)
Description: Not as attractive as other tetras but interesting nevertheless. The body is elongate and moderately compressed laterally. The head is blunt for a tetra and the median fins are deep olive green, dark brown, or almost black. The background body color is tan or gold and is often suffused with golden flecks on the scales that reflect the light.
Aquarium suitability: If this fish is kept in small schools of up to eight individuals, it will do well. It should be housed with other peaceful fish in a well-planted tank.
Breeding information: The eggs are laid on the underside of broad-leaved plants and hatch after about 24 hours. Keep the aquarium dark during the incubation time and feed the fry with infusorians. Remove the parents to keep them from eating the newly laid eggs.

Colossoma macropomum

Common names: Pacu, Tambaqui, Black-finned pacu
Range: South America, throughout the Amazon River basin
Size: 28 inches (71 cm)
Description: The body is ovate and compressed laterally. The fins are uniform black and the body is deep brown with fine scales that reflect the light in a spangled pattern. Young specimens have dark spots across the flanks that fade with age. This is a very big fish with an arched back and large eyes.
Aquarium suitability: Young specimens can be kept in a normal aquarium for a few months, but they will soon outgrow all but the largest aquarium. Ideally, an aquarium of 200 gallons (750 liters) or more is required to house this fish properly. It is a herbivore and can be fed on lettuce, spinach, canned peas, fruits, oatmeal, and anything else that will fit in its enormous mouth.

Thayeria boehlkei

Common name: Penguin tetra
Range: South America, in the Rio Araguaia, Brazil, and the Peruvian Amazon
Size: 3¼ inches (8 cm)
Description: Easily identifiable with the bold black stripe that extends from the operculum to the caudal peduncle, where it angles downward to the margin of the lower caudal lobe. Above this stripe, the dorsal region is pale olive-brown and below it the belly is silver. In males, there is a lighter gold stripe above the black one that ends in a gold spot on the caudal peduncle.
Aquarium suitability: An easy fish to keep and one that can be kept singly or in small groups. It is a peaceful community fish that does best if it is provided with a well-planted aquarium with floating plants to diffuse the lighting.

Metynnis argenteus

Common name: Silver dollar
Range: South America, mainly Guyana
Size: 5 inches (12.7 cm)
Description: Many *Metynnis* species are called silver dollars because of their silver bodies and disk shape. However, this is the original silver dollar that was introduced to the hobby many years ago. The sides are silver and the leading edge of the anal fin is red. Juveniles often have small spots on the sides.
Aquarium suitability: This fish prefers subdued lighting and places to hide. It is herbivorous and will decimate a well-planted aquarium.
Breeding information: Parent fish will not eat their eggs or young. About 2,000 eggs are laid and fall to the aquarium bottom. Hatching takes place after three days and the fry become free-swimming a week later.

Metynnis hypsauchen

Common name: Silver dollar
Range: South American Amazon and Paraguay river basins, and north Guyana Shield River
Size: 6 inches (15 cm)
Description: Fully grown specimens can inflict serious bites because of their powerful jaws and sharp dentition. Adults have a red tinge to the belly and the median fins are dark brown. Juvenile fish are uniformly silver with a pale pink anal fin.
Aquarium suitability: Silver dollars are best in a tank of their own. Alternatively, keep them in small groups along with other hardy and aggressive fish. They should not be kept with barbs, which will result in fin-nipping and territorial squabbles.
Breeding information: Males adopt a brighter, more reddish color than the females at breeding time. The eggs are demersal and sink to the bottom after being laid among floating plants.

Metynnis maculatus

Common name: Spotted metynnis
Range: South America: Amazon and Paraguay river basins
Size: 7 inches (18 cm)
Description: Juveniles have spotted flanks. These spots are often carried over into adulthood when the colors darken with age. The body coloration can be silver or silvery-green. The anal fin is pink with a clear margin and the teeth and jaws are well developed.
Aquarium suitability: Take care when handling this fish—it has a powerful dentition and can inflict serious bites. For the best results, it should be kept in soft water with an ideal pH of 6.8. This is a plant eater, so it is advisable to use plastic plants as aquarium decoration. Diffused lighting will bring out the colors of this species.

Myleus pacu

Common name: Brown pacu
Range: South America, principally the Rio Essequibo
Size: 8 inches (20 cm)
Description: The overall body color of this species is silvery-brown, making it quite easy to identify. Adult fish are gray-brown with a darker head. In juveniles the tail is white and darkens with age. The dark anal fin often has a reddish tinge to it.
Aquarium suitability: This is another species with powerful jaws and sharp teeth, so care should be taken when handling it or hand feeding. Most aquarium foods are snapped up readily but it should be provided with an ample supply of greenstuff such as spinach and peas.
Breeding information: As far as it is known, there are no records of this fish having ever been successfully bred in captivity.

Myleus schomburgkii

Common names: Disk tetra, Black-barred myleus
Range: South America, in the middle and lower Amazon River basins as well as the Rio Nanay and the upper Orinoco
Size: 16½ inches (42 cm)
Description: The Disk tetra is characterized by the bold black bar that extends vertically from the dorsal fin to the anal fin. The back is pale olive-brown and the sides are silver to light bronze, often with a spangled effect in certain light conditions. There is a dull, reddish-orange blotch that runs from the lower two-thirds of the operculum to a point below the angle of the pectoral fin base.
Aquarium suitability: For it to do well, this species needs soft, slightly acidic water. It should be kept in groups of several individuals in a large tank with lots of hiding places and plenty of free-swimming space.

Myloplus rubripinnis

Common names: Redhook myleus, Redhook dollar
Range: South America: Amazon and Orinoco river basins and north and eastern Guyana Shield rivers
Size: 15 inches (38 cm)
Description: The body coloration is silver with a shimmering effect in certain light. The throat is yellow in adults and the nape is olive green. The tail is deeply forked and the upper and lower lobes are pink to dull red. Perhaps the most signifying feature of this species is the extended anal fin. This is hook-shaped and is bright red in color, though yet to show on this immature fish.
Aquarium suitability: The Redhook dollar can inflict serious wounds if it is handled incorrectly. However, it is not aggressive in a community setup, even as an adult fish. Nevertheless, it needs places to hide and a very large tank because of its ultimate adult size. Several together are extremely attractive.

Mylossoma duriventre

Common names: Mylossoma, Silver dollar
Range: South America, in the Amazon, Orinoco, and Paraguay-Paraná river basins
Size: 10 inches (25 cm)
Description: Similar in appearance to several other so-called silver dollars but this species has a much deeper belly and shallower dorsal region. There are also up to six shadowy bars on the sides of juveniles that are sometimes present in adult fish. The anal fin is darker than the other median fins and often has a black margin. The tail is more or less truncate, with a white or clear margin.
Aquarium suitability: Not often seen for sale in dealers' tanks but this species does turn up occasionally. Like other silver dollars, this is a plant eater, so plastic plants are needed in its aquarium. Provide plenty of cover and slightly soft water.

Piaractus brachypomus

Common names: Red-bellied pacu, Pirapitinga, Red pacu
Range: South America, in the upper Amazon basin
Size: 18 inches (45.7 cm)
Description: Like many other pacus and piranhas, juveniles have black spots on the flanks. Adult fish are silver-spangled and olive-colored dorsally, with silvery-white bellies. The pectoral, pelvic, and anal fins are red with clear bases and the tail is moderately forked, often with a black margin. The body is discoid and laterally compressed.
Aquarium suitability: This is a peaceful fish by nature. It can be kept in a community tank with ease. However, once it starts to grow, small tank-mates are in danger of being eaten despite the fact that this is essentially a herbivorous fish. A good filter is required because of this fish's metabolism. Use large lumps of driftwood and rocks for hiding places.

Pygocentrus nattereri

Common names: Red piranha, Red-throated piranha
Range: Paraguay: Paraná, Amazon, and Essequibo river basins
Size: 12 inches (30 cm)
Description: Red piranhas have a reputation for attacking in large shoals and stripping flesh from any creature that enters the rivers they inhabit. However, many of these stories are exaggerated. They vary in color, both with age and environment. Younger specimens are bluish-gray dorsally, with delicate olive green flanks and numerous metallic silver spots that fade with age. As their name implies, the throat and belly is red in adults.
Aquarium suitability: Piranhas are timid and appreciate sheltered areas in the aquarium provided by broad-leaved plants and pieces of bogwood. Feed them beef heart, earthworms, and fish. They require high levels of oxygen and good water flow, so external power filters and power-heads are a must.

Pygocentrus piraya

Common names: Piranha, Sao Francisco piranha, Piraya
Range: South America: Amazon River region and Rio Sao Francisco, Brazil
Size: 24 inches (61 cm)
Description: This is the true piranha and the most fearsome. However, its reputation as a voracious predator is not strictly true. It is quite a timid fish. It is similar to the preceding species and has a red belly for a greater part of its life. This species has a tufted adipose fin, which is unique to this fish. It is also one of the biggest piranhas.
Aquarium suitability: This fish can be kept in an aquarium without too many problems. A large aquarium with excellent filtration and water flow is required. All foods are accepted but it should be provided with regular fresh protein foods such as frozen silversides and freshwater shrimp.

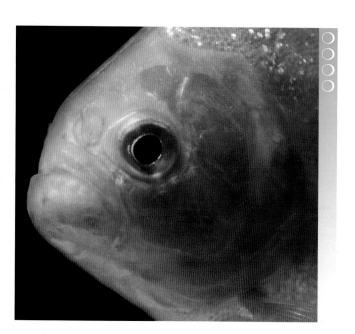

Order: Siluriformes

The order Siluriformes contains all the catfish that one can find in freshwater streams, lakes, and rivers throughout the world in both tropical and subtropical regions. There are well over 2,000 different known species of catfish and these are split up into more than 410 genera. The genera are currently grouped into 34 families. This makes it a very large order, second only in size to the order Perciformes, which is comprised of 148 families.

However, almost all members of this order are found in freshwater; only two families, Ariidae and Plotosidae, contain species that are truly marine living. There are many species that live in brackish water and some that can tolerate high levels of salinity, but these are not strictly sea fish and are therefore well within the scope of this book. Quite a few of the freshwater species are well known to aquarists who keep tropical fish, and each has his favorites. For the tropical fish hobbyist, there is a rich selection, with many bizarre and spectacular species widely available.

For the marine aquarist, the selection is poor, with only one species that is usually imported. Generally catfish are scavengers and bottom-dwellers, therefore it is odd that they are so poorly represented in the seas of the world. It could be that through the process of evolution, too much competition developed with families of fish from other orders, such as the blennies, gobies, and goatfish. This may have forced them to seek nutrition in freshwater. Nevertheless, for the freshwater aquarist there is a wide choice of catfish available for the home aquarium.

Ictaluridae (North American freshwater catfish)

Fish from this order are restricted in distribution to North America, from southern Canada to Guatemala. The common characteristics of this group of catfish are as follows: the skin is naked, there are four pairs of barbels on the head, the dorsal and pectoral fins have a spine, and the dorsal fin usually has six soft rays. Three species of blind catfish are known from deep wells and ditches near San Antonio, Texas, and another species from a well in northeastern Mexico. The family contains seven genera with about 45 species. These are *Ictalurus* (channel catfish) with about nine species, five of which are found only in Mexico and Guatemala; a single species of *Trogoglanis*; *Ameiurus* (bullheads) with seven species; *Noturus* with about 25 species; and *Prietella, Satan,* and *Pylodictis,* each with a single species. There is a fossilized record of the ictalurids that dates back to the Paleocene period. In North America, channel catfish are bred commercially and raised as popular food fish.

Ictalurus punctatus

Common name: Channel catfish
Range: Central drainage systems of the United States, southern Canada, and northern Mexico
Size: 52 inches (132 cm)
Description: The back is usually olive to gray in color, darkening to black with age. The belly is white or pale cream and there are numerous dark spots scattered along the flanks. The tail is deeply forked and clear, with a black margin in juveniles. Adult fish often have tails that are pinkish-brown.
Aquarium suitability: Small specimens of about 2 inches (5 cm) are frequently available to the hobbyist. They are cute and lively at this stage. Nevertheless, these catfish grow to an enormous size and will eventually outgrow even the largest aquarium.
Breeding information: Although this fish is bred in holding pens as a commercial food fish, it has never been bred within the confines of an aquarium because of its large adult size.

Bagridae (Bagrid catfish)

Species in this family are highly varied in size and range from a few inches to several feet in length. *Chrysichthys grandis* from Lake Tanganyika attains a length of 6 feet 8 inches (200 cm) and weighs several hundred pounds. Generally, a spine precedes the dorsal fin and there is an adipose fin present. This is variable in size. These fish have serrated pectoral spines and they are without scales. There are usually four pairs of well-developed barbels around the mouth. A few species are kept as ornamental aquarium fish but, for the most part, this group comprises some important food fish for local inhabitants where they occur in the wild. There are 30 genera within this family and about 220 species in all.

Bagrid catfish are found throughout Africa and Asia and the number of species on each of these two continents is approximately the same. All of the species are found in freshwater and those found in Asia have a distribution from Japan to Borneo. Only a few species of bagrid catfish find their way into dealers' tanks. These are reviewed here.

Batasio affinis

Common names: Golden tiger lancer, Tiger lancer, Bengal lancer
Range: Southeast Asia: Mayanmar in tropical streams and freshwater rivers
Size: 4 inches (10 cm)
Description: This is a small catfish, pink to olive in color. There are several black markings on the sides and fins that give a clue to its identity. These do not occur in other catfish. There is a large black spot behind the operculum and a second large spot in the midbody region. A distinct black bar extends obliquely down the body from the apex of the spinous dorsal fin. The anal and caudal fins are often pale yellow.
Aquarium suitability: This is an active catfish that needs plenty of free-swimming space and good water quality. Feeding is not a great problem and it does well in a community tank if it is kept with several other individuals of its own kind.

Mystus vittatus

Common name: Striped dwarf catfish
Range: Asia, including India, Pakistan, Sri Lanka, Nepal, Bangladesh, Malaysia, Laos, Vietnam, and Cambodia
Size: 8¼ inches (21 cm)
Description: The body is elongate and somewhat compressed, with the maxillary barbels extending beyond the pelvic fins. The background body color can be from silver to light gold. There are several (usually three to five) longitudinal bluish-brown stripes along the sides and there is a large dark spot present behind the operculum.
Aquarium suitability: This is a great fish for a medium-sized community tank because it does not grow too large. Although it may be shy at first, it will soon settle down to tank life if there are enough hiding places. It is generally peaceful, but it is not to be trusted with very small fish.

Siluridae (Old World catfish)

The silurids are the Old World catfish that have their origins in Europe and Southeast Asia. Sometimes they are referred to as "sheatfish." Currently there are 89 described species in 12 genera, the largest of these being *Kryptopterus* with 20 species and *Ompok* with 18 species. Some species are suitable for aquarium life, but many are not. Nevertheless, the group is diverse with some species entering brackish water, although none of them are solely marine living.

The dorsal fin is short, often having less than seven rays. In contrast, the anal fin is very long with between 41 and 110 rays. There are no nasal barbels but there are one or two pairs of barbels on the lower jaw. Some very large species belong to this family, including the European Wels catfish, *Silurus glanis*, which attains a maximum length of 16½ feet (5 meters) and weighs upward of 725 pounds (330 kg) and is much sought after by anglers. Because of the diversity and vast differences in size between species, only two examples have been chosen here to represent this family, but there are others that occasionally find their way into dealers' tanks.

Kryptopterus bicirrhis

Common names: Glass catfish, Ghost catfish
Range: Southeast Asia, mainly Sumatra, Java, Borneo, and Thailand
Size: 5½ inches (14 cm)
Description: There are quite a few so-called glass catfish and they are difficult to identify with any degree of certainty. Most species belong to the Schilbeidae family, which will be dealt with next. This species, however, does not possess an adipose fin. The body is transparent, with scattered patches of pigment on the head and underbelly. The swim bladder can clearly be seen in the body cavity adjacent to the pectoral fins.
Aquarium suitability: In an aquarium this is a peaceful community fish. Several should be kept in the same tank for the best result. It is a diurnal catfish that should not be kept alongside aggressive species. Most aquarium foods are accepted.

Ompok bimaculatus

Common names: Butter catfish, Gulper catfish
Range: Southern Asia, from Afghanistan to China, Thailand, and Borneo, often in muddy water and sandy streams
Size: 18 inches (46 cm)
Description: In the wild this species moves into freshly inundated flood plains to feed during the flood season. The body is generally deep brown to grayish-brown. The dorsal fin is short along its base and is held high during swimming. There is no adipose fin present but the anal fin is very long. There is a bold black spot present on the shoulder that is the main key to identifying this species.
Aquarium suitability: The Butter catfish is not to be trusted with small tank-mates. It is constantly on the move and does well in a tank in a group of three or more. Provide plenty of swimming space and a varied diet for the best results.

Schilbeidae (Glass catfish)

Species from this family are found throughout southeast Asia and Africa. The dorsal fin is usually present, but absent in *Ailia* and *Paralia* species. When it is present, it is short and often prominent with a single spine. There are about 18 genera with 45 species. Usually there is an adipose fin present and the base of the anal fin is very long and separate from the caudal fin. The anal fin has between 24 and 90 rays. Several of the genera lack pelvic fins and species from this family are usually found swimming in open waters. There are usually four pairs of barbels present around the mouth.

At this moment in time the author feels that the African and the Asian genera in this family grouping do not form a monophyletic taxon, and more work needs to be done. The species are found in freshwater environments and do not occur in marine or brackish-water areas. During the breeding season the parent fish do not guard their eggs. At least four species are known by the common name African glass catfish, which is confusing to many hobbyists. These are *Pareutropius buffei*, *Pareutropius debauwi*, *Parailia congica*, and *Paralia pellucida*. Two of these species are described here in greater detail.

Parailia congica

Common names: African glass catfish, Congo glass catfish
Range: Western Africa, in the Congo basin
Size: 3½ inches (9 cm)
Description: This species lacks both the adipose and the dorsal fins. The body is transparent with numerous small brown spots on the sides. There is a long pair of barbels on the upper jaw and two shorter pairs and a rudimentary pair on the lower jaw. A dark brown stripe extends dorsally to the tip of the upper caudal lobe.
Aquarium suitability: A well-planted tank and excellent water quality are necessary to keep this fish happy with its surroundings. Small groups fair better than single fish. This is a relatively shy and peaceful community fish that should be given live food at least once a week. It is very sensitive to rapid changes in water quality.

Pareutropius debauwi

Common names: Flag-tailed catfish, African glass catfish
Range: Central Africa and the Niger river basin
Size: 3¼ inches (8 cm)
Description: The snout is broad and an adipose fin is present. There is a dorsal stripe of olive brown that runs from the nape, over the back to the caudal peduncle. A broad black stripe extends from behind the eye to the tail. The rest of the body, including the belly, is silvery-white.
Aquarium suitability: Single fish do not do well, so stock groups of six or more. The tank should have subdued lighting. Feed supplements of live food and various frozen foods.
Breeding information: Simulate the rainy season through frequent partial water changes. Up to 200 white eggs are laid among plants. Eggs hatch after 72–84 hours but the fry are difficult to raise. They are best fed on rotifers—*Brachionus* spp.

Pangasiidae (Shark catfish)

This is a small family of sharklike fish with two genera and 21 species. Due to their shape they are often referred to as "shark cats" or "iridescent sharks." The largest, *Pangasius gigas*, grows to about 10 feet (300 cm) and weighs up to 660 pounds (300 kg). Generally, the dorsal fin is set forward on the back and there is an adipose fin present. The eyes are quite large. The tail is moderately forked and the body is somewhat compressed. There are no nasal barbels present and only two pairs of barbels, one pair of which are chin barbels.

These fish are known throughout southern Asia from Pakistan to Borneo. Primarily these are freshwater fish, although some species will enter brackish water. None are found in a marine environment. Most species grow too large for the average aquarium and they get very nervous if they are not given enough room to swim. Commercially, two species are significant food fish. These are *Pangasius bocourti* and *P. hypophthalmus*, which are farmed by the Vietnamese on the Mekong Delta. Surging imports of the cheaper Vietnamese catfish filets has threatened the U.S. catfish industry.

Pangasius hypophthalmus

Common names: Asian shark catfish, Siamese shark, Iridescent shark, Sutchi shark
Range: Fast-flowing rivers throughout Southeast Asia, particularly Thailand
Size: 40 inches (100 cm)
Description: The body is elongate with a deeply forked tail. The eyes are large and the body is iridescent bluish-silver. Juveniles have two broad white stripes that extend parallel from behind the operculum to the tail. These fade with age. The head is moderately depressed, giving the snout a blunt appearance.
Aquarium suitability: The Iridescent shark grows quite large and needs plenty of space in a large show tank. It is a shy fish with poor eyesight and is easily frightened. It is a relatively peaceful fish that will not harm smaller tank-mates that it cannot swallow.

Pangasius sanitwonsei

Common names: Paroon pangasius, Giant pangasius
Range: Asia, in the Chao Phraya and Mekong basins
Size: 10 feet (300 cm)
Description: Juveniles have a stubbier snout and are not as colorful as the previous species. The head is broad and the tips of the dorsal, pelvic, and pectoral fins have extended filaments in adults. This is an important food fish with considerable commercial significance. Large individuals are known to feed on waterfowl and dogs, which are often used for bait.
Aquarium suitability: Small individuals are frequently seen for sale but do not do well in a captive environment for more than a year or so because they soon outgrow their tank. This is a large fish that needs special care in a very large aquarium with excellent filtration. Most foods that are offered will be accepted with gusto, including small live fish and freshwater shrimp.

Clariidae (Airbreathing catfish)

The family comprises 13 genera with about 100 species from Africa, Syria, and southern and western Asia. The dorsal fin base is very long, without a leading spine, and may be separate or continuous with the caudal fin. The caudal fin is rounded and the pectoral and pelvic fins are absent in some species. There are usually four pairs of barbels around the mouth. Some species can move short distances on land. Air breathing is attained with a labyrinthic organ with its commencement at the gill arches. Some of the African species are known to burrow in mud and have small eyes. These species often lack or have rudimentary pectoral and pelvic fins. The body is scaleless.

One species of walking catfish, *Clarias batrachus*, has been introduced to Florida waters, where it thrives. Because of this, importing most species is banned in the United States and also in Germany, which faces a similar problem with some of the more temperate species. Several species from Somalia, India, and southwestern Africa are blind.

These are primarily freshwater fish. None have been reported entering brackish water environments.

Clarias batrachus

Common name: Walking catfish
Range: Southeast Asia from India to Malaysia and Indonesia
Size: 20 inches (51 cm)
Description: There are three color variations of this species. The first has a body color that is slate gray to olive-brown and males have a black spot on the dorsal fin. The second variation is a natural albino variety that is white with pink eyes. A third variety exists that is white and salmon pink, sometimes sprinkled with black spots, with normal eyes.
Aquarium suitability: Because of its invasive and predatory nature, this fish is now banned in the United States and Germany. It needs a large tank with a tight-fitting hood. Even then, this fish may climb out. It has very strong dorsal muscles and has been known to lift an aquarium hood that had three house bricks on top of it! Almost any food is acceptable to this fish.
Breeding information: There are only a few reports of this fish ever being bred in captivity and the majority were purely by accident, rather than by design. The male wraps himself around the female after a series of courtship maneuvers and up to 500 eggs are laid in a hollow in the substrate. These hatch after 36 hours and the fry become free-swimming after an additional two days.

Ariidae (Sea catfish)

The family comprises 14 genera with about 125 species. Most of these are entirely marine living, although some species are known to enter freshwater and a few species occur only in freshwater. Generally, the caudal fin is deeply forked and there is an adipose fin present. There are usually three pairs of barbels, although some species lack the nasal barbels. The dorsal and pectoral fins have spines. These catfish are mouthbrooders—the male carries the relatively large eggs in its mouth until they hatch. Most of the species available to the hobbyist grow far too large for the average aquarium and they are usually very aggressive. One fish frequently seen for sale is the Tete sea catfish. This is a marine fish that often enters brackish or fresh water. Although it is attractive and shown in many aquariums throughout the world, it requires special care.

Hexanematichthys seemanni

Common names: Tete sea catfish, Colombian shark catfish, Shadowfin catfish
Range: Central and South America, in Pacific rivers and estuaries from Mexico to Peru
Size: 13¾ inches (35 cm)
Description: The head, nape, and back is golden-brown and the belly is white. The pectoral, pelvic, and anal fins are black with white margins and the dorsal fin is light brown. The dorsal spine is often black, but may sometimes be gold. The lateral line is prominent and white with black upper and lower margins.
Aquarium suitability: Adult specimens are entirely marine living, but juveniles are happy in brackish water or freshwater for short periods of time. Unless the hobbyist is willing to cater for the different water requirements of this species throughout its life, it should be left to the experts.

Mochokidae (Upside-down catfish)

This family is restricted to the lakes and rivers of Africa and includes the so-called squeakers as well as the upside-down catfish. There are about 10 genera with 189 described species. Almost 75 percent of the species are placed in the genus *Synodontis*. Specimens from the African rivers tend to live in softer water than those found in lakes, which have a greater toleration for hard water. Most species are nocturnal but once they have settled down to tank life, some will become diurnal.

Generally speaking, they make good community fish, although some adult fish will often eat very small tank-mates. The adipose fin is usually very large and the tail is deeply forked. The dorsal and pectoral fin spines are very sturdy and have a locking mechanism. Three pairs of barbels are present but there are no nasal barbels. Some species have their lips and part of their barbels modified into an oral sucker. Quite a few species have spines, so they should be netted with care. Others emit squeaking noises when they are distressed; these are appropriately called "squeakers." One or two species are able to discharge small electrical charges when they are disturbed.

Synodontis angelicus

Common names: Angel catfish, Black clown catfish, Angel synodontis
Range: Tropical western Africa, in the Zaire River throughout Cameroon, the Democratic Republic of the Congo, and Zaire
Size: 10 inches (25 cm)
Description: A very striking catfish that has a dark brown to black body coloration. The fish is squat, with a high back and tall dorsal fin. The tail is deeply forked and the barbels are white. The entire body and head is covered in small white spots. The median fins, pectorals, and pelvic fins are also spotted, but these are fused in many cases to form stripes and bars.
Aquarium suitability: The Angel catfish is a firm favorite with hobbyists. It is a community fish but it needs good water quality. A large tank is preferred, with hiding places and plenty of free-swimming space. Feeding should be done in the evening.

Synodontis brichardi

Common names: Britchard's synodontis, Banded synodontis
Range: Western Africa, in the Congo river system
Size: 8 inches (20 cm)
Description: The streamlined body makes this species slightly different in form to others of this genus. This is because the body is more elongate and the back is lower. The background body color is dark brown to black and the sides are adorned with a series of narrow white or pale cream bars. Sometimes the bars can take on a reticulated pattern. The markings of the Banded synodontis usually become more intense toward adulthood.
Aquarium suitability: This fish can become diurnal quite easily. However, it is inclined to chase small tank-mates at night. Do not keep this with species that are less than 2 inches (5 cm) in length. Plants should be firmly planted or in pots because it tends to dig and root around looking for food.

Synodontis eupterus

Common name: Feather-fin catfish
Range: Central Africa, in the tributaries of Lake Chad in Niger and Chad as well as the White Nile in the Sudan
Size: 6 inches (15 cm)
Description: As far as the coloration is concerned, this species is the reverse of *Synodontis angelicus*. The body is white to cream and suffused with small brownish-black to intense black spots. The fins are spotted and, in the case of the caudal fin, can fuse together to form bands and stripes. The back is high, with a tall dorsal fin, and there are three pairs of barbels present.
Aquarium suitability: Use floating plants to diffuse the tank lighting. Feed live food and frozen brine shrimp regularly. Dried food is taken if it is in pellet form rather than flake. This is a peaceful community fish.

Synodontis flavitaeniatus

Common names: Orange-striped squeaker, Pajama catfish
Range: Central Africa, the Democratic Republic of the Congo
Size: 7¾ inches (19.5 cm)
Description: The background body color is cream to pale orange-yellow, which darkens dorsally. The tail is deeply forked and there are three sets of barbels around the mouth. The sides and head of this species are marked with broad dark brown to blackish stripes and blotches. These markings are sometimes reticulated or have wavy borders. The upper and lower lobes of the tail are darkly striped with clear margins.
Aquarium suitability: The pajama catfish is very attractive and it has filaments on its barbels. It is an easy species to keep and will not uproot plants. It is not aggressive to its own kind and several of them can be kept in a large tank along with species like the Congo tetra.

Synodontis multipunctatus

Common names: Cuckoo catfish, Multispotted catfish
Range: East Africa, along the shoreline of Lake Tanganyika
Size: 8 inches (20 cm)
Description: Thanks to the striking pattern of spots, this fish is relatively easy to identify. The background body color is pale cream to tan and the dorsal fin and deeply forked tail are black with clear or white margins.
Aquarium suitability: Larger fish should have a tank with plenty of rocky caves for hiding places. Its diet should consist of algae, fish eggs, frozen brine shrimp, and pellet food.
Breeding information: The breeding pair waits for a pair of cichlid mouthbreeders to spawn. The eggs of the catfish are then released among the cichlid eggs. The female cichlid then picks them up, believing them to be her own, and cares for them in her mouth. The young fry feed on the yolk sacs of the cichlid fry.

Synodontis nigriventris

Common name: Upside-down catfish
Range: Western Africa, among heavy vegetation along the banks of the Zaire and Kasai rivers
Size: 4 inches (10 cm)
Description: This fish swims upside down under broad-leaved plants and rocky overhangs for much of its life. Because of this, its belly is darker than the rest of the body to camouflage it from predators. The body and fins are tan to light brown and the fins are sprinkled with brown spots. The body is adorned with brownish-black blotches and spots that vary between specimens.
Aquarium suitability: Subdued lighting should be provided for this fish. This is best done by utilizing floating plants such as water lettuce and *Salvinia* spp. It is a peaceful fish that can be kept in a community setup. Most popular aquarium foods are accepted with relish.

Synodontis notatus

Common name: Domino synodontis
Range: Central Africa, the Democratic Republic of the Congo
Size: 11 inches (28 cm)
Description: The background body color of this species is silvery gray to orange-tan, which often darkens dorsally. The belly is more or less white and there are three pairs of barbels present around the mouth. The number of dark spots on the sides of the fish can vary a great deal, hence its common name. There may be no spots at all, or up to 12 spots adorning the sides. However, between one and three large spots are usually present.
Aquarium suitability: Although this species has gotten a bad name for being predatory and aggressive, the author has not found this to be the case. Larger specimens may be aggressive toward their own kind but this is a relatively peaceful community fish that will accept most foods that are offered.

Synodontis ocellifer

Common names: Ocellifer catfish, Ocellated synodontis
Range: Western Africa, in numerous river systems
Size: 4¾ inches (12 cm)
Description: Easily confused with other species of its genus, this particular fish has a light sprinkling of dark spots on a tan body. The spots often appear as ocelli because of the lighter margins around them. The tail has mixed-size spots that are often fused together to form short bars. The head is somewhat darker than the rest of the body.
Aquarium suitability: This is a peaceful fish that does well on a diet of catfish pellets, bloodworms, tubifex, and flake food. Provide plenty of hiding places and a stable water temperature for the best results. The tank should be relatively large. During the initial introduction, take care not to net this species out of the bag and damage the serrated spines on the fins.

Synodontis schoutedeni

Common names: Electric squeaker, Leopard catfish
Range: Central Africa, the Democratic Republic of the Congo
Size: 6¾ inches (17.2 cm)
Description: Unlike the previous species, the body pattern of this fish more closely resembles that of a leopard. The background color is light orange-tan. There are numerous spots and blotches on the sides that are often somewhat reticulated in form. The spots on the head and fins are smaller than on the rest of the body. The electric sensory organ that it possesses is located dorsally, and is formed by modified striated muscle.

Aquarium suitability: Quite a rare species and one not often seen in dealers' tanks. It is a harmless catfish that is usually peaceful with its neighbors. Most foods that are offered will be accepted eagerly but its diet should include live food occasionally.

Breeding information: Like other catfish, it is oviparous and there is distinct pairing during breeding. Even so, this fish has not been bred in captivity so far.

Doradidae (Thorny catfish)

The family is divided into 30 genera with about 74 species. Thorny catfish are characterized by the row of lateral bony plates that extends along the body. There are three pairs of barbels but the nasal barbels are absent. There is usually an adipose fin and the dorsal fin has a single spine with four to six soft rays. The fish can produce sound using movements of the pectoral spine or by vibrating the swim bladder. This phenomenon has given rise to the frequently used term "talking catfish" that has been attributed to these species. The larger species grow to about 30 inches (76 cm) and are unsuitable for a tropical freshwater aquarium except as juveniles. These are freshwater fish and none are found in brackish water or marine environments. There are scattered occurrences throughout South America but their range is primarily Brazil, the Guianas, and Peru.

Thorny catfish swim at lower levels near the substrate. They are primarily nocturnal and like to burrow in the substrate. They are hardy and can withstand a wide pH range. Nevertheless, they prefer soft water with a pH of 6.5–6.8. Most species are good community fish but they prefer a tank with subdued lighting or lighting that is diffused through the use of floating plants.

Amblydoras hancockii

Common names: Hancock's catfish, Croaking spiny catfish, Talking catfish
Range: South America, in slow-moving waters of the Amazon basin and its tributaries
Size: 6 inches (15 cm)
Description: There is often a marbled effect to the body markings of this species and the exact pattern varies between individuals. There are several blotches and streaks on the sides and the fins are spotted. The single dorsal spine is darker than the rest of the fin. Usually there is a brown or black stripe present that extends sublaterally from the midbody region.
Aquarium suitability: Very much a nocturnal species and one that will seldom be seen during daylight hours. Its diet of regular aquarium foods should be supplemented with weekly feedings of live food such as mosquito larvae and bloodworms.

Agamyxis pectinifrons

Common names: Talking catfish, White-spot doradid, Spotted talking catfish
Range: South America, in shallow flood plains of eastern Peru and Ecuador
Size: 6 inches (15 cm)
Description: The body is deep brown to black with a sprinkling of white spots over much of the sides, head, and fins. The dorsal fin is high and frequently held erect. There is a series of spiny plates on the sides that runs laterally from the operculum to the caudal peduncle. Of the three pairs of barbels, two are on the lower jaw and one is on the upper jaw.
Aquarium suitability: Although this is a nocturnal species, it can become diurnal. It is great for a community tank unless it is kept with very small fish. In this case it is not to be trusted and may eat them. Use fine gravel in the tank, as this fish likes to burrow.

Platydoras costatus

Common names: Chocolate catfish, Chocolate doradid, Striped raphael catfish
Range: South America, principally the Putumayo and Amazon rivers in eastern Peru
Size: 8½ inches (21.6 cm)
Description: The Chocolate catfish is easily identified with its horizontally striped livery of pale tan and chocolate brown to brownish-black. There are two bold stripes present. The first extends from the nape to the upper lobe of the tail. The second and lower one runs from the snout to the lower lobe of the tail. There is also a black bar through the dorsal fin.
Aquarium suitability: Provide plenty of hiding places in a well-planted aquarium. This species is quite intolerant of its own kind and fighting can ensue. However, little harm is done. Most foods are accepted and it will also graze on algae.

Pimelodidae (Long-whiskered catfish)

The body is naked and devoid of scales. An adipose fin is present and there are three pairs of barbels surrounding the mouth. These are very long, often reaching as far back as the tip of the anal fin or the base of the tail. There are no nasal barbels and the dorsal fin may or may not have spines. The body is elongate and the spine is well developed. Generally they are nocturnal creatures and some species will undertake extensive upstream spawning migrations. The family comprises 56 genera with about 300 species. The largest of these, *Brachyplatystoma filamentosum*, is known to grow to about 10 feet (3 meters). Almost all catfish in this family are predatory to a degree. In an aquarium they should only be kept with fish that are the same size or larger than themselves. Essentially, they swim at or near the bottom of slow-moving rivers, lakes, and streams of Central and South America, as far north as the southernmost regions of Mexico. Lundberg et al (1988) described a six-million-year-old fossil that appears to be identical to a living species. Three subfamilies are recognized: Rhamdiinae, Pimelodinae, and Pseudopimelodinae. Some authors recognize the latter taxon as a separate family.

Batrochoglanis raninus

Common names: Bumblebee catfish, Mottled catfish
Range: South America: Amazon River basin, Guyana, and French Guiana
Size: 8 inches (20 cm)
Description: The head is broad and depressed and the pectoral fins are large. The background body color is brownish-black and the head and nape are covered in small white spots. There are three broad orange-yellow bars present. The first of these bars arches over the back, behind the head, to the pectoral bases. The second extends vertically from the adipose fin to the anal fin and the third is across the base of the tail.
Aquarium suitability: This is a fish that can be kept in small groups. It should never be housed in the same tank as other fish that are smaller than 3 inches (7.6 cm) in length, because they will be considered food for this predator.

Perrunichthys perruno

Common name: Reticulated pimelodid
Range: South America, mainly the Rio Negro and its tributaries in southern Venezuela and Brazil
Size: 24 inches (61 cm)
Description: The body pattern resembles that of a tortoiseshell. There are large, dark brown, irregular-shaped blotches and spots over much of the body and fins. These are separated by thin tan to light brown lines. The median fins tend to be spotted rather than blotched, whereas it is the opposite with the paired fins.
Aquarium suitability: The tank should be at least 72 inches long (183 cm) or a minimum of 100 gallons (378 liters), with plenty of free-swimming space and rocky hiding places. If plants are being used, they should be large and well rooted in the substrate. Suitable tank-mates include arowana, large cichlids, and large characins. Generally, this catfish will only accept live food.

Phractocephalus hemioliopterus

Common name: Redtail catfish
Range: South America, in the Amazon and Rio Negro
Size: 40 inches (100 cm)
Description: The body coloration of this species can vary considerably with both age and between individuals. The upper half of the body is usually black or brownish-black and there is often black in the pelvic region. The rest of the lower body, throat, and belly is white or light cream. The tail is grayish-brown to bright orange-red and the fins are black, usually with white margins or leading edges.
Aquarium suitability: A large nocturnal predator, it is immobile by day, but at night it will cruise the tank in search of prey. This means that any other tank-mate is in danger if it is small enough to be eaten. As with the previous species, it should only be housed with other large fish such as large loricarids or cichlids.

Pimelodus blochii

Common names: Bloch's catfish, Fourline catfish
Range: South America; Gulf of Paria and Amazon, Essequibo, and Orinoco basins
Size: 13 inches (33 cm)
Description: In its natural habitat, fruit forms the greater part of this fish's diet. In this way, fruit seeds are subsequently voided and eventually form new plants once the rainy season has passed. The background body color is silvery white, darkening dorsally. There are four deep brown longitudinal stripes that extend from the opercular region to the tail. There is a small black saddle immediately in front of the dorsal spine.
Aquarium suitability: Although this fish can be initially quite shy, it soon settles into tank life. Provide plenty of rocks and caves in a well-planted aquarium and this fish will feel at home.

Pimelodus maculatus

Common name: Spotted pimelodus
Range: South America, principally the Paraguay River in Paraguay and the Rio Velhas in Brazil
Size: 10 inches (25 cm)
Description: This species has a large, squat head that is depressed. The base coloration is silvery-brown with a lighter-colored belly. The tail is deeply forked and there are three pairs of barbels around the mouth that are very long. The body and fins are covered in dark brown spots, which are larger dorsally.
Aquarium suitability: A very hardy catfish, but one that needs live food on a weekly basis to keep it healthy and happy. Earthworms are a good live food source. It will eat small fish at night, so it should only be kept with other large fish. The pectoral fins are serrated and can easily get caught in a net or pierce the skin, so care must be taken in handling this species.

Pimelodus pictus

Common names: Pictus cat, Spotted pimelodella, Angelicus catfish
Range: South America, Colombia, and Venezuela
Size: 8 inches (20 cm)
Description: The head is large and usually darker in color than the rest of the body, which is pale brownish-silver. There are large, transparent black spots on the body and fins. The caudal fin markings can often include black streaks and bars where the spots are fused together.
Aquarium suitability: A well-planted tank with a good filtration system is required. Use floating plants to diffuse the light so that this fish appears more often during the day. Hiding places of rocks and driftwood should be included. This is a hardy species that will accept most aquarium foods, but it should be given live food occasionally to keep it in condition.

Pseudoplatystoma fasciatum

Common names: Tiger shovelnose catfish, Barred sorubim
Range: South America, in the Rio Negro in Peru and the Rio Lebrijo in Venezuela
Size: 24 inches (61 cm)
Description: One of the major characteristics of this fish is its flat snout that is shaped like a duck's bill. The body is silver to silvery-brown and has a striking color pattern of wavy vertical black bars and spots. The median and paired fins are suffused with small black spots and the upper part of the head is also spotted. The belly is cream-colored or white.
Aquarium suitability: Juveniles are great aquarium fish. Unfortunately, they grow quite large and will eventually need a large show tank. Young specimens are not to be trusted with any fish smaller than they are. If the tank has plants, these should be well rooted or in sturdy pots.

Sorubim lima

Common names: Shovelnose catfish, Duckbill catfish
Range: South America, in the Amazon, Orinoco, Paraná, and Paranaíba river basins
Size: 20 inches (51 cm)
Description: The snout is bill-formed and the lower jaw recedes considerably. The head is broad and depressed and the body is elongate. There is a broad black stripe in the upper lateral region that extends from the snout to the caudal fin. Above this the dorsal region is tan to light brown. Below this stripe, the belly and throat are silvery-white. Adults often have a pinkish-red anal fin and tail.
Aquarium suitability: This fish makes a spectacular display when several individuals are kept in a very large show tank of 200 gallons or more. Their tank-mates can be large arowana, large cichlids, and giant gouramis.

Aspredinidae (Banjo catfish)

Although approximately 60 species have been described and assigned to this family, many of them should be considered as subjective junior synonyms of earlier described species. The family comprises 13 genera with about 35 valid species.

Banjo catfish are named because of their overall body shape. The depressed head is somewhat ovate and the body and caudal peduncle are slender, giving the fish a banjo shape when viewed from above. They are an unusual group of fish because their skin is keratinized and covered with tubercles. This skin is periodically shed like some amphibians and reptiles. There is no adipose fin and the opercular aperture is reduced to a mere slit. There is little or no locking mechanism on the dorsal spine and the tubercles on the body are arranged in longitudinal rows.

These fish can swim normally using undulations of the body and fins, but they are also capable of short bursts of speed along the substrate using a form of jet propulsion, when water is thrust from their gill slits. Most species in this family are omnivores and will feed on benthic invertebrates, terrestrial insects, plants, and aquatic debris. Quite a few species will also enter brackish water.

Dysichthys coracoideus

Common name: Banjo catfish
Range: South America, Amazon River system
Size: 6 inches (15 cm)
Description: The body color resembles that of a rotting or decaying leaf. This is its camouflage against predators. Overall, the body is mottled light and dark brown, usually with a black or dark brown dorsal fin that has a white trailing edge. Behind the pectoral fins there is a row of dark brown blotches. The dorsal region is often lighter in color than the belly. There are numerous lighter spots over much of the body, fins, and head.
Aquarium suitability: A strange fish that is more interesting than attractive. It can remain hidden for weeks and only appear when it is hungry. When they are housed with boisterous fish that are eager for food, this fish may go hungry because they are not the fastest movers at the feeding table.

Callichthyidae (Armored catfish)

The armored catfish have two rows of overlapping bony plates on each side and the swim bladder is encased in bone. The mouth is small and ventral, with one or two pairs of barbels and other short sensory processes on the upper and lower jaws. There is a spine present on the dorsal, adipose, and pectoral fins. Some species have the ability to move short distances across land using the air in the vascular hindgut. There are currently two subfamilies with eight genera and about 161 species. Of these, roughly 130 species belong to the genus *Corydoras*, the largest siluriform genus. The callichthyids are found throughout South America in a variety of habitats. Some are very small and make ideal candidates for a tropical freshwater aquarium. Others may reach a length of over 6 inches (15 cm) and even though they are still relatively small, the South American natives consider them food fish and will cook them within their bony-plated body armor. According to reports, they are very tasty. They are bottom-dwellers that live on detritus and other aquatic debris as well as microcrustaceans, other aquatic invertebrates, and terrestrial insects. Their habitat is usually an area where there is plenty of oxygen-rich water, from creeks to large rivers and flooded areas. However, they may also inhabit muddy or swampy areas where there is little or no oxygen.

Brochis splendens

Common names: Emerald catfish, Green brochis, Emerald cory, Short-bodied catfish

Range: South America, mainly the western Amazon basin

Size: 4 inches (20 cm)

Description: Similar in appearance to *Corydoras aeneus* at first glance, this species has a much deeper body and the head is more pointed. In addition, the scales are somewhat iridescent green or bluish-green.

Aquarium suitability: The Emerald catfish is ideal for a community tank. If it is kept with large, aggressive fish, it will not do very well.

Breeding information: Group spawning often occurs between several males and females. The eggs are laid on roots, leaves, and stone, or on the tank glass. Remove the parents and provide a constant water current. The fry hatch after five days.

Callichthys callichthys

Common name: Armored catfish

Range: South America, in brackish rivers and estuaries in Brazil, Guyana, Paraguay, Peru, and Venezuela

Size: 7 inches (18 cm)

Description: This is an unusual catfish that is fairly elongate with a flat belly and a broad head with small eyes. The body is brown to light tan and the body plates reflect the light, giving the fish a green or violet sheen. The head and dorsal region are sprinkled with numerous black spots and there are three pairs of barbels present around the snout.

Aquarium suitability: Ideally suited to a brackish-water tank, especially if it is planted with mangroves. This species is not suitable for a normal freshwater setup. It is a nocturnal catfish that is best kept with archerfish, monos, and scats.

Corydoras adolfoi

Common name: Adolf's cory

Range: South America, principally in the fast-moving tributaries of the Rio Negro in Peru

Size: 2½ inches (6 cm)

Description: This species is easily identified. There is a bold, black dorsal stripe present that extends from the first rays of the dorsal fin to the upper region of the caudal peduncle. The second black marking is a broad bar that runs from the nape, through the eye, to the throat. Behind the nape, between the origins of the two margins, there is a bold orange bar that extends to the operculum.

Aquarium suitability: A good community fish and one that is peaceful toward its tank-mates. It likes to school, so several can be kept in the same tank. Don't house it with large predators because it has no defense and will be eaten.

Corydoras aeneus

Common name: Bronze cory
Range: South America, from the Rio de la Plata in Venezuela; also known from the rivers of Trinidad
Size: 3 inches (7.6 cm)
Description: The body coloration is somewhat variable. Generally, the dorsal region and flanks are silvery-blue and the belly region varies from white to light brown. A triangular patch extending downward from the nape to the operculum is often pink in color, but may also be yellowish-brown. The fins are clear to bronze and the upper row of bony plates may have a greenish tinge in certain light.
Aquarium suitability: A peaceful community fish that is ideally suited to a tank containing discus, gouramis, tetras, and killifish. Most foods are eagerly eaten, including flake food, insect larvae, bloodworms, and whiteworms.

Corydoras agassizii

Common names: Silverstreak corydoras, Agassiz's corydoras
Range: South America, mainly Brazil and Peru
Size: 2¾ inches (7 cm)
Description: The snout below the eye is often blue and there is a dark bar above the eye that extends to the nape. There is a broad triangular bar of yellow that runs from the first dorsal ray to the operculum. Behind this is an indistinct blue bar. The body is suffused with regular horizontal rows of black spots that become vertical rows on the tail.
Aquarium suitability: A peaceful, undemanding fish that is recommended for novice aquarists. They can be kept in small groups and are great for a community tank. This species will not harm other fish. It is omnivorous and will feed on the waste food and detritus that has fallen to the substrate, thus combating tank pollution.

Corydoras arcuatus

Common names: Skunk cory, Arched cory
Range: South America in the Amazon tributaries
Size: 2 inches (5 cm)
Description: The body is stocky and the back is arched. The belly is flat and white in color. The median fins are colorless and the rest of the body is silver to tan. There is a prominent black stripe that curves subdorsally over the back from the snout, through the eye, to the lower lobe of the caudal fin.
Aquarium suitability: The Skunk cory is a bottom-dweller that likes plenty of shade and hiding places. It likes to forage for food in the substrate, so this should be soft and loose enough that it can feed correctly. Make sure enough food falls to the bottom.
Breeding information: Spawning is quite rare in an aquarium and is usually initiated by adding cooler water. Only 20–30 eggs are laid on plants and these should be removed to a rearing tank.

Corydoras atropersonatus

Common name: Fairy catfish
Range: South America: upper Amazon River basin, Ecuador, and Peru
Size: 1¼ inches (4.5 cm)
Description: Although this species is often confused with
C. sychri, it is much smaller and has a blunter snout. The spots are also much bolder. The body is silvery-white with small spots over much of the dorsal region and sides. There is a bold black bar through the eye and the fins are relatively clear of markings.
Aquarium suitability: A peaceful fish, which is ideal for a community tank containing tetras and the like. The substrate should be fine and not sharp-edged in any way, otherwise barbel damage will ensue. It is best kept in small groups of its own kind in a medium to large show tank with other fish.

Corydoras barbatus

Common names: Giant cory, Bearded catfish, Banded catfish, Barbatus catfish
Range: South America, in coastal rivers and streams from Rio de Janeiro to São Paulo
Size: 5 inches (12.7 cm)
Description: This species is variable in color and markings. Generally, the elongated body is tan to light brown and the fins are spotted with deep brown. Numerous dark spots adorn the head and anterior half of the body. These are often so close together that they form a reticulated pattern. The belly is white and there is often a broad brown stripe from the midbody region to the tail.
Aquarium suitability: A peaceful community fish that is quite hardy. It is the largest species in this genus and needs plenty of hiding places. Most aquarium foods are accepted.

Corydoras hastatus

Common names: Dwarf corydoras, Pygmy corydoras, Tail spot pygmy catfish
Range: South America, in the tributaries of the Paraguay and Amazon rivers
Size: 1 inch (2.5 cm)
Description: This species is easy to identify. It is a small fish with a prominent arrowhead marking on the caudal peduncle and a white V-shaped (sometimes U-shaped) marking behind this on the tail. The body is translucent with a narrow stripe mid-laterally, and the head is often tan.
Aquarium suitability: A tiny species that should be kept in small schools along with peaceful tank-mates. Most foods are accepted, including flake, brine shrimp, whiteworm, and insect larvae. Provide plenty of hiding places in a tank containing broad-leaved plants. It is a mid-water swimmer that likes plenty of water flow.

Corydoras incolicana

Common name: Incolicana cory
Range: South America, in the Rio Inçana and the upper Rio Negro in Brazil
Size: 2½ inches (6 cm)
Description: The nape is dark and there is a broad pinkish-yellow band present behind the operculum. The dorsal and caudal fins are sprinkled with black spots and flecks, as is much of the body and flanks. The belly and pelvic fins are white and the snout often contains flecks of gold.
Aquarium suitability: This is a shy and nonaggressive fish that is best kept in small groups along with other peaceful tank-mates. It will accept most foods, including whiteworms, insect larvae, tubifex, and brine shrimp, along with flake and frozen foods.

Corydoras julii

Common name: Leopard corydoras
Range: South America: the Rio Negro and Paranaíba river basins
Size: 2¾ inches (6.5 cm)
Description: The Leopard corydoras is very similar in appearance to *C. trilineatus* and is often confused with this species. However, there are notable differences. This species has distinct spots on the head that are small and not fused together. It is also somewhat smaller than *C. trilineatus* as an adult.
Aquarium suitability: For the best results in an aquarium, this species should be kept in small groups of six or more. It is an interesting fish that will literally go to sleep on a rock with its companions during the day. Later, as if by command, one will begin to swim and go back to work foraging for food and its companions will follow. A great fish for a community setup.

Corydoras melanistius

Common name: Bluespotted corydoras
Range: South America, in the coastal rivers of the Guianas
Size: 2 inches (5 cm)
Description: An attractive catfish, it has a black vertical bar through the eye and a second black bar that is oblique and runs from the dorsal fin to the middle of the operculum. The head has a gold sheen and the rest of the body is covered in fine spots that may give a bluish, shimmering effect in certain light conditions.
Aquarium suitability: A great community fish, but make sure that several are kept together. This species hates being alone.
Breeding information: About 70 or 80 eggs are laid after cooler water is added to the breeding tank. Most of these will be laid on the glass sides or on flat rock surfaces. Remove the parents after spawning. Eggs hatch after four days and the fry are free-swimming two days later.

Corydoras melini

Common name: Bandit corydoras
Range: South America: the upper Negro and Meta river basins
Size: 2 inches (5 cm)
Description: An oblique black bar is present that extends from the dorsal fin to the lower part of the caudal peduncle. There is also an equally bold bar that runs from the nape, through the eye, to the throat. The rest of the body color is silvery-white, often with a pinkish tinge. The opercular region usually has a gold sheen.
Aquarium suitability: This species can be quite shy initially. If it is kept in small groups of three or more, it will settle down to aquarium life much more quickly. Most *Corydoras* species like to be in the company of their own kind, so if you intend to buy this fish, buy more than one.

Corydoras metae

Common name: Masked corydoras
Range: South America, in the Meta River basin
Size: 2 inches (5 cm)
Description: Although this is quite a small species, it is a very attractive fish. The markings are bold and the background body color can be either shimmering gold or silver. There is a bold black bar through the eye and a broad black stripe is present that extends from the anterior base of the dorsal fin, through the base of the adipose fin, to the caudal peduncle.
Aquarium suitability: Another peaceful member of this genus that is recommended for novice aquarists. They can be kept in small groups and are great for a community tank. This species will not harm other fish and has a placid nature. It is omnivorous and will feed on the waste food and detritus that has fallen to the substrate.

Corydoras paleatus

Common names: Peppered corydoras, Paleatus cory
Range: South America, along the river margins of eastern Brazil to the Rio de la Plata basin
Size: 4 inches (10 cm)
Description: The belly color of this species can vary from white to pinkish-orange. The silver to orange-brown body is covered in numerous dark spots and patches that vary from dark brown to black.
Aquarium suitability: A peaceful fish ideal for a community tank containing tetras and similar. The substrate should be fine and not sharp-edged in any way to avoid barbel damage. It is best kept in small groups in a medium show tank with other fish.
Breeding information: The females are usually larger than the males. Adding cooler water induces spawning, and the eggs are laid in Java moss or similar plants.

Corydorus punctatus

Common names: Spotfin corydoras, Spotted cory
Range: South America; principally found in Compagnie Creek, which is a tributary of the Surinam River
Size: 2 inches (5 cm)
Description: The upper two-thirds of the silvery-white body is covered in small black spots that become somewhat reticulated toward the nape. The fins are also spotted but those on the caudal fin are arranged in vertical rows, giving the impression of narrow bars. There is a large black blotch at the apex of the dorsal fin.
Aquarium suitability: Although this is one of the smaller of the *Corydoras* species, it is very attractive and endearing. Small groups make delightful additions to a community tank and will accept most foods that are offered.

Corydoras panda

Common names: Panda catfish, Panda cory
Range: South America, in slow-moving tributaries of the Peruvian Amazon, particularly the Ucayali River
Size: 2 inches (5 cm)
Description: The body color varies from white to pale bronze. A bold black bar is present from the nape, through the eye, to the cheek. The fins are white or pale tan with the exception of the dorsal fin, which is black.
Aquarium suitability: A very peaceful fish that should be kept in small groups of four or five in a community setup. Use fine gravel as a base medium and feed on a variety of aquarium foods.
Breeding information: Females are larger, plumper, and less colorful than the males. Breeding this species is not easy. The small number of eggs are laid in Java moss or on a flat surface.

Corydoras pygmaeus

Common name: Pygmy corydoras
Range: South America; in large aggregations mainly in the Rio Madeira and its tributaries in Brazil
Size: 1 inch (2.5 cm)
Description: The body is white to tan and there is a short stripe below the pectoral fins that extends to the base of the anal fin. A bold black stripe runs from the snout to the tail, making this fish easy to identify.
Aquarium suitability: A peaceful community fish that should be kept in small groups where possible. Single specimens do not do well in an aquarium.
Breeding information: This is quite an easy species to breed in low-populated tanks. The eggs are laid on broad-leaved plants and the male will pick out the infertile eggs and remove them. Once the fry hatch, they can be fed on liquid fry food.

Corydoras rabauti

Common names: Rust corydoras, Rabaut's cory, Rusty cory
Range: South America, in various rivers and tributaries throughout Brazil and Peru
Size: 2¼ inches (5.5 cm)
Description: *Corydoras rabauti* can easily be confused with several other species from this genus. However, this fish is distinct because it lacks the bar through the eye and the broad and oblique black stripe extends subdorsally from the nape to the middle of the caudal peduncle.
Aquarium suitability: This is another good addition to a community aquarium. A small group of these can turn out to be real characters in a tank! They are always there at feeding time and will often encourage other, newer additions to feed on aquarium food because of their eagerness to take any food that is offered to them.

Corydoras reticulatus

Common names: Network catfish, Reticulated catfish
Range: South America, principally along the banks of slow-moving rivers in Iquitos, Peru
Size: 2¾ inches (7 cm)
Description: As with all *Corydoras* species, the body is deep and squat, with an arched back. The background coloration of the body is silver to light tan. The spots covering much of the body and fins are fused together and form reticulated lines and streaks over the body and head. The caudal fin has a similar pattern of spots fused to form narrow bars, and there is a large white-margined black spot present at the apex of the dorsal fin.
Aquarium suitability: The Reticulated catfish is particularly undemanding in its requirements and is an ideal fish for the novice aquarist. It is a peaceful community fish that can be kept with barbs, danios, small tetras, and gouramis.

Corydoras robineae

Common name: Bannertail catfish, Mrs. Schwartz's cory
Range: South America, in the Rio Negro, Brazil
Size: 2½ inches (6 cm)
Description: This is currently the only known *Corydoras* catfish with a black and white horizontally striped "flag tail." The rest of the body carries a series of spots and horizontal stripes against a background coloration of silvery-white.
Aquarium suitability: This is a peaceful fish that should be kept in groups of three or more in a tank containing fine gravel. It requires good water quality and a varied diet of fresh and flake food. Whiteworms are a real treat for most armored catfish.
Breeding information: Very hard to breed in captivity. Lower the breeding aquarium temperature to 65°F to induce spawning after conditioning the pair at 77 °F for seven days. They usually spawn at night on the aquarium glass or other flat surfaces.

Corydoras schwartzi

Common name: Schwartz's catfish
Range: South America, in the Rio Purus basin
Size: 2 inches (5 cm)
Description: *Corydoras schwartzi* has a series of spots that form vertical bars in the caudal region and horizontal rows of stripes along the body. There is a broad black bar present that runs from the nape to the cheek. The operculum is streaked with gold and the background body coloration is silvery-white.
Aquarium suitability: Keep in small groups of three to five for the best results. This is a peaceful catfish that is ideal for any community setup. Feed a varied diet of dried foods and fresh protein such as whiteworms, *Daphnia*, and bloodworms.
Breeding information: The female is larger than the male. A well-planted tank is a prerequisite for any breeding success.

Corydoras seussi

Common name: Seuss's cory
Range: South America, principally the Mamoré River basin
Size: 2½ inches (6 cm)
Description: The first ray of the dorsal fin is orange in color. The head is brown and the sides of the body are grayish-black. The tail is adorned with spots that are arranged into vertical bars and the pectoral and pelvic fins are orange in color.
Aquarium suitability: Providing good water quality and fine gravel will keep this fish happy. Failure to do this will result in barbel abrasion and poor health. Feed a varied diet and keep in a community setup in small groups of three or more for the best results. A well-planted aquarium is preferred to one that is sparsely planted.
Breeding information: Current information suggests that this species has not yet been bred in captivity.

Corydoras sterbai

Common name: Sterba's cory
Range: South America: Rio Guaporé and Mato Grosso, Brazil
Size: 2½ inches (6 cm)
Description: The head is dome-shaped and the squat body has an arched back, like most members of the genus. The head is dark and covered with light spots and blotches. The body can be silver or white, sometimes with a deep-bluish tinge, and the spots are arranged in narrow horizontal stripes along the sides. The caudal fin has spots that form vertical bars.
Aquarium suitability: The tank should have fine sand or rounded gravel so that this fish does not suffer from barbel degeneration. Bogwood and plants are ideal to provide hiding places. Feed a varied diet and keep in small aggregations for the best results. This is quite an easy fish to keep.

Corydoras trilineatus

Common names: Three line cory, Threestripe corydoras
Range: South America, in the Ambiyacu and Ucayali rivers in Peru
Size: 2¾ inches (7.3 cm)
Description: All *Corydoras* species have two rows of bony plates that cover each side of the fish, and this species is no exception. The body is speckled with dark spots that are brownish-black or deep black in color. The median fins are beige to light bronze in color and the upper portion of the dorsal fin is black. The spots on the caudal fin are frequently fused together to form irregular vertical bands.
Aquarium suitability: An undemanding species that will take most foods that are offered. This makes it an ideal fish for the beginner. It can be kept with most nonaggressive fish, including tetras, livebearers, danios, and gouramis.

Dianema longibarbus

Common name: Porthole catfish
Range: South America: the Rio Negro, in the region of Manaus, and also in slow-moving tributaries of the Peruvian Amazon
Size: 4 inches (10 cm)
Description: The background body coloration is silver to light brown, depending on the age of the fish. There are two rows of bony plates on the sides and the belly is silvery-white. Small dark brown spots cover much of the body and head, and the barbels are more elongated than those of the *Corydoras* genus.
Aquarium suitability: Provide a tank with strong filtration that develops little or no current for the best results. This species does not like strong water movement. A shady aquarium with floating plants to block out much of the light is preferred. This is a nocturnal fish that can become diurnal after a period of time. Most aquarium foods are accepted.

Loricariidae
(Suckermouth armored catfish)

Aquarists revere this family of unusual fish to the point of creating entire Web sites dealing only with these species. Their popularity is founded on the individual characteristics that these fish possess. Despite their ungainly and somewhat grotesque appearance, catfish from this family have a way of endearing themselves to hobbyists.

This may sound a bit too enthusiastic in the description of this family, but it is not so. They are simply fascinating and, if this does not sound believable, the reader is advised to purchase one and put it in a community aquarium—then they will know what it means to keep this fish in a captive environment. They are one of the mainstays of the freshwater aquarium hobby. Of course, one of their most endearing characteristics is that they will eat algae and help clean up the aquarium.

The family comprises some 80 genera with about 695 species. The mouth is situated ventrally and may be with or without conspicuous barbels. If there is an adipose fin present, it usually has an anterior spine. The body is generally elongate and has bony plates. These fish are found in swift-flowing streams and rivers in Central and South America, principally Panama and Costa Rica.

Ancistrus hoplogenys

Common names: Blueseam pleco, Whitefin pleco
Range: South America, in the Amazon, Essequibo, and Paraguay river basins
Size: 6¼ inches (15.8 cm)
Description: Juveniles sometimes have fine white spots over much of the body and head. At this stage, the mouth is surrounded with barbels that usually recede with age. Adult fish have a dark brown to deep black body with distinct bluish-white margins to the dorsal and caudal fins.
Aquarium suitability: This is a nocturnal species that is ideal for a cichlid tank. It is a peaceful fish that requires no special care once it has settled in. The tank should be well planted, with plenty of hiding places made up of rocks and driftwood.
Breeding information: The 100 or so eggs are laid in caves or holes in the substrate. The male guards them for six to seven days.

Ancistrus temminckii

Common name: Bristlenose plecostomus
Range: South America: shallow pools and fast-flowing tributaries of the Saramacca, Surinam, and Maroni river basins
Size: 5 inches (12.7 cm)
Description: In adults, the body is dark brown to black and the large fins are light beige in color. Numerous spots cover much of the body and head and these are light to dark brown. The fins, particularly the dorsal and caudal fins, are covered in dark spots. There is an array of tentacle-like antennae present on the upper surface of the snout that extend toward the nape.
Aquarium suitability: A peaceful fish that is ideal for a community tank. It should be provided with lots of hiding places and plenty of free-swimming space. This fish is a great character once it has settled down to aquarium life. Plenty of water flow should be provided along with a varied diet.

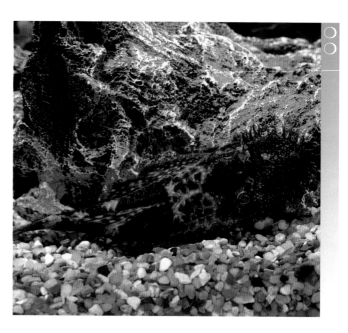

Dasyloricaria filamentosa

Common name: Whiptail
Range: South America, in small creeks and streams of the Rio Magdalena, Colombia
Size: 24 inches (61 cm)
Description: The mouth is ventral and shaped like a suction cup. This catfish has an elongated body and several rows of bony plates. The coloration is generally light tan with many brown and black blotches and spots over much of the body and fins. There are several dark vertical bands present from behind the dorsal fin to the tail.
Aquarium suitability: Very sensitive to changes in water quality and medications. This is a peaceful species that makes a good community fish if it is kept with others of a similar nature.
Breeding information: Very difficult to breed in captivity because females do not spawn very often.

Dekeyseria pulcher

Common names: Clown pleco, Tiger plecostomus
Range: South America: in the Canal Casiquiare basin and the upper Negro and Orinoco rivers
Size: 4 inches (10 cm)
Description: As with the previous species, the mouth is shaped like a suction cup. The large head is broad and flat and the body is covered in large bony plates. The coloration is particularly striking, consisting of vertical bands of contrasting black and white over much of the body and fins. There are two barbels located at the ventrally situated mouth.
Aquarium suitability: This is a peaceful community fish that feeds on excess algae in the aquarium. It is quite easy to care for if there is enough algae there for it to eat. If not, it should be fed on frozen or tablet-form greenstuff foods. They need a large tank because of their ultimate size, plus hiding places.

Farlowella acus

Common names: Needle catfish, Twig catfish
Range: South America, in southern tributaries of the Amazon River system
Size: 10 inches (25 cm)
Description: The body is very elongate and arrowlike, with large fins and tail. The background body coloration can be quite varied but it is generally light tan to beige. The barbels are rudimentary and there is a broad black stripe present that extends from the snout midlaterally to the caudal fin. The pectoral and pelvic fins are tan with black or dark brown spots.
Aquarium suitability: Try to keep in pairs rather than single individuals; these fare better in aquariums. This species can be a picky eater if there is not a great deal of algae in the tank. It is a nocturnal feeder, so it should be fed late in the evening on algae flake. Do not feed too much, as this species is likely to overeat.

Glyptoperichthys gibbiceps

Common names: Sailfin plecostomus, Leopard pleco
Range: South America in the middle and upper Amazon and Orinoco basins
Size: 20 inches (51 cm)
Description: One of the most significant identifying features of this fish is its very high dorsal fin. The background body color is cream to light brown. Most of the body and fins are covered with large brown or black spots that often fuse together to produce an almost continuous dark body color. However, these fins are more lightly spotted.
Aquarium suitability: The Leopard pleco is a nocturnal species that feeds predominantly on algae.
Breeding information: Unfortunately, this fish has never been bred under aquarium conditions. However, they are commercially bred in fishponds in Florida and Southeast Asia.

Hypancistrus zebra

Common name: Zebra pleco
Range: South America, on rocky substrates in fast-flowing areas of the Rio Xingu in Brazil
Size: 3½ inches (8.9 cm)
Description: It is said that no two specimens of this species are alike in coloration. Therefore, a generalization must be used to describe this fish. Basically, the background body color is white to silver. Overlaying this is a series of bold stripes that extend onto the head and fins in a distinctive pattern.
Aquarium suitability: The Zebra pleco is one of the most strikingly attractive fish in the freshwater aquarium hobby. It is a small, shy fish that needs peaceful tank-mates and other bottom-dwellers that will not compete for food. Plenty of hiding places should be provided, as this is a seminocturnal fish. Feed on brine shrimp, chopped zucchini, lettuce, and spinach.

Hypostomus plecostomus

Common names: Plecostomus, Suckermouth catfish, Pleco
Range: South America: Venezuela in the Rio del Plata, Trinidad, and southern Brazil in fast-flowing rivers and streams
Size: 24 inches (60 cm)
Description: Only one pair of barbels are present on this large fish. Juveniles are attractive, with a body coloration that varies quite considerably. Generally, the body color is light tan to beige with numerous dark spots or blotches over much of the body and fins. The spotted dorsal fin is very high when it is erected and makes this species easy to identify.
Aquarium suitability: Small specimens are great for a moderately sized community setup. However, once they grow, they should be transferred to a larger aquarium where they have enough free-swimming space. Feed on a varied diet that includes plenty of greenstuff. This is an easy fish to keep.

Hypostomus punctatus

Common names: Common pleco, Suckermouth catfish
Range: South America, in fast-flowing rivers and coastal drainages of southeastern Brazil
Size: 12 inches (30 cm)
Description: Juveniles, such as the one shown here, have light and dark brown spots with a pale background body color. As the fish grows, the lighter spots recede and the body color changes to orange-brown with deep brown spots. The spots can form bands and stripes on the fins, particularly the caudal fin.
Aquarium suitability: An excellent fish for a community aquarium and entirely suitable for the beginner once the tank is mature. It is a nocturnal species but older specimens often become diurnal. This fish will even greet its owner at feeding time by swimming to the front glass to wait for food. In ideal conditions, this fish will often take food from its owner's hand.

Leporacanthicus galaxias

Common names: Galaxy pleco, Vampire pleco
Range: South America, in the tributaries of the lower Amazon, Madeira, Tocantins, and Guamá rivers
Size: 8¼ inches (21 cm)
Description: Males have a larger dorsal fin and the coloration is generally more pronounced. The body is deep brown to brownish black and is covered in fine spots that may be white, light yellow, or orange. Some specimens from the Ventuari River basin in the upper Orinoco have a white or yellow tail margin.
Aquarium suitability: Most aquarium foods are accepted once this fish has settled in. In the wild it is found in fast-flowing streams and rapids. Because of this, it should be housed in a tank that has a strong water flow. It is an ideal community fish that can be kept with cichlids and tetras alike.

Liposarcus anisitsi

Common name: Snow king plecostomus
Range: South America, in a variety of habitats in the Paraguay River system of Brazil and Paraguay
Size: 24 inches (60 cm)
Description: In the dry season in its natural habitat, this fish will live in burrows and wait, without water, until the rains return. It is an amazing fish that has a broad head and a relatively slender body. The general coloration is light gray to white with a profusion of dark spots over much of the body, head, and fins.
Aquarium suitability: Small tanks are only suitable for fish that are under 5 inches (13 cm) in length. After that, they need to be removed to larger aquariums. They will eat small fish, so make sure that this species is housed with tank-mates that are large enough to defend themselves. Ideal species would be cichlids, large characins, and other large catfish.

Otocinclus affinis

Common names: Midget catfish, Golden otocinclus, Dwarf otocinclus, Midget sucker catfish
Range: South America, in rivers around Rio de Janeiro, Brazil
Size: 1½ inches (3.8 cm)
Description: Although this is a small fish, it is quite attractive. The median fins are clear of color and the body is white or pale cream. A bold black stripe runs from the snout to the tail, often ending in a blotch on the caudal peduncle.
Aquarium suitability: This species is inclined to be a plant-eater if it does not get enough greenstuff in its diet, or if there is insufficient algae available. It is a peaceful community fish.
Breeding information: Add cooler water to induce spawning. Roughly 20–40 eggs are laid on leaves and the glass walls of the tank. Remove the parents after spawning and slowly raise the water temperature back to normal.

Panaque maccus

Common name: Clown pleco
Range: South America, in the Apuré and Caroni river basins
Size: 4½ inches (11.5 cm)
Description: Often confused with *Peckoltia vittatus*, which has broad white bands and narrower dark ones. The light stripes of the Clown pleco are white to pale yellow. The fins are striped and the body color varies from brown to grayish-black. The head is adorned with light-colored spots and bars.
Aquarium suitability: A great fish for a community tank and one that is peaceful and friendly. Most "off the shelf" foods are eagerly accepted once it has overcome its initial shyness. This diet should be supplemented with fresh and frozen foods such as brine shrimp, whiteworms, and bloodworms. The aquarium should be well planted with an assortment of suitable hiding places.

Panaque albomaculatus

Common names: Orange spot pleco, Mustard spot pleco
Range: South America, in the fast-flowing upper reaches of the Marañon, Napo, and Ucayali rivers
Size: 5 inches (12.7 cm)
Description: This is an attractive species with a high dorsal fin. The background body color varies from chocolate brown to deep black. The head, body, and fins are covered in small white, yellow, or pale orange spots that can vary greatly in number. The pelvic and pectoral fins are large and the tail is moderately forked.
Aquarium suitability: Provide plenty of hiding places in rocks and driftwood for the best results. This is a good community fish that will live peacefully with most cichlids and other aggressive fish. Feed on sinking pellets, flake, and wormlike foods.

Panaque nigrolineatus

Common names: Royal plecostomus, Royal panaque, Black-lined panaque
Range: South America, mainly from the Putumayo River in southern Colombia
Size: 16 inches (40.7 cm)
Description: This is an amazing catfish with bright red eyes. The body is deep chocolate brown with numerous black wavy stripes through the body, fins, and head. The dorsal fin is sail-like and held very high and the mouth is shaped to form a sucker. In most specimens, there is a broad white bar across the caudal peduncle and a second across the base of the tail.
Aquarium suitability: Provide a strong water current and plenty of places to hide among rocks and driftwood. This is a nocturnal species that is aggressive toward its own kind but generally peaceful to other community fish.

Sturisoma aureum

Common names: Giant whiptail, Golden whiptail
Range: South America: Colombia, in the upper reaches of the
Rio Magdalena
Size: 8 inches (20 cm)
Description: Juveniles of this and other *Sturisoma* species are
difficult to distinguish from one another because of their similar
colors. This species is the smallest member of the genus. The
background body color is pale brown and has numerous fine
spots. A bold and uneven black stripe extends from the snout
to the midbody, where it breaks into fused or individual spots
toward the tail. In adults, the upper lobe of the caudal fin
extends into a long filament.
Aquarium suitability: Although this fish is not suitable for the
complete novice, it is relatively easy to keep and feed. All forms
of algae are its main diet but other foods are also accepted.

Panaque suttonorum

Common names: Blue-eyed plecostomus, Blue-eyed panaque
Range: South America, principally in Colombia in small, swift-
flowing rivers and streams
Size: 18 inches (45.7 cm)
Description: Despite the overall lack of color, this is an extremely
attractive fish. Much of the body is covered in bony plates and
the general body coloration is black. The iris of the eye is bright
blue and the mouth is ventral and formed into a suckerlike
mechanism. The striking features of this species are the high
dorsal fin and the contrast of the black body with blue eyes.
Aquarium suitability: This catfish is very peaceful toward other
tank inhabitants and makes an ideal aquarium fish. It is a
nocturnal fish, so feed it toward the evening rather than in the
middle of the day. This way, it will not die of malnutrition. It is
a real character in the aquarium once it has settled in.

Order: Gymnotiformes

Within this order there are 31 genera with 150
valid species; another 33 species have not yet been
described. No doubt these figures will increase as more
understanding is gained from this group. Nelson (1994)
describes this order as having six families. However, the
monospecific family Electrophoridae is now vacant and
its single species, the electric eel (Electrophorus electricus),
has recently been placed within the family Gymnotidae.
There are five families, the other four being Apteronotidae,
Hypopomidae, Rhamphichthyidae, and Sternopygidae.
Species from three of these families will be discussed in
greater detail later.

Generally, the body form of these fish is eel-like,
sometimes tubular, but without a pelvic girdle. The dorsal
fin is completely absent and the anal fin is very long. This
is often used in a rippling manner to create forward and
backward motion. There are restricted gill openings and
electric organs are present in most species. These may be
myogenic or neurogenic. They are used to stun prey when
they are myogenic, or to emit low- to high-frequency
electrical tones and charges for defense in the case of the
neurogenic organs.

Apteronotidae (Ghost knifefish)

Apteronotids are species that are easily recognized. They
are the only South American knifefish that have a caudal
fin, although in most cases it is rudimentary. The eye is

usually very small and there is a fleshy longitudinal strip present dorsally that is attached to the posterodorsal midline.

They also have a high-frequency neurogenic organ that emits warning tones up to 750 Hz in adults. The family comprises some 13 genera currently with 52 valid species. At the time of writing, another 12 new species are being prepared for publication. It is expected that the total number of valid species will greatly increase over the next few years.

The body is rounded, or partially so, and the anal fin is very long. They are found in deep river channels and in floodplains. One species is known to eat freshwater sponges from submerged tree trunks and other wooden debris. Only two species are regularly imported for the aquarium trade and this is definitely a fish best left to the experienced aquarist.

Apteronotus albifrons

Common names: Black ghost knifefish, Ghost knifefish
Range: South America, in the Amazon and Paraguay rivers in Brazil, Ecuador, Guyana, and Peru
Size: 19 inches (48.3 cm)
Description: The overall body coloration is velvet-black. The anal fin is very long and the caudal fin is rudimentary. There are two white bands present. The first of these is at the base of the anal fin and extends dorsally. The second band is narrower and is on the caudal peduncle.
Aquarium suitability: A tank measuring at least 40 inches (152 cm) is the minimum requirement for keeping this fish. As an adult, it will require a much larger tank. Provide plenty of hiding places with thoughtful placing of rocks and driftwood. Do not worry if the Black ghost knifefish lies on its side—this is its natural resting posture.

Sternarchella schotti

Common names: Brown ghost knifefish, Little-scale knifefish
Range: South America: this species is widespread throughout the Amazon River basin
Size: 16 inches (40 cm)
Description: Quite an attractive and interesting species that has an elongate body with a short snout. It is an easy fish to identify because the body is deep brown to black with a narrow white dorsal stripe that extends from the tip of the snout to the tail. The tail is also tipped with white.
Aquarium suitability: Do not be alarmed if this fish lies down on its side at the bottom of the aquarium—it is a natural trait. It is a good community fish, but one that is not to be trusted with bite-sized tank-mates. Although this is quite a hardy species, it should be provided with a varied diet that includes live food such as bloodworms, whiteworms, *Daphnia*, and insect larvae.

Gymnotidae (Naked-back knifefish)

Currently there are 28 extant species from two genera. They are restricted to freshwater areas of Central and South America. The body is eel-like and either strongly compressed laterally or rounded. The anus is situated behind the throat and the anal fin extends from below the pectoral fins to the tip of the tail, where it ends in a point. The dorsal fin, pelvic girdle, and pelvic fins are completely absent. These are nocturnal species that are capable of giving off a weak electrical charge. They usually inhabit quieter and deeper water of large rivers and swamps. In fast-flowing streams they will often bury themselves in the substrate. Adult fish do not guard their eggs once laid. Recently, the family Electrophoridae, with its single species, *Electrophorus electricus*, has been included. This species is known as the Electric knifefish.

Hypopygus lepturus

Common name: Slender tail knifefish
Range: South America, in the Amazon and Orinoco river systems and the Guianas
Size: 4 inches (10 cm)
Description: The head and anterior part of the body is rounded and the rest of the body is laterally compressed. The background body color is light brown to yellow-tan, with numerous dark brown wavy bands that narrow ventrally. It is found in sandy areas of slow-moving waters and swamps and will bury itself in the substrate to survive if they dry out.
Aquarium suitability: Provide plenty of floating plants to diffuse the aquarium lighting. This fish needs a tank with plenty of hiding places. It is a peaceful fish with tank-mates of a similar size but small tetras may be considered food. Generally it will not tolerate its own kind or similar species.

Sternopygidae (Glass knifefish)

Glass knifefish are restricted to the humid neotropics of South America, from the Rio Tuira in Panama to the Rio de la Plata of Argentina. The family comprises a total of six genera with 30 valid species. However, this is expected to rise over the next couple of years. Already there are another 11 species that are in manuscript preparation before being announced to the zoological world. This would then bring the total number of species to 41, with many more expected as research continues.

Like all knifefish, the body is culteriform (knife-shaped) with an elongate, laterally compressed body and a long anal fin that is used for locomotion. In most species, the eye is larger in diameter than other South American knifefish. They have a variety of habitats, from deep river channels, floodplains, mountain rivers, and small streams.

Usually their diet consists of small invertebrates and other aquatic life, such as small fish fry, that they find among the roots of aquatic plants. They cannot be considered as a food fish and commercially remain only of interest to the aquarium hobby.

Eigenmannia virescens

Common names: Glass knifefish, Green knifefish
Range: South America, in the Amazon basin on floodplains and in slower-moving rivers and creeks
Size: 18 inches (46 cm), though females are considerably smaller
Description: *Eigenmannia virescens* is an interesting fish because its body is translucent and the bone structure can be clearly seen when it is viewed from the side. Two fine black stripes are present along the body. One is a midlateral stripe that extends from the operculum to the tail, the other is situated just below this and runs from behind the pectoral base toward the tail, where it becomes indistinct. The head is dark beige to brown.
Aquarium suitability: This fish can be kept in small groups that make an attractive display in a community tank. It is a peaceful species so long as its tank-mates are not small enough to eat. Combine them with catfish, small cichlids, and angelfish.

Order: Atheriniformes

Generally, fish of this order have two distinct dorsal fins and a weak or absent lateral line. The anterior dorsal fin usually has a weak spine and most species have deciduous cycloid scales. The pelvic fins may be thoracic, subabdominal, or abdominal. The order encompasses eight families, 47 genera, and about 285 species. Many authors include most of the families noted here within the order Cyprinodontiformes. I follow Nelson (1994) and place the following families in the Atheriniformes taxon: Bedotiidae (Madagascar rainbowfish), Melanotaeniidae (Rainbowfish), Pseudomugilidae (Blue eyes), Atheriniformes (Silversides), Notocheiridae (Surf sardines), Telmatherinidae (Celebes rainbowfish), Dentatherinidae (Tusked silversides), and Phallostethidae (Priapiumfish). This is reasoned by four of the derived common characters of Cyprinodontiformes and Beloniformes, which should be recognized as sister groups of Antheriniformes. These are: second infraorbital bone absent, first epibranchial with expanded base, second and third epibranchials reduced in size, and first pharyngobranchial completely absent. There is also an absence of spines in the fins and only one dorsal fin is present. Fossil records of this group date back 45 million years to the middle Eocene period.

Bedotiidae (Madagascar rainbowfish)

Madagascar rainbowfish differ from the silversides and other rainbowfish because of their bone structure. In the *Bedotiidae*, the last six or seven caudal vertebrae are thickened and the medial process of the pelvic girdle is asymmetrical. There are one or two other minor differences, including the presence of a single elongate infraorbital bone behind the lachrymal. Many authors recognize this family as a subfamily of Melanotaeniidae. There are two genera: *Bedotia* with four species and *Rheocles* (Rheocloides) with about six species. All of them inhabit freshwater areas of Madagascar, particularly the Manantenina, Maningory, and Anjozorobe, and they are also found in Lake Alotra and in the tributaries of Betsikiboba on the western slopes of Madagascar. The adult fish do not guard their eggs.

Some species of *Rheocles*, such as *Rheocles sikorae*, were thought to be extinct. Recently, though, specimens have been collected from five forest stream areas near the town of Marolamba, Madagascar. Although the species is well known to local residents, in view of its apparently restricted current range, it has been placed on an international list of endangered species and is not imported for the aquarium trade.

Bedotia geayi

Common names: Madagascar rainbowfish, Red-tailed silverside
Range: Madagascar, in mountain streams
Size: 6 inches (15 cm)
Description: The body is elongate and moderately compressed laterally. Two horizontal, dark bluish stripes are present. The first of these is bold and extends from the snout to the caudal peduncle, whereas the second is less distinct and runs from the belly along the anal fin base. The first dorsal fin is short and often colorless. The second dorsal has a black submarginal stripe. The anal and caudal fins also have black submarginal stripes.
Aquarium suitability: This is a schooling fish that is ideal for a community tank. Provide plenty of free-swimming space and a varied diet of *Artemia*, *Daphnia*, insect larvae, chopped spinach, and flake food.

Melanotaeniidae (Rainbowfish)

The family is comprised of fish that are found in northern and eastern Australia, Papua New Guinea, and various surrounding islands. There are six genera encompassing some 53 valid species. The genera are *Cairnsichthys*, *Chilatherina*, *Glossolepis*, *Iriatherina*, *Melanotaenia*, and *Rhadinocentrus*. Generally, the body is elongate and laterally compressed. There are two dorsal fins present. The first of these has three to seven spines, and the second has 10–30 soft rays. The lateral line is weak or completely absent. The posterior pelvic ray is attached to the abdomen along its entire length. Rainbowfish are found mostly in freshwater, although some species will enter brackish water for at least part of their lives. As a rule, the females are less colorful than the males and have a tendency to be more uniform in color.

Chilatherina bleheri

Common name: Bleher's rainbowfish
Range: Indonesia; known only from Lake Holmes in the Mamberamo River system of West Papua
Size: 4¾ inches (12 cm)
Description: The back is light olive and the sides are dull green in color, changing to pastel yellow and pink toward the tail. The posterior dorsal, anal, and caudal fins are pink or red and there is an indistinct bluish-green stripe that extends from behind the operculum midlaterally toward the tail.
Aquarium suitability: This is a good fish for a community tank and looks especially attractive in a small school of five or six. Most foods are accepted within a few hours but live food will make them feel at home. Try mosquito larvae, tubifex, and whiteworms for the best result. An occasional feeding of *Daphnia* also works wonders!

Glossolepis incisus

Common names: West Papua rainbow, New Guinea red rainbowfish, Red rainbowfish
Range: Indonesia, in areas of dense water vegetation around Lake Sentani, West Papua
Size: 6 inches (15 cm)
Description: Males are deep copper to bright red in color. Females tend to be light bronze. The body is compressed and large adults have arched backs. The anal fin extends from the mid-belly region to the caudal peduncle and the tail is deeply forked. There are two dorsal fins present and the posterior one has a longer base than the anterior one. The throat and snout of both sexes is generally a light silver.
Aquarium suitability: This is a lively schooling fish that should be kept in small groups of five or more individuals. Single fish do not do well in a community setup.

Glossolepis wanamensis

Common names: Emerald rainbowfish, Lake Wanam rainbowfish
Range: Papua New Guinea, known only in Lake Wanam
Size: 3½ inches (9 cm)
Description: A median yellow stripe runs from the snout over the nape and along the two dorsal bases. The upper sides are yellowish-green to iridescent green and the ventral region is bright orange in dominant males. Female flanks are yellow.
Aquarium suitability: A reasonably large tank is required if they are to be kept in small groups, as they are active swimmers. This species is an ideal choice for a large show aquarium. Feed a varied diet with frequent water changes to enhance the colors.
Breeding information: Like *G. incisus*, the fry are difficult to feed unless cultured rotifers are being used. Raise the water temperature to 81–86°F (27–30°C) to induce spawning.

Melanotaenia affinis

Common name: North New Guinea rainbowfish
Range: Oceania: Papua New Guinea and West Papua
Size: 4½ inches (11.5 cm)
Description: Males have an olive to bronze upper body and white lower body. A broad stripe extends midlaterally from the eye to the tail; immediately above this is a narrower yellow stripe. The second dorsal and anal fins are yellow with blue margins. There are several geographical color morphs. One, known as the Pagwi variety from the Sepic River, is similar in coloration, although the upper body is greenish-blue. The midlateral stripe is blue, but the upper and lower margins are bright orange-red from the midbody region to the tail.
Aquarium suitability: One of the first rainbowfish from New Guinea to be imported, it is a firm favorite among aquarists. The feeding and care of it is the same as other rainbowfish.

Melanotaenia boesemani

Common names: Boeseman's rainbowfish, Bicolor rainbow
Range: West Papua, mainly in the Ajamaru Lakes region of the Vogelkop peninsula
Size: 6 inches (15 cm)
Description: This is the only rainbowfish that has a vertical half-and-half coloration. In dominant males the front half of the body is bright bluish-gray, while the posterior part and fins are ostensibly orange-red. Secondary males and females are much lighter in color, often with several vertical bands of light and dark extending from the dorsal base to the ventral region.
Aquarium suitability: A good schooling species for a community tank. Planting should be carried out along the rear and sides of the tank, leaving plenty of free-swimming space. This species requires a varied diet of live and flake foods.

Melanotaenia duboulayi

Common names: Duboulay's rainbowfish, Crimson-spotted rainbowfish
Range: Australia, particularly drainage systems of northern New South Wales and southern Queensland
Size: 3½ inches (9 cm)
Description: Considerable color variations exist with this species. The body can be silvery bluish-green or specimens may be deep blue with yellowish nuances. A narrow pink or magenta sublateral stripe extends from the midbody region to the caudal base. The median fins can also vary in color from dull magenta to pale yellow-green.
Aquarium suitability: Again, this is a community fish that is best kept in groups of five or six individuals. Provide a varied diet of whiteworms, insect larvae, tubifex, frozen adult brine shrimp, and flake food for the best results.

Melanotaenia fluviatilis

Common names: Murray River rainbowfish, Australian rainbowfish
Range: Western Australia, in inland waterways and ponds as well as the Murray-Darling River system
Size: 3¼ inches (9 cm)
Description: Dominant males have olive backs and greenish-turquoise flanks. The belly is silvery-white and the dorsal and anal fins often have black margins. Secondary males and females are not so brightly colored. Mature males have a higher first dorsal fin that extends over the first few rays of the second dorsal fin when it is depressed.
Aquarium suitability: The tank should be large and well planted, with plenty of free-swimming space. All rainbowfish should be kept in small groups, not as single specimens. They are essentially carnivores, so they should be fed the appropriate diet.

Melanotaenia lacustris

Common name: Lake Kutubu rainbowfish
Range: Oceania, in Lake Kutubu and the Soro River in the southern highlands of Papua New Guinea
Size: 4 inches (10 cm)
Description: Mature males have a high anterior dorsal fin. The body is laterally compressed and slender but grows deeper with age. Males are larger than females and more brightly colored. The body can be varying shades of blue, from cobalt blue to light turquoise, but can also be steel blue or aquamarine.
Aquarium suitability: Like all rainbowfish, this species prefers plenty of aquarium plants and free-swimming space in its tank.
Breeding information: In the wild it breeds between October and December. The 100–200 eggs are laid over a few days on plants. The eggs hatch 6–10 days later. The fry are small and need to be fed on enriched rotifers or infusorians for the first week.

Melanotaenia herbertaxelrodi

Common name: Lake Tebera rainbowfish
Range: Oceania: Lake Tebera in the southern highlands of Papua New Guinea
Size: 3½ inches (9 cm)
Description: Males develop a high nape with age. The body is laterally compressed, becoming deeper as the fish grows. The body coloration is yellow, with a bluish-black midlateral stripe that extends from the snout to the base of the tail. The anal and dorsal fins can be red or yellow in color but the dorsal fins are usually yellow.
Aquarium suitability: A very popular fish in the hobby but one that is not often seen for sale. Their diet should consist of terrestrial insects as well as aquatic insect larvae, small aquatic crustaceans, and flake food. Plenty of free-swimming space in a well-planted aquarium is required.

Melanotaenia maccullochi

Common names: Black-lined rainbowfish, Dwarf rainbowfish
Range: Australia, principally northern Queensland
Size: 2 inches (5 cm)
Description: There are several color variations of this species. This is probably due to the fact that the locations in which they are found are isolated from one another, allowing for color diversification. Generally, males have a higher first dorsal fin than females and are more colorful. The body color of the male is gray-green with a bluish hue dorsally and light greenish-silver ventrally. The sides are adorned with seven fine black stripes that extend from the opercular region to the base of the tail. The dorsal and anal fins have black stripes submarginally, often red marginally.
Aquarium suitability: Great for a community setup when they are kept in small groups and fed on a varied diet.

Melanotaenia nigrans

Common names: Dark rainbowfish, Black-banded rainbowfish
Range: Northern Australia, from Kimberly, Western Australia, to the Cape York Peninsula, Queensland
Size: 4 inches (10 cm)
Description: This is the type species of the genus. Coloration is very distinct. A bold bluish-black stripe extends midlaterally from the snout to the base of the tail. Above this, the dorsal region is light olive-brown. Below the stripe, the ventral region is silver. Color variations exist where the body takes on a bluish sheen, often with blue or yellow fins.
Aquarium suitability: The tank should be well planted and have plenty of space for a small school to swim. Single specimens do not do well in a community tank, so keep them in a group of five or six. Like all rainbowfish, they need a varied diet for optimal success.

Melanotaenia parkinsoni

Common name: Parkinson's rainbowfish
Range: Oceania: between the Kemp Welsh River and Marine Bay, Papua New Guinea
Size: 4¾ inches (12 cm)
Description: The background body coloration is bluish-silver, often with a light rose-pink chest. Seven fine orange-yellow stripes extend between the scale rows from behind the operculum to the base of the tail and there is an orange-yellow spot. Mature males have bright yellow fins and often develop a blotchy orange-yellow coloration on the flanks.
Aquarium suitability: A school of five or six of this species will require quite a large, well-planted aquarium because of their eventual adult size. Try to duplicate their natural diet, which comprises small aquatic crustaceans, terrestrial insects, algae, and insect larvae.

Melanotaenia praecox

Common name: Dwarf rainbowfish
Range: New Guinea, in the entire Mamberamo River system
Size: 3 inches (7.6 cm)
Description: Both sexes have bright, metallic-blue bodies that are strongly compressed laterally. Males have broad red margins to the dorsal and anal fins and the tail is red with a clear margin. Females often have the same fin coloration but may also have yellow fins, depending on the region from which they were collected.
Aquarium suitability: This is a good fish for a community tank if several are kept together in a small school. Groups of three or fewer will not do well. The tank should have subdued lighting to bring out the colors of this beautiful fish. Use floating plants to provide shaded areas if there is high-intensity lighting over the aquarium.

Melanotaenia splendida australis

Common name: Western rainbowfish
Range: Western Australia, in the Pilbara and Kimberly regions as well as the western region of the Northern Territory
Size: 4 inches (10 cm)
Description: There are no less than five subspecies in what has become known as the "Splendida group." The main identifying feature of this subspecies is the presence of crosshatch or zigzag lines on the lower flanks (not seen clearly in the photo). The tail is bright red and the margins of the dorsal and anal fins are also red. In certain light, the body has a greenish-blue iridescence but not as much as in *M. praecox*, a similar-looking species. A series of seven yellow-orange stripes is present between the scale rows. These extend from the operculum to the base of the tail.
Aquarium suitability: This is an easy species to keep and breed and can be recommended for the complete novice.

Melanotaenia splendida splendida

Common names: Splendid rainbowfish, Cape York rainbowfish, Pink-tailed rainbowfish
Range: Australia, in streams and tributaries east of the Great Dividing Range, Queensland
Size: 4¾ inches (12 cm)
Description: There are many color varieties, depending on where they are collected. Mature males have a high first dorsal fin that extends over the first few rays of the second dorsal fin when it is lowered. Generally, the body coloration is dull yellow between the scales and each scale has a light blue edge, except behind the operculum and on the lower flanks. In these areas, the scales are edged in amber-yellow. The fins have red margins and are spotted red or yellow submarginally.
Aquarium suitability: Like other rainbowfish, they make good candidates for a community tank if kept in small schools.

Melanotaenia trifasciata

Common names: Jewel rainbowfish, Three-stripe rainbowfish
Range: Australia, in streams and river systems from the Northern Territory to Queensland
Size: 5½ inches (14 cm)
Description: A broad black midlateral stripe extends from the snout to the base of the tail. This is sometimes interrupted in the midbody region. There are extreme color variations possible, depending on where they are collected. Generally, though, the background body color is pale olive-brown to drab orange but it can also have an iridescent bluish sheen. The fins may be yellow, orange, pink, red, or any combination of these colors.
Aquarium suitability: A small school of this fish makes a spectacular show in a large tank. Vitamin supplements should be added to their food to enhance their striking colors. Use floating plants to diffuse the light to show them off at their best.

Pseudomugilidae (Blue-eyes)

The family comprises three genera, *Kiunga*, *Pseudomugil*, and *Scaturiginichthys*, and 17 species. *Pseudomugil* contains 15 species and the remaining two genera are monotypic. These are slender-bodied fish that are found in brackish and fresh water. There are two dorsal fins present. The anterior dorsal fin is usually much higher than the posterior one and is frequently more of a spike than a fin. In one case, the pectoral fins are set low on the body and the caudal fin is rounded. In others, the pectoral fins are not low and the tail is moderately to deeply forked. Their collective common name originates through the fact that most species do actually have blue eyes. The distribution of the family is restricted to New Guinea, adjacent islands, parts of eastern Indonesia, and northern and eastern Australia.

Pseudomugil connieae

Common name: Popondetta blue-eye
Range: Southeast Papua New Guinea, in creeks around Popondetta
Size: 2 inches (5 cm)
Description: The body is slender. The forehead is somewhat depressed and the pectoral fins are fairly elongated. Males have longer dorsal fins. The body is bluish-green on the flanks and the first third of the body is yellow. The dorsal and anal fins have white margins and black stripes below this. The anterior dorsal fin is tipped with yellow. Females are similarly colored but the coloring is less intense.
Aquarium suitability: This species needs somewhat harder water and requires frequent water changes to keep it healthy. Weekly 25 percent water changes are recommended. Its diet should consist of algae, brine shrimp, mysid shrimp, and *Daphnia*.

Pseudomugil furcatus

Common name: Forktail rainbowfish
Range: Papua New Guinea, in clear freshwater streams that have an abundance of aquatic plant life
Size: 2 inches (5 cm)
Description: The body is elongate and moderately compressed and the forehead and nape are somewhat depressed. Males and females are similar but the female's coloration lacks the intensity of the male's. The body coloration is yellow-green with a yellow throat and belly. The pectoral and pelvic fins are yellow with occasional tinges of red, and the dorsal and anal fins have yellow margins. The upper and lower lobes of the tail have black margins and broad yellow submargins. The female fish lacks the black margins.
Aquarium suitability: This is a great fish for a community tank if it is kept with other fish of a similar size.

Pseudomugil gertrudae

Common name: Spotted blue-eye
Range: Australia, in southwestern New Guinea, the Northern Territory, and northern Queensland
Size: 1¼ inches (3.2 cm)
Description: The body coloration is greenish-silver, with small black spots arranged in rows along the sides. The median fins are covered with small black spots and the pectoral fins are bright yellow in color. There is a small red spot at the angle of the pectoral axil. Males have longer fins and the first rays of the pelvic and anterior dorsal fins are greatly extended. Females are lighter in color and have fewer body spots.
Aquarium suitability: This tiny fish is one of the most attractive of all the blue-eyes. It is an ideal subject for a small tank. Several together make a great show but they need a varied diet of insect larvae, *Artemia*, whiteworms, and algae.

Pseudomugil signifer

Common names: Australian blue-eye, Pacific blue-eye
Range: Australia, widely distributed in various marine, brackish-water, and freshwater habitats along the eastern coast
Size: 1¾ inches (4.5 cm)
Description: The body color is olive green dorsally and greenish silver ventrally. Each scale is edged in black, creating a crosshatch pattern on the sides. The eye is blue and the median fins are bright yellow to dull yellow, as are the ventral fins. In males, the first rays of the dorsal, pelvic, and anal fins are extended with black margins. The dorsal and ventral margins of the tail are white and black submarginally. Females are less brightly colored and have shorter fins.
Aquarium suitability: A fine dark-colored substrate is best to show off this species in groups of five or more. Provide plenty of free-swimming space and a moderate water circulation.

Telmatherinidae
(Sailfin silversides, Celebes rainbowfish)

This family comprises five genera with a total of only 17 species. The genera are *Kaliptatherina*, *Marosatherina*, *Paratherina*, *Telmatherina*, and *Tominanga*. In spite of the fact that there are only a few species in this group, they are extremely diverse in their habitat requirements. Some species live in freshwater, others in brackish water, and there are species that live in a totally marine environment among mangrove roots. At least one species lives solely in mangrove swamps.

The characteristics of this group are that the lateral line is thin, weak, or absent; there are teeth on the vomer; the rostrum is short; the anterior dorsal fin has four to eight spines; and the posterior dorsal has eight to 11 soft rays. The lateral line series, when present, is usually 31 to 41 scales. Species in this family closely resemble the rainbowfish and the silversides, although their cladistic relationship to other antheriniforms remains uncertain. As a group, they are restricted in their geographical range and are found only in Sulawesi and the islands of Misool and Batanta off the western coast of New Guinea.

Marosatherina ladigesi

Common names: Celebes rainbowfish, Celebes sailfish
Range: Asia, in the Bantimurung area of south Sulawesi, Indonesia, in slow-moving water that is rich in plant life
Size: 3½ inches (9 cm)
Description: The two dorsal fins are widely separated and the anterior one is short. The posterior dorsal fin is high and its first few rays are almost separated into a distinct fin. The first few rays of the anal fin are also partially separated and the tail is moderately forked. The eye is yellow and the background body color is yellow-brown with a bluish iridescence. There is a midlateral stripe present that extends from the midbody region to the base of the tail.
Aquarium suitability: Use floating plants to diffuse overhead lighting. This is a brackish-water species that should be kept with others that can tolerate slightly brackish conditions.

Order: Cyprinodontiformes

This order encompasses quite a large group of fish. There are eight families, 88 genera, and about 807 species. The strangest of all the genera is *Anableps* because these species have adapted eyes. The eyes, situated on top of the head, are divided by a band of epithelium (tissue) into upper and lower parts, with separate corneas and retinas. They swim with their head almost out of the water and the lower pair of pupils sees underwater—looking out for predators—whereas the upper pair has been adapted for seeing above the water surface to look for prey. Fish from the family Cyprinodontidae resemble carps but there are teeth present in both jaws, a complete absence of barbels, and the head and body are scaled. Species from this group are found in brackish or freshwater. Of the eight families in this group, only fish from three families are of real interest to the hobbyist. The compilation and monophyly of this taxon is recognized on the basis of several derived characters and follows the detailed anatomical study of L. R. Parenti in his paper, *A Phylogenetic and Biogeographic Analysis of Cyprinodontiform Fishes* (1981) and the taxonomic study by Nelson (1994). The caudal fin is symmetrical, supported internally by a single epural; the first pleural rib is from the second vertebrae rather than the third; there is an alveolar arm to the premaxillae; and the pectoral girdle is low-set with a scalelike postcleithrum. The families share additional characteristics: the lateral line canal and pores are mainly on the head, the body's lateral line is represented by pitted scales, a paired narial opening, pelvic fins and girdle are present or absent, and only the upper jaw is bordered by premaxilla. The males are much more brightly colored.

Species from this order are popular aquarium fish and they are also used for experimental purposes, particularly genetic studies. The egg diameter can vary from 0.3 mm to about 3 mm and the embryonic development from six days to over one year. Some rivulines and poeciliids can be found in freshwater, brackish water, or they may be entirely marine living.

Aplocheilidae (Rivulines)

The family is recognized as having two subfamilies: Aplocheilinae (Old World Rivulines), with eight genera and about 185 species, and Rivulinae (New World Rivulines), with 12 genera and more than 130 species. Some of these fish are termed "annuals" because adults spawn during the rainy season and bury their eggs in the substrate. In the dry season, the parent fish die but the eggs survive and hatch during the first rains of the following season. Growth is very fast; these fish spawn and the cycle is repeated. In extended dry periods and drought, the eggs can survive well into the following rainy season. "Killifish eggs" are often available to the hobbyist in their dry form. Old World Rivulines are found in Africa south of the Sahara to South Africa, and in the Indian subcontinent, the Seychelles, Sri Lanka, and the Indo-Malaysian archipelago as far as Java. New World Rivulines are restricted to southern Florida, through Central America to Uruguay. Several of these species are self-fertilizing hermaphrodites where the eggs are internally fertilized and then laid.

Aphyosemion amieti

Common names: Amiet's lyretail
Range: Western Africa, in rain-forest pools, creeks, and streams in western Cameroon
Size: 2¾ inches (7 cm)
Description: Females are similar to males but with less intense markings and shorter fins. Typically, the male has a bluish-green back and a pale yellow ventral region. A series of red blotches and streaks extends horizontally behind the operculum to the caudal peduncle. The median fins are blue or green with bright red spots.
Aquarium suitability: One male should be kept with several females in a shallow, species-specific tank for the best results. The aquarium should have a tight-fitting cover because this species is known to jump out of the water when it is frightened.

Aphyosemion ahli

Common name: Ahli's lyretail
Range: Western Africa, in streams and swamps from Cameroon to Equatorial Guinea
Size: 2½ inches (6 cm)
Description: The background body color is pale olive-brown changing to yellow-ocher dorsally. The front half of the body and head are covered with bright red spots and streaks whereas the rear part is adorned with a series of red vertical bands and streaks. The dorsal fin is red with a yellow margin and blue submargin. The lobes of the tail are bright yellow with red submargins, and the center of the tail is blue with red spots.
Aquarium suitability: This species is happy in a community tank with fish of a similar size and peaceful nature. Provide lots of plants and cover for their protection and feed a varied diet of live and frozen fare, supplemented with flake and tablet foods.

Aphyosemion australe

Common names: Lyretail panchax, Orange lyretail, Cape Lopez lyretail
Range: Western Africa, in shallow, slow-moving rivers, particularly in the rain forests of Gabon
Size: 2½ inches (6 cm)
Description: The background body color of the males can be greenish-brown, brownish-orange, or reddish-orange. There are numerous small red spots present on the head and the anterior part of the body. The dorsal and anal fins are generally orange or brown with yellow margins and broad red submargins. The tail is lyre-shaped with a broad red center. The upper and lower lobes are yellow. Females are less colorful and lack the lyre tail.
Aquarium suitability: This species prefers peat filtration. The tank should have a partial cover of floating plants to diffuse the overhead lighting. This is a good community fish if kept in pairs.

Aphyosemion bitaeniatum

Common name: Two-striped aphyosemion
Range: Africa, in small brooks and rain-forest streams in the southern areas of Togo, Benin, and Nigeria
Size: 2 inches (5 cm)
Description: The body is silvery-blue and brownish-red dorsally. Males have long filaments on the dorsal, anal, and caudal fin extremities. The dorsal and caudal fins are orange-red with numerous red spots. The anal fin may be yellow, bluish-white, or orange-red.
Aquarium suitability: This is not a seasonal fish. It is ideal for a well-planted freshwater aquarium and a good community fish. The tank water should be mildly acidic with a pH of 6.5–6.8.
Breeding information: Eggs are laid on fine-leaved plants and are difficult to spot because they are very small for killifish eggs. These should be removed to a separate rearing tank.

Aphyosemion calliurum

Common name: Banner lyretail
Range: Africa, in brooks, small streams, and swamps from southern Nigeria to southwestern Cameroon
Size: 2 inches (5 cm)
Description: The body color varies from bluish-green to yellow and the ventral region is lighter than the rest of the body. In males, the dorsal and anal fins have greatly extended ray filaments, as do the upper and lower lobes of the tail. The dorsal, anal, and caudal fins typically have broad yellow margins and there are numerous red spots on the head and sides. Females lack the showy fin filaments.
Aquarium suitability: Quite a difficult fish to keep in an aquarium because it does not travel well. The aquarist should only buy a pair, and they should be feeding in the dealers' tank. Provide floating plants to diffuse the lighting.

Aphyosemion coeleste

Common name: Sky-blue killi
Range: Africa: southern Congo and Gabon, in swampy areas of rain-forest streams and inland plains
Size: 2 inches (5 cm)
Description: The female is olive green dorsally with a yellow ventral region. Males are brightly colored. The body is pale blue with a yellow dorsal region and head. The dorsal scales have red edges and there are numerous spots and streaks of red on the head. The caudal fin has a blue center and the upper and lower lobes are yellow marginally and red submarginally. The dorsal and anal fins are similarly marked.
Aquarium suitability: The tank water should be made slightly acidic using peat filtration. Plenty of cover should be provided using plants and driftwood. Keep in pairs or trios with other fish of a similar size and peaceful nature.

Aphyosemion splendopleure

Common name: Splendid killifish
Range: Africa, in streams and rain-forest brooks of southeastern Nigeria, Cameroon, Gabon, and Equatorial Guinea
Size: 2¼ inches (5.5 cm)
Description: In males, the dorsal, anal, and caudal fins have extended yellow extremities. The body is variable in color and may be blue with a violet iridescence, deep violet-red, or pinkish-yellow. There is often a shadowy black midlateral stripe present that extends from the operculum to the caudal peduncle. The central caudal fin rays are often blue in mature males and the anal fin may have a red margin.
Aquarium suitability: Try to keep this species in pairs. Males can often be aggressive toward one another but generally this is a peaceful fish. The tank should be heavily planted with the addition of floating plants to diffuse strong overhead lighting.

Aphyosemion poliaki

Common name: Poliaki
Range: Western Africa, in small rain-forest streams and brooks in southwestern Cameroon
Size: 2 inches (5 cm)
Description: Males are quite variable in color. The sides may be yellow to olive-brown, darkening dorsally. The numerous red spots on the head may be fused together to form horizontal or diagonal stripes on the snout and around the eye. The median fins have yellow margins with darker submargins and the anal fin is pale blue.
Aquarium suitability: Quite difficult to keep unless the tank conditions are optimal. The water should be slightly soft and there should be plenty of plants in the tank. Most foods are accepted, including flake food. Nevertheless, live food should be given to these species on a weekly basis.

Aphyosemion striatum

Common names: Red-lined killifish, Red-striped killifish
Range: Western Africa, in shallow rain-forest streams of northern Gabon
Size: 2 inches (5 cm)
Description: The background body color is pale blue to greenish-blue and the nape is olive green to olive-yellow. The body, head, and tail have bright red spots that are arranged in horizontal rows. These are frequently fused together to form stripes. The pectoral, anal, and pelvic fins are yellow, often with red margins. The dorsal fin is blue or greenish-yellow with two bold red stripes. One of these is marginal and the other is at the dorsal fin base.
Aquarium suitability: Small tetras make ideal tank-mates for this species. Use a dark substrate and provide plenty of plants and other hiding places made from rocks and driftwood.

Aplocheilus lineatus

Common names: Striped panchax, Lineatus panchax, Sparkling panchax, Golden wonder killifish, Golden killifish
Range: India and Sri Lanka, at various altitudes and in a variety of habitats such as streams, ponds, and paddy fields
Size: 4 inches (10 cm)
Description: Females less colorful than males. A typical male has an olive green to yellow body. The sides and flanks are covered in yellow to gold spots that are arranged in horizontal rows. The dorsal and anal fins are yellow with red margins and the margins of the upper and lower lobes of the caudal fin are also red or orange-red.
Aquarium suitability: The aquarium should have a tight-fitting hood because this fish tends to jump out of the water if it is frightened in any way. Use floating plants to diffuse strong overhead lighting. Most foods, including flake, are accepted.

Aplocheilus panchax panchax

Common name: Blue panchax
Range: Southeast Asia, from India throughout the Indo-Malaysian archipelago to Borneo, in ponds and canals
Size: 3¼ inches (8 cm)
Description: The background body coloration is greenish-blue on the flanks and olive to bronze dorsally. There are six to eight horizontal rows of fine red spots present that extend from the operculum to the tail.
Aquarium suitability: This species needs a varied diet of insect larvae, flake food, tubifex, brine shrimp, *Daphnia*, and small fish fry. It is a lively, surface-dwelling predator that is best kept with catfish and small cichlids.
Breeding information: Between 150 and 300 eggs are laid on a regular basis. These hatch in 10–14 days. The fry can be fed on brine shrimp and crushed flake once yolk sacs are consumed.

Fundulopanchax filamentosus

Common name: Plumed lyretail
Range: Africa, in stagnant pools, swamps, and ponds throughout western Africa from Togo to Cameroon
Size: 2½ inches (6 cm)
Description: This species is easily identified by the three bold diagonal red bars that extend a short distance from above and behind the eye in both males and females. Females lack the intense red spots on the body and fins. Males have a broad red stripe through the anal fin and lower lobe of the tail (the photograph at left shows a male).
Aquarium suitability: Most seasonal killifish prefer to be kept with their own kind in a separate aquarium. This particular species should be kept in pairs or one male with two females. Feed on flake food supplemented with live foods such as tubifex and brine shrimp.

Fundulopanchax gardneri gardneri

Common name: Blue lyretail
Range: Africa: the lower part of the Beno and Cross River area in humid forest streams and swamps
Size: 2½ inches (6.5 cm)
Description: Coloration may vary considerably depending on where the species was collected. Generally, males have a green body with a blue iridescence. The body is marked with irregular spots and there are red streaks on the head. The dorsal fin and upper and lower lobes of the caudal fin have a bold red stripe submarginally, and yellow margins.
Aquarium suitability: This is not a seasonal killifish and it is much easier to keep than the preceding species. Provide plenty of cover using plants, rocks, and bogwood. Use a dark substrate to bring out the true colors of the male. Two males in the same tank will show a great deal of aggression toward each other.

Fundulopanchax sjoestedti

Common names: Blue gularis, Golden pheasant
Range: West Africa, in rain-forest pools and swampy ponds and marshes from the Ivory Coast to Cameroon
Size: 4 inches (10 cm)
Description: Typically, the male's body has a bluish-green background coloration with red spots around the head and several narrow vertical bands on the flanks that are also red. The fins are green with red spots and bold red margins. Females are reddish-brown. There is a gold color morph that is olive-brown dorsally with greenish-gold flanks.
Aquarium suitability: The aquarium should contain plenty of hiding places formed by rocks and plants. Using a dark substrate will bring out the true colors of this attractive species.
Breeding information: This species buries its eggs in the substrate, so peat moss should be used in the breeding tank.

Nothobranchius guentheri

Common name: Redtail notho
Range: Africa, in seasonal pools and streams of Zanzibar and eastern Tanzania
Size: 2¼ inches (5.5 cm)
Description: The background body color of the male can range from golden yellow to bluish-green. The tail is almost always deep red, as is the caudal peduncle. The body is suffused with bright red spots that are arranged in rows to form a series of dense, chevron-shaped bars on the flanks. Females are much less colorful.
Aquarium suitability: This is a seasonal fish that usually lives for less than a year in an aquarium. It is quite an aggressive fish and males will fight one another during the breeding season. Keep one male with several females in a well-planted aquarium for the best results.

Nothobranchius rachovii

Common name: Bluefin notho
Range: Southeast Africa, in ponds, streams, and floodplains of Mozambique and South Africa
Size: 2½ inches (6 cm)
Description: An extremely attractive fish that has a turquoise body and median fins. Each scale has a red margin on the sides and flanks, whereas those around the head tend to be overall red in color. The rounded caudal fin has a black margin and a broad red submargin.
Aquarium suitability: The substrate should be dark and the tank should be well planted, with plenty of cover and hiding places made of rocks and driftwood. This fish is best kept in a species-only aquarium with one male and several females. However, two or three *Corydoras* catfish will not disturb this species and will add interest.

Pachypanchax playfairii

Common name: Golden panchax
Range: East Africa, in small freshwater and brackish-water streams of Zanzibar, the Seychelles, and Madagascar
Size: 4 inches (10 cm)
Description: The dorsal region is olive-brown in color and the sides of the body are yellow with a greenish iridescence. There are numerous reddish-brown spots arranged in horizontal rows along the sides, from the operculum to the tail. The fins are similarly marked and the anal and caudal fins have black margins. Females are dull orange-brown with a black spot at the dorsal fin base.
Aquarium suitability: Best kept with small African cichlids, catfish, and hatchetfish. The tank should be quite heavily planted, with plenty of hiding places. Floating plants should be used to diffuse strong overhead lighting.

Pseudepiplatys annulatus

Common names: Banded panchax, Clown killie, Rocket panchax
Range: Western Africa, in small rain-forest and savanna streams of Guinea, Sierra Leone, and Liberia
Size: 1½ inches (4 cm)
Description: This is an easy fish to identify because of its distinct coloration. Males and females are similarly marked but the colors of the male are more intense. The body is silvery-white with four broad bluish-black bars.
Aquarium suitability: Not an easy fish to keep in an aquarium and one that should be left to an expert. The water conditions need to be perfect and frequent partial water changes are necessary to keep this species happy in its captive surroundings. Provide a varied diet of tubifex, *Cyclops*, *Daphnia*, flake food, and brine shrimp.

Poeciliidae (Livebearing tooth-carps, Egg-laying tooth-carps)

There are 30 genera in this family containing about 300 species. Two-thirds of these belong to the subfamily Poeciliinae (Livebearers), with many hybrids. Almost all of the species are popular aquarium fish. Livebearing tooth-carps originate from North, Central, and South America. As aquarium fish they are easy to keep, colorful, and there are many varieties, color morphs, and hybrids. They are easy to breed because they give birth to live young, which gives them a great advantage over egg-laying species. Generally they are small- to medium-sized fish that are ideal for a community tank. But they are also cannibalistic and will eat their young if the tank is not well planted or if the young fry are not removed to a separate rearing tank.

Heterandria formosa

Common names: Least killifish, Het, Mosquitofish
Range: North America, from the Cape Fear River drainages of North Carolina to Louisiana
Size: 1½ inches (3.8 cm)
Description: This species is olive-yellow dorsally with a white belly. It is an easy fish to identify because there is a broad black midlateral stripe present in both males and females.
Aquarium suitability: The Least killifish is initially a shy species that feels more at home in groups in a well-planted aquarium. Once settled, though, they are bold and inquisitive and will accept most foods that are offered.
Breeding information: Around 15–60 young fry are released after a short gestation period. The fry do not need to be removed from the breeding tank because the parents will not eat them. Feed the young on brine shrimp and crushed flake.

Gambusia affinis

Common name: Mosquitofish
Range: Central America, including Mexico, in ponds and marshes; introduced into other countries for mosquito control.
Size: 2¼ inches (6 cm)
Description: The Mosquitofish is found in both brackish and fresh water. Females are much larger than males and both sexes resemble colorless guppies, to which they are closely related. The sides of the body are silver and each scale has a narrow black margin. The back is pale olive-brown and the belly is white. The dorsal, anal, and caudal fins often have a sprinkling of black spots.
Aquarium suitability: This is a relatively drab fish that is not very popular with hobbyists. However, it is easy to keep and breed and will survive most beginners' mistakes because it can adapt to a wide variety of temperatures and water qualities.

Poecilia latipinna

Common name: Sailfin molly
Range: North America, from Virginia to northern Mexico in coastal marshes and rivers in fresh, brackish, or salt water.
Size: 4¾ inches (12 cm)
Description: The back is olive green and the belly is white. Females are larger than males and lack a gonopodium (the modified anal fin used for fertilizing eggs within the female). There are five fine horizontal stripes present on the body. Also, there are several dark vertical bars on the chest that are sometimes indistinct. The sail-like high dorsal fin and broad tail are translucent with mottled black and white spots and blotches.
Aquarium suitability: This is a firm favorite with European aquarists and there are many color variations that have been developed. It is an easy fish to keep and one that will accept most foods. It is tolerant of most aquarium conditions.

Poecilia reticulata

Common names: Guppy, Millions fish
Range: Central America, in Venezuela, Trinidad, and Barbados; now bred in Singapore and the United States
Size: 2¾ inches (7 cm)
Description: The size given here is for an adult female. Males are considerably smaller. In the wild, this species is not very colorful and is usually olive green, sometimes with spots and blotches. Tank-bred specimens show considerably more color, as can be seen in the accompanying photograph, which shows a pronounced orange coloration of the caudal fin.
Aquarium suitability: The Guppy is an ideal fish for the complete novice and will survive most beginners' mistakes. The tank should be well aerated and have plenty of plants and hiding places. It is a peaceful fish that is best kept in small groups with both males and females together.

Varieties of *Poecilia reticulata*

Poecilia reticulata (Yellow veiltail—male)

Poecilia reticulata (Yellow veiltail—female)

Poecilia reticulata (Yellow snakeskin—male)

Poecilia reticulata (Yellow snakeskin—female)

Poecilia reticulata (Red veiltail—male)

Poecilia reticulata (Red/Black veiltail—male)

Poecilia reticulata (Red snakeskin—male)

Poecilia phenops

Common names: Black molly, Painted molly, Short-finned molly, Pointed-mouth molly

Range: North and Central America, in fresh and brackish water areas from Mexico to Colombia

Size: 4¾ inches (12 cm)

Description: There are many color variations of this species including black, orange, and white with black spots. The wild form has an olive green back and bluish flanks. The caudal fin is rounded and the body is moderately compressed. Males have a modified anal fin (gonopodium) that is used to fertilize the eggs of the female.

Aquarium suitability: The Molly is an easy species to keep in all its forms and colors. There are no special requirements regarding its aquarium or diet. This is a good community fish.

Poecilia phenops (Black molly, top, and Dalmation molly)

Poecilia velifera

Common names: Green molly, Mexican sailfin molly, Sailfin molly, Yucatán sailfin molly

Range: Mexico and the Yucatán peninsula, in brackish and fresh water.

Size: 6 inches (15 cm)

Description: Males are more colorful than females, with a large dorsal, or sail, fin that is pale orange to blue with iridescent spots and spangles. The tail is often blue and is also spotted. Breeding males usually develop orange throats.

Aquarium suitability: This species is ideal for a brackish-water aquarium but does not do well in a completely freshwater environment. Specimens adapt much more easily to marine aquariums than they do to freshwater ones, where they become prone to disease. Once settled in and happy with the tank, most foods will be accepted.

Xiphophorus helleri

Common names: Swordtail, Green swordtail
Range: Central America, in a variety of habitats in Mexico, Belize, Guatemala, and Honduras
Size: 4 inches (10 cm)
Description: Wild specimens have an olive green back and a light-colored breast. The fins are pale orange and there is an orange-red stripe present from the operculum to the tail. Males have a swordlike extension formed by the lower rays of the caudal fin (most noticeable in the Red lyretail sword below). Due to years of selective breeding, specimens seen in the hobby differ in coloration and sometimes fin shape.
Aquarium suitability: Generally quite peaceful, and suitable for a community tank. Older males tend to be quite aggressive toward other fish under cramped conditions. A well-planted tank with plenty of free-swimming space is recommended.

Xiphophorus helleri (Green swordtail—male)

Xiphophorus helleri (Green swordtail—female)

Xiphophorus helleri (Red swordtail—male)

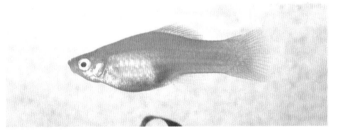

Xiphophorus helleri (Red swordtail—female)

Xiphophorus helleri (Red lyretail sword—male)

Xiphophorus maculatus (Mickey Mouse platy)

Xiphophorus maculatus

Common names: Mickey Mouse platy, Platy, Moonfish
Range: Central America, from Mexico to Honduras in rivers that flow to the Atlantic coast
Size: 2 inches (5 cm)
Description: The caudal fin is typically fan-shaped and convex. Wild specimens are not as colorful as those that are raised within the aquarium hobby. They are olive-brown dorsally with bluish-silver flanks. The flanks and caudal peduncle sometimes show shadowy dark bars. There are many color variations available that have been brought into the hobby through years of selective breeding.
Aquarium suitability: This is often the first fish that beginners will purchase. It is hardy and easy to keep. It is also a good community fish that is peaceful and undemanding.

Xiphophorus variatus

Common names: Variegated platy, Variatus platy
Range: North America, in the shallow, slow-moving rivers of southern Mexico
Size: 2¾ inches (7 cm)
Description: Similar to the previous species but with some distinct differences: the back is higher than that of *X. maculatus* and the belly is somewhat more rounded. The body coloration is varied, even with wild-caught specimens. However, the body is generally yellow or orange with or without black blotches.
Aquarium suitability: This is a firm favorite with both beginners and experienced aquarists. They are a good choice for a community setup and, because they are usually first at the "feeding table," they will often induce fish with more fastidious eating habits to feed in competition with them.

Xiphophorus variatus showing color variations

Cyprinodontidae (Pupfish, Flagfish)

The cyprinodonts differ from others of the Cyprinodontiformes group mainly because of fin form and fin ray variations. However, the dentition also plays a key role in their classification. In addition, the dorsal processes of the maxillaries are medially extended and almost meet at the midline. The lateral arm of the maxilla is also expanded. In reproduction, the eggs are always fertilized externally.

Pupfish and flagfish are found in a variety of environments in fresh water, brackish water, and also coastal marine areas. Their range extends from the United States through Central America to the northern areas of South America. Representatives are also found in North Africa and the Anatolian region of the Mediterranean. The 11 species of *Alphanius* are found from Northern Africa, Spain, Italy, Greece, Turkey, and the Saudi Arabian peninsula to Iran. The family is comprised of two subfamilies, nine genera, and about 100 species. Very few are suitable for the home aquarium. One such species, the American flagfish (*Jordanella floridae*), is extremely popular with hobbyists.

Jordanella floridae

Common name: American flagfish
Range: North and Central America, from Florida to the Yucatán Peninsula, in ponds, swamps, lakes, and marshes
Size: 2¼ inches (6 cm)
Description: The body is stocky and moderately compressed. The dorsal region is olive and the belly is cream to white. There are numerous olive spots on the flanks and a series of pale greenish-blue spots that are often arranged in rows along the sides. There is a large black ocellus present at the center of the flank and another white-edged black ocellus on the posterior portion of the dorsal fin.
Aquarium suitability: The American flagfish is an attractive species that is very hardy and easy to keep. It is peaceful and will not harm its neighbors. Provide plenty of cover using plants, rocks, and driftwood and it will soon settle down.

Order: Perciformes

This is not only the largest order within the class Osteichthys (bony fish); it is by far the largest order in the subphylum Vertebrata (vertebrates). With almost 9,300 valid species, the order Perciformes represents almost 25 percent of all known vertebrates! This makes it a very large order; it is split into 148 different families.

It is an unbelievably varied order and ichthyologists and taxonomists cannot agree over the exact divisions and groupings of the various families. In any event, for the aquarist the family listings are far more important and these remain unaffected in the somewhat simplified arrangement as it is shown in the following pages.

The order Perciformes groups together all perchlike fish as well as modified forms of these. It includes the vast majority of the modern bony fish. To be more specific, this order includes the economically important game fish, such as tuna, mackerel, and swordfish, and the cichlids and anabantids of the freshwater tropical fish hobby. A large proportion of all reef fish is included but there are also pelagic and oceanic fish represented, such as skipjack, bonito, marlin, billfish, and albacore. These are well known and highly prized by anglers.

When possible—or when one exists—common family names have also been included to give the reader an idea of the extent and scope of fish encompassed in this order. In all of the sections on freshwater and brackish water fish, frequent reference has been made to marine fish. Certainly many of them will be familiar, even though they may have nothing whatsoever to do with the freshwater aquarium hobby. To some, this could be looked upon as a digression away from the main theme of this book, but this is not so. It is an effort to provide a means for the aquarist to see the overall picture of fish in general and

aquarium fish in particular, which their nearest relatives are, taxonomically speaking, and what the relationship is from one particular group to another. It all helps to build a deeper understanding of this hobby.

Of the 148 families included in the order Perciformes, some of these families are considered as suitable for a reef or marine aquarium—others are suitable for a tropical freshwater aquarium. But many of these species are so rarely imported or so difficult to keep that we can discount them from the outset. The families covered in the following sections contain those species that are most commonly seen for sale to hobbyists, and these have been chosen carefully to indicate their suitability for a home aquarium.

Ambassidae (Asiatic glassfish)

The family Ambassidae is referred to as Chandidae by some authors. Fish from this group are found in the sea, in brackish waters such as tidal estuaries and mangrove swamps, or in freshwater rivers and streams. This latter case is particularly so in Madagascar and India. Asiatic glassfish are found throughout the western Indo-Pacific as far as Australia. The family comprises eight genera (*Ambassis, Chanda, Denariusa, Gymnochanda, Paradoxodacna, Parambassis, Priopis,* and *Tentracentrum*) with about 42 species. Most species have a transparent to semitransparent body and in some cases they are completely scaleless. The dorsal fin usually has seven to eight spines and seven to 11 soft rays. The anal fin has three spines and seven to 11 soft rays. One species, *Paradoxodacna piratica,* actually eats the scales of other fish as the main part of its diet. More than half of the described species are placed in the genus *Ambassis* and 22 species are found solely in fresh water.

Hobbyists have known about Asiatic glassfish for several years but they have never been popular aquarium fish because of their colorless body and lackluster appearance. Interest in them has blossomed recently, but for all the wrong reasons. Some unscrupulous exporters have adopted extreme methods in order to increase business volume: they took a few simple translucent species and dyed them.

Now, because of the unethical artificial coloring of some *Parambassis* species for the aquarium trade and the large losses that result from this practice, wild populations of these fish have been greatly reduced and are rapidly nearing the point where they will be declared endangered. It only requires visits to some main retail outlets to see that few naturally colored specimens are available to the hobbyist.

The trade names of the artificially colored fish are as varied and numerous as their different colors but include Glass tetra, Painted tetra, Painted glassfish, Neon glassfish, and many other created "common names." The list is endless, but the trade names all spell death. The reader should be made aware of such activities for the sake of his or her pocket and the well-being of the fish.

Notes on artificially colored aquarium fish

The process of painting or dyeing fish is an extremely cruel method used to increase fish sales. Most individuals believe that fish do not feel pain, therefore injecting them with dyes or pigments is a perfectly acceptable practice. After the process, many of these fish typically exhibit red, blue, orange, or green on part or the whole of the body, but the dyes used on most are not as bright or gaudy as those used to inject glassfish. In this case, small pockets of dye are injected just below the skin using a large needle. The other method used is to dip a large number of specimens into a caustic or acidic solution to strip them of their slime coat and then dip them into a vat of dye. Of the fish that survive either of these processes—and only a small percentage do—their life span can be measured in months, not years. It is estimated that 80 percent of these fish do not survive longer than three months. A cursory look in a dealer's tank will prove this. Most specimens seen for sale show obvious signs of stress and/or disease. For the fish that reach the retail outlets, there is little chance of their survival.

Many reputable wholesalers of aquarium equipment and plants refuse to deliver to stores that carry these fish. It should be considered to be unethical and inhumane to traffic in these fish and it is hoped that the aquarist will not support it in any way, shape, or form.

Artificially colored glassfish in a dealer's tank. These are sold under the trade names "Painted tetras" or "Painted glassfish."

Parambassis baculis

Common name: Himalayan glassfish
Range: Asia, in the Himalayan region and the central plains of the Ganges River
Size: 2 inches (5 cm)
Description: The body is strongly compressed laterally and has a translucent clear-glass appearance, so the internal bone structure is clearly visible. This is an active fish that prefers the dense vegetation of river margins in its natural habitat.
Aquarium suitability: Unpainted specimens are rarely available and it was not possible for the author of this book to obtain a natural specimen (see page 224).
Breeding information: Specimens not dyed artificially can live and breed under aquarium conditions. However, this is not easy. The several hundred eggs are laid in nests built among plants and the parents will guard their young against predators.

Parambassis ranga

Common name: Indian glassfish
Range: Asia, in Pakistan, India, Bangladesh, Thailand, and Malaysia
Size: 3¼ inches (8 cm)
Description: There is little to choose between the outward characteristics of this and the previous species. Certainly the hobbyist would be hard-pressed to differentiate between the two species. Both are translucent and both are commercially dyed for the aquarium trade. This particular species has a slightly different bone structure and is generally deeper-bodied than *P. baculis*.
Aquarium suitability: Again, untreated natural fish are relatively easy to keep and feed. Dyed specimens are usually short-lived, lose their fluorescent color after about six months, and often die before this happens.

Centrarchidae (Sunfish)

Sunfish began to appear in North America around 20 million years ago in the Miocene period. By the late Miocene period five million years ago, species were widespread west of the Rocky Mountains. Now there is only one extant centrarchid, the Sacramento perch, that is native west of the Rocky Mountains. Almost all sunfish are nest builders, with the male hollowing out a small depression in the substrate with his tail. Once the eggs are laid, it is the male who guards them until they hatch. There are eight genera in this family with about 32 species. The largest species, *Micropterus salmoides* (Largemouth bass) may reach a length of 33 inches (84 cm) and is revered throughout the United States as a top sport fish for anglers. This, along with other bass, has been introduced to areas beyond the natural range.

Lepomis microlophus

Common name: Redear sunfish
Range: North America, in ponds, lakes, and river drainage to the Atlantic and Gulf coasts from Florida to Texas
Size: 15 inches (38 cm)
Description: The Redear sunfish is not very attractive in its juvenile stage (shown on the next page). As it grows, the black bars become more intense and the dorsal and throat regions become a burnished gold color. Specimens that are about a year old develop a bright red spot on the upper part of the operculum. At this stage the black bars (usually 10) break up into vertical rows of spots and blotches. This attractive fish lives for about seven years.
Aquarium suitability: They are relatively slow-growing and will accept most foods in an aquarium. As they grow larger, they should be removed to a bigger or show aquarium.

Monodactylidae (Moonfish, Monos)

Members of this family are sometimes called Moonfish or Fingerfish (The generic name *Monodactylus* means "single finger"). There are two genera with five species and the general characteristics are that they have strongly compressed bodies, often silvery colored. In the juveniles belonging to the genus *Monodactylus*, the pelvic fins are present but in adults they are vestigial or completely absent. They have a single broad-based dorsal fin partially covered with scales.

The range of these fish is widespread throughout the Indo-Pacific from Africa to Australia, often in brackish water and mangrove roots and sometimes even entering freshwater rivers. The three species belonging to the genus *Monodactylus*—*M. argenteus*, *M. falciformes*, and

M. sebae—are often kept in freshwater tropical aquariums. However, they seem to fare better in brackish water.

The eastern Australian species *Schuettea woodwardi* is similar in appearance to *M. argenteus* but is much smaller, seldom exceeding 2 inches (5 cm). This and the remaining species have normal pelvic fins and the scales are cycloid. All the species are fast-swimming and are constantly on the move in search of food, usually in small schools among rocks or in sandy areas of lagoons.

Monodactylus argenteus

Common names: Malayan angelfish, Mono, Silver dollar, Singapore angel, Fingerfish
Range: The Red Sea, and the entire tropical Indo-Pacific, from Africa to Polynesia
Size: 9 inches (23 cm)
Description: Two vertical bars are present, one through the eye and the other behind the opercle. These fade as the fish reaches adulthood. In juvenile specimens the dorsal fin is orange. This fish is capable of living in marine, brackish, or freshwater.
Aquarium suitability: This is a popular aquarium fish usually sold acclimatized to freshwater. To acclimatize it to brackish water, the "drop by drop" method, discussed in the section on introducing fish, should be used over a period of about an hour. Monos should be kept in small groups. Young fish are inclined to nip fins.

Monodactylus sebae

Common names: African moony, Sebae angelfish, African mono, Fingerfish
Range: Eastern Africa, from the Canary Islands and Senegal to Angola, in lagoons, estuaries, and mangroves
Size: 9¾ inches (25 cm)
Description: The Fingerfish has a much deeper body than the previous species and there is less yellow in the body and fin coloration. The background body coloration is silver and there is an intense black ocular bar. A second bar extends from the nape to the throat and a third can be seen from the trailing edge of the dorsal fin to the forward part of the anal fin.
Aquarium suitability: This is not a fish for the beginner. If it is kept in freshwater it will develop disease within a few days (usually white spot) and never really recover from it. This is a fish that does best in brackish water if it is acclimatized slowly.

Toxotidae (Archerfish)

There is only one genus in this family with six described species. They each have a small anal fin with three spines and a dorsal fin with about four strong spines along with 15 to 18 soft rays. Essentially, these are coastal fish that live in estuaries and in freshwater from India to the Philippines and Australia and Polynesia. These fish have the ability to forcefully eject drops or squirts of water from their mouths onto overhanging vegetation in order to down insects from the leaves, which can then be eaten once they have dropped into the water. It is amazing how accurate these droplets can be. The archerfish can adjust for water refraction and still hit their intended target with relative ease. Most archerfish are found in and around mangroves in brackish or freshwater streams. Only one species is regularly imported, *Toxotes jaculatrix*.

Toxotes jaculatrix

Common names: Archerfish, Banded archerfish
Range: India, Asia, and Oceania, in brackish mangrove estuaries, rivers, and streams
Size: 12 inches (30 cm)
Description: The archerfish is well known for its ability to eject beads of water at a high velocity out of the water to overhanging vegetation, directed at insects such as flies. It is a surface-feeder that will also eat floating debris and plant matter. The body is silvery-white, darkening to gold dorsally, with four or five black saddles that extend to the midbody.
Aquarium suitability: This species is great for a brackish aquarium with an open top and hanging lighting. It will keep your living room clear of all flying insects that are attracted to the light. It will also spit water out of the tank if you enter the room. The message is clear then—they need to be fed!

Teraponidae (Tiger perches, Target perches)

There are 16 genera in this family with about 45 species. Thirteen of these are confined to New Guinea, but most species are found in Australia. In general, the tiger perches are known from Africa, India, the Indo-Australian archipelago, Australia, and from Japan to Fiji and Samoa. These are marine coastal, brackish, or freshwater fish with ovate to oblong bodies that are moderately compressed laterally. The anterior portion of the swim bladder is often used for sound production. The dorsal fin usually has a notch between the spinous and soft dorsal rays and the spinous rays can be lowered into a groove or depression that is modeled by a sheath of the dorsal scales.

Although several species are occasionally imported for the aquarium trade, only one has become a favorite among aquarists. This is the bold Target perch, *Terapon jarbua*, which can live equally well in saltwater or freshwater. I have seen shoals of these fish in freshwater streams in Southeast Asia, and stood in the sea to have them scurry around my ankles looking for food when the sand was disturbed.

Terapon jarbua

Common names: Target perch, Target grunt, Crescent perch, Jarbua terapon
Range: Tropical Indo-Pacific, from East Africa and the Red Sea to Australia and Japan, in marine, brackish, or fresh water
Size: 14¼ inches (36 cm)
Description: This fish can be recognized easily because of the curved, crescent-shaped stripes along the body. There are also horizontal stripes on the tail and a large black blotch on the spinous portion of the dorsal fin. Older specimens have tinges of yellow on the pelvic and anal fins. When viewed from above, this species has a pattern like a bull's-eye.
Aquarium suitability: Basically, this is a brackish-water species and salt must be added to make it feel entirely at home. It should not be kept with small fish that can easily fit into its mouth. Nevertheless, it is safe with Scats, Monos, and Archerfish.

Cichlidae (Cichlids)

The Cichlidae family is perhaps the most diverse and incredible example of vertebrate evolution. The immense size of it and the ecological interactions and rapid evolution has provided an important key to the many contingencies that promote speciation. Cichlids have many different feeding behaviors that are not found among other fish. Their parenting is more intense and often unique to this family. It is impressive how many behavioral and physical changes have been made through intense speciation. Although the fundamental body plan of cichlids is fairly consistent, they have developed into an amazing array of colors, shapes, sizes, and dentition patterns.

There are no concrete figures on how many species there are in this family, or even the number of genera.

This is because new species are being discovered on almost a daily basis. The author of this book estimates that there are in excess of 140 genera with more than 2,500 species. This makes it a very large family indeed.

The fundamental fact that no genera exist on more than one continent indicates the degree of endemism that cichlids have established. Cichlids mainly inhabit freshwater, although some can be found in brackish water. A few species will even migrate into the sea to enter other estuaries and river systems. Those that live in isolation in lakes, such as the African Rift Lakes, appear to have the highest degree of diversification. It is thought that up to 2,100 species could be extant in these lakes.

Cichlids can be characterized apart from all other freshwater fish by two unique features: they have a single nostril on each side of the snout and the lateral line is incomplete. Almost all cichlids are relatively small in size and their body form is very diverse. Some species are elongate and tubular, whereas others are perchlike or even disk-shaped. Many species have extended dorsal and anal fins, whereas those in fast-flowing waters are more streamlined. Generally, sexual dimorphism is common among species in this family, with the male exhibiting much more color than the female, particularly during the breeding season. Males are also generally larger than their partners; a profound case of this can be seen with the harem-forming *Neolamprologus callipterus*, where the male is a massive 30 times larger.

Cichlid mating takes on many forms and systems. The most basic form is monogamy with males and females pairing, usually because of color differences. Courtship rituals usually follow before the eggs are laid. The eggs are then cared for by one or both parents. However, some are polygynous, and males fertilize the eggs of several females. Polyandry is another example, where females mate with several males. In a few cases there may be promiscuous spawning (polygynandry), where many males and females congregate together in mass spawning. Basically, there are two kinds of egg breeding in this family. The first is substrate breeding, where the eggs are laid and fertilized on the substrate or plants. The second is mouthbreeding, where the eggs are raised in the mouth of the fish and sometimes even fertilized there. Parental care of cichlid young is typical of most species.

They are usually very territorial, both in feeding and space needs. Very few freshwater fish defend feeding areas, but cichlids do, often with extreme aggression. Nevertheless, they make charming subjects and are one of the most popular groups of fish to keep and breed.

Aequidens pulcher

Common name: Blue acara
Range: Central America to northern South America, including Trinidad and Tobago, in a variety of habitats
Size: 8 inches (20 cm)
Description: The body shape of this fish is ovate and the nape is quite broad. Its color can vary a great deal, from light olive to gray to grayish-black. The individual scales are marked with yellow or pale blue spots. There are often five to eight vertical bars on the body behind the operculum, but these are not always present. There is a bold black spot above the lateral line and below the dorsal, sometimes with several smaller blotches.
Aquarium suitability: Provide plenty of hiding places along with hardy plants and this fish will do well. This is a greedy fish that will live and grow well in a tropical aquarium with other bold and hardy fish.

Aequidens rivulatus

Common names: Green terror, Rivulatus
Range: South America: in coastal streams from the Esmeraldas River in Ecuador to the Tumbes River in Peru
Size: 8 inches (20 cm)
Description: Older males develop a large bump on the nape. The body is ovate and the caudal fin is rounded, often with a yellow or pink margin. The body is olive green dorsally with lighter green on the flanks. The scales have dark green spots that are often arranged into horizontal stripes, and the cheeks have an array of turquoise lines and spots.
Aquarium suitability: Use robust plants in a large aquarium if you intend to keep this species, as it is inclined to burrow in the substrate. It likes rocky areas and driftwood with plenty of space to swim. The Green terror is quite aggressive, so care should be taken in choosing its tank-mates.

Altolamprologus calvus

Common name: Pearly lamprologus
Range: East Africa, in crevices and rocky caves of Lake Tanganyika
Size: 5½ inches (14 cm)
Description: The body is somewhat elongated and compressed laterally. It is marked with 10 to 12 vertical bars behind the operculum. The head is adorned with broad diagonal bars and the flanks and median fins of juveniles are suffused with pearly white spots that fade with age.

Aquarium suitability: Although this is quite a shy fish when it is newly introduced to an aquarium, once it feels safe it will enter out into the open water from its hiding place and begin to explore its new home. Use rocky cover and provide it with lively and hungry tank-mates for the best results.
Breeding information: The water should be hard, with a pH of around 7.5. There should be more females in the breeding tank than males. Spawning usually takes place in a small crevice and roughly 200 yellow-green eggs are laid. The parents guard the eggs at this time. The fry will hatch after two days and start to feed a little over a week later.

Altolamprologus compressiceps

Common name: Compressed cichlid
Range: East Africa, in rocky holes and crevices around the shores of Lake Tanganyika
Size: 6 inches (15 cm)
Description: This is a deep-bodied fish that is strongly compressed laterally. The body is beige to light brown and there are 10 dark vertical bands present from the head to the caudal peduncle. These bands tend to fade with age. In some specimens, the flanks have orange-brown spots and fine blotches.
Aquarium suitability: Although this is a typical cichlid in that it is quite territorial, it is also a shy fish when it is first introduced into an aquarium. Given time, it will develop into quite a character if it is kept among other robust species.
Breeding information: Caves are required, in which the breeding pair can lay up to 300 eggs. Fry require rotifers as first food.

Amphilophus citrinellus

Common names: Midas cichlid, Lemon cichlid, Red devil
Range: North and Central America, from southern Mexico to Costa Rica, in a variety of river systems
Size: 12 inches (30 cm)
Description: Generally, the overall body color is a uniform yellow, orange, orange-red, or white. The tail is rounded and the forehead is marginally concave. Behind this, the nape develops a cranial lump with age, giving this fish a bizarre appearance.
Aquarium suitability: The Midas cichlid tends to be very aggressive toward its tank-mates, particularly around spawning time. It will dig into the substrate and uproot any live plant.
Breeding information: Up to 1,000 eggs are laid on a vertical smooth surface. The female guards the eggs and the male defends the territory. The eggs hatch after three days and are transferred to previously dug pits, where the parents continue their guard.

Amphilophus labiatus

Common names: Red devil, Large-lipped cichlid
Range: Nicaragua, in Lake Managua and Lake Xiloa
Size: 10 inches (25 cm)
Description: As with the previous species, this fish also develops a large cranial lump on its forehead, but the color and markings are different. In this case, the body color can be gray, yellow, white, or orange to orange-red, although it is generally a mix of colors. The caudal fin is rounded and the dorsal and anal fins are pointed at the tips of the trailing edges. A rare red form also exists, but this is seldom caught and available to the hobbyist.
Aquarium suitability: The Red devil can be very pugnacious and should not be kept with small fish that it will eat. In a tank with hiding places and sturdy cichlids, it will not be a problem.
Breeding information: As with *A.citrinellus*, this species will guard its fry in a pit until they are free-swimming.

Amphilophus longimanus

Common name: Red breast cichlid
Range: Central America, from southwestern Honduras to Nicaragua
Size: 7 inches (18 cm)
Description: There are some similarities that can confuse the hobbyist into thinking that this is a Firemouth cichlid (see page 261). Closer inspection will reveal the difference. The belly is bright red and the back is gray-green to greenish-brown. There are several dull dorsal bars present that extend to the lateral line. A series of black blotches run horizontally from behind the operculum to the caudal peduncle.
Aquarium suitability: If this species is kept with other cichlids, it will usually behave itself. If it is kept in a community tank, it will terrorize other tank inhabitants. Hardy, well-rooted plants are required because this fish will burrow into the substrate.

Apistogramma agassizii

Common name: Agassiz's dwarf cichlid
Range: South America: found in shallow, slow-moving tributaries of the Amazon River in Brazil and Bolivia
Size: 3½ inches (9 cm)
Description: The caudal fin is rounded but mature males have extended central rays. Generally, the dorsal base is deep black and the dorsal margin is bright red, as is the tail.
Aquarium suitability: This species can be kept in small groups in peat-rich, slightly acidic water. A male will form a harem with several females.
Breeding information: The breeding tank should have a pH of 6.0–6.5. The male will court and mate with each female. Each of these will lay about 150 eggs in a crevice. The female guards the eggs, which hatch after 72 hours. The fry are moved to shallow depressions and become free-swimming a few days later.

Anomalochromis thomasi

Common names: Dwarf jewel, Butterfly cichlid, African butterfly cichlid
Range: Western Africa, in southern Guinea, southwestern Sierra Leone, and western Liberia, in tributaries of the Moa River
Size: 4 inches (10 cm)
Description: The body color ranges from silver to yellow-brown. There are five black bands on the sides that can be quite indistinct or appear as blotches. Iridescent spots adorn the individual scale margins and these may be yellow, green, or turquoise. With age, these darken to purple or deep blue.
Aquarium suitability: Arrange the tank so that the substrate is dark in color, with plenty of plants and rocks. This will enhance the fish's color and make it feel at home. Leave plenty of space for swimming and use rocks for resting places and potential spawning areas. This is a peaceful cichlid.

Apistogramma borellii

Common names: Umbrella cichlid, Yellow dwarf cichlid
Range: South America, usually in shallow swamps and rivers along the Paraguay River
Size: 2¾ inches (7 cm)
Description: Although this species is similar to *A. agassizii* in form, there are distinct differences. In this case, the head and throat are yellow and the dorsal region and flanks are bluish-green. The first rays of the pelvic fins are extended in adult males. The midbody stripe is indistinct and often reduced to a short stripe toward the base of the tail.
Aquarium suitability: Can be kept with other *Apistogramma* species, catfish, and characins. It can be territorial during the breeding season, but it will not harm plants. It is advisable to keep one male with several females.
Breeding information: This is quite a hard fish to breed.

Apistogramma cacatuoides

Common names: Cockatoo cichlid, Cockatoo dwarf cichlid
Range: South America, in floodplains and rivers along the border of Brazil and Peru
Size: 3½ inches (9 cm)
Description: There are many color variations of this species, depending on its geographic origin and breeding regime. Most commonly, the background body color is olive to gray with orange or yellow median fins. The second, third, and fourth dorsal fin rays are extended, as are the first rays of the pelvic fins. The upper and lower lobes of the tail and the soft dorsal and anal fins all display a ray extension in mature males.
Aquarium suitability: Subdued lighting using floating plants should be provided for this fish. It is quite territorial and males are pugnacious at breeding times. Ensure that there are plenty of hiding places in the rocks and plants.

Apistogramma trifasciata

Common names: Blue apistogramma, Three-stripe dwarf cichlid
Range: South America, in lagoons and ponds in the headwaters of several rivers in southwestern Brazil and Paraguay
Size: 2½ inches (6 cm)
Description: Although this fish's species name is *trifasciata*, which means "three stripes," it has only two. The third band that was originally described is, in fact, a black margin to the anal fin and an indistinct diagonal streak from the operculum to the ventral region. There are two horizontal stripes present on the sides. The first of these is along the base of the dorsal fin. The second is much broader and occurs midlaterally from the eye to the caudal peduncle.
Aquarium suitability: As with other species of this genus, three to four females should be kept in a tank with one male. Create hiding places for each female using rocks and driftwood.

Archocentrus nigrofasciatus

Common name: Convict cichlid
Range: Central America, from Guatemala to Panama
Size: 6 inches (15 cm)
Description: The Convict cichlid is easy to identify because of its distinct markings. Eight or nine vertical black bars are present on a white or gray background. The dorsal and anal fins have yellow or greenish tinges and the belly, operculum, and throat may be pink or mauve.
Aquarium suitability: Not suitable for a community tank that contains tetras and livebearers. It is quite aggressive and males will often kill their own mate. It is best kept with other similar-sized cichlids or in small groups of its own kind.
Breeding information: Eggs are laid on a flat rock and are guarded by both parents. The fry become free-swimming after seven days. Parents will continue brood care for four weeks.

Astronotus ocellatus

Common names: Oscar, Velvet cichlid
Range: South America, with a wide distribution from the Orinoco River basin to the Paraguay River
Size: 14 inches (35.6 cm)
Description: There are several different color morphs of this species. The background body color ranges from gray to black. A marbled ring pattern distinguishes this fish from all other cichlids and it may be pink or deep red. There is a distinct ocellus on the caudal peduncle in most specimens (visible in this photograph).
Aquarium suitability: Oscars are great fish to have in a large show aquarium of 150 gallons (568 liters) or more. They make an impressive sight. Use potted plants with rocks to cover the pots and root systems. A good filtration unit is a prerequisite for an Oscar tank.

Aulonocara baenschi

Common names: Nkhomo-benga peacock, Baensch's peacock, Yellow peacock cichlid, Yellow regal cichlid
Range: East Africa, in rocky and sandy areas of Lake Malawi
Size: 6 inches (15 cm)
Description: There are several color morphs of this species, including one with a blue head. However, the specimen shown here is the one that is most commonly imported for the aquarium trade. The upper half of the body is predominantly yellow, with eight or nine faint bluish bands. The throat and belly is bluish and the median fins are also blue with yellow margins.
Aquarium suitability: This fish requires a tank with lots of rocks and caves. Use sturdy, hard-water plants such as *Anubias* spp. and *Cryptocoryne* spp. The tank should have a coral sand substrate and the water is best kept at a pH of 7.5 to 8.8.

Aulonocara hansbaenschi

Common names: Peacock cichlid, African peacock, Aulonocara Fort Maguire
Range: East Africa, among rocks in Lake Malawi
Size: 6 inches (15 cm)
Description: Some species in this genus are very difficult to identify with any degree of certainty. This one is no exception. This is because several color morphs exist within Lake Malawi in different locations. The body is usually indigo blue or gray with seven to nine vertical black stripes. The head is indigo blue with an iridescent sheen. The trailing edges of the dorsal and anal fins may be blue or yellow.
Aquarium suitability: Provide plenty of rocks and caves for this fish and use a coral sand substrate. If hardy plants are used to decorate the tank, it will usually leave them alone. It requires hard water with a high pH for it to do well.

Aulonocara jacobfreibergi

Common names: Fairy cichlid, Lake Malawi butterfly cichlid
Range: East Africa, in rocky and sandy zones of Lake Malawi
Size: 5 inches (12.7 cm)
Description: Many color variations are known of this particular species. However, the forehead and upper back is usually light brown. The flanks and throat are deep indigo and there are about nine vertical bars along the sides of the body. The dorsal and caudal fins are blue and the anal fin is red and black with a blue margin.

Aquarium suitability: A peaceful fish that can be kept in a community setup without too much trouble if it is housed with other robust fish. As with other members of this genus, it should be fed on a varied diet of bloodworms, mosquito larvae, tubifex, pellet food, and flake food.
Breeding information: The male has egg spots on the anal fin. After the female has spawned, she collects the eggs up into her mouth. She mistakes the spots on the anal fin of the male as eggs and sucks at them. He then releases sperm to fertilize the eggs in her mouth.

Cheilochromis euchilus

Common names: Malawi thick lip, Big-lipped cichlid, Euchilus
Range: East Africa, rocky coastlines of Lake Malawi
Size: 13 inches (33 cm)
Description: A moderately compressed fish with a large head. The background body color is pale tan to dull gold. There are two brownish-black stripes present. The first stripe is subdorsal and extends from the nape to the upper part of the caudal peduncle. The second runs from the operculum to the tail. Juveniles (as seen here) have bold bars that fade with age.
Aquarium suitability: Use a large tank to house this species and provide plenty of caves and other hiding places. Broad-leaved, well-rooted plants should be used.
Breeding information: The female lays 30 to 60 eggs on a rocky surface before taking them into her mouth. The "dummy egg method" (as described above) is used in fertilization.

Cichla ocellaris

Common names: Peacock cichlid, Peacock bass, Lukanani
Range: South America, in large rivers and lakes of Venezuela and Brazil, including the lower Amazon and the Orinoco River
Size: 36 inches (91 cm)
Description: A large fish with a very large appetite. The back is olive green and the belly is deep red in adult specimens. There is a large, white-margined black ocellus stretching into the tail and three broad black bands on the sides in the midbody region. The flanks are golden yellow to dull bronze.
Aquarium suitability: The ultimate size of this fish makes it a poor choice for the freshwater aquarist, unless he has a very large aquarium and plans on something really spectacular as a show tank. The filtration system should be adequate for this fish's enormous appetite and the copious waste it produces. It is a very aggressive fish, but it will not damage plants.

Cichlasoma festae

Common names: Guayas cichlid, Red terror, Festa's cichlid
Range: South America, in the rivers and estuaries of western Ecuador
Size: 20 inches (50 cm)
Description: Males are light green, sometimes iridescent green, with six to eight blue or black bands. The belly and throat regions are rose pink and the dorsal fin is bright blue. Females are more brightly colored during the spawning season, when they are bright orange-red. There is a large, white-margined black ocellus on the upper portion of the tail.
Aquarium suitability: This is quite a pugnacious fish that is extremely territorial. It is not recommended for a community tank unless its tank-mates are large and robust. The aquarium should have plenty of hiding places among rocks and driftwood. Plants will be dug up unless they have mature rooting systems.

Cichlasoma grammodes

Common name: Sieve cichlid
Range: North and Central America, in lakes and rivers from Mexico to Guatemala
Size: 12 inches (30 cm)
Description: Juveniles are olive-brown with a horizontal row of black blotches midlaterally. These fade with age. Males develop red spots on the margins of each scale and the flanks are often greenish-blue, as is the anal fin.
Aquarium suitability: A robust species that is both aggressive and territorial, so care should be taken in choosing its tank-mates. Cichlid pellets seem to be the best food for it, but live food should be given on a twice-weekly basis as a supplement.
Breeding information: Keep an eye on the parents once spawning has occurred—they are inclined to fight with one another. Keep a dividing glass handy in case this happens.

Cichlasoma octofasciatum

Common name: Jack Dempsey
Range: Central America, in slow-moving water in swamps and bogs from Guatemala and Belize to Honduras
Size: 8 inches (20 cm)
Description: Juveniles have two ocelli on the sides. The first is in the midbody region and the second is at the base of the tail. The body coloration is brown to black and the scales are highlighted with spots that range from gold to dark blue or purple-mauve. Vertical bars sometimes appear on the flanks and are shown at will for aggression or defense. In males, the margin of the dorsal fin is bright red.
Aquarium suitability: This is quite an aggressive fish that is often intolerant of its tank-mates. Provide a large tank with plenty of caves, rocks, and bolt-holes for the best results. Plenty of water movement should be provided.

Cichlasoma portalegrense

Common names: Black acara, Port acara
Range: South America, in the rivers and tributaries of the Rio de la Plata in southern Brazil, Bolivia, and Paraguay
Size: 10 inches (25.5 cm)
Description: The background body color is greenish-blue in males, whereas females show reddish-brown tones. There is often iridescence in reflected light. A broad midlateral stripe is present that extends from the eye to the caudal fin. This is sometimes reduced to a row of dark spots.
Aquarium suitability: The Black acara is a peaceful but territorial fish that has a tendency to burrow into the substrate. However, it can be kept in a community setup with other fish of a similar nature.
Breeding information: Frequent partial water changes will prompt spawning. Both parents care for eggs and subsequent fry.

Cichlasoma salvini

Common names: Yellow belly cichlid, Salvini, Tricolor cichlid, Salvin's cichlid
Range: North and Central America, in slow-moving water from southern Mexico to Honduras
Size: 6 inches (15 cm)
Description: Juveniles undergo a remarkable color change before they reach adulthood. They have a greenish-blue iridescence with a midlateral spot and a second spot near the tail. Adult fish have a bright yellow head and belly and two rows of dark spots along the sides. The first of these is subdorsal and the second runs from the eye to the tail.
Aquarium suitability: This is a territorial fish that can be kept with other, medium-sized cichlids and catfish in a relatively large show tank. A varied diet of live and frozen food should be given to help develop its beautiful colors.

Cleithracara maronii

Common name: Keyhole cichlid
Range: South America, in the Rio Maroni on the border between Suriname and French Guiana
Size: 4 inches (10 cm)
Description: There is a characteristic dark blotch present on the body that is often said to resemble a keyhole, hence its common name. In some cases this is more of an ocellus. If frightened, the colors on the fish become considerably darker until the danger has passed.
Aquarium suitability: It requires a well-planted tank with lots of cover and hiding places. This is not an aggressive cichlid and can be kept with catfish, gouramis, and small schooling fish.
Breeding information: Parents will often eat their first brood, but will spawn again within days. Both parents fan the eggs with their fins and pick out the unfertilized ones.

Crenicichla lepidota

Common name: Pike cichlid
Range: South America: Brazil, Bolivia, Paraguay, Uruguay, and northern Argentina, among floating vegetation
Size: 18 inches (46 cm)
Description: The body is elongate and torpedo-shaped. This fish is dark olive green dorsally with a yellow-white belly and throat. A dark brown lateral stripe extends from the snout, through the eye, to the caudal peduncle. Short dark bands adorn the sides of the body, but these do not extend to the belly. There is much variation in markings that is dependent on the actual geographic location of the specimen.
Aquarium suitability: Use floating plants with plenty of root systems to them. Provide hiding places such as rocks and caves for the best results. This species needs plenty of space and is a predator that will swallow any fish that will fit into its mouth.

Crenicichla notopthalmus

Common names: Two-spot pike cichlid, Dwarf pike cichlid
Range: South America, in the Amazon River to Manaus, among floating vegetation
Size: 6 inches (15 cm)
Description: This fish has a typical pike cichlid shape, elongated and cylindrical. The dorsal region is deep orange-tan in color and the belly is brownish-white. A broad dark stripe runs from the snout to the tail and the back has small spots. There is a black ocellus present on the caudal fin.
Aquarium suitability: Although not particularly aggressive, this fish should be housed with other robust cichlids, pacus, and piranha. It requires plenty of swimming space and floating plants to make it feel at home in a captive environment.
Breeding information: The Dwarf pike cichlid has rarely been bred in captivity and little is known of its breeding habits.

Cynotilapia afra

Common names: Dogtooth cichlid, Red-dorsal afra
Range: East Africa, in the open water of Lake Malawi
Size: 4¾ inches (12 cm)
Description: Males are blue with six to eight darker blue bands that are sometimes distinct. The dorsal and caudal fins may be yellow or turquoise, depending on the individual fish, and the pectoral fins are clear. In males, there are three or four orange-brown "egg spots" on the anal fin.
Aquarium suitability: Use coral sand as a substrate to provide an alkaline buffer and keep this fish in hard water. It can be quite aggressive, so it needs caves and plenty of plant cover.
Breeding information: One male should be kept with several females. Once the eggs are laid, the female will take them in her mouth and nudge the egg spots on the anal fin of the male, trying to suck them in. The male then fertilizes the eggs in her mouth.

Cyphotilapia frontosa

Common names: Humphead cichlid, Frontosa
Range: East Africa, in Lake Tanganyika
Size: 14 inches (35 cm)
Description: The body is white or bluish-gray with five or six broad vertical black bands. The median and pelvic fins are generally blue with a hint of violet. Mature males develop a large cranial lump on the forehead.
Aquarium suitability: Humphead cichlids are seminocturnal feeders, so they should be fed in the early morning or late evening. Keep several females to each male for the best results with this fish. A coral sand substrate and plenty of crevices should be provided.
Breeding information: Up to 50 eggs are laid in a cave and the male fertilizes these. The female incubates them in her mouth for four to five weeks.

Cyprichromis leptosoma

Common names: Black-finned slender cichlid, Blue flash
Range: East Africa, in open water near rocky drop-offs of Lake Tanganyika
Size: 5½ inches (14 cm)
Description: The body is slender and elongate. There are many color morphs of this species that vary based on geographic origin. The tail may be blue or bright yellow. The dorsal and anal fins are often bright blue, sometimes with yellow tinges, or they may be deep indigo blue. The head can be yellow or blue.
Aquarium suitability: Provide plenty of swimming space for this fish and ensure the tank has a cover on it, because this fish is inclined to jump, particularly during courtship. It should be kept in groups of six or more, with more females than males.
Breeding information: Breeding is quite difficult because they spawn in open water.

Cyrtocara moorii

Common names: Blue lump head, Blue dolphin cichlid, Hump-head
Range: East Africa, over sandy areas of Lake Malawi
Size: 10 inches (25 cm)
Description: The deep body and fins are generally blue with seven or eight darker blue bars on the sides. Mature males develop a large cranial lump on the forehead, which is frequently gray in color.
Aquarium suitability: Coral sand should be used as a substrate to maintain a high pH. Provide plenty of rocky caves and crevices in which the fish can hide. This fish will thrive on a varied diet of flake food, aquatic insects, and tubifex.
Breeding information: The female lays about 50 eggs, which are then fertilized by the male. She then takes them into her mouth and broods them for 20–24 days.

Dimidiochromis compressiceps

Common name: Malawi eyebiter
Range: East Africa, in the sandy areas of Lake Malawi, among dense growths of tape grass
Size: 10 inches (25 cm)
Description: The body is elongate and strongly compressed laterally; the head is triangular. Males are silvery-blue while females are generally silver. The anal fin of the male is orange-red with several clearly defined egg spots. The dorsal fin is mottled with black streaks and spots, and the soft rays are extended in mature males.
Aquarium suitability: This is a predator with a large mouth, and it should not be housed with small fish. Despite this, it should be kept with nonaggressive tank-mates. It needs plenty of room to swim, so a large tank is a necessity. Live feeder fish are an ideal diet for the Malawi eyebiter.

Eretmodus cyanostictus

Common names: Tanganyika clown, Striped clown goby, Striped goby cichlid
Range: East Africa, on pebbly bottoms in Lake Tanganyika
Size: 3¼ inches (8.5 cm)
Description: The body is elongate with a shallow, sloping forehead. Because of this, and the fact that the upper jaw protrudes over the lower one, the fish appears to have a long snout. The body color is gray to light brown with seven or eight vertical yellow bands. Like many gobies and blennies, this fish likes to rest on its pelvic fins on the substrate.
Aquarium suitability: Strongly territorial toward its own kind, but otherwise a peaceful fish that can be kept in a community tank. Feed algae, mosquito larvae, live foods such as *Daphnia* and frozen brine shrimp, and flake foods.

Etroplus maculatus

Common name: Orange chromide
Range: India and Sri Lanka, in coastal areas and brackish-water rivers
Size: 3½ inches (9 cm)
Description: The color and markings of this fish can vary considerably, depending on where it was collected. The body is compressed laterally and somewhat oval-shaped. The color may be yellow or orange, with or without a midlateral black spot. Juveniles sometimes have a row of spots that fade with age.
Aquarium suitability: This is an ideal choice for a brackish-water aquarium. Pairs should be kept rather than individual fish. Provide plenty of hiding places using rocks and driftwood.
Breeding information: Pairs form monogamous bonds. Once hatched, fry are transferred to pits and the parents continue to care for them for up to four months.

Etroplus suratensis

Common names: Green chromide, Banded chromide
Range: Southeastern Asia, in freshwater, brackish water, and seawater at different times of the year
Size: 18 inches (46 cm)
Description: Juveniles are usually white with eight dark bands. Older fish are olive green to greenish-brown with less distinct bands. The anal fin can have a blue iridescence and the colors become enhanced at breeding times.
Aquarium suitability: The Green chromide is best kept in a brackish-water aquarium along with other chromides. Use robust plants because it is a notorious plant-eater. They should be kept in groups of at least six, as this is a schooling fish.
Breeding information: Up to 1,000 eggs are laid on a rock or in a cave and both parents care for them. These hatch very quickly, in about 36–50 hours. The fry become free-swimming a week later.

Geophagus brasiliensis

Common names: Pearl cichlid, Mother-of-pearl eartheater
Range: South America, along the rocky banks of coastal rivers in Brazil
Size: 12 inches (30 cm)
Description: The body is moderately compressed and the forehead is rounded, especially in adult males. The body color varies from yellow to brown and each scale carries a blue, yellow, or green spot. The median fins have elongated rays and retain a similar pattern to the body, but with blue coloring. Adult males develop humps on their foreheads.
Aquarium suitability: Adult fish require a large tank and a gravel substrate. Arrange the tank so that it has enough substantial hiding places and caves. Plants should be kept in pots in the gravel so that they cannot be uprooted. Tank-mates should be similar in size.

Geophagus steindachneri

Common name: Redhump eartheater
Range: South America, in the upper reaches of the Rio Magdalena and its tributaries in Colombia and Venezuela
Size: 10 inches (25 cm)
Description: The background body color can vary from green to gold. The male develops a nuchal hump on the forehead with age, which can be yellow or red. Often there are irregular dark spots on the sides of the body and the scales can be iridescent.
Aquarium suitability: Males can be quite aggressive but females are not at all territorial. A large tank is recommended, with a sand or gravel substrate.
Breeding information: Up to 150 bright yellow eggs are laid on a rock, which are immediately taken into the female's mouth along with the male's sperm. These are then incubated for about 15 to 20 days.

Gymnogeophagus balzanii

Common name: Argentine humphead
Range: South America, in swamps and slow-moving water along the Rio Paraguay and Rio Paraná in Paraguay and Argentina
Size: 6 inches (15 cm)
Description: The male develops a large hump on its forehead with age. The back can be gray or brown, and the belly and lower flanks are usually yellow to brown. Some specimens have five to eight dark vertical bands on the sides. The tail is often reddish-brown.
Aquarium suitability: Rocks and driftwood should be used to provide hiding places. Although this fish can be territorial, it is generally calm and peaceful when surrounded by nonaggressive species. Keep one male with two or more females and feed them on a wide variety of foods.

Haplochromis obliquidens

Common name: Zebra haplochromis
Range: East Africa, in coastal regions of Lake Victoria and the Victoria Nile
Size: 5 inches (13 cm)
Description: The coloration and markings can vary a great deal dependent on sex, mood, dominance, population, and spawning season. A dominant male is the most colorful. The back is bright orange-red and the flanks are yellow or yellow-green. There are several vertical bars on the body and the fins are multicolored. Females and secondary males are less colorful.
Aquarium suitability: Males are very territorial and will guard quite a large area of the tank. The tank should be planted with areas of well-rooted tape grass and *Anubias* for the best results. The tank-mates for this species should be similar-sized and robust.

Hemichromis bimaculatus

Common names: Jewelfish, Jewel cichlid, Two-spotted jewel cichlid

Range: Western Africa, in forested streams of the Niger River watershed in Guinea, Ivory Coast, Mali, and Sierra Leone

Size: 6 inches (15 cm)

Description: The lower jaw, snout, and cheeks are generally bright red. Numerous small spots and streaks are present on the head and these vary in color from yellow to turquoise. There is a dark spot on the operculum. Dorsally, the body is light olive green and the belly can be light red or orange. At breeding time, these colors intensify with small iridescent spots covering the entire body—hence the name.

Aquarium suitability: The Jewel cichlid tends to uproot plants not strongly rooted and is best kept in compatible pairs. Provide plenty of hiding places constructed from rocks and bogwood.

Hemichromis lifalili

Common names: Blood-red jewel cichlid, Lifalili jewel cichlid

Range: Central Africa, found in tributaries of the Congo and Ubanghi rivers

Size: 5 inches (13 cm)

Description: Generally, the body is bright red with numerous yellow to turquoise spots. A dark spot is present midlaterally. As with the previous species, there is a dark spot on the operculum. The dorsal and caudal fins have turquoise margins.

Aquarium suitability: This species requires good filtration and well-aerated water for it to do well. Like *H. bimaculatus*, it is inclined to be very territorial, particularly at breeding time.

Breeding information: The male digs a spawning pit, in which 250 to 350 eggs are laid and fertilized. The male then abandons the female and the brood. The female mouthbreeds the eggs and fry until they are large enough to fend for themselves.

Herichthys carpintis

Common name: Pearlscale cichlid

Range: North America, in the Rio Panuco river system of northern Mexico

Size: 12 inches (30 cm)

Description: The body is moderately compressed laterally and during the breeding season it is deep black with many iridescent turquoise and green spots. The iris of the eye is deep red in color.

Aquarium suitability: This species grows quite large and needs a good-sized tank with roots and caves for shelter. It is pugnacious and territorial, so it should only be combined with other large cichlids. Most foods are accepted eagerly.

Breeding information: Up to 500 eggs are laid, which are guarded and cleaned by both parents. The female digs a pit and when the fry emerge after five to seven days, they are transferred there. They become free-swimming a week later.

Herichthys cyanoguttatus

Common names: Texas cichlid, Rio Grande cichlid
Range: North America, in the Rio Grande, the Rio Pecos, and the Rio Conchus in Mexico
Size: 12 inches (30 cm)
Description: The body is compressed with a high back. Mature males develop a cranial hump on the forehead. The trailing edges of the dorsal and anal fins are extended in adults. The body color varies from gold, through greenish-gray, to dark brown. Numerous gold spots cover much of the body and there is a black spot on the caudal peduncle. In front of this there is often a row of dark blotches that extend horizontally.
Aquarium suitability: Needs a large tank with plenty of open swimming area as well as hiding places. Provide strong aeration and use floating plants as cover for the best results. This is quite an intolerant species that will eat small fish.

Heros severus

Common names: Banded cichlid, Severum
Range: South America, in still or slow-moving water in the Amazon basin northward to the Orinoco basin
Size: 12 inches (30 cm)
Description: There are many color variations, but the most commonly seen color morph is olive green dorsally with a gold-green belly. The anal region is often orange-red. There are seven or eight dark vertical bands along the sides that fade with age.
Aquarium suitability: Great for a community tank containing other medium to large fish. The Banded cichlid is a peaceful species and very hardy. Keep them in pairs or small groups.
Breeding information: The water should have a pH of 6.0–6.5 and be of a slightly higher temperature than is normal for a cichlid tank. Up to 1,000 eggs are laid on rocks. The female cares for the eggs and the male defends the territory.

Herotilapia multipinosa

Common name: Rainbow cichlid
Range: Central America, in shallow muddy river margins of rivers with dense vegetation, from Honduras to Panama
Size: 6 inches (15 cm)
Description: The body is generally golden yellow with a black lateral stripe that extends from the eye to the caudal peduncle. In some fish this stripe is broken into a row of black blotches.
Aquarium suitability: Fine gravel or sand should be used as a substrate. Provide dense planting with tape grass, *Anubias*, and *Cryptocoryne*, with plenty of caves and hiding places. This is a hardy and peaceful species that is inclined to be territorial.
Breeding information: After the eggs are laid in crevices, the male fans and guards the eggs until they hatch two or three days later. He then moves them to small pits and continues to guard the fry until they can fend for themselves.

Hypselecara temporalis

Common names: Emerald cichlid, Chocolate cichlid
Range: South America, in Lake Hyanuary, Lake Saraca, and the Hutay River in Brazil
Size: 12 inches (30 cm)
Description: Emerald cichlids do not show their true colors until they are adults. Juveniles are bright to dull yellow in color with a large black spot midlaterally. The belly, throat, and cheeks are often red. Older males develop a deep emerald green back, particularly toward the tail, and the rest of the body can be deep red.
Aquarium suitability: A large tank is required for this fish. It will uproot most plants unless they are long-established or in pots in the substrate. Despite its size, it is good in a community setup and peaceful to other tank-mates, though sometimes it can be intolerant of its own kind.

Julidochromis dickfeldi

Common names: Blue julie, Brown julie, Dickfeld's julie
Range: East Africa, near the Zambian shores of Lake Tanganyika, particularly in rocky areas
Size: 4 inches (10 cm)
Description: The body is elongate and torpedo-shaped with three dark gray or black stripes that extend from the head to the caudal peduncle. The background body color may be white, pale brown, or bluish-gray. The lowest stripe runs through the eye to the tip of the snout.
Aquarium suitability: Despite its small size, a large tank and plenty of caves are required for this species. It needs a lot of space and is strongly territorial, particularly to its own kind.
Breeding information: A compatible pair is required if any success is to be achieved. Around 40 eggs are laid on the roof of a cave and both parents will aggressively defend these.

Julidochromis marlieri

Common names: Marlier's julie, Checkerboard julie
Range: East Africa, along the southwestern shores of Lake Tanganyika
Size: 6 inches (15 cm)
Description: A striking fish with the typical body shape of this genus. Adults develop a hump on the nape. The body is light beige to golden yellow, with three to four dark brown lateral stripes. Crossing these are five to eight vertical bands, which together form a checkerboard pattern. The median fins are suffused with spots and have white margins.
Aquarium suitability: Very territorial to its own kind but generally peaceful with other species. It can be combined with other hardy Lake Tanganyika cichlids, unless there are insufficient hiding places. This will inevitably result in territorial squabbles.

Julidochromis ornatus

Common names: Ornate julie, Golden julie, Yellow julie
Range: East Africa, in rocky areas close to the shores of Lake Tanganyika
Size: 3¼ inches (8 cm)
Description: One of the most attractive representatives of this genus, the Ornate julie exhibits the typical three-stripe color pattern, but the fins are often bright yellow, particularly in mature males. In secondary males, the fins are usually pale yellow with dark spots and the belly is yellow.
Aquarium suitability: Fine gravel or coral sand should be used as a substrate, along with plenty of rocks and caves, which the species will need for breeding. A few hardy plants can be included in the setup. The wise aquarist will ensure that the tank has a tight-fitting lid—this fish is inclined to jump if it is frightened.

Julidochromis regani

Common names: Convict julie, Regan's julie, Striped julie
Range: East Africa, in Lake Tanganyika
Size: 12 inches (30 cm)
Description: Similar to the previous species, but the body is more elongate. The background body color varies from pale cream to dull yellow. The median fins are mottled and spotted, often with a black submargin and a blue-and-white margin. The body is marked with three or four horizontal deep brown stripes.
Aquarium suitability: Like all *Julidochromis* species, it is aggressive toward its own kind and very pugnacious toward all other fish during the breeding period. Try to avoid keeping this fish with others that are small enough to swallow.
Breeding information: About 300 eggs are laid on the ceiling of a cave and hatch after two to four days. The parents continue their care for six to eight days, after which fry emerge.

Julidochromis transcriptus

Common name: Masked julie
Range: East Africa, along the northwestern coast of Lake Tanganyika
Size: 2¾ inches (7 cm)
Description: This fish is easy to identify because of the seven or eight broad black bars along the sides. There is also a saddlelike bar across the nape. The background body color is white or pale yellow, although in some specimens it appears that the reverse is true and the base color is black with white or yellow bars. The dorsal, anal, and caudal fins have bright turquoise margins.
Aquarium suitability: The care of this species, as well as its breeding pattern, is the same as others of this genus. They require a varied diet that should include insect larvae, aquatic insects, tubifex, finely chopped meat, algae, spinach, flake food, bloodworms, and pellets.

Labeotropheus fuelleborni

Common name: Blue mbuna
Range: East Africa, along rocky shores of Lake Malawi
Size: 7 inches (18 cm)
Description: The body is elongate and the upper jaw extends over the lower one. Males are generally blue with 10–12 darker blue vertical bands that are sometimes indistinct. Females are often very similar, although some are pale orange or white with large black blotches over much of the body.
Aquarium suitability: Probably the most peaceful of all the mbunas. The tank should have plenty of rock work, but no plants—they will be eaten. Use strong aquarium lighting to promote algal growth on the rocks.
Breeding information: Use hard, alkaline water and a pair will spawn quite easily. About 60 eggs are mouthbred in the female's throat. Fry are free-swimming after three to four weeks.

Labeotropheus trewavasae

Common names: Scrapermouth mbuna, Red-finned cichlid
Range: East Africa, in Lake Malawi, in areas where there are plenty of algae-covered rocks
Size: 4½ inches (11 cm)
Description: The body shape is the same as the previous species and the soft rays of the anal and dorsal fins are extended to points in adults. Coloration is also similar, but in this case the dorsal fin is bright red in adult males. Sometimes this red also appears in the caudal and anal fins.
Aquarium suitability: Because this is quite an aggressive and territorial fish, it should only be housed in a tank with other mbunas. Hiding places are particularly important.
Breeding information: Several females should be kept with a single male. Anywhere from 12 to 40 eggs are mouthbred and fertilized by the dummy egg method. Fry emerge three or four weeks later.

Labidochromis caeruleus

Common names: Blue streak hap, Electric yellow mbuna, Yellow labid
Range: East Africa, at various depths and habitats in Lake Malawi
Size: 4 inches (10 cm)
Description: The forehead is curved and the body is elongate. The body coloration is bright yellow and the iris of the eye occasionally has a short black bar running diagonally through it. The median fins are yellow with black margins and the pelvic fins are black with blue streaks along the leading edges.
Aquarium suitability: The aquarium should be arranged with some rock structures that extend almost to the water surface and with plenty of hiding places within the rocks. The substrate should be coral sand in order to buffer the pH and keep the water alkaline.

Lamprologus ocellatus

Common name: Ocellated shell-dweller
Range: East Africa, in sandy and muddy areas of Lake Tanganyika
Size: 2½ inches (6 cm)
Description: This is a tiny fish that lives in shells scattered on the substrate. Its body color varies from pale tan to light brown. There is an indistinct white midlateral stripe on the body. This extends from the operculum to the tail. Below this, a second stripe runs parallel to it. Often the throat, belly, and chest display an iridescent violet color (usually males) and there are large black ocelli on the operculum.
Aquarium suitability: Ideally, a fine sand substrate should be used for this fish. Along with this, there should be a scattering of large shells from land snails so that each fish has one.
Breeding information: Spawning occurs in the female's shell.

Laetacara curviceps

Common name: Flag acara
Range: South America, in slow-moving rivers and lakes throughout the Amazon River system
Size: 3½ inches (9 cm)
Description: An oval-shaped fish with a rounded caudal fin. The body coloration can vary a great deal but generally the dorsal region and head are olive to gray. The flanks may be green or blue, and this color increases in intensity toward the caudal peduncle. A black midlateral stripe is present in most cases and this extends horizontally from the eye to the midbody, accompanied by a cream- or yellow-margined ocellus.
Aquarium suitability: This species will not harm plants and, with the exception of the breeding season, can be kept with other peaceful community fish such as large tetras and gouramis. Most foods are accepted eagerly.

Lobochilotes labiatus

Common name: Zebra cichlid
Range: East Africa, at great depth in rocky areas of Lake Tanganyika
Size: 16 inches (41 cm)
Description: Juveniles have a light tan body with 10 to 12 narrow brown vertical bands. As the fish grows in size, these bands become more distinct and the body deepens to a rich greenish-white or greenish-brown, and the bands turn dark gray. The lips of the adult fish are thick and well developed.
Aquarium suitability: Juveniles can be kept in a 48-inch (122-cm) tank, but larger individuals need a lot more space. The tank must have lots of free-swimming space with plenty of hiding places. Keep one male with several females. This is a very aggressive, predatory fish that should be left to the expert fishkeeper.

Melanochromis auratus

Common names: Golden mbuna, Malawi golden cichlid, Auratus
Range: East Africa, along the rocky shores of Lake Malawi
Size: 5 inches (12 cm)
Description: The body is golden yellow with three black horizontal stripes. Each of these stripes has a parallel white stripe close to it. The tail is often spotted, but the other fins are golden yellow. Mature males are much darker and, depending on the geographic location where the fish is found, may have a black background body color with turquoise or blue stripes.

Aquarium suitability: This fish is quite pugnacious and can be very intolerant of its tank-mates unless plenty of space is provided. One male should be kept with several females in a "Malawi tank" with other similar species.

Breeding information: Parents form a matriarchal family with one male in a spawning tank. Spawning occurs with the female laying just 10 to 30 eggs. These are taken into her mouth, where the male fertilizes them. He should then be removed from the tank. The fry emerge after one week and can be fed on small fry foods.

Melanochromis chipokae

Common name: Chipokae mbuna
Range: East Africa, in rocky coastal areas of Lake Malawi
Size: 4¾ inches (12 cm)
Description: Females are very similar in appearance to *M. auratus*, but they lack the white horizontal stripes next to the black ones. Males have light blue horizontal stripes and may be completely blue as adults.

Aquarium suitability: Probably the most aggressive of all the mbunas, this fish is a real killer that will take over any tank and squabble with anything that encroaches its territory—which usually means the whole aquarium. During the spawning season, it will try to kill any fish that challenges its territory.

Breeding information: Up to 40 eggs are laid and the female takes them in her mouth. Fertilization takes place via the "dummy egg" phenomenon. Remove the male at this point.

Melanochromis parallelus

Common name: Parallel striped mbuna
Range: East Africa, in rocky inshore areas of Lake Malawi where there is an abundance of food
Size: 5 inches (13 cm)
Description: The body is elongate and torpedo-shaped. Juveniles and females have white bellies and yellow-white bodies. A bold horizontal stripe extends from behind the eye to the tail. A second stripe runs from the nape, along the dorsal base, to the trailing edge of the soft dorsal fin. The dorsal fin is black submarginally with a white margin. Males are black with three or four indigo blue stripes.
Aquarium suitability: This is a very hardy fish, but quite aggressive, especially toward its own kind. The substrate should comprise coral sand or very fine gravel. Coral sand is the best choice because it will help buffer the pH of the aquarium.

Melanochromis johannii

Common names: Bluegray mbuna, Johannii, Johann's mbuna
Range: East Africa, in stony areas between huge sedimentary rocks around the coasts of Lake Malawi
Size: 4¾ inches (12 cm)
Description: The body shape reflects that of other mbunas. The color is variable and depends on the sex of the fish and its age. Juveniles and females tend to have a dark body with three yellow or cream stripes that extend from the operculum to the tail. Males have a similar body pattern but the dark background body color is often deep indigo and the stripes are bright blue.
Aquarium suitability: Keep this fish with other mbunas of a similar size. For the best results, keep one male with several females and provide plenty of rock caves and crevices in which the fish can hide. Feeding this fish is not a problem if a wide variety of foods are offered.

Melanochromis vermivorus

Common name: Purple mbuna
Range: East Africa, in a variety of habitats in Lake Malawi
Size: 6 inches (15 cm)
Description: Similar to the previous species, but the body is dark blue. Dorsally, there is a row of white to turquoise blotches that extend from the upper lip to the soft dorsal fin. These sometimes form a stripe. Below this there is a bolder stripe, similarly colored, and a third stripe that runs from the operculum midlaterally to the base of the tail. Females are smaller than males and lack the "egg spots" on their anal fins.
Aquarium suitability: Keep a single male with several females. This is a very aggressive species, so plenty of hiding places in its tank are a prerequisite if any success is to be achieved. It can be kept in a community setup with other similar-sized mbunas.
Breeding information: This species is difficult to breed in captivity.

Mesonauta festivus

Common names: Flag cichlid, Festivum, Festive cichlid
Range: South America, specifically from the upper tributaries of the Amazon in Bolivia and Paraguay
Size: 6 inches (15 cm)
Description: This species has recently undergone revision that has resulted in its division into five separate species. It is an oval-formed fish that is moderately compressed. The belly is usually white and it is greenish-gray to dark olive dorsally. A dark oblique stripe runs from the eye to the base of the soft dorsal fin. The median fins are often suffused with irregular rows of spots.
Aquarium suitability: For a cichlid, this is quite a timid fish. It should never be housed in a tank with Neon or Cardinal tetras, though, because these small fish form a great part of its natural diet! It should be kept in a tank along with other peaceful cichlids.

Mikrogeophagus ramirezi

Common names: Ram cichlid, Dwarf cichlid, Butterfly cichlid, Ram, Venezuelan ram
Range: South America: in brooks, swamps, and lagoons of the Orinoco River in Venezuela and Colombia
Size: 3½ inches (9 cm)
Description: The body is moderately elongate and the dorsal fin is high. The belly is often pink, and the rest of the body is blue in older specimens. The iris of the eye is red and there is a black stripe running through it that extends from the nape to the throat. The median fins carry many blue spots and the pelvic fins are a dull orange-red. There is a bold black spot present behind the operculum in the middorsal region.
Aquarium suitability: Plenty of plants are needed for this species to feel completely at home. Floating plants help to diffuse strong aquarium lighting and bring out its true colors.

Nannacara anomala

Common name: Goldeneye cichlid
Range: South America, in streams and slow-moving waters of western Guyana
Size: 3½ inches (9 cm)
Description: Several color morphs are common with this particular species. Generally, the female is less colorful than the male. Males are dark olive green dorsally and the flanks are bluish-green. One or two lateral stripes are present that extend from the operculum to the caudal peduncle. The anterior portion of the dorsal fin is red and the dorsal margin is white.
Aquarium suitability: The tank should be well planted with plenty of hiding places that have been constructed using bogwood and rocks. Except during the spawning season, this is a peaceful community fish.

Neolamprologus brichardi

Common names: Fairy cichlid, Lyretail cichlid
Range: East Africa, around rocky shorelines of Lake Tanganyika
Size: 4 inches (10 cm)
Description: The body is elongate and laterally compressed. The upper and lower outer rays of the caudal fin are extended to give this species a characteristic lyretail. The body color is pale tan with small yellow spots on the flanks. The iris of the eye is bright blue and there is a short horizontal bar present that runs from the eye to the operculum. Above this is a golden yellow spot on the operculum.
Aquarium suitability: Plenty of free-swimming space should be provided for this fish. Use coral sand as a substrate to buffer the pH and keep it alkaline. Provide rocks and caves into which the fish can retire.

Neolamprologus leleupi

Common name: Lemon cichlid
Range: East Africa, in coastal areas of Lake Tanganyika
Size: 4 inches (10 cm)
Description: The body is elongate and bright yellow in color. Juveniles have large eyes in relation to the rest of the body. At this stage, the first rays of the pelvic fins have white edges. The tail is fan-shaped and the lips are relatively large.
Aquarium suitability: This is a peaceful fish that can be kept in a community aquarium. Coral sand should be used as a substrate and the tank should be well planted with hardy species. Provide plenty of rocks and caves and a varied diet for the best results.
Breeding information: Roughly 150 eggs are laid on the ceiling of a cave. The female cares for the eggs and the male guards the surrounding area. The fry hatch after three days and feed from their egg sacs for an additional three to four days.

Neolamprologus longior

Common name: Elongated lemon cichlid
Range: East Africa, in rocky shore areas of the eastern side of Lake Tanganyika
Size: 4 inches (10 cm)
Description: Similar to the previous species, but in this case the body is somewhat more elongate and not always yellow. The body color can vary from pale tan or yellow to dull orange. There is often a violet area present under and behind the eye that extends onto the operculum.
Aquarium suitability: A varied diet is required to bring out the true colors of this fish. The ideal foods for this and other Lake Tanganyika cichlids are insect larvae, aquatic insects, flake food, crustaceans, and pellet foods.
Breeding information: This is a cave-breeder and the breeding techniques are the same as others of this genus.

Neolamprologus tetracanthus

Common name: Fourspine cichlid
Range: East Africa, in rocky and sandy inshore areas of Lake Tanganyika
Size: 8 inches (20 cm)
Description: The background body color can vary from pale tan to deep violet-green. The body and dorsal fin have fine horizontal rows of spots that give the impression of narrow stripes running along the body and radiating out into the caudal fin. On the anterior part of the body these are pearly white, but on the flanks they are bright turquoise blue.
Aquarium suitability: This is a peaceful fish that is only aggressive toward its own kind. Therefore it is ideal for a Lake Tanganyika community tank. Do not combine with fish that are considerably smaller than this fish, or they will be eaten.

Neolamprologus pulcher

Common names: Daffodil cichlid, Daffodil brichardi
Range: East Africa, in areas of heavy aquatic vegetation around the shores of Lake Tanganyika
Size: 4 inches (10 cm)
Description: Adult males develop a cranial hump on the nape. The caudal fin is typically lyre-shaped with greatly extended upper and lower fin rays. The body varies from pinkish-tan to yellow, sometimes with a pale mauve iridescence. The margins of the median fins are bluish-white and there is a yellow spot at the angle of the pectoral fin. Males are slightly smaller and more colorful than females.
Aquarium suitability: Provide plenty of robust plants for this species. *Anubias* and *Cryptocoryne* are ideal for this purpose but they should be kept in pots in the substrate to keep them from becoming uprooted.

Neolamprologus tretocephalus

Common name: Five-barred cichlid
Range: East Africa, in rocky areas of Lake Tanganyika
Size: 6 inches (15 cm)
Description: The body is cream to white with five broad black vertical bars. A sixth bar is incomplete and runs from the nape to the eye. Adult males have blue median fins that get very dark in color during breeding times. The pelvic fins are blue with white leading edges. The throat and chest are usually lighter in color than the rest of the body.
Aquarium suitability: Adult fish need a large tank with plenty of room to swim. Provide caves and crevices to ensure that this species feels at home in a captive environment.
Breeding information: The water should be quite hard and the water temperature should be around 79–82°F (26–28°C) for any breeding to take place.

Nimbochromis linni

Common name: Elephant-nose cichlid
Range: East Africa, along the rocky coasts of Lake Malawi
Size: 14 inches (35.6 cm)
Description: This species has large lips and a protruding upper jaw with a concave throat. This gives the impression that it has a trunk rather than a snout. The body color is variable to the extreme. Males are mottled blue or have blue on the head. Females are mottled brown and often have vertical bands on the tail. The male possesses distinct egg spots on the anal fin.
Aquarium suitability: This is a predator that will eat small fish, so care should be taken in choosing its tank-mates. Males tend to be quite aggressive, so it should be housed with other robust cichlids in a large tank with plenty of rocks and well-rooted plants. Most foods are accepted eagerly.

Nimbochromis livingstonii

Common name: Livingstoni
Range: East Africa, in reed beds and sandy areas of Lake Malawi
Size: 12 inches (30 cm)
Description: The tail in adults is truncate. The color varies between sexes. The female has a creamy white background color with bold brown blotches over much of the body and fins. Males are similarly colored, but the blotches are a darker bluish-black and the lighter areas are bluish-white.
Aquarium suitability: This is a predator that will lie on its side waiting for prey. It will play dead until a suitable small fish comes within its reach to be snapped up. For this reason it should only be housed with similar-sized fish.
Breeding information: A large breeding tank is required. Up to 100 eggs are mouthbred by the female for 21 to 25 days. The resultant fry can be fed on all the usual fry foods.

Nimbochromis polystigma

Common name: Polystigma
Range: East Africa, along rocky coastlines of Lake Malawi
Size: 10 inches (25 cm)
Description: The coloration of the female is different than the male. Females have a creamy white body with brown blotches. Males, on the other hand, have a bluish head and a white to golden yellow body. The blotches that cover much of the body range from slate gray to bluish-green. Yellow egg spots are present on the anal fin.
Aquarium suitability: A large, heavily planted tank is required with plenty of hiding places. This is a predator that will eat small fish, so care should be exercised in choosing its tank-mates.
Breeding information: About 30 eggs are laid and fertilized using the dummy egg method. The female mouthbreeds these for 21 to 24 days. Remove all other fish from the breeding tank.

Nimbochromis venustus

Common names: Giraffe cichlid, Venustus
Range: East Africa, in sandy areas of Lake Malawi
Size: 10 inches (25 cm)
Description: Juveniles have white bodies, yellow bellies, and dark brownish-black patches over much of the body. Adult males tend to be yellow with blue on the head and median fins and bluish-black blotches on the body.
Aquarium suitability: Although this is a very aggressive fish toward its own kind and other tank-mates, it is also quite intelligent and will try to get your attention when it is not chasing other fish. It should be given plenty of free-swimming space and many hiding places. The Giraffe cichlid will flourish on a twice-weekly diet of live foods along with daily dried foods. Close to spawning, females should not be frightened, otherwise the eggs will be prematurely expelled.

Oreochromis mossambicus

Common names: Mozambique tilapia, Mozambique mouth brooder
Range: East Africa, in freshwater, brackish water, and saltwater
Size: 20 inches (51 cm)
Description: The body color is deep olive green to bluish-gray, with a silver iridescence. The belly is usually lighter with faint reddish tinges during the breeding period. The median fins have red margins and the pectoral fins can be pink, orange, or red in adults. This species has been artificially introduced throughout Africa, Indonesia, and the southern United States as a food fish.
Aquarium suitability: Although this fish is belligerent toward its own kind, it is generally peaceful with other large cichlids. It is a heavy eater and grows fast, so a good filtration system is needed to deal with the copious amount of waste that it produces.

Parachromis friedrichsthalii

Common name: Yellowjacket cichlid
Range: North and Central America, from Mexico to Costa Rica
Size: 10 inches (25 cm)
Description: There are many color morphs of this species but the most common one has a bright yellow body with 10 to 12 irregular vertical bars. Another morph, such as the one seen here, is yellow with a horizontal row of midlateral spots that sometimes join to form a stripe running from the operculum to the tail.
Aquarium suitability: Although this fish does not eat plants, it is an active digger and will uproot most plants that do not have a good root system. It is a highly pugnacious species that can only be kept in a tank with other large cichlids.
Breeding information: About 400 eggs are laid on smooth rocks. After 72 hours, the eggs hatch and the fry are moved to pits. After another five days, the fry are free-swimming.

Parachromis managuensis

Common names: Guapote tiger, Managua cichlid, Jaguar cichlid
Range: Central America, in still and slow-moving water throughout Nicaragua, Costa Rica, and southern Honduras
Size: 20 inches (51 cm)
Description: The normal body color is creamy white to light gray with an overlay of dark spots and blotches. This color pattern continues onto the fins, but no two color patterns are the same on individual specimens. The iris of the eye is usually bright red.
Aquarium suitability: Young fish can be kept in a small aquarium. However, they grow quite fast and get very large, at which point they will need to be moved to a larger tank; aquarists should plan accordingly. Use potted or plastic plants as decoration because it will uproot anything that is not secure in the substrate.

Pelvicachromis pulcher

Common names: Rainbow krib, Common krib, Purple cichlid, Kribensis
Range: Central Africa, in slow-moving rivers with plenty of vegetation; in the Niger River delta of southern Nigeria
Size: 4 inches (10 cm)
Description: Males have elongated fin rays on the dorsal, anal, and caudal fins. There are two dark brown stripes present: the first extends from the nape along the base of the dorsal fin, and the second runs from the snout to the tail. Above this second stripe, the body is yellow-green, and below the stripe, the belly region is often bright mauve, deep magenta, or purple.
Aquarium suitability: A dark substrate should be used to enhance the colors of this fish. Floating plants will reduce strong lighting and make this fish feel at home. The aquarium should have plenty of plants and rocky hiding places.

Placidochromis electra

Common names: Deep-water hap, Deep-water haplo, Hap electra
Range: East Africa, in intermediate zones between rocky and sandy substrate in Lake Malawi
Size: 8 inches (20 cm)
Description: The head and snout are steeply angled and the mouth has a slightly protruding upper jaw. There are six to eight vertical bars present on the body that tend to fade with age. The boldest of these is the first bar, which extends from the first rays of the dorsal fin to the throat. The rest of the bars are less distinct. Generally, the body is silver to pale blue and the fins are darker with a black or dark blue stripe submarginally.
Aquarium suitability: A good-natured fish that needs plenty of room for it to grow. Given a large tank with lots of crevices, plants, and hiding places, this fish will be in its element.

Protomelas taeniolatus

Common name: Red empress
Range: East Africa, in coastal regions of Lake Malawi
Size: 8¼ inches (21 cm)
Description: Females are generally brown with horizontal stripes. Males are very colorful as they reach maturity and often have red flanks and fins, and a blue head and throat. The median fins carry pearl-like spots of bluish-white, red, and blue, and the dorsal fin margin is white.
Aquarium suitability: An aggressive fish in any size of tank, males will defend a large territory. The tank should be equipped with dozens of rocky hiding places and caves. Keep only one male and choose robust and hardy tank-mates.
Breeding information: After an elaborate courtship, with the male vibrating and showing his colors, the female lays up to 60 eggs. Egg and fry care is the same as for Lake Malawi cichlids.

Pseudotropheus aurora

Common name: Aurora cichlid
Range: East Africa, in Lake Malawi, around the Likoma Islands and Mdemba Bay
Size: 4¼ inches (11 cm)
Description: Males are generally light blue or light turquoise with seven indistinct broad vertical bars along the sides. The throat, belly, and pelvic fins are yellow, as is the iris of the eye. Females are far less colorful and tend to be drab brown in color.
Aquarium suitability: The tank should be set up using a coral sand substrate with lots of rocky crevices and retreats for this fish. Use robust plants such as *Anubias* spp. and tape grass. Strong lighting is a must to promote a good growth of algae.
Breeding information: Up to 75 eggs are laid on a flat rock and the female incubates these in her mouth for 18 to 21 days. As soon as the fry emerge, they should be fed on rotifers such as *Artemia*.

Pseudotropheus barlowi

Common name: Golden fuscoides
Range: East Africa, around the Mbenji and Maleri islands of Lake Malawi
Size: 4 inches (10 cm)
Description: The body is bright yellow in color. The fins are often mottled with blue and yellow spots in adults. The dorsal fin is blue submarginally with a yellow margin in adult males. Females tend to be less colorful.
Aquarium suitability: This is an aggressive species for its size and should be kept with similar-sized Lake Malawi cichlids.
Breeding information: Quite an easy fish to breed. Up to 50 eggs are laid on a flat rock. The female takes these into her mouth and the male fertilizes them using the dummy egg method. These are then incubated for 20 to 22 days before being released as free-swimming fry.

Pseudotropheus crabro

Common names: Bumblebee mbuna, Hornet cichlid
Range: East Africa, among rocks and stony outcrops along the coastlines of Lake Malawi
Size: 4 inches (10 cm)
Description: The background body color is usually dull yellow with an overlay of eight or nine broad vertical black bars. Sometimes these bars stop short of the belly, leaving it light yellow. In other geographic areas, specimens may show one or two horizontal stripes in a crisscross pattern.
Aquarium suitability: Hard water and coral sand as a substrate are prerequisites for this fish. Leave open areas for swimming space and provide plenty of rocky cover and robust plants.
Breeding information: The male should be kept with several females. Around 50 eggs are fertilized using the dummy egg method. The female then broods these for 20 to 25 days.

Pseudotropheus elongatus

Common names: Elongate mbuna, Slender mbuna
Range: East Africa, the rocky coastlines of Lake Malawi
Size: 5¼ inches (13.5 cm)
Description: Somewhat more elongate than other mbunas, this species has a light to dark blue body with six to eight dark vertical bands. The body color of juveniles is usually bluish-white and the bands are quite pronounced. In older specimens, the bands on the flanks fade and become less distinct.
Aquarium suitability: This is one of the most aggressive of all the Lake Malawi cichlids. If a single female is housed with this fish, it will most likely kill it. Keep several females with a single male, because males form a polygamous relationship with females. Provide plenty of live food in a varied diet.
Breeding information: About 30 to 40 eggs are fertilized in the mouth and incubated for three weeks prior to being released.

Pseudotropheus socolofi

Common names: Pindani, Eduard's mbuna
Range: East Africa, eastern coast of Lake Malawi
Size: 4¾ inches (11 cm)
Description: There are many color morphs of this species, which often leads to confusion over the exact scientific name. Specimens may be light blue, dark blue, or yellow. Blue morphs usually have dark dorsal and anal fin margins.
Aquarium suitability: Requires plenty of hiding places and free-swimming space. It is best to build rock structures toward the surface, leaving caves and crannies in which the fish can hide. This species will not harm robust plants.
Breeding information: Several females are required for every one male. Up to 60 eggs are laid and fertilized using the dummy egg method. The female broods the eggs for 20 to 25 days, after which the blue-colored fry emerge.

Pseudotropheus tropheops

Common names: Tropheops, Blue mbuna
Range: East Africa, along the rocky coastlines of Lake Malawi
Size: 4¾ inches (11 cm)
Description: Color morphs of this species vary a great deal. Males may be bright yellow with a bluish-white anal fin, as in the photograph here, or they can be deep bluish-gray with eight dark bands along the sides.
Aquarium suitability: A relatively peaceful mbuna that requires hard alkaline water if it is to do well. It can be quite quarrelsome with others of its own kind, but seldom is any real damage done. This fish will accept all the usual cichlid foods.
Breeding information: Breeding is moderately difficult and several females should be included in the breeding tank with a single male. Up to 50 eggs are laid and, once fertilized using the dummy egg method, the eggs are mouthbred for 21 to 24 days.

Pseudotropheus zebra

Common names: Zebra mbuna, Zebra Malawi cichlid, Zebra cichlid, Nyasa blue cichlid
Range: East Africa, around the rocky coastlines of Lake Malawi
Size: 6 inches (15 cm)
Description: The most common color morph of this species is the one shown here. Nevertheless, specimens vary a great deal depending on the mood of the fish and its geographic origin. White and albino morphs are relatively common.
Aquarium suitability: A 48-inch (122-cm) tank is the minimum size that the Zebra mbuna needs—it likes lots of swimming space and is quite territorial. Use coral sand as a substrate with plenty of rocky hiding places. Most foods are greedily accepted.
Breeding information: Keep several females to each male. Up to 60 eggs are laid and they are fertilized in the female's mouth. She will incubate these for 20 to 25 days before releasing them as fry.

Pterophyllum altum

Common names: Deep-bodied angelfish, Altum angelfish, Deep angel, Orinoco angel
Range: South America, in the Orinoco and Negro river systems of Venezuela
Size: 9 inches (23 cm)
Description: The body is disk-shaped and strongly compressed laterally. It is also deeper-bodied than *P. scalare* (page 260) and the fins are longer. Generally, the background body color is silver to olive green. There are three or four vertical bands present, the first of which is from the nape, through the eye, to the throat.
Aquarium suitability: The tank needs to be well planted and the water should be slightly acidic. This can best be achieved using peat-filtered water. It is a peaceful fish that can be kept in a community setup, providing its tank-mates are not small enough to be eaten.

Pterophyllum scalare

Common names: Angelfish, Freshwater angelfish
Range: South America, in slow-moving rivers and lakes of Brazil, Peru, and Ecuador
Size: 6 inches (15 cm)
Description: Like the previous species, the body is disk-shaped and strongly compressed laterally. There are many color varieties of this species, such as the "calico" one shown here. The most common coloration is silver with three to four vertical black bars. The fins are long and stand tall and erect.
Aquarium suitability: This is a peaceful cichlid and juveniles can be kept in small aquariums. Larger specimens need plenty of swimming space and a wide variety of foods. Most Angelfish available are bred in captivity.
Breeding information: Pairs are quite easy to breed. Around 1,000 eggs are laid on a vertical flat surface (see page 288).

Sciaenochromis ahli

Common name: Electric blue hap
Range: East Africa, in rocky and sandy zones of Lake Malawi
Size: 6¼ inches (16 cm)
Description: Females are brown, sometimes with 10 to 12 vertical dark-colored bars. Males are much more colorful and are a bright blue that can vary in intensity but can rival the blue of some saltwater fish. They also have faint bars on the sides.
Aquarium suitability: The ideal aquarium should have rock structures with plenty of caves and hiding places. Use coral sand as a substrate and keep with other similar-sized cichlids. One male should be kept with several females.
Breeding information: The tank water should be hard and alkaline. Females incubate the eggs for a period of 19 to 23 days. After fry are released, they are looked after for another week.

Symphysodon aequifasciatus

Common names: Blue discus, Brown discus, Green discus
Range: South America, in the Amazon River basin from Colombia to Peru
Size: 6 inches (15 cm)
Description: Many authors attribute the three color varieties to the existence of three separate subspecies. In this book, however, the three color morphs are handled as a single species. The body is disk-shaped. There are nine vertical bands on the body at the juvenile stage, but these fade with age. The dorsal and anal fins are deep blue-green with a red iridescence and the head is often veined with turquoise streaks.
Aquarium suitability: Tall tanks are better for this fish, regardless of their water capacity. Soft water should be provided using a peat filter, and frequent partial water changes are necessary to keep this fish healthy.

Symphysodon discus

Common name: Red discus
Range: South America, in the Amazon, Madeira, Negro, Purus, and Xingo river systems
Size: 8 inches (20 cm)
Description: The body is somewhat rounder than the previous species, but equally compressed laterally. The background body color is generally red with a suffusion of turquoise spots and streaks. The fins are similarly marked. Juveniles are dull brown.
Aquarium suitability: Provide plenty of hiding places and excellent water quality. Frequent water changes are mandatory for this species. A moderately-planted aquarium with soft water will make this fish feel at home. No Discus should be kept singly.
Breeding information: The fry attach themselves to the parents a few days after hatching. They feed initially on a milky secretion produced by gland cells in the parent fish's skin.

Thorichthys meeki

Common name: Firemouth cichlid
Range: North and Central America, in shallow lakes, springs, and streams from southern Mexico to Belize
Size: 6 inches (15 cm)
Description: The head is large and the snout is somewhat pointed. Generally, the body is light to dark gray with six or seven shadowy vertical bands. There is a large blotch present on the lower part of the operculum and juveniles have a large midlateral spot. The throat and belly are bright red.
Aquarium suitability: A peaceful cichlid that can be kept in a community tank with similar-sized fish. Plants should be well rooted, as this fish is inclined to burrow.
Breeding information: Firemouths are easy to breed in a separate aquarium. Up to 500 eggs are laid on a smooth, clean surface. The eggs hatch after three days and the fry are moved to pits.

Tilapia buttikoferi

Common name: West African tilapia
Range: West Africa, in clear streams and rivers from Guinea-Bissau to western Liberia
Size: 13 inches (33 cm)
Description: The background body color ranges from deep gray to dark brown. The median fins are black, usually with pale or white margins. The snout is pale gray, darkening toward the nape, and the body carries a series of eight to nine bold white or yellow bands.
Aquarium suitability: The tank should be well planted with robust species. Create hiding places from driftwood and rocks to provide cover. Suitable tank-mates can include larger catfish and other cichlids. Adults are usually very aggressive.
Breeding information: Breeding is fairly difficult and should be done in a separate aquarium.

Tropheus moorii

Common name: Blunthead cichlid
Range: East Africa, in rocky shallows of Lake Tanganyika
Size: 5½ inches (14 cm)
Description: The body is compressed and the back is high and slopes steeply to a large head. The body color is dark brown or black with a broad yellow or orange-red midbody bar that extends onto the dorsal fin. There are several color morphs of this species, but the one described is the most common.
Aquarium suitability: Try keeping this fish in small groups of its own kind as juveniles. These will be less aggressive as they grow, but won't accept later additions. Strong lighting will increase the growth of algae, which is a vital part of its diet.
Breeding information: The female scatters up to 15 large eggs before taking them into her mouth. These are then fertilized by the male. Incubation time is about four weeks.

Tropheus duboisi

Common name: Duboisi
Range: East Africa, in rocky zones of Lake Tanganyika
Size: 4¾ inches (12 cm)
Description: Adults are deep gray or black with a broad yellow or black vertical bar behind the pectoral fins. This is a striking fish with a steeply sloping nape. Juveniles are black with bold white spots over much of the body and head.
Aquarium suitability: Many aquarists find that juveniles are more attractive than adults. This is a peaceful fish that may occasionally prove to be territorial. Provide plenty of hiding places and choose hardy tank-mates of a similar size.
Breeding information: Often difficult, females spawn via the dummy egg method in open water and the eggs drop into rocky crevices before being picked up by the female. Up to 15 eggs are mouthbred for about four weeks before release.

Vieja maculicauda

Common name: Blackbelt cichlid
Range: North and Central America, from southern Mexico to the Panama Canal
Size: 12 inches (30 cm)
Description: Juveniles have a horizontal row of spots that extend from the midbody to the caudal peduncle. These fade with age and a broad black vertical bar appears in the midbody region and also on the dorsal fin, giving this fish its common name. At this stage, the belly and throat turn red, as does the caudal fin. Some specimens also have red on the soft portions of the dorsal and anal fins.
Aquarium suitability: An attractive species that can be very aggressive, particularly around breeding time. It should only be kept with other large cichlids in a suitably large tank with lots of cover and free-swimming space.

Scatophagidae (Scats)

Nelson (1994) places this family in the suborder Acanthuroidei rather than in its earlier percoid position. He does not, however, specify the number of species and may be unsure. Two genera are recognized with four species and one subspecies in this family and, in the case of *S. argus*, numerous color morphs.

Species from this family occur throughout the tropical Indo-Pacific and also in brackish waters and estuaries, with occasional specimens entering freshwater. They are deep-bodied fish that are laterally compressed. The head is small and the single dorsal fin is deeply notched. The scales are small and extend onto the head and the median fins. They have small, square, and terminal mouths, and the anal fin has four spines. Outwardly, they are similar in appearance to the Butterflyfish, although unlike these, the pelagic larvae lack the bony plates on the head. Brackish water species are scavengers that will often feed on human excrement. The diet of marine-living specimens is algae and small benthic invertebrates.

The family is well known to freshwater aquarists but it must be remembered that these are predominantly marine-living species. For the beginner they offer an ideal opportunity to experiment with a brackish-water aquarium without a great deal of cost. These fish are usually quite inexpensive and they are very hardy. Being scavengers by nature, they will accept most aquarium foods that are offered.

Scatophagus argus

Common names: Spotted scat, Common scat, Argus fish, Scat
Range: East Africa to the central Indo-Pacific
Size: 12 inches (30.5 cm)
Description: The coloration of the adult fish ranges from grayish-silver to light brownish-silver. The body is suffused with dark circular spots throughout its life. Young fish are sometimes red in the dorsal and ventral regions (but not as much as the next species). This species is found in tidal rivers, estuaries, and mangrove swamps.
Aquarium suitability: This is an ideal fish for the beginner who wishes to establish a cheap brackish-water aquarium. The Scat will eat practically anything and is easy to keep. Unfortunately, they tend to get discarded once the aquarist has gained enough confidence to try his hand at keeping species that have a less boisterous disposition.

Scatophagus atromaculatus

Common names: Red scat, Mia-mi
Range: Central Indo-Pacific, from Sri Lanka to Australia
Size: 12 inches (30.5 cm)
Description: Adult specimens have a pinkish cast to the silvery body coloration. They are irregularly spotted over much of the body. Juveniles have red on the forehead and the base of the dorsal fin. In addition, the dorsal and anal fins are red with black blotches. Very young fish have six dark vertical bars on the body that become indistinct as the fish grows.
Aquarium suitability: Young fish are very attractive and easy to keep. They look effective in a small shoal and feeding is not a problem; this is a greedy fish. For the best results, they should be kept with other brackish-water species such as Monos (*Monodactylus argenteus*) and the Spot-banded scat (*Selenotoca multifasciata*).

Eleotridae (Sleepers and gudgeons)

Unlike the true gobies, the pelvic fins on these fish are separate and do not form a sucking disk to adhere to the substrate. However, the bases of the fins are quite close together. Eleotrids are found as far north as the Atlantic seaboard of North America and as far south as New Zealand. They can be found in a variety of habitats in seawater, brackish estuaries, and in freshwater. The family comprises some 35 genera with about 150 described species. The six freshwater species in New Zealand are found in fast-flowing streams. The larvae and subsequent fry are thought to drift down to the ocean, where they grow to adulthood, returning only to freshwater to spawn in a similar manner to salmon and sea trout.

The largest species, *Dormitator maculatus*, found from North Carolina to Brazil, grows to 24 inches (61 cm).

There are two dorsal fins present, and the anterior dorsal fin has two to eight flexible spines. The eyes are far up on the head and the mouth is never inferior. The arrangement of the two subfamilies, Butinae and Eleotrinae, raises some important questions, for it may be that Butinae is a paraphyletic taxon.

Mogurnda adspersa

Common names: Purple spotted goby, Purple spotted gudgeon
Range: Australia, principally the Murray-Darling river system of Victoria, New South Wales, and Queensland
Size: 5½ inches (14 cm)
Description: The body color ranges from pale cream in juveniles to dull yellow-ocher in adults. A suffusion of reddish-purple and white spots covers much of the body and fins. In some specimens there is a horizontal row of dark spots that extend midlaterally

from the middle of the body to the caudal peduncle, where it ends with a bluish-black ocellus.
Aquarium suitability: The Purple spotted goby is a territorial fish that is best kept in small groups to even out its aggressive behavior. A large tank is also important. It will frequently take in large gulps of sand and expel this through its gill openings after filtering it for food.
Breeding information: Little is known of the breeding habits of this fish, other than it spawns on a hard substrate where there is plenty of aquatic vegetation.

Anabantidae (Climbing gouramis)

The Anabantidae, or climbing perch family, consists of three genera with about 30 described species. *Ctenopoma* and *Sandelia* encompass species that live in Africa, whereas *Anabas* species are found in Southeast Asia. The land exploits of *Anabas* species are well known and some are said to have the ability to climb shrubs and trees! Anabantids possess a suprabranchial organ that is labyrinthine. This functions as an auxiliary breathing apparatus that enables them to breathe aerially as well as underwater. As the fish gulps air, the air is passed to the labyrinth, where small capillaries can absorb the oxygen. When the next gulp of air is taken, it forces out the oxygen-depleted old air from the labyrinth and expels it though the opercula. This enables many species to live in stagnant water with a low oxygen level, or in submarginal areas where little water is present. Most anabantoids (species of the suborder Anabantoidei, including the families Anabantidae, Belontiidae, and Osphronemidae) build a nest of bubbles. This is usually among floating plants. The male constructs this and the female lays her eggs in the bubbles. After this, the male cares for the eggs.

Ctenopoma acutirostre

Common names: Leopard gourami, Leopard ctenopoma, Spotted climbing perch
Range: Central Africa, in sluggish streams of the Congo River basin in Zaire
Size: 6 inches (15 cm)
Description: The background body color is yellowish to dark tan. Numerous large brown spots and blotches are present over much of the body, head, and fins, giving this fish a leopardlike appearance. In juveniles, there is a large yellow-edged black ocellus on the caudal peduncle that becomes less distinct with age. Females have fewer spots on the fins.
Aquarium suitability: A large, peaceful bottom-dwelling fish that can be kept in a cichlid tank or with other large community fish. It is predatory by nature and an active hunter, so care should be taken regarding the size of its tank-mates.

Helostomatidae (Kissing gourami)

This family is monophyletic; therefore it contains only one species, *Helostoma temminki*. The interesting aspect of this species is the adaptation of the gill structures. Numerous gill rakers form a sophisticated filtering system on the gill arches that adapts the fish to filter feeding. In addition, the hornlike teeth on the lips are well equipped to scrape algae off of rocky substrate and other surfaces. The dorsal fin is continuous and not notched, with 16 to 18 spines and 13 to 16 soft rays. The anal fin mirrors this in length, and has 13 to 15 spines and 17 to 19 soft rays.

The Kissing gourami is known for its "kissing" behavior, for it actually appears to kiss others of its kind. There are many theories as to why this occurs, but none have been proven. Some authors attribute it to aggression, others to territorial signals. Whatever is true, much more investigation is required.

The pectoral fins are set low on the body and the pelvic fins have extended first rays. The most distinctive characteristic of the Kissing gourami is the mouth. In addition to the fact that it is terminal rather than superior, it is highly protrusible—as its common name would indicate.

Helostoma temminki

Common name: Kissing gourami
Range: Southeast Asia, in lakes, ponds and rice paddies in Thailand, Malaysia, Sumatra, and Borneo
Size: 12 inches (30 cm)
Description: The body is compressed and somewhat oval-shaped with a pointed snout. Two color morphs exist. The first has an olive green body with a green iridescence, whereas the second has a pinkish-white body with a white iridescence.
Aquarium suitability: Sturdy-leaved plants should be used in the tank, as this species is a plant eater. Use floating plants for cover and combine with other labyrinths. If it is hungry, it will suck at the sides of slow-moving fish.
Breeding information: Spawning is aggressive, with lots of splashing at the water surface. Up to 1,000 eggs float to the surface and attach to plants. These hatch after 50 hours.

Osphronemidae (gouramis)

The family Osphronemidae has recently been revised and now includes Belontiidae with its three subfamilies. Gouramis are uniquely adapted to stagnant waters in tropical areas because of their labyrinth organ. All of them inhabit freshwater in Africa and southeast Asia. They are found in Pakistan, India, China, Korea, and the Indo-Australian archipelago. One species, the Siamese fighting fish (*Betta splendens*), has been bred for over 100 years and current captive-bred specimens hardly resemble their wild counterparts. The family contains 13 genera with about 49 species.

Most gouramis are small but they have a variety of body shapes. Some species have elongate cylindrical bodies, and others may have deep bodies that are strongly compressed. Generally, the anal fin base is much longer than the dorsal fin base. The first ray of the pelvic fin is often greatly extended and is used as a tactile sensing organ. Species from this family are important for insect control. Stagnant water and heavy vegetation makes an ideal breeding ground for insects, particularly mosquitoes, yet these conditions suit gouramis perfectly. It is estimated that an adult or subadult fish of the genus *Betta* consumes 10,000 to 15,000 mosquito larvae annually.

Betta splendens (Red and Blue)

Betta splendens

Common name: Siamese fighting fish
Range: Southeast Asia in sluggish or stagnant ponds, rice paddies, and streams in Cambodia and Thailand
Size: 3 inches (7.6 cm)
Description: The original wild *Betta splendens* is quite a drab fish. It is reddish-tan with several dark brown horizontal stripes that run from the head to the caudal peduncle. However, decades of selective breeding have produced brightly colored varieties that can be any color in the spectrum. Even two-colored specimens are often seen for sale. Males have longer fins than females.
Aquarium suitability: Males should not be kept together or they will fight. Care should be taken to keep this fish in a tank with peaceful tank-mates. Fin-nippers will see this fish as fair game because of its long, flowing fins and damage them.

Betta splendens (Purple bicolor)

Betta splendens (Red/Tan bicolor)

Colisa fasciata

Common names: Banded gourami, Giant gourami
Range: Asia, in still or sluggish waters throughout India, Bengal, Myanmar, and northern Thailand
Size: 4 inches (10 cm)
Description: The first pelvic fin rays are greatly extended and the caudal fin is fan-shaped. The background body color is olive-brown to dull orange dorsally, while the belly is often orange with a turquoise iridescence. There are several oblique bars present on the flanks that may be green, yellow, or turquoise.
Aquarium suitability: Ideal for a small, well-planted aquarium with other peaceful fish. During the acclimation period, this fish can be relatively timid. Once settled though, it is much bolder.
Breeding information: The male embraces the female after he has built a bubble nest. Up to 1,000 eggs are released, which the male gathers into the nest. They hatch 24 hours later.

Colisa lalia

Common name: Dwarf gourami
Range: Asia, in vegetation-rich floodplains of Assam, India, and Myanmar
Size: 2¼ inches (5.5 cm)
Description: Normal coloration consists of an orange-red body with numerous slightly oblique vertical bands that are greenish-blue or turquoise. The pelvic fins are elongated into sensory feelers. There are many different color varieties.
Aquarium suitability: This is an excellent community fish if it is housed with other peaceful species. Its tank should be well planted and have a light cover of floating plants such as *Riccia*.
Breeding information: The male constructs a bubble nest that includes plant debris. Successive spawnings produce 400 to 600 eggs, which the male blows into the nest. The male cares for the eggs but should be removed when the eggs hatch 24 hours later.

Macropodus opercularis

Common names: Paradise fish, Paradise gourami
Range: Asia, in still and sluggish water throughout China, Korea, Taiwan, southern Vietnam, and Okinawa
Size: 4 inches (10 cm)
Description: The fins are long and flowing in adults. Generally, the male is bluish-gray to greenish-brown dorsally. The flanks carry numerous dull orange vertical bars and the operculum and caudal peduncle also have orange markings.
Aquarium suitability: Juveniles are ideal for a community setup, but adult fish can get very aggressive. Provide plenty of cover, including floating plants and rock structures, for the best results.
Breeding information: The courtship is active and the male collects up to 1,000 eggs that are released and spits them into a bubble nest. He guards them until they hatch 24 to 27 hours later. The fry are free-swimming after three days.

Osphronemus goramy

Common name: Common gourami, Giant gourami, True gourami
Range: Southeast Asia; originally from Java and Sumatra but now throughout the region as a food fish
Size: 28 inches (71 cm)
Description: The snout is sharply angled in juveniles and the body is reddish brown to dull orange with numerous narrow brown bands. Adults are very large and are dark brown dorsally with brown flanks and fins. The scales on the flanks are iridescent silver. The head is usually lighter colored than the rest of the body and the snout is blunt.
Aquarium suitability: This fish requires a very large tank because it grows quickly. The filtration system should be powerful enough to handle the tremendous amount of waste that it produces.

Sphaerichthys osphromenoides

Common name: Chocolate gourami
Range: Southeast Asia, in still and slow-moving water in western Borneo, Malaysia, and Sumatra
Size: 2½ inches (6 cm)
Description: The body is strongly compressed and the fins are long and flowing. The background body color is chocolate brown with four yellow to white bands. There is a black spot present on the upper region of the caudal peduncle and the mottled brown median fins have yellow margins.
Aquarium suitability: A peaceful but timid fish that is best kept with tank-mates of a similar nature. A pair will fare a lot better in a community tank than will single individuals.
Breeding information: Breeding is difficult but not impossible. The male mouthbreeds 20 to 30 eggs for two to three weeks, after which they emerge as very small fry.

Trichogaster chuna

Common names: Honey dwarf gourami, Honey gourami
Range: Asia, in clear water and well-oxygenated pools in northern India, and Bangladesh
Size: 1¾ inches (4.5 cm)
Description: The body coloration of this species can resemble one color variety of *Colisa lalia* (see page 267). Generally, the body is reddish-orange to pale orange. Males develop darker colors at breeding time and the lower part of the head, throat, and forward portion of the anal fin become dark green or black.
Aquarium suitability: The Honey dwarf gourami is a great community fish if it is kept with other fish that have a placid nature. It requires a varied diet with occasional live food supplements to keep its colors. Males can become quite aggressive at spawning time.
Breeding information: The same pattern as *C. lalia*.

Trichogaster labiosus

Common name: Thick-lipped gourami
Range: Asia, in still water in ponds, rice paddies, and lakes in India and Myanmar
Size: 2¼ inches (5.5 cm)
Description: The bases of the anal and dorsal fins are long and the first rays of the pelvic fins are greatly extended. Males are dark orange-brown dorsally and somewhat lighter, often with turquoise, ventrally. A series of yellow to turquoise vertical bands extend along the sides of the fish and the lips are thick.
Aquarium suitability: Can be kept in a small tank with other gouramis, armored catfish, and barbs. It is a peaceful fish except in the breeding season when it may become aggressive. A small group looks terrific in a moderately-sized show tank.
Breeding information: The breeding details are the same as *C. lalia*, except *T. labiosus* builds a larger bubble nest.

Trichogaster leerii

Common names: Pearl gourami, Lace gourami, Mosaic gourami, Platinum gourami
Range: Southeast Asia, in slow-moving rivers, lakes, and pools in Borneo, Sumatra, Malaysia, and Thailand
Size: 5 inches (13 cm)
Description: The nape and dorsal region are deep olive green and the flanks are somewhat lighter. The throat and chest are yellow and orange-red in mature males. There is a horizontal black line present that extends from the snout to the caudal peduncle. The pelvic fins are extended to the extreme and the flanks and median fins are suffused with pearly white spots.
Aquarium suitability: This is a very attractive fish and one of the author's personal favorites. If the tank is arranged in dark colors this fish will look its best. They should be kept in pairs or trios and are great community fish with others of a similar nature.

Trichogaster microlepis

Common names: Moonlight gourami, Moonbeam gourami
Range: Southeast Asia, in still and slow-moving waters of Cambodia and Thailand
Size: 6 inches (15 cm)
Description: The first rays of the pelvic fins are extended to the extreme—in fact, far longer than others of this family. The flanks are white with a silver iridescence and the dorsal region is whitish-olive with a green iridescence. Juveniles have a yellow iris. This changes to red with age.
Aquarium suitability: Provide plenty of hiding places for this species, as it can be quite timid in a community tank, even with other peaceful fish. The tank should also be well planted to provide additional cover. Its diet should include flake food, insect larvae, tubifex, *Artemia*, *Mysus*, chopped spinach, and blanched chopped lettuce.

Trichogaster pectoralis

Common name: Snakeskin gourami
Range: Southeast Asia, in rice paddies, shallow pools, and swamps in Cambodia, Thailand, and southern Vietnam
Size: 12 inches (30 cm), though much smaller in captivity
Description: The dorsal region is deep olive green to brown and the dorsal fins are long and flowing. The flanks are greenish-gray to tan with a silver iridescence. There is a black stripe present in juveniles that extends from the snout to the tail. This fades with age, leaving just a spot on the caudal peduncle. The dorsal region and flanks are often marked with a series of dark vertical bands that give a snakeskin effect.
Aquarium suitability: Peaceful and hardy, this is a great fish for a community tank. There are two color morphs that hobbyists have bred. The first is the true color described above and the second is the more popular blue-green "opaline" color.

Trichogaster trichopterus

Common name: Three-spot gourami
Range: Southeast Asia, in muddy or clear streams, lakes, and ponds throughout the Indo-Australian archipelago
Size: 6 inches (15 cm)
Description: This is a fish that is easy to identify. The pelvic fins are greatly extended and the body is a mottled blue that can give a snakeskin effect. There are two bold spots present. The first occurs in the midbody region and the second is on the caudal peduncle. The third "spot" is actually the fish's dark eye.
Aquarium suitability: This is a very peaceful fish, ideal for a community aquarium. Males can become slightly aggressive at breeding time, but otherwise it is a tranquil fish.
Breeding information: Up to 1,200 eggs are laid and the male corrals them into a bubble nest. The fry hatch in 20 to 30 hours and are free-swimming after five days.

Order: Tetraodontiformes

The preceding pages dealt only with fish belonging to the huge order Perciformes. The last group of fish described in this book is considerably smaller. It contains nine families with approximately 100 genera and 339 extant species.

Regarding the characteristics of the fish of this order, the body is variable in form, with modified scales. These may be plates, spines, or shields, or they may be hidden under tissue, such as is the case with the triggerfish. Some families have a modified stomach that enables the fish to inflate with a rapid intake of water when it is angry or frightened. These fish are known as puffers. A lot of species are able to produce an audible sound by grinding their pharyngeal teeth together. Most triggerfish can enlarge their bodies in anger or in fright by extending their stomachs downward. They possess a movable pelvic bone that enables them to do this.

The order contains two suborders, the first of which contains the spikefish and triplespines. This is the suborder Triacanthoidei, incorporating two families. These are Triacanthodidae (with 15 species, mostly from deep water) and Triacanthidae (with seven shallow-water benthic species). These are of little interest to the freshwater aquarist and will not be dealt with further in this book.

The second suborder, Tetraodontoidei, is of greater interest to the hobbyist and 25 species are described on the following pages. It contains the triggerfish, filefish, boxfish, trunkfish, cowfish, pufferfish, and porcupinefish. The suborder is split into three superfamilies, although the exact placing of the family Ostraciidae is, at the moment, very sketchy and uncertain.

Tetraodontidae (Pufferfish)

The family is made up of two subfamilies with 19 genera and 121 species. These are fish that are able to inflate their abdomens by taking in water (or air, when they are removed from the water). They have no ribs, no pelvic fins, and their skin is very tough, sometimes with short spines on the belly. There are no scales and the fins do not possess spines. The tail is often rounded or truncate.

The alkaloid poison tetrodotoxin is present in the flesh of some species but the largest accumulation is in the viscera, particularly the liver. This can often prove fatal if these fish are eaten.

Some species are confined to freshwater, particularly those of the genera *Colomesus*, *Takifugu*, and *Tetraodon*. These are of particular interest to the freshwater aquarist. In addition, quite a few different species are found in brackish water and mangrove swamps throughout the Indo-Pacific region.

The Spotted Puffer (Tetraodon fluviatilis) *is typical of its species. Its hardy, characterful demeanor hides a voracious predatory appetite.*

In the first subfamily, Tetraodontinae, the bodies are widely rounded when viewed from the front. The gill opening extends below the middle point of the pectoral axil and there are one or sometimes two well-defined nostrils on each side of the head. The dorsal fin is set well back on the body and the anal fin is more or less below it. There are about 95 species, the largest of which grows to a length of 36 inches (91 cm).

Canthigastrinae, the second subfamily, contains fish with laterally compressed bodies when they are not inflated. The skin is scaleless and coarse, and the gill opening ends at the midpoint of the pectoral axil. These are predominantly marine fish and will not be dealt with further in this book.

Pufferfish are quite hardy under aquarium conditions, but they can be voracious predators. They should never be trusted with smaller tank-mates. Even ones that are larger than them may be attacked and bitten to the point of debilitation. At this point, the pufferfish will devour bite-sized pieces of them at will. Also, many hobbyists like to show off their new charges to friends by provoking them until they inflate themselves as a defense to the attack. This is not a good idea. Many species have difficulty deflating and this induces a great deal of stress and can bring about the onset of disease.

Pufferfish are great subjects for large aquariums with other very large tank-mates. They are true characters with a high level of intelligence and easy to keep if they are given a varied diet and are properly cared for.

Order: Tetraodontiformes

Order	Suborder	Superfamily	Family
Tetraodontiformes	Triacanthoidei		Triacanthodidae
			Triacanthidae
	Tetraodontoidei	Balistoidea (Leatherjackets)	Balistidae
			Monacanthidae
		Ostracioidea	Ostraciidae
		Tetraodontoidea	Triodontidae
			Tetraodontidae
			Diodontidae
			Molidae

The entries in **bold** type
are dealt with in detail
in the following pages.

Tetraodon biocellatus

Common names: Figure-eight puffer, Eyespot pufferfish
Range: Southeast Asia, in freshwater streams in Thailand,
Malaysia, and Borneo
Size: 3¼ inches (8 cm)
Description: This is a freshwater puffer with a dark olive green
back and a white belly. Two yellow-edged black ocelli are
present. The first of these is seen below the dorsal base, and the
second on the caudal peduncle. The upper half of the body is
covered with curved yellow reticulations and circles, which often
form a large figure eight on the back.
Aquarium suitability: Juveniles are very peaceful but older fish
tend to be somewhat pugnacious. This species will not eat flake
foods and should be fed live and frozen foods such as cockle and
brine shrimp.
Breeding information: After a short period of courtship near
the substrate, the pale, glassy eggs are laid on plant leaves.
The male guards and cares for these until they hatch in six to
seven days.

Tetraodon nigroviridis

Common name: Green puffer
Range: Southeast Asia, in fresh and brackish waters of India, the Indo-Australian archipelago, and the Philippines
Size: 8 inches (20 cm)
Description: The belly is white and the back is greenish-yellow. The small dorsal and anal fins are vertically opposite one another and the body is rounded. The upper half of the body is suffused with large brown spots. These are larger on the anterior of the fish and diminish in size and become less reticulated toward the belly.
Aquarium suitability: Juveniles are peaceful, whereas older specimens are territorial and scrappy. Nevertheless, they can be kept in a community setup with other similar-sized fish. Two adult males will usually fight until one dies.
Breeding information: Spawning will only take place in brackish water. The pale, glassy eggs are laid on the substrate or on plant leaves. The male guards the eggs, which hatch after six to seven days. The fry will only accept minute live foods.

Phylum: Arthropoda (Jointed-limb animals)

The late English zoologist S. M. Manton reclassified the phylum Arthropoda assuming that the established classification was polyphyletic. Crustacea was raised to phylum status, along with Uniramia and Chelicerata, in the belief that these three groups of animals were not derived from a common ancestor. This theory has been followed by many biologists and authors for a number of years.

However, in this present book the author prefers to retain the older, established classification of this large group of animals, with a few changes that reflect recent research. Since the Cambrian period, between 600 and 500 million years ago, the three groups have diversified. Nevertheless, they still retain many common characteristics.

In arthropods, the skin is relatively thick, often with a chitinous exoskeleton. In most species this is molted during the larval stages or as the creature grows. The body possesses bilateral symmetry and there is a well-developed nervous system with highly developed sense organs. The eyes are compound and consist of many smaller rudimentary eyes joined together to form compact and effective units. Many of the species have antennae with accompanying sensory organs, and in all species the body is segmented, usually with three pairs of walking legs attached, but often more. Millipedes have over a hundred pairs of legs. All arthropods have similar blood systems and sex organs. Their eyes and muscular structure are characteristic of the phylum.

The arthropods are the only group of animals, with the exception of the vertebrates, that possess jointed legs. The phylum is very large and encompasses over a million described species, but the number is probably a great deal higher if one includes the species that have yet to be filed. This makes up over two-thirds of all the known species in the animal kingdom. It is a diverse group that contains over 50,000 species of spiders, 32,500 species of crustaceans (although this will probably be nearer 60,000 once all the species have been described), and an incalculable number of insects. This latter group is the largest and representatives are found in all climates of the world and in every milieu.

Of course, it would not be possible to chart the whole phylum down to order level on a single page because of its sheer immensity, nor is it necessary because many dwell on land. However, the important groups are displayed in the chart here, along with a breakdown to order level of those that will be discussed in greater detail in the following pages. Bold type indicates groups that are of particular interest to the tropical freshwater aquarist.

There are three subphyla that make up this group of animals. The first subphylum, Uniramia, is divided into two superclasses, encompassing a total of eight classes. The subphylum contains millipedes, centipedes, and all the insects of the world. It is a large group and is only mentioned briefly so that the reader can see how they all fit into the grand scheme of things.

Subphylum: Chelicerata

The subphylum contains three classes, the first of which is Arachnida. This large class contains all of the land-dwelling spiders, scorpions, ticks, and mites. The only truly aquatic representatives belong to the order Acari, which contains marine and aquatic mites as well as terrestrial and parasitic animals. The few species are usually from the family Halacaridae.

The second class, Pycnogonida, encompasses more than 1,200 species of sea spiders. This is an exclusively marine group of animals that are often less than 1.0 mm in length, although some deep-sea species may grow to 20 inches (50 cm). These animals are outside the scope of this book.

The third class in the subphylum Chelicerata is small, but Merostomata is of considerable interest.

Class: Merostomata

The class is small and contains only one order with a single family and three genera, encompassing four species. The chart on page 278 shows the complete taxon as it is currently known.

Horseshoe crabs—or King crabs, as they are sometimes called—are not, in fact, crabs. They are more closely related to spiders and scorpions than to crustaceans. They are placed in the order Xiphosura along with the long-extinct sea scorpion, which died out some 300 million years ago. This beast reached a length of 10 feet (3 meters) and was, in evolutionary terms, closely related to the trilobites that came into being in the Cambrian period 570 million years ago but are also extinct, having died out in the Permian period more than 230 million years ago. The horseshoe crabs reached their peak of development toward the end of the Cretaceous period between 80 and 60 million years ago. At that time there were many species and these had a wide distribution over much of the earth's surface. There are many fossilized records and, although most of the species are now extinct, those few that remain have retained more or less the same form up to the present day. They can be considered "living fossils" and one of the oldest groups of creatures known to man.

These creatures are bottom-dwellers, preferring sandy or muddy seabeds, where they can burrow and plow through the surface in search of morsels of food. They are

Jointed-limb Animals

Phylum	Subphylum	Superclass	Class	Subclass	Superorder	Order

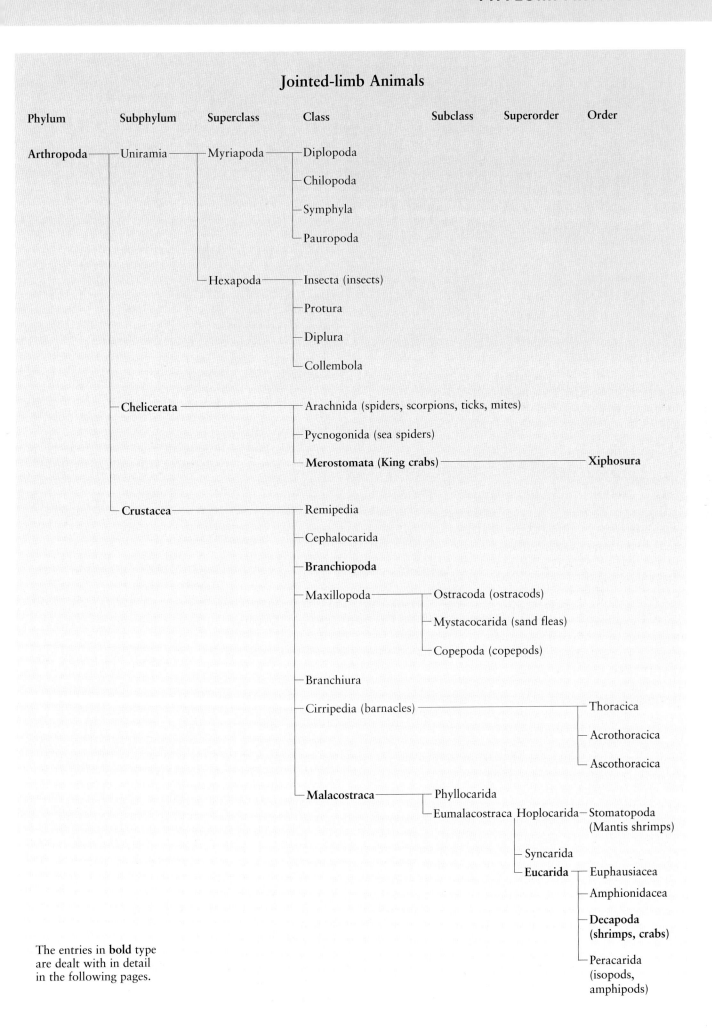

Arthropoda — Uniramia — Myriapoda — Diplopoda

Chilopoda

Symphyla

Pauropoda

Hexapoda — Insecta (insects)

Protura

Diplura

Collembola

Chelicerata — Arachnida (spiders, scorpions, ticks, mites)

Pycnogonida (sea spiders)

Merostomata (King crabs) — **Xiphosura**

Crustacea — Remipedia

Cephalocarida

Branchiopoda

Maxillopoda — Ostracoda (ostracods)

Mystacocarida (sand fleas)

Copepoda (copepods)

Branchiura

Cirripedia (barnacles) — Thoracica

Acrothoracica

Ascothoracica

Malacostraca — Phyllocarida

Eumalacostraca — Hoplocarida — Stomatopoda (Mantis shrimps)

Syncarida

Eucarida — Euphausiacea

Amphionidacea

Decapoda (shrimps, crabs)

Peracarida (isopods, amphipods)

The entries in **bold** type are dealt with in detail in the following pages.

omnivorous scavengers of considerable value because they feed on dead marine worms and mollusks such as bivalves. They will also feed on algae and other organic matter. The heavily armored carapace affords ample protection against predators and it appears that they have little in the way of natural enemies. Perhaps this is why they have been around for so long!

A horseshoe crab molts its shell as it grows in order to form a larger one to accommodate its increase in body size. This is also the case with most crustaceans. The carapace splits along the forward edge and the horseshoe crab literally scrambles out of its old shell with the new one already forming. On contact with salt or brackish water, a chemical reaction takes place and it starts to harden, becoming leathery at first and harder later.

The sexes are separate and the male is much smaller than the female. During the breeding season, they move inshore into the intertidal zone or into brackish water to deposit and fertilize the eggs. The eggs are laid in a scooped-out hollow in the sand or silt, which is usually about 6 inches (15 cm) deep. As they are deposited they are fertilized by the male, who mounts onto the back of the female, grasping her with the second modified appendages (the pedipalps), becoming inseparable until the mating is completed. The number of eggs laid varies between species from 250 to 1,000. Each female can lay eggs in up to a hundred separate nests before she is exhausted. The eggs develop into larvae, which hatch after a period of two to three weeks. At this stage, they are about a millimeter long. These undergo a series of molts over the next three years until they acquire the adult form.

In Southeast Asia, and particularly Hong Kong, the eggs are also considered to be of great food value. These are removed from the female and eaten stir-fried. In Thailand the eggs are also fried and mixed with a little

of the strange blue-colored blood that these creatures possess. In some areas, the live animals themselves are caught and ground up into meal to be used as pig or chicken food or occasionally as soil fertilizer.

The blue blood coloration comes from the presence of copper-rich proteins (hemocyanin) within the blood plasma. In contrast to other animals, which have red blood corpuscles that contain iron-rich encapsulated proteins (hemoglobin), the blue-colored, copper-rich hemocyanin is in large molecules that are without the encapsulated structure of the hemoglobin and freely distributed throughout the plasma. This phenomenon has its uses in medical science and the blood is very important as a diagnostic aid. Its particular color, consistency, and chemical composition is ideally suited to testing gram-negative bacterial infection such as blood poisoning and also for the testing of meningitis in humans.

Order: Xiphosura (Horseshoe crabs and King crabs)

Of the four extant species in this order, only one is found in the Atlantic. This is *Limulus polyphemus*, which is the only representative of its genus. This species is restricted to the western Atlantic seaboard, from Nova Scotia to Florida and the Caribbean, and is described on the next page. They enter brackish water during the breeding season and can easily be kept in large brackish-water aquariums. The other three species are found in various regions of the Indo-Pacific.

There are two representatives of the genus *Tachypleus*, and these are widespread in the northern part of the Indo-Pacific, from India to Japan and from southern China to Indonesia. They are *T. gigas*, which grows to about 20 inches (50 cm), and *T. tridentatus*, which is slightly larger

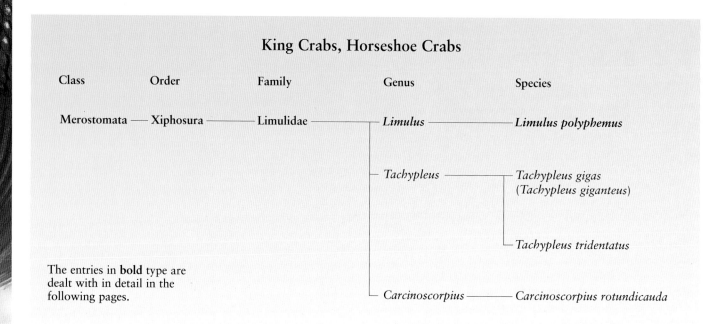

King Crabs, Horseshoe Crabs

Class	Order	Family	Genus	Species
Merostomata —	Xiphosura —	Limulidae —	**Limulus** —	**Limulus polyphemus**
			Tachypleus —	*Tachypleus gigas* (*Tachypleus giganteus*)
				Tachypleus tridentatus
			Carcinoscorpius —	*Carcinoscorpius rotundicauda*

The entries in **bold** type are dealt with in detail in the following pages.

at 24 inches (60 cm). These two species are often found together, particularly around the shores of Hong Kong. Here it is possible to pick up both specimens from the beaches of Tai Long Bay in the east, and around the shores of Cheung Chau Island in the west during the breeding season. The tails of these species have a more or less triangular cross-section.

Carcinoscorpius rotundicauda has, as the Latin specific name implies, a rounded to oval tail cross-section unlike the other three species, and this makes it easy to identify. It is the only species in its genus and is endemic from India to Brunei. This horseshoe crab is ubiquitous in the Bay of Bengal, where specimens are known to enter brackish

water during the breeding season, particularly the mouths of the Ganges in Bangladesh and the Irrawaddy delta in southern Burma. The species is the smallest of the four and seldom reaches a size of more than 14 inches (35 cm). It is also known from the Malaysian archipelago and as far east as the Philippines.

Most of these species have appeared in dealers' tanks at one time or another. As a general rule, they require a special aquarium, so beginners should refrain from buying them simply because of their appearance. It is for this particular reason that they are often displayed in large public aquariums and zoos throughout the world.

Limulus polyphemus

Common name: Atlantic horseshoe crab
Range: Tropical and subtropical western Atlantic
Size: 18 inches (46 cm)
Description: The carapace coloration ranges from light tan to deep gray. There are 11 spines on the upper surface of the anterior, or prosoma, and these are arranged in three longitudinal rows. The center row has three spines, the first of which is between and well below the compound eyes. The first of the four

spines in the outside rows is situated near the inside margins of the eyes.
Aquarium suitability: Feeds well on whole mussels or cockles. Troublesome specimens can be removed from the water, inverted, and fed pieces of food by hand without any adverse effects. A large aquarium with plenty of sandy spaces (with room to turn), interspersed with large rocks, is the best for this species. The brackish-water tank should be well-established, well-lit, and have plenty of water movement, as well as a good power filter.

Subphylum: Crustacea

Crustaceans are predominantly marine creatures, but there are some freshwater representatives and a few that have managed to venture onto land, although most of this latter group have retained their aquatic ties for breeding, feeding, or larval development. The subphylum encompasses seven classes with 32,500 described species and an estimated 6,000 undescribed ones. They are an extremely varied group, both in size and form. They range from the microscopic, some of which are parasitic, to the large lobsters and crabs of the Indo-Pacific, which often weigh many pounds. However, most of the species are small, and these animals are of major importance to the marine food chain because they make up a great part of the planktonic life in the sea and many larger animals rely on them as their primary food source. The commercial importance of these animals is without question. Edible shrimps, crabs, and lobsters are on the daily menus of most restaurants throughout the world and the peoples of some island groups rely on these creatures for a great part of their daily protein intake.

In freshwater aquatic environments, crustaceans are well represented, and in some cases they are the dominant group. These tropical species are often highly colored and are particularly attractive in a tropical freshwater aquarium. Countless microscopic species belonging to this group inhabit freshwater areas. They are a vital part of the interstitial community and play an important role in the ecological stability of various waterways. They have a long fossil history and extant species are everywhere in one form or another.

As far as the biological features of these creatures are concerned, the body can generally be divided into two parts—if you have ever peeled and eaten a prawn or shrimp, you will know what I mean! Despite this, there are three distinct regions of the body, or four if the fanlike tail of some species is included. The first is the head, which includes the mouth, the compound eyes, two pairs of antennae, and the mouth appendages. The eyes are often on long stalks and the mouth appendages are used for mastication and feeding. There are three pairs of these, which are situated behind the mouth. These are known as the mandibles, the maxillules, and the maxillae. In some species, one of the pairs is developed into claws. The next region is the thorax, which bears the main digestive system and reproductive organs. The number of body segments, appendages, and walking legs varies a great deal depending on the species. The thorax is almost always fused with the head into one section (the cephalothorax). The third region is the segmented abdomen and this usually has strong tail muscles. There may be a tail fan, or telson, present in some species, which has been developed from the last pair of ventral appendages. This is used for swimming backward. Other appendages on the abdomen are often developed into swimming legs. At the base of these and other appendages are the respiratory devices or gills. In minute species, the latter are not always present, as many of them respire directly through their body walls.

The cephalothorax has a carapace of layered chitin and calcium carbonate. This is often pigmented and brightly colored, as are the chitinous shields that cover the segments of the abdomen. The carapace covers the organs in the head and also the digestive and reproduction organs in the thorax. There is often a projecting spine (rostrum) between the eyes; in some species this is highly developed.

Unlike insects, which only molt once they have reached the adult size and form, crustaceans are continually growing and have to molt periodically so that the shell-like exoskeleton can accommodate the increase in body size. To do this, the creature takes in water, allowing the body to swell up so that the exoskeleton splits at a point between the thorax and the abdomen. The animal then extricates itself backward out of the old shell, leaving behind a perfect but fragile replica of its own form. It is fragile because there are no longer any attached muscles to support the separate sections of the exoskeleton. Once this has been completed, a new exoskeleton begins to form, and when this has hardened the body is deflated in order to make room for more growth. At the molting stage of its life, the crustacean is at its most vulnerable because of its soft body. This is why many of these creatures will find a cave or crevice in which to carry out the molt. Most of them do this at night, when the risk of being eaten by predators is at its lowest. The complete molting process can take anywhere from a few hours to several weeks, depending on the species.

Usually the sexes are separate and a large percentage of these animals brood their young. There are exceptions, of course, with the parents laying and fertilizing the eggs. In all cases however, the young go through some sort of larval stage. During this part of their lives they are known as nauplii.

Crustaceans make ideal subjects for aquariums but it must be remembered that many species, such as large freshwater crabs, crayfish, and lobsters, are quite capable predators themselves. These are usually not to be trusted with small fish or some of the slow-moving invertebrates that may be present in a tropical freshwater aquarium.

Class: Branchiopoda

This is a group of animals that is almost exclusively from freshwater, or from saline seas and salt lakes. The reader may wonder why a group of predominantly very tiny inland water species has been included at this point in the book. The reason is that they are important to the tropical freshwater aquarist as a live-food source.

The class encompasses four orders with over 900 species of mainly small crustaceans, and includes water fleas known as *Daphnia* and also the saline crustaceans known as brine shrimp, or *Artemia*. The genera *Cyclops*, *Moina*, and *Diaptomus* also belong to this group. A simplified chart of the class is shown here. There are only a few truly marine representatives present and these are planktonic animals belonging to the order Cladocera.

Generally, the body has easily recognizable segments and, when it is present, the carapace can occur as two halves of a protective shell similar to that of the bivalve mollusks. In some species the body is squat and shortened, while in others it may be elongate. The thoracic appendages are usually leaf-formed, with gills at the base of each pair. They have multiple functions and are used for swimming, feeding, and respiration. The compound eyes are usually in pairs but this is not always the case, and there may be additional simple eyes present. The first pair of antennae and the first pair of mouth appendages are usually rudimentary or completely absent. The sexes are separate and the females are dominant. Eggs often develop into young without being fertilized, especially when the water conditions are good. With adverse conditions, such as a decrease in oxygen or an increase in salinity, eggs are produced by sexual reproduction and are thick-walled and resistant to dehydration.

The first order, Anostraca, contains a group of creatures that are without a carapace. They include freshwater species and also the commercially important genus *Artemia*, or brine shrimp, which is found in great numbers in American salt lakes such as the Great Salt Lake in Utah and Mono Lake in California. But they are also found in other salt lakes throughout the world, such as Chaplin Lake in Canada, the lakes south of Tianjin in Hebei province of China, and Shark Bay in Western Australia. In addition, Brazil, Italy, Argentina, and France have flourishing commercial breeding stations for these creatures.

There is some disagreement as to how many species of brine shrimp there are. Most authors use the name

Artemia salina to cover all species from this genus, but it is probable that this particular species is extinct. It is known that one species, *Artemia franciscana*, is cultured in quantity for the aquarium trade in the National Wildlife Refuge in the San Francisco Bay area. Although this is classified as an "Environment Protected Water," it is licensed by the U.S. Fish and Wildlife Service for the production of these crustaceans. This is usually as a cost-effective byproduct of desalination plants, which provide freshwater to the local areas.

Physically, these crustaceans are small, relatively long-bodied animals that have 20 or more segments. Depending on the species, the first 12 to 18 segments have leaf-formed appendages used for swimming and for filtering food. There is no carapace present and the first pair of antennae is rudimentary. The second pair is longer and, in males, these are developed into claspers to hold the female during copulation. The eggs are in shells and produce larvae that develop through the nauplii stages into adults. When, however, the salinity of the water increases to the point where the specific gravity is over the level of 1.130, the eggs are deposited with thick shells that are resistant to drying out. This means that in areas where inland salt lakes have a tendency to dry out during the summer months, the eggs can remain dormant and hatch later during the rainy season. These "time eggs" (cysts) are an ideal source of live food to the aquarist. The eggs are easily hatched and inexpensive to obtain. They have the added advantage of being free of parasites and bacteria. Recently, eggs with chemical shells have become available so that the aquarist need no longer worry about the irritating empty shells that are sometimes difficult to separate from the nauplii.

The order Cladocera contains species that usually have a carapace formed as a bivalve shell to cover the thoracic appendages and body but leave the head free. The abdominal terminus is often curled forward and is armed with spines and claws, which are used to clean the carapace. Predatory species have a greatly reduced shell, which usually only covers the brood pouch. They are small creatures that are often transparent, and often only a few millimeters long. The eyes are compound and are fused together at the median line of the head to form one large eye. The first antennae are small but the second pair is greatly enlarged and these are used for swimming. There are four to six pairs of appendages on the thorax and these are generally leaflike. They are used for respiration and for filtering food particles from the water. In the few predatory species, the limbs are cylindrical and used to grasp prey. The young are developed in the brood pouch, protected by the carapace. In this order the young do not usually have a larval stage.

There are two suborders, Haplopoda and Eucladocera. Haplopods are freshwater animals; the few marine representatives of this group belong to the second suborder, Eucladocera.

Branchiopods (Water Fleas)

Class	Order	Suborder
Branchiopoda	Anostraca	
	Notostraca	
	Conchostraca	
	Cladocera	Haplopoda
		Eucladocera

Daphnia (usually *Daphnia pulex*) belong to this order and are well known to freshwater aquarists.

Class: Malacostraca

To attempt to describe the diversity of the animals encompassed within this class seems, on the surface, to be a little superfluous. One has only to look at the daily menu of a good seafood restaurant to know the sort of creatures that are being dealt with here. Crabs, lobsters, prawns, shrimps, and crayfish are well known throughout the world. This particular group of animals is diverse to the extreme, and many of the creatures have a meaningful commercial significance. These are not all marine-dwelling creatures, though: the freshwater crawfish group is a case in point.

The body of these animals usually has 14 segments. The first eight of these form the thorax and the last six form the abdomen. Appendages are present and may be developed into claws or walking and swimming legs. The compound eyes are sometimes highly developed and may appear on stalks, and have a high degree of sensory perception. As with most species in this large phylum, the carapace is molted periodically to allow for growth.

There are two subclasses, the first of which is Phyllocarida. Phyllocarids are rather primitive and ancient creatures that have been around in our seas for about 300 million years. Most of them are extinct; there is only one extant order, with bottom-dwelling and planktonic species. The thorax and part of the abdomen are covered with a bivalved carapace that has a hinged portion to cover the head. The eyes are compound, often at the end of raised stalks, and the antennae are long.

The second subclass contains five orders, some of which are of little interest to the tropical freshwater hobbyist. The order Stomatopoda encompasses a group of creatures that are not uncommon in aquariums, although they are often undesirable. These are crustaceans that are commonly known as mantis shrimps. However, these animals do not usually inhabit freshwater.

Euphausiacea, the second order in this subclass, is of interest. For some years now, Pacific krill has been available frozen for use as marine fish food (usually *Euphausia pacifica*, but sometimes *Euphausia sanzoi*). Krill are oceanic crustaceans that often occur in large aggregations. They are an important part of the marine food chain for many fish, manta rays, and whales. Typically, krill seldom reach a length of much more than 1 inch (3 cm). They are usually colorless to pink but some deepwater species can be bright red. As food for tropical freshwater fish, they are second only to brine shrimp. If marine krill are washed and treated with vitamins, and then fed to carnivorous tropical fish, the result is startling: colors are enhanced and the general well-being of the fish is readily apparent after only a few days.

The third order, Decapoda, is of particular interest and will be dealt with in some detail in the following pages, since it contains many attractive and ornamental species for the tropical fish tank.

The last order in this class is Peracarida. Apart from containing the small, bottom-dwelling isopods and amphipods such as the sea-slaters, which resemble wood lice, and sand hoppers, the order also incorporates the small shrimps known as opossum shrimps. These are another alternative food source for tropical freshwater fish. The expert aquarist may be familiar with some species but not relate them to the opossum shrimps because they have a variety of names in the hobby, such as mysid shrimps, *Mysus*, or sometimes just mysids. Mysid shrimps (usually *Neomysis vulgaris*) are available frozen or, in some areas, as live food. They are an excellent food for many African Rift Lake cichlids.

Order: Decapoda (Shrimps, Prawns, Lobsters, Hermit crabs, True crabs)

The order contains about 68 families, with a total of almost 9,000 described species. The commercial importance of this group of animals is well known. In many lands, the economy relies heavily on lobster and crab fishing. A whole industry has been built up around shrimp fishing and also the capture of other animals, such as scampi, within this diverse group.

As far as the marine and freshwater aquarists are concerned, species from this group are in constant demand. They are excellent scavengers that will take care of any uneaten food that is left in the aquarium and also keep excessive growths of algae under control. In the last few years, many species suitable for tropical freshwater aquariums have emerged onto the wholesale market. These include brightly colored lobster and shrimp that are highly decorative and offer an unusual, if not sensational, talking point. Many species are surprisingly easy to keep and the selection of species available to the hobbyist is growing fast.

Breeding crustaceans in an aquarium is, at the moment, a largely hit-or-miss affair. In fact, this is the case with most freshwater invertebrates. It is known that many crustaceans carry the eggs tucked among the thoracic legs and that they later hatch and become shrimp larvae. Many larvae are planktonic, though, and are carried away by the currents until they go through a series of molts before settling to the substrate.

Palaemonites pugio

Common names: Ghost shrimp, Glass shrimp
Range: North America, in freshwater streams, shallow rivers, and canals throughout the southern United States
Size: 1½ inches (3.8 cm)
Description: Unlike other ghost and grass shrimps, this species prefers lightly brackish or fresh water. It is almost entirely transparent and this makes it difficult for predators to see. Adults have fine black lines on the carapace. These animals feed on algae and small benthic invertebrates.
Aquarium suitability: A group of these shrimp can be kept in a community tank and they will scavenge and help keep the aquarium clean. Avoid keeping large fish, such as cichlids and large tetras, with this invertebrate because they will only see it as food. These shrimp are very hardy in an aquarium and do a lot of good scrounging in the gravel for uneaten food and detritus.

Cherax cainii

Common names: Electric blue marron, Blue marron, Blue crayfish, Blue lobster
Range: Western Australia, in rivers and streams southward from Geraldtown
Size: 16 inches (40 cm)
Description: Often misidentified as *Cerax tenuimanus*, which has a similar coloration to this species but has many more hairs on the carapace. In *C. cainii*, the carapace is quite smooth. The natural color of this species is brownish-black, but beautiful blue examples are collected and bred in outdoor pens for the aquarium trade. In this case, the carapace may be pinkish-blue to deep blue.
Aquarium suitability: A species that is active during the day but needs plenty of hiding places and a large show tank to feel at home. This is a species that can be bred in captivity if a large enough tank is available.
Breeding information: Females carry up to 350 eggs that hatch after 21 days. The resulting nauplii are difficult to raise but will reach a size of 4 inches (10 cm) in just eight months if they are fed and protected correctly.

Phylum: Mollusca (Mollusks)

In terms of numbers of species, the mollusks represent the largest group of aquatic animals and the second largest in the whole of the animal kingdom, after insects. No one knows for certain how many species there are in this phylum but over 120,000 have been described so far. Mollusks are found in the sea, in freshwater, and there are also terrestrial species. It goes without saying, therefore, that a comprehensive coverage of this phylum is not possible in a book of this nature, and no attempt is being made here. Although the phylum is grouped into seven classes, only species from two of these classes are of interest to the tropical freshwater aquarist and these have been indicated in bold type in the chart shown on page 286. There is much controversy over the exact taxonomy of the gastropods at the moment. Until this is resolved, however, this book will be based on the conventionally accepted taxonomy of this group of mollusks.

Throughout history, these creatures have made their impression on the world as we know it. Mollusks evolved at the beginning of the Cambrian period, about 550 million years ago, and there are many fossilized records of their development. Many species are an important food source to fish, other invertebrates, land animals, birds, and humans.

Characteristically, the mollusk has two things that set it apart from other invertebrate groups. The first is a mantle, which is a fleshy dorsal cape that covers the mantle cavity where the gills, primitive kidney, anus, and sense organs are situated. This is unique in that, in many species, it has special glands that produce the calcium carbonate shell. Each species has its own shell form that reflects its feeding habits and lifestyle. In some species the mantle can be extended over the shell as camouflage or as a brightly colored warning to predators. In most cases it also protects the shell and gives it a highly polished appearance, such as that of the cowrie shells.

The second feature that is exclusive to the mollusks is the radula. This is present in almost all gastropods and is a long ribbonlike organ bearing chitinous teeth. This is used to grasp and scrape at food.

In most species there is a head region present, with the exception of the bivalves. There is a bulbous lump of tissue known as a visceral mass that encloses the gut and other internal organs. A foot is present, used for locomotion and for burrowing into the sediment for protection. In some species, such as the octopus, this is highly developed and its tentacle-like arms with rows of suckers are, in fact, an extension or splitting of the muscular foot.

Class: Gastropoda

In the gastropods, the body is asymmetrical and consists of a head with tentacles, eyes, a radula, a ventral foot, a visceral mass, and a mantle. The one-piece shell is spiraled when present and the body can be fully retracted into it. In some marine species the shell is internal, or completely absent. The visceral mass is large and covered by the mantle. It contains the heart, reproductive organs, anus, and a large part of the gut. A feature of the gastropods is that the visceral mass and mantle are twisted 180 degrees to the rest of the body, which means that the mantle cavity containing the gills and anus is set well forward, above and behind the head. This twisting, or torsion, usually occurs during the free-swimming larval stage of the mollusk's life. As a result of this torsion the

The Malayan sand snail is a welcome addition to the sandy aquarium. They will constantly turn over the sand, letting oxygen get in, and will also eat waste that gets into the sand.

gut, along with the nervous system, becomes twisted into a U-shape. The creeping ventral foot is often highly modified in swimming and burrowing forms.

Of the three subclasses of gastropods, the first is Prosobranchia. These are mostly aquatic and have shells that are thick and strong. In the few terrestrial species the shell is a great deal thinner and lighter to carry. The radula is often highly developed and is used to scrape at algae or sometimes detritus.

In the subclass Opisthobranchia, the shell is often absent or completely encapsulated by the mantle. The branchia, or internal gills, are smaller and regressive, but often there are more sophisticated external gills present as with the nudibranchs (*nudibranch* literally means "naked gill"). The radula is developed according to the specific feeding requirements of the species involved—this feature

is an important aid to taxonomists in identifying the species. In most species, detorsion takes place after the larval stage and the body more or less straightens out.

The final subclass, Pulmonata, contains mostly land-dwelling species and freshwater species. These are mollusks that lack gills but part of their mantle cavity is developed into a respiratory organ for breathing in air or water. The familiar garden slugs and snails belong to this group, as do pond snails and tropical freshwater mollusks.

Because of the ongoing controversy of the taxonomy of this group, it has been decided to restrict the species here.

Pomacea paludosa

Common name: Florida apple snail
Range: North America (Florida) and Cuba, in dense aquatic vegetation
Size: 2½ inches (6 cm)
Description: The shell is globose and the aperture is large and with a deep umbilicus. The color can vary from yellow to green to dark brownish-black with dark spiral bands. The foot is dark to pale gray with black on the upper side of the body. In clear water, the shell sometimes has reddish streaks. This snail will often leave the water and become amphibious.
Aquarium suitability: In low-oxygen water, this species will climb plant stems to the water surface and respire air to fill its secondary lung system. This is a Florida swamp snail that will breed readily under aquarium conditions. The eggs are pinkish-white and adhere to emerging stems of plants.

Planorbis corneus

Common name: Ramshorn snail
Range: North America and Europe, in still and slow-moving water with a high degree of vegetation
Size: 1½ inches (4 cm)
Description: The thin shell is opaque and resembles the curling horn of a ram. The blood in this snail contains hemoglobin and sometimes the body has very little pigmentation and will look red. If the water is low in oxygen, it will climb to the water surface and breathe air.
Aquarium suitability: If the aquarist wants to have a healthy plant growth in the tank, this species should be avoided at all costs. It reproduces quickly and will devour any and every plant. It is literally the "lawn mower" of the aquarium snails. In a tank that contains plastic plants, it is an excellent choice to keep algae under control.

Mollusks

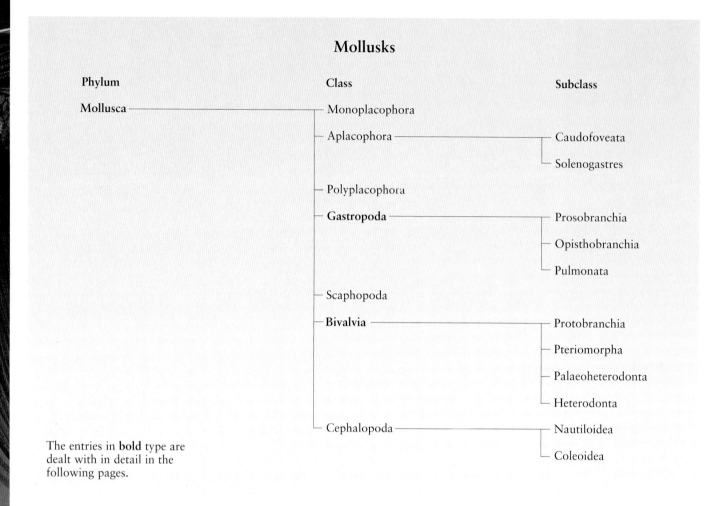

Phylum	Class	Subclass
Mollusca	Monoplacophora	
	Aplacophora	Caudofoveata
		Solenogastres
	Polyplacophora	
	Gastropoda	Prosobranchia
		Opisthobranchia
		Pulmonata
	Scaphopoda	
	Bivalvia	Protobranchia
		Pteriomorpha
		Palaeoheterodonta
		Heterodonta
	Cephalopoda	Nautiloidea
		Coleoidea

The entries in **bold** type are dealt with in detail in the following pages.

Class: Bivalvia

The commercial importance of the mollusks belonging to this class is unquestionable and throughout the world they are an important food source. Clams, mussels, cockles, oysters, and scallops all belong to this group. Collectively they are known as bivalve mollusks. Generally, the body is laterally compressed and enclosed between two shell halves (valves). These are hinged dorsally with a ligament of tissue that controls the opening of the two valves. To facilitate this, two large muscles (adductor muscles), counteracting one another, hold the two halves of the valve together. Two mantle folds are present and these are joined to enclose the mantle cavity, which contains a pair of specialized gills. In many bivalves, the mantle folds are joined along the posterior edges to form siphons. These tubelike structures control the flow of water in and out of the mantle cavity. They carry oxygen and food to the gills, where the nutrients are collected by cilia on the modified and enlarged gill structures. The head is greatly reduced, often to a pair of sensory palps, and there is no radula present. The foot is well developed in burrowing species and can be extended some distance between the valves to assist in burrowing. In sessile species, it is greatly reduced but in many cases a special gland is present that produces a threadlike secretion that, on contact with the minerals in the water, hardens into a horn-shaped, elastic thread. These are known as byssus threads and are used by the mollusk to attach itself to the substrate.

The sexes can be separate or hermaphroditic. In some species, such as in some clams, the sex can change several times throughout the life of the animal. In most marine species, fertilization takes place in the water, although in some cases, such as the European oyster, fertilization of the eggs takes place within the mantle cavity; the sperm is carried there by the water. The young hatch and become free-swimming larvae. A second stage, also pelagic, occurs before the mollusk develops its benthic form.

Bivalve mollusks are found in the sea in great numbers, but there are a few species that inhabit freshwater. They are bottom dwellers that are to be found in a variety of habitats. Most of them are filter feeders but some are carnivorous and scavenging species. Most of the species are sessile, although some scallops can swim for short distances by rhythmically clapping their valves together to create a primitive form of propulsion.

Order: Veneroida
(Cockles, Clams, Razor shells)

This, and the closely related order Myoida, belong to the subclass Heterodonta. This is a very large group of mollusks, many of which are unsuitable for the tropical freshwater aquarium. In the order Myoida, only a few species may be encountered in an aquarium, usually on rocks and plants taken from the wild. Most of the species in this group are burrowing mollusks. Ship worms, such as *Teredo navalis* and *Bankia setacea*, from the family Teredinidae, are not worms but mollusks. They also belong to this order and are responsible for a great deal of damage to harbor pilings, marine timber structures, and wooden boats because of their boring activities.

In contrast, the order Veneroida contains species that are not only beneficial to our natural world; they are also a valuable food source. The clams of the genus *Tridacna* are well known to aquarists and also to gourmets worldwide, although there are now strict ecological controls regarding their export. In spite of this, they are being reproduced both as a food and for the aquarium trade on a large scale. The giant clam (*Tridacna gigas*) belongs to this genus. It can grow to over 4½ feet (137 cm) and attain a weight in excess of 440 lb (200 kg). Freshwater mussels are often seen for sale in the aquarium trade and are quite easy to keep if they are given the correct substrate.

Corbicula fluminea

Common name: Freshwater clam
Range: Southeast Asia in freshwater streams, lakes, and rivers of Burma and Thailand
Size: 2 inches (5 cm)
Description: This species burrows into the substrate and opens its shell slightly to filter food. The shell halves more or less mirror one another and have black and brown irregular stripes across them. Some specimens have a pale green background color, whereas with others it may be yellow.
Aquarium suitability: This is an excellent filter feeder that is easy to keep. Do not keep with invertebrate-eating fish such as puffers. Clams are intolerant of copper, so if this is to be used to treat diseased fish, ensure that the clams are removed first and are not returned until all the copper has been eliminated via chemical filtration. Clams bury themselves in the substrate, so this should be of medium grade or finer.

part five

BREEDING
AQUARIUM FISH

Breeding techniques

One of the most important themes in the successful culture of tropical fish is the feeding and nutrition of the fry. It is where most of the major mistakes are made, and will continue to be made, unless the aquarist understands the prerequisites. It is not only the type of food used that will reflect in the success of a fish brood, but also the nutritional quality of the food itself. This should be of a standard that allows the fry to develop as healthfully and naturally as possible within the glass walls of an aquarium.

In order to establish organisms on which very small fish fry can be fed, we need to set up a food chain. This is not as difficult as it sounds. The aquarist should not panic and draw away from the problem from the start. The food chain begins with single-celled algae, which are produced to feed rotifers (*Brachionus* spp.). These are then used as food for the fish fry—it is as simple as that!

Of course there are problems. But these have nothing to do with the culture of algae and rotifers; this is relatively easy when you know how. The main problems lie in the ability of the fish breeder to produce a food that is nutritional enough to keep the larvae healthy and provide a good growth rate. The procedures for this will be discussed later in this chapter.

Many biologists and hobbyists question the morals of the hybridization and "line breeding" of certain tropical fish species to produce bizarre forms and colors. They believe it to be somehow cruel and an exploitation of nature. Nevertheless, in nature this often happens without the intervention of humans, particularly with fish. If a species cannot find a mate in the wild, it will often mate with a similar but different species in order to fulfill its inherent reproductive role. There are many examples of this in the marine environment as well as in freshwater.

Our intervention in producing bizarre-shaped fish is nothing new, nor should it be a controversial subject. The Chinese have been culturing goldfish (*Carassius auratus*) and koi carp (*Cyprinus carpio*) for hundreds of years. This has resulted in some really exotic forms. The black moor, the telescope-eyed moor, the lacy shubunkin, and the comet-tailed shubunkin are just a few examples of line breeding and hybridization. These are all well-known and well-loved ornamental pond fish. So why not have ornamental aquarium fish, too? Nature will preserve the integrity of the species, because no one can affect that. But line breeding and hybridization can produce some excellent ornamental fish for the aquarium trade, such as the Peacock cichlids.

The courtship and spawning of a pair of Golden panchax (Pachypanchax playfairii) is shown in this sequence of photographs. The male approaches the female, showing his spread fins. He coaxes her to the breeding site and they come together side by side so that the male can fertilize the eggs as they are laid.

A large shoal of fry of Madagascar rainbow fish (Bedotia geayi).

Livebearers

The term "livebearers" refers to a group of fish that give birth to live young (viviparous) rather than laying eggs (oviparous). However, it is a misconception to assume that the female livebearer does not produce eggs. Indeed she does, and these are fertilized in her egg duct. The male is able to achieve this because his anal fin is specially adapted into a hollow spike. Juvenile males have a normal anal fin, but as the fish grows, this changes to become a rodlike projection (gonopodium) that can be moved forward or backward and from side to side. Depending on the species, this can vary in length. The male approaches the female from the side and slightly to the rear. For a brief moment he will touch the female's egg duct with his gonopodium, which is near the vent, and fertilization takes place. The eggs eventually hatch and grow inside the egg duct until they reach the free-swimming stage. At this point the female expels them one at a time. The young fry in her egg duct are folded once, with their heads next to their tails. As each is expelled it soon straightens out and begins to swim for suitable cover. Females can give birth to four or five broods from a single fertilization. Distinguishing a ripe female is easy if the fish is not black, such as a Black molly: there is a large darkened area near the vent and it appears somewhat swollen. This is known as the gravid spot. Mature males and females can be distinguished by the shape of the anal fin, but with some species it is not so apparent. This is particularly the case with some platies.

Nature has a way of controlling species that are sexually prolific and livebearers are very fecund. In this case, it is cannibalism by the parent fish that reduces the numbers. If the young are to be saved, it is better to remove them to a separate rearing tank or remove the parents.

Egglayers

Oviparous fish have evolved separate breeding procedures depending on the species. In each case the eggs are laid by the female and fertilized by the male. Egg-scatterers that drop nonadhesive eggs (such as danios) are different from those that scatter or drop adhesive eggs (such as barbs). Then there are those fish that carefully build a nest of bubbles and lay their eggs near it so that the male can spit each individual egg into the nest. Many cichlids carefully lay eggs on a flat surface that has been previously cleaned by one or both parents to minimize the risk of fungal infection on the eggs.

Floating plants, such as *Riccia*, are ideally suited to those fish that spawn at or near the surface, and whose

A female Blue tetra (Boehlkea fredcochui) *ready to spawn.*

eggs are adhesive. Fish that scatter nonadhesive eggs, which drop to the substrate, need an entirely different approach. The most effective method of preventing the eggs from being eaten by the parents or other fish is to use marbles as a substrate. The eggs will drop between them and develop as fry without any fish being able to get at them.

Those species that lay eggs and care for them also have different procedures. The eggs can be laid in previously dug pits, on the roof of a cave, or on a flat surface such as bogwood or rock. It is up to the aquarist to determine the general breeding habits of the fish in his charge and equip the aquarium accordingly if breeding is intended.

Fry that are hatched generally have a yolk sac that supplies nourishment until it becomes free-swimming and is able to feed on fine foods. The time frame until this yolk sac is used up varies a great deal between individual species. Some fish offer additional nourishment to the fry as they reach the free-swimming stage. This is particularly the case with the Discus—the fry will attach themselves to the sides of the parent and feed on secretions that are given off through the skin.

Mouthbreeders

There are many cases of this phenomenon among fish in both the marine and freshwater environments. Mouthbreeding means that the eggs are incubated in the mouth of one or both parents. Even when the eggs are hatched, the parent fish may continue to hold the larvae until they are released as free-swimming fry. In many cases parenthood does not stop there. At the first sign of danger, the parent will collect up the fry into its mouth and hold them there until the danger has passed.

In some cases, the eggs that are laid are fertilized and then taken into the mouth to incubate. In others, they are actually fertilized in the female's mouth. A classic example

of this occurs with many cichlids that originate from Lake Malawi in East Africa. Here, nature has provided an ingenious solution.

Many Lake Malawi male cichlids have prominent yellow spots on their anal fins. To the female, these look like eggs. These spots represent "dummy eggs." When the female has laid her eggs she carefully takes them into her mouth to incubate them. But at this stage they are unfertilized. Seeing the bright spots on the male's anal fin, she mistakes these as eggs that she has missed and mouths his anal fin. At this point the male releases his sperm and the eggs in her mouth are fertilized. Biologists and ichthyologists call this the "dummy egg method."

Care should be taken not to feed mouthbreeders that are incubating eggs, or the female may swallow the eggs by accident. This is not always the case, but as a rule of thumb it is good general practice unless it is otherwise stated. The amount of time that the eggs and larvae are incubated varies greatly between species, but it is generally a period of three weeks or more. Despite this, the young fry emerge better equipped to deal with their own survival. Because of the limitations of the size of the parent fish's mouth, fewer eggs are laid than oviparous species and this can be as few as 10 eggs or as many as 80 eggs.

The culture of rotifers (Brachionus spp.)

The mass culture of rotifers, such as *Brachionus* spp., costs a great deal of time and the aquarist must be aware of this. He must also be aware of the fact that they have little in the way of nutrition to offer fish larvae. One must be clear about this. It is only utilized because of its ability to reproduce rapidly, reaching a size that is attractive to the fish larvae and fry, and that through its swimming movements is made especially tempting. But as a food it is very poor.

It is the responsibility of the aquarist and fish breeder to ensure that these organisms are changed into high-quality food with an excellent nutritional value. This process is called "enrichment." It is based on the fact that these organisms will take in any particles that are of the right size. So the possibility exists, through the clever feeding of nutritional elements that are important foods for fish fry, that *Brachionus* becomes a living nutritional capsule. A simple form of this enrichment would be to feed *Brachionus* cultures on singled-celled algae. But this is not as easy as it sounds. Many of the singled-celled algae that are responsible for "green water" are totally unsuitable as food source for these organisms. Even if the correct alga is used, there is always the danger that other stronger and more robust algae can take over the culture, thereby destroying them as a food source for the rotifers. For this reason many experienced fish breeders utilize the correct alga from a test tube in order to establish a culture and prevent contamination. Professional fish breeders use this sterile method so that large cultures of single-celled algae can be produced and utilized for the feeding of these organisms. Unfortunately for the aquarist, there is no way for him to check whether or not the algae remain uncontaminated. There is a great risk that the algal culture can become contaminated with low-grade algae. In this case, the best method is to periodically throw away the algal culture and start fresh with another batch from the calibrated starter culture.

A very good product, and one that is suitable for the hobby aquarist, is the Micro Algae Disc from Aquaculture Supply. This is a pure culture of microalgae from the genus *Nanochloropsis* and is of an extremely high quality. It lends itself ideally to the growth and enrichment of *Brachionus* rotifers. In addition, its growth is strong and competitive, so the danger of contamination is not as critical as it is with other algae species. Despite this, it is advisable to start another algal culture every six months or so. Aquaculture Supply also offers a handbook, which deals with the culture of rotifers.

After removing enough *Brachionus* from the plankton culture to satisfy the feeding requirements of the fish fry, further enrichment can be applied. There are a number of products available that were originally developed for mariculture. The ones that are recommended—because they produce successful results—are Selco and Super Selco from Inve/Artemia-Systems. These are complex mixtures based on fish and invertebrate oils. They are specifically developed to provide the fish fry with all the important nutritional elements that they require, in the form of *Brachionus*.

Some time ago, a new product became available, Algemac-2000 from Aquafauna-Biomarine. It consists of spray-dried alga (*Schizochytrium*) and produces good results because it is not oil-based. This is an advantage for the fry, since the raising tank does not become as dirty as it does with other substances.

Enrichment techniques can sometimes be a problem for the novice breeder. Enrichment means packing the *Brachionus* with as many nutrients as possible, so the rotifers must be incubated in a thick suspension of an enrichment medium. It is recommended that this be done at a temperature of 82–86°F (28–30°C). Bacteria tend to form quickly under these circumstances and they use up a lot of oxygen, so the air being pumped into the culture should be fairly strong to counteract this.

Generally speaking, *Brachionus* should be left in this suspension for a period of three to four hours, followed by an additional three to four hours in a freshly prepared suspension. After this procedure, they can be carefully washed in fresh water and fed to the fry.

The procedure for enriching rotifers must be well organized. When the lights switch on over the fry container at 8:00 a.m., the larvae must be fed immediately.

This means that the enrichment of the *Brachionus* must take place at 2:00 a.m. and at 5:00 a.m. A good idea here is using a dosing unit connected to a timer so that the enriching medium is added to the culture at a predetermined time. After the *Brachionus* has been enriched, it will maintain its quality for about six hours. If a 12-hour feeding regime is being used, a new enriched culture must be used after the first six hours.

It is sometimes difficult for the aquarist to get hold of some of the enriching media that have been developed for mariculture. This is understandable, since manufacturers are not really interested in such small orders for their products. The solution to this problem is simple: get together with other fish breeders. An organized group of amateur breeders can obtain these essential materials without too many problems.

Choosing the parent fish

This is not easy. Many fish species are not sexually dimorphic, which means that you cannot differentiate between the male and female. If the aquarist is unsure and intends to breed his fish, then he should take advice from a knowledgeable aquarist or dealer. But even this doesn't always work. Some fish can be sexed, but there are others that are very difficult to differentiate by anyone other than the expert. The form of the fins is often a good indicator of the sex of the fish. Other species are often easy to tell apart, but they may belong to a group of fish that is especially difficult to breed. Rainbowfish are often sexually dimorphic, but again they are difficult to breed successfully under artificial conditions.

Some fish often show no differences between the male and female, but breeding pairs will usually separate themselves from a group and defend their territory at all costs. Again, this is not always the case. A dominant male fish may pursue his partner and bite her fins, or the female might pursue the male. There are many species that outwardly appear to be archenemies when two are kept in an aquarium together, but they could be a breeding pair.

In general, it can be said that to obtain a pair of fish for breeding, a certain amount of experience is required, along with a great deal of understanding of fish behavior.

An attempt has been made throughout this book to include breeding details alongside each individual fish species, where these details are known and where space allows. However, this is only general information and the eager hobbyist is advised to refer to a specialized reference if they are going to take breeding seriously.

Feeding and rearing fish fry

Up until recently there were frequent discussions and articles in aquarium magazines dealing with the optimal size of the organisms that are fed to fish larvae. The newcomer to fish breeding should always check whether or not feeding with rotifers is effective. It is no use simply looking into the fry tank and observing them, because they sometimes take other suspended matter in the container. Very often they show typical feeding characteristics at exactly the time when there is no more food in the container. The only sure way is to remove one of the fry and place it under a microscope. By lightly pressing the foil against the fry and glass, the stomach contents can be examined. *Brachionus* is digested very quickly, with the exception of the so-called mastax (a feeding apparatus of the rotifer), which often remains in the stomach longer than the rest of the *Brachionus*. These—and any other remains—can be examined in order to determine the amount of success in the feeding rate of the fish fry.

In most cases brine shrimp nauplii are used as the second food source for most of the smaller fish fry. These are usually given when the fry are large enough to accept larger organisms as food. Most aquarists feed brine shrimp nauplii to fish fry as soon as they are hatched and begin feeding. Although at this stage they are small and easily caught, it is not a good practice. Like rotifers, brine shrimp are of very little nutritional benefit to the fish larvae. By far the best method—and one that brings the most success—is to prolong the period where *Brachionus* are fed to the fry until such time as the fry are able to eat larger organisms. In this critical phase the brine shrimp nauplii should be enriched in much the same way as the rotifers. Since newly hatched brine shrimp are unable to feed, they should be left to develop into their own second larval stadium and then placed in a suspension of *Nanochloropsis* and other enriching products. The amount of time that they are kept in this suspension is not as critical but should be kept to about 12 hours, followed by another 12 hours in a fresh suspension. After this they can be washed in fresh water and fed to the fish larvae. Naturally, at this stage the brine shrimp are considerably larger, which is why the feeding period with *Brachionus* should be extended. The idea is to create a continuous diet of high-quality food during the developing stages of the fish fry.

There are brine shrimp nauplii available that are guaranteed to have an especially high nutritional value. These are from specially chosen cysts that deliver nauplii of "super-nutritional value." Unfortunately, the eggs are very expensive and the results obtained by fish breeders are not very positive.

Magazine articles about breeding successes with one species or another— and their accompanying photographs—often show the results of dietary deficiencies of which the breeder is unaware. This usually manifests itself through slow growth, bad colors, malformed fish, low survival rate, or even no surviving fish at all.

Measuring the survival rate of a fish brood is an important indicator of the success of the fish breeder. This involves is the number of fish that go through the initial growth stage and become juvenile fish in relation to the number of hatched fry on the first day. Beginners and experienced breeders would profit a great deal if they periodically employ this method to measure their success rate.

So how does one accurately measure the survival rate of a batch of newly hatched fish fry? It sounds simple to the uninitiated, doesn't it? Just count them. Have you ever tried to count 400 tiny fry swimming about in a tank? If you have, then you will know the problem. With many species the task is relatively uncomplicated, since the eggs are usually laid on a flat piece of the substrate in an orderly manner (see photograph opposite). A camera is required to take a photograph of the batch of eggs. The eggs can then be inspected and counted in a quiet moment, but these are still eggs and not newly hatched fry.

The eggs are then transferred, along with the piece of substrate, to the fry container. After hatching has taken place, the piece of substrate can be removed and the aquarist can count the eggs that have not hatched. This is subtracted from the number of eggs that were laid— simple as that. The aquarist then knows exactly how many of the fry actually hatched. With other species it can be considerably more difficult, but I am confident in the resourcefulness of most aquarists once they are shown the way!

The number of fish that have gone through the growth stages and become healthy young fish should then be counted and this can be stated as a percentage of those that were hatched. The resultant figure is termed the survival rate.

If the results are considerably less than the minimum expected figures, other aspects should be investigated. These include not only the feeding of the fry, but also the breeding pair. Their diet is also vital and must be as varied and nutritious as possible. Water quality must also be checked and any shortfalls corrected before the next attempt at breeding is undertaken.

Examination of fish larvae under a microscope results in the death of the larva under scrutiny. For the biologist this is an everyday occurrence, an element of "quality control," if you like. The aquarist shies away from such a practice, often thinking, "This could be the only one that survives." The failure to carry out such examinations is misguided. It is far better to sacrifice one or two larvae for a high survival rate than to lose most of them through a lack of understanding.

Among the cichlids, angelfish are particularly easy to breed in the aquarium. The male and female select and peck clean a small patch on a vertical rock or leaf and eventually the female will lay eggs on it.

Glossary

Acclimatization: the process of gradual introduction of a newly-acquired fish to its aquarium. This is normally done by allowing the water in the aquarium to mix slowly with the water containing the fish, thus ensuring that any change in water does not produce shock.

Activated charcoal: a filter medium used in both internal and external filters to remove toxic substances, such as phenol, from the water.

Aerobic bacteria: bacteria that thrive in an oxygen-rich environment and break down organic waste into nitrate.

Alga: a photosynthetic plant that reproduces by spores and lacks true vascular tissue, flowers and seeds.

Anaerobic bacteria: bacteria that live in an oxygen-poor environment and utilize the oxygen from nitrate to produce nitrogen.

Antenna: sensory appendage on the head of crustaceans and catfishes.

Anterior: pertaining to the front, the forward region.

Anus: the external opening of a digestive tract from which wastes are voided.

Arborescent: tree-like in form.

Axil: the acute angular region between the underside of the pectoral fin and the body of a fish. It is equivalent to the armpit of man.

Bar: an elongated color marking that is vertical in orientation with more or less straight sides.

Barbel: slender sensory tentacle, usually in pairs on the chin of certain fishes.

Basal: towards the base or area of attachment.

Base medium: material such as sand or gravel that is used to cover the floor of an aquarium or the base of a sub-sand filter.

Benthic: bottom dwelling.

Bifid: divided into two equal parts or lobes.

Bilateral symmetry: symmetry where the body is divided along a single longitudinal and vertical plane into two identical halves.

Bioluminescence: active light that is created by living organisms.

Biomass: the amount of living matter in a given area.

Bio-system: the term used to describe an aquarium that employs bacterial filtration.

Blade: the leaf-like structure of an aquatic plant, sometimes called a frond.

Brackish: a mixture of seawater and fresh water found in estuaries and the like.

Calcareous: composed of calcium carbonate.

Calcified: containing deposits of calcium carbonate within its structure.

Carapace: the chitinous or calcareous skin or shell that encloses part or all of the body of crustaceans.

Carnivore: a flesh-eating animal.

Caudal fin: the tail fin (the term "tail" may indicate any portion of an organism that is posterior to the anus).

Caudal peduncle: in fish, the part of the body between the posterior bases of the dorsal and anal fins. This is usually the narrowest part of the fish.

cf. : an abbreviation of the Latin word "conferre" meaning to compare with the formal description. Used in tentative species identifications.

Chloroplast: plastid containing chlorophyll.

Cirrus: a small, fleshy appendage that is often jointed or flexible; the plural is cirri.

Cladistic analysis: the phylogenetic approach to classification where the method seeks to resolve which two taxa of a group of three or more have the closest genealogical relationship.

Cladogram: a dichotomously-branching diagram that is constructed to show paired lineages (sister groups) that each is given or understood to have the same taxonomic rank.

Class: a group of related organisms in a category ranking below phylum and above order.

Classification: the practice of arranging items into categories or groups. There are two main approaches to the systematic classification of organisms. These are the cladistic and the synthetic approaches.

Community tank: an aquarium containing several different species of fishes living in peaceful coexistence.

Compressed: laterally flattened.

Cytoplasm: protoplasmic content of a cell other than the nucleus.

Dendritic organ: an organ composed of cells similar to the chloride cells in the gills of fishes and the salt cells of birds.

Denticles: small teeth.

Depressed: vertically flattened.

Dichotomously branched: in plants, having each division of a branch or fork divided into two equal parts.

Dimorphic: where there is a marked difference in the appearance of the two sexes.

Dominant: having the greatest influence or abundant and conspicuous.

Dorsal: the upper surface or back of an animal.

Ecology: the study of the distribution and abundance of organisms relative to their respective environments.

Ectoparasite: an external parasite, one that lives on the outside of the body.

Emaciated: of a starved appearance.

Emarginate: used to describe the inward curving border of the caudal fin in fishes.

Evolution: the origin of the species by development from earlier forms.

Evolutionary analysis: see Synthetic analysis.

Family: a collective term used to incorporate all similar genera into one group of like-creatures.

Filter bed: the filtering medium that removes debris from the water.

Fry: young fish, normally free-swimming.

Gastrovascular cavity: the stomach area in some invertebrate animals.

Genus: a collective term used to incorporate like species into one group (plural—genera).

Gonad: the organ that produces eggs or sperm.

Herbivore: a plant-eating animal.

Hermaphrodite: a creature that possesses both male and female reproductive organs.

Heterosporus: producing spores of two different sizes: the larger spore effectively functioning as the female spore and the smaller functioning male.

Homosporus: in plants, a characteristic where the plant only produces one kind of spore.

Hydrometer: a calibrated instrument used for measuring the specific gravity of a liquid, in this case seawater.

Ichthyology: The science and study of fishes.

Inert solids: particles, which are chemically inactive and therefore safe.

Inflorescence: the part of the plant where leaves

and roots are developed and often bulbous.

Interorbital space: the space at the top of the head between the eyes.

Invertebrates: animals without backbones.

Iridescent: displaying or reflecting an interplay of rainbow or metallic colours, glowing or shining.

Junior synonym: the first scientific name to be published is the senior synonym; any others are junior synonyms of the species.

Lamella: thin plate or scale.

Lanceolate: Lance-like, shaped like the head of a spear.

Larva: a pre-adult form that hatches from an egg and often leads a different life to that of the adult organism.

Lateral line: a sensory canal running along the sides of a fish.

Life-support system: a system where the conditions to support life are produced artificially.

Lunate: sickle-shaped; normally used to describe the form of the tail of a fish.

Mantle: in mollusks, the part of the body wall that produces the shell and encloses the visceral mass within the mantle cavity.

Median fins: the dorsal, anal, and caudal fins.

Metamorphosis: broadly speaking the transformation of a larva to the adult form.

Monophyly: sharing a common ancestor.

Monotypic: a genus containing a single species.

Myogenic: referring to electric organs that are derived from muscle cells.

Nape: the dorsal part of the head.

Neurogenic: referring to electric organs that are derived from nerve cells.

Ocellus: an eye-like marking in one colour, bordered by a ring of another colour.

Omnivore: an animal that is both flesh and plant-eating.

Operculum: a calcareous or chitinous plug that closes the aperture of a tube or shell in invertebrates. In fish, it refers to the gill cover, which consists of four bones: the opercle, preopercle, interopercle and subopercle.

Order: the category of taxonomic classification ranking above family.

Oviparous: egg-laying.

Orbital: refers to the orbit or eye.

Palp: sensory appendage near the mouth.

Parasite: an organism that lives on or in the body of a host animal or plant and from which it obtains nourishment, detrimental to the host.

Pectoral fin: situated on each side of the body in fishes, behind the operculum.

Permeable: porous, through which molecules may pass.

pH: the negative decimal logarithm of a hydrogen-ion concentration in moles per litre, giving the measure of acidity or alkalinity of a solution. In other words a unitless index from 0 to 14 used to describe the degree of acidity or alkalinity of a substance. Zero is the highest degree of acidity and 14 is the highest degree of alkalinity, a pH of 7 being the neutral point, related by formula to a standard solution of potassium hydrogen phthalate, which has a value of 4 at $15°$ Centigrade.

Pharyngeal teeth: groups of teeth on the gill arches of certain fishes.

Pharynx: the forward part of the gut.

Photosynthesis: the process by which plants convert carbon dioxide and water into carbohydrates and chlorophyll under the influence of energy derived from light.

Phylogeny: evolutionary history.

Phylum: the basic sub-division of a kingdom (plural—phyla).

Pinnate: having branches on opposite sides of a main axis in a feather-like form.

Pinnule: the sub-branch of a feather-like branch or arm, particularly in the case of algae and crinoid echinoderms.

Plastids: small bodies in the cytoplasm of a plant cell containing pigment or food.

Posterior: pertaining to the rear, the tail region in some species.

Predator: an animal that hunts to catch food.

Premaxillary: the forward most bone forming the upper jaw in fishes.

Proboscis: a protrusion or projection, often tubular, from the head region of some animals.

Protoplasm: viscous translucent substance forming the main constituent of cells in organisms. The basis of life in animals.

Pyriform: pear-shaped.

Ray: the bony or spinous elements of the fins that function as a support for the membranes.

Reagent: a substance with a known reaction to a given chemical or given water conditions.

Rhizoid: the root-like part of a plant.

Rhizome: the stolon of a plant, a horizontal stem.

Rudiment: primitive or undeveloped and unable to carry out its normal function.

Sagittate: shaped like a modern arrowhead.

Sensu lato: broadly speaking, in the broad sense of.

Sensu stricto: strictly speaking, in the strict sense of.

Serrate: saw-like, or notched along a margin.

Siliceous: composed of silicon dioxide.

sp. : abbreviation for species.

Specific gravity: the weight of a substance when compared to that of pure water at standard pressure and temperature ($4°C$) e.g. SG 1.022 = 1.022 times heavier than pure water at $4°C$.

Spinule: a small spine.

spp. : the plural form of sp. where more than one particular species is involved.

Stolon: the horizontal rhizome or runner of the plant, which connects upright fronds.

Supraorbital: the area bordering the upper edge of the eye.

Substrate: the surfaces or substances on which organisms are growing.

Symbiosis: two unlike creatures living and associating with one another for the benefit of one or both partners.

Synonym: an invalid scientific name of a creature that has been put forward, or proposed, after the accepted name.

Synthetic analysis: evolutionary analysis in which the classification is based on a synthesis of knowledge concerning both the genealogical relationships and the perceived degree of evolutionary or genetic similarity or divergence from other groups.

Telson: the chitinous or calcareous tailpiece of crustaceans.

Thorax: the area of the body behind the head in crustaceans.

Thoracic: referring to the thorax or chest region.

Tracheophyte: a vascular plant that has water-carrying tissue termed "tracheids" in their tissue, enabling the plant to evolve larger and more elaborate structures.

Truncate: square-margined; refers to the caudal fin of some fishes that have tails with vertical terminal borders and slightly rounded corners.

Ventral: the underside of the body, opposite of dorsal.

Yolk sac: the yolk-containing sac, which is attached to the embryo; common in newly

Bibliography

Unlike most aquarium books that list other works for further reference in terms of their popularity and availability in bookstores, this listing is somewhat different. Although many of the books are currently available, there are others that are not. Some scientific journals and papers have been used during the research for this book and these are not generally accessible to the average aquarist. Many of these are available—or at least photocopy versions—by writing to the various museums or publishers concerned. A small fee is usually payable. I have found them all extremely helpful.

Books that are unavailable or out of print can usually be found in a reference library (another helpful institution). The aim of this bibliography is twofold. Firstly as a summary of the source information used, and secondly as an informative listing of related works and magazine articles that the reader may want to read for further information about a particular aspect of the hobby.

The authors are listed in alphabetical order in bold type and the name of the book or periodical appears in italics. The date of the publication is in brackets after the author's name. Where two authors are involved both have been named in the order that they appear in the publication. Where more than two authors are involved, the name of the compiler or senior author is given with the suffix "*et al*" e.g. Axelrod, H. R. *et al*. Where two or more publications from the same year and by the same author are cited, the year reference is suffixed with the letters, a, b, c, etc, in lower case, in the order in which they were published.

Allen, G. R. (1983) *Kiunga ballochi*, A New Genus and Species of Rainbowfish (Melanotaeniidae) from Papua New Guinea. *Tropical Fish Hobbyist*. Vol. 32 (2).

Allen, G. R. (1990) Les Poissons arc-en-ciel (Melanotaeniidae) de la Péninsule de Vogelkop, Irian Jaya, avec description de trois nouvelles espèces. *Aquariol*. 16. 1990.

Allen, G. R. (1997) A new species of rainbowfish (Melanotaenia: Melanotaeniidae) from the Lakekamu Basin, Papua New Guinea. *Aquariol*. 24. 1997.

Allen, G. R. (1998) A new genus and species of Rainbowfish (Melanotaeniidae) from fresh waters of Irian Jaya, Indonesia. *Aquariol*. 25. 1998.

Allen, G. R. & Moore, R. (1981) *Pseudomugil paludicola* a new Species of Freshwater Blue-eye (Melanoaeniidae) from Papua New Guinea. *Aquariol*. 7 1980.

Allen, G. R. & Renyaan, S. J. (1998) Three New Species of Rainbowfishes (Melanotaeniidae) from Irian Jaya, Indonesia. *Aqua*. 3. No. 2.

Axelrod, H. R. et al. (1991) *Dr. Axelrod's Atlas of Freshwater Aquarium Fishes (Sixth Edition)* TFH Publications, Neptune City, New Jersey.

Bridges, W. (1970) *The New York Aquarium Book of the Water World*. The New York Zoological Society, American Heritage Publishing Co., Inc., New York.

Froese, R. & Pauly, D. Editors. (2005) *Fish Base*. World Wide Web electronic publication. www.fishbase.org, version (03/2005).

Goemans, R. (1999) *Live Sand Secrets*. Marc Weiss Companies, Inc., Ft. Lauderdale, Florida.

Hargreaves, V. B. (1978) *The Tropical Marine Aquarium*. McGraw-Hill Book Company, New York.

Hargreaves, V. B. (1989) *The Tropical Marine Aquarium (Revised Edition)* David & Charles (Publ.) Ltd, Newton Abbot.

Hargreaves, V. B. (2004) *The Complete Book of the Marine Aquarium*. Thunderbay Press, San Diego.

Hoek, C. van den, et al. (1993) *Algen (3 Auflage)* . Georg Thieme Verlag, Stuttgart.

Horst, K. & Kipper, H. E. (1989) *Die Optimale Aquarienkontrolle*. Aquadocumenta Verlag GmbH, Bielefeld.

Innes, W. T. (1966) *Exotic Aquarium Fishes (19th Edition)* Metaframe Corporation, Maywood.

Lundberg, J. G. et al. (1988) *Phractocephalus hemiliopterus* (Pimelodidae, Siluriformes) from the Upper Miocene Urumaco formation, Venezuela: a further case of evolutionary stasis and local extinction among South American fishes. *J. Vertebr. Paleont*. 8(2): 131-138.

Manton, S. M. (1973) Arthropod phylogeny – a modern synthesis. J Zool. London., **171**, 111-130.

Manton, S. M. (1977) The Arthropoda: Habits, Functional Morphology and Evolution. Oxford University Press, London.

Nelson, J. S. (1987) The next 25 years: vertebrate systematics. *Canadian Journal of Zoology*., Vol 65. 4. P. 779-785.

Nelson, J. S. (1994) Fishes Of The World (3rd Edition). John Wiley & Sons, New York.

Oliver, A. P. H. (1975) *The Hamlyn Guide to Shells of the World*. The Hamlyn Publishing Group Ltd, London.

Parenti, L. R. (1981) A phylogenetic and biogeographic analysis of cyprinodontiform fishes (Teleostei, Atherinomorpha). *Bull. Am. Mus. Nat. Hist*. 168 (4): 335-557.

Reveal, J. L. (1997) *PBIO Lecture Notes – Selected Families of Angiosperms: Rosidae*. Norton-Brown Herbarium, University of Maryland.

Silberstein, M. & Campbell, E. (1989) *Elkhorn Slough*. Monterey Aquarium Foundation, Monterey, California.

Tunze, A. et al. **(1995)** Aquarium Ecology: A supplementary approach. The mechanisms of biotechnological water cultivation. Tunze Aquarientechnik GmbH, Penzberg.

Index

Acknowledgments

During the preparation and research for this book I was in constant contact with some of the top European and American aquarists, manufacturers throughout the world, and countless naturalists and ichthyologists in order to produce an authoritative work. It is only fair that I thank them all for their help. In order to do this, some logical order has been necessary for the amount of people involved therefore I have chosen to list them country-by-country.

In the UK, my eternal gratitude must go to Professor Ray Gibson of Liverpool John Moores University first and foremost, for the enormous amount of help he gave me with my previous book, which he also proof read, and for his continued support. I thank my long-time buddy Adrian Jefferys of Leeds, Roy Meeke of Interfish, Ossett, Liz and Mike Donlan of Valley Publishing, Accrington, and Don Attewell of Newnham Court Pet Centre, Maidstone. In addition I would like to thank world class photographers John Clipperton and his buddy, Alan Hill, who pulled out all the stops for me to obtain photographs of some of the more elusive species. Also my own brother, Anthony Hargreaves, who has almost half a century of experience in the keeping and raising of ornamental fishes, produced some excellent photographs for this book. Thanks Tony!

In the USA, Shawn Underwood of Petco USA was of some considerable help during the production of this book. From Monterey Bay, Dr. Steve Webster, senior marine biologist at the Monterey Bay Aquarium, helped me in no small way. My thanks go to Mark Hamran and Del Goins of www.aquariumplant.com, South Dakota, for their assistance regarding the aquarium plants featured in this book. Del, in particular, was a great help in putting together so many species for me to photograph. As well, I should not forget Dr. John E. Randall of the Bishop Museum in Honolulu who, albeit unintentionally, has shown me the disciplines that one must observe in pursuit of accuracy and truth. Also, I should like to thank Steve Dalrymple of Zoo Med, San Luis Obispo, California, Robert Fenner of San Diego, California, Ray Meyers, Aimee Stone, Richard Anderson and Daniel Kershing of Pet Fun, Salinas, California, who allowed me to photograph many of the fish and invertebrate species featured in this book. My thanks are also extended to Keri Dunneboil of All-Glass Aquarium, Co., Franklin, Wisconsin, fellow author and friend Bob Goemans Ph.D. of Tucson, Arizona, and Lou Dell of American Marine Inc., Ridgefield, Connecticut. Adam Duarte loaned me his aquarium to take some of the photographs, thanks Adam! Ron, Nancy, and Caryle Smith also allowed me the peace and quiet to enable me to write uninterrupted and deserve a special thank you. But there is also the crew at 'The Ocean Floor' in Goleta, Santa Barbara to thank too, including Dustin Grossman, Craig Gutshall and Anne Curtis - these guys are really nice and gave me "carte blanche" to take photographs in their facility.

In Canada, my sincere thanks are extended to Professor Joseph S. Nelson of the Department of Biological Sciences, University of Alberta for his helpful comments regarding the subject of systematics, 'Thanks Joe!'

In Australia Dr. Gerald R. Allen is a trusted colleague and old friend. His help with the rainbowfishes was very valuable. Thanks for your help and continued encouragement, Jerry!

In Hong Kong, I am indebted to Mr. Richard Wong and Mr. Y. K. Luk of the Fish Marketing Organization, Kowloon for allowing me the opportunity to have a 'free hand' in the Sai Kung Nature Reserve, where many field trips were undertaken. Dr. Margaret Cope of the University of Hong Kong was also a great help to me.

In Germany, I must thank Dr. Manfred Schluter and Klaus Hansen, both of Aqua Medic, Bissendorf, Erika Schoedder and Karl Buschke of 'aqua connect', Gau-Odenheim. In addition, Mr. Hans-Peter Schmidt of Cologne and Klaus Stuerzenhofecker of Hatern were a great help with regard to bacteria cultures in aquarium filter systems. Also my thanks go to the inimitable Hans E. Baensch of Mergus Verlag, Melle.

In Switzerland, Karl-Friedrich Korner of AQ Marketing AG, Luzern has supported me for some years now, by providing me with a high quality sea salt mix so that I could carry out additional brackish-water aquarium research.

In Israel, Neil Marks and Eli Nissenberg of Red Sea, Eilat, Israel deserve my thanks. Neil was especially quick in pulling out all the stops for me when I was faced with a difficult dilemma.

Without the generous help and support of these people, this book would never have been completed.

Picture Acknowledgments

tl=top left, tr=top right, c=centered, bl=bottom left, br=bottom right

All photos **Vincent B. Hargreaves** with the excption of:
Alan Hill: page 196(tl), 203(t), 214(bl), 237(c), 240(bl), 245(tl), 246(tl), 248(c), 253(tl), 254(tl), 291
All Glass Aquarium Company: page 13, 14, 27
American Marine Inc.: page 28(tr)
Anthony Hargreaves: page 176(c), 185(c), 189(tl), 220(bl), 259(bl), 260(bl), 261(tl), 268(c)
Aqua Medic: page 16(br), 17(tl), 19, 20, 47(bl)
Dohse Aquaristik: page 22
Interpet: page 17(br), 23, 24
JBL GmbH, Germany: page 30, 31, 33, 35
John Allan Aquariums: page 12
John Clipperton: page 149(c), 151(c), 153(bl), 158(c), 161(bl), 168(bl), 179, 186(bl), 188(bl), 200(c)
Klaus Hansen: page 47(tr)
Maximal-Bio-Systems: page 25
Neil Sutherland: page 1, 2, 3, 4-5, 9, 38, 40, 41, 42, 44, 53, 56-57, 122-123, 128, 134(c), 136(bl), 138(tl), 139(b), 140(bl),

141(tl), (c), 144(bl), 152(bl), 154(c), 157(bl), 160(bl), 161(tl), 163(tl), (c), 166(bl), 177(c), 178(tl), 181(bl), 183(tl), (c), (bl), 185(tl), 186(tl), 194(c), 195(c), (bl), 196(bl), 198(c), 199(tl), 226(bl), 227(b), 246(bl), 249(t), 256(c), 260(tl), 261(c), 263(c), 267(bl), 270(bl), 273, 288-289, 295
Photomax: page 49, 64(bl), 65(bl), 66(c), (bl), 72(c), 73, 74(bl), 83(c), 103(tl), 112(c), 113(tl), 129(t), (c), 133(bl), 134(tl), (bl) 135(c), (bl), 145(bl), 150(tl), (bl), 151(tl), 153(tl), 157(tl), 162(bl), 163(bl), 164(c), 165(c), 166(bl), 167(bl), 171(bl), 174, 175(t), 176(bl), 177(bl), 180(c), 182(bl), 180(c), 182(bl), 185(bl), 187(tl), 188(tl), 190(tl), 191(c), 192(c), 194(tl), 197(c), 198(tl), 199(c), 201, 209(bl), 212(tl), (c), 213(tl), (c), 214(tl), (c), 215(c), (bl) 216(bl) 217(tl), 218(c), 219(tl), 220(c), 227(tl), 228, 229(c), 232(c), 233(c), 235(t), 238(tl), 241(tl), 243(c), 245(c), 248(bl) 250(c), 251(bl) 252(bl) 254(bl) 255(c), 257(c), 260(c) 261(bl) 262(tl), (bl) 263(bl) 265, 266(tl), (bl) 269(c), (bl) 270(tl), (c), 271, 272, 274-275, 279, 284
Selzle: page 29(br)
Tunze Aquarium Technical Systems: page 28(br), 29(tr), 45